Higher Education and National Development

Contemporary universities in many parts of the world are subject to changes driven by the collapse of the former Soviet empire, by the triumph of neoliberal economic policies and by the mobility of capital and the ease of communication that are features of the global economy. They are also responding to the reconfiguration of social, political and economic structures in which global, regional, national and local identities compete for attention. Nowhere, perhaps, have all these changes been more dramatically felt than in the Baltic States that are the source of and focus for a number of contributions to this volume.

Universities are increasingly expected not merely to respond to these changes but to drive economic and social development in the new environment, contributing to business competitiveness and innovation through (in the language of the contemporary discourse): 'knowledge transfer', 'research-based business start-ups', 'demand-led education and training', the development of 'the learning society' and the contribution of higher level skills to 'the knowledge economy'. At the same time, perhaps, they struggle to retain a sense of more traditional roles in the formation of an intellectual leadership, the education of a democratic citizenry or the cultivation of a wise, as well as a skilled, community.

The intersection of these changes in society and higher education provides the themes for this wide-ranging text by an international group of contributors. *Higher Education and National Development* includes concrete illustration of these developments, analysis and critique. It will be valuable reading for all higher education researchers and policy makers.

David Bridges was Pro-Vice-Chancellor of the University of East Anglia until 2000 when he became founding Director of the Association of Universities in the East of England. **Palmira Jucevičienė** is Professor of Kaunas University of Technology, Head of the Department of Educational Systems and Director of the Institute of Educational Studies. **Robertas Jucevičius** is Professor and Head of the Strategic Management Department at Kaunas University of Technology. He is also Director of the Business Strategy Institute at the same University. **Terence McLaughlin** was formerly Professor of Philosophy of Education at the London Institute of Education. **Jolanta Stankevičiūtė** is a Research Associate at the Von Hugel Institute, St Edmund's College, Cambridge. She was previously an Associate Professor at Kaunas University of Technology.

Higher Education and National Development

Universities and societies in transition

Edited by David Bridges,
Palmira Jucevičienė,
Robertas Jucevičius,
Terence McLaughlin and
Jolanta Stankevičiūtė

LONDON AND NEW YORK

First published 2007
by Routledge
2 Park Square, Milton Park, Abingdon, Oxon OX14 4RN

Simultaneously published in the USA and Canada
by Routledge
711 Third Avenue, New York, NY 10017

Routledge is an imprint of the Taylor & Francis Group, an informa business

First issued in paperback 2012

© 2007 Selection and editorial matter, David Bridges, Palmira Jucevičienė, Robertas Jucevičius, Terence McLaughlin and Jolanta Stankevičiūtė; individual chapters, the contributors

Typeset in Times by Wearset Ltd, Boldon, Tyne and Wear

All rights reserved. No part of this book may be reprinted or reproduced or utilized in any form or by any electronic, mechanical, or other means, now known or hereafter invented, including photocopying and recording, or in any information storage or retrieval system, without permission in writing from the publishers.

British Library Cataloguing in Publication Data
A catalogue record for this book is available from the British Library

Library of Congress Cataloging in Publication Data
A catalog record for this book has been requested

ISBN13: 978-0-415-51400-2 (pbk)
ISBN13: 978-0-415-33110-4 (hbk)
ISBN13: 978-0-203-39233-1 (ebk)

Terence H. McLaughlin

Terry McLaughlin, one of the authors and co-editors of this book, died on 31 March 2006 shortly after completing work on the manuscript. Terry was a colleague and friend dear to all those who have contributed to this volume, which we dedicate to him with gratitude and affection.

Contents

List of figures	x
List of tables	xi
List of contributors	xii
Acknowledgements	xiv
Introduction	1
DAVID BRIDGES AND TERENCE MCLAUGHLIN	

PART I
Universities, societies and transitions: setting the scene   11

1 Comparing and transferring: visions, politics and universities   13
   ROBERT COWEN

2 Conceptions of the university and the demands of contemporary societies   30
   RICHARD SMITH

PART II
Universities and transitions in conceptions of society   41

3 The development of higher education for the knowledge society and the knowledge economy   43
   PALMIRA JUCEVIČIENĖ AND RIMANTAS VAITKUS

4 The role of the university in the development of the learning society   55
   PALMIRA JUCEVIČIENĖ

5 The concept of the 'intelligent country' 72
ROBERTAS JUCEVIČIUS

PART III
Universities and economic development 85

6 Concepts of development: the role of education 87
FLAVIO COMIM

7 The role of the university in regional economic development 103
DAVID BRIDGES

8 Regional universities in the Baltic Sea region: higher education and regional development 120
KAZIMIERZ MUSIAŁ

PART IV
Universities and the demands of the economy 133

9 The role of higher education in national innovation systems in Central and Eastern Europe 135
SLAVO RADOŠEVIĆ AND MONIKA KRIAUČIONIENĖ

10 Bridging knowledge and economy: technology transfer and higher education 161
ARŪNAS LUKOŠEVIČIUS

11 The changing requirements for business management and business education in the 'countries in transition': combining cultural and institutional perspectives 176
GIEDRIUS JUCEVIČIUS

12 Competence development for the knowledge-driven economy 190
DAIVA LEPAITĖ

13 Concepts of a service university 201
ARILD TJELDVOLL AND AUKSĖ BLAŽĖNAITĖ

PART V
Universities and social, civic and ethical demands 213

14 Higher education as an agent of social innovation 215
BRIGITA JANIŪNAITĖ AND DALIJA GUDAITYTĖ

15 The role of the university in community development: responding to the challenges of globalization 227
IRENA LELIŪGIENĖ AND VIKTORIJA BARŠAUSKIENĖ

16 Higher education and its contribution to public health: tackling health inequalities through health policy development in Lithuania 237
VILIUS GRABAUSKAS

17 Spirituality and citizenship in higher education 250
HANAN A. ALEXANDER

18 Higher education, scientific research and social change 265
SIR BRIAN HEAP

PART VI
Universities, societies and transitions in perspective 279

19 The audit and 'embrace' of quality in a higher education system under change 281
BARBARA ZAMORSKI

20 Universities and societies: traditions, transitions and tensions 293
TERENCE MCLAUGHLIN

Index 310

Figures

9.1	Innovation expenditures in manufacturing, by economic activity	139
9.2	Relationship between employment and working age population with third level education in new member states	142
9.3	Relationship between employment and working age population with third level education in EU-15	142
9.4	Partners of innovative activities in Lithuanian enterprises	156
16.1	Comparison of age-specific mortality between the group with university education and the group with primary education	239
16.2	Differences in average life expectancy of Lithuanian population by age and educational background	240
16.3	Low-birth-weight proportions by educational level of mothers	241
16.4	Proportion of regular smokers in Lithuanian population by education	242
16.5	Proportion of frequent strong alcohol users in Lithuanian population by education	242
16.6	Proportion of persons using mostly vegetable oil for cooking, in Lithuanian population aged 20–64 between 1994 and 2000	244
16.7	Proportion of Lithuanian population aged 20–64 using vegetable oil for cooking, by educational level, 1994 and 2000	244
16.8	Trends in proportion of regular smokers in Lithuanian population aged 20–64 between 1994 and 2000	245
16.9	Proportion of regular smokers by educational level in Lithuanian population aged 20–64 in 1994 and 2000	246

Tables

9.1	High-tech and medium-high-tech manufacturing and knowledge-intensive services (KIS) in EU-15 and in new member states and candidate countries	140
9.2	Share of R&D personnel by institutional sectors, 2001	144
9.3	R&D personnel as percentage of labour force, by institutional sectors in 2000	145
9.4	R&D expenditure as a percentage of GDP, by institutional sectors in 2001	146
9.5	Relative number of graduates and annual changes	147
9.6	Ranking of sources of information by importance for enterprises	150
9.7	Tertiary graduates in science and technology, 2002	151
9.8	Public expenditure on tertiary level education	152
9.9	Lifelong learning: percentage of working age population participating in education and training	153
9.10	Assessment of supply, demand and linkages in the Lithuanian education system	154
9.11	Sources of R&D funding and performance by institutional sectors in Lithuania, 2003	155
10.1	Ways of developing technological innovations in 1999	170

Contributors

Hanan A. Alexander teaches in the Faculty of Education at the University of Haifa and is a Fellow of the Van Leer Jerusalem Institute, Israel.

Viktorija Baršauskienė is Professor and Dean of the Faculty of Social Sciences, Kaunas University of Technology, Lithuania.

Auksė Blaženaitė is an Assistant Professor at the Department of Strategic Management, Institute of Business Strategy, Kaunas University of Technology, Lithuania.

David Bridges is Chair of the Von Hügel Institute at St Edmund's College, Cambridge and Fellow of the College. He is also Executive Director of the Association of Universities in the East of England and Professorial Fellow at the University of East Anglia.

Flavio Comim is an economist and Fellow of St Edmund's College, Cambridge.

Robert Cowen is Emeritus Professor of Education at the Institute of Education, University of London.

Vilius Grabauskas is Professor and Head of the Department of Preventive Medicine, Faculty of Public Health at Kaunas University of Medicine and Chancellor of the University, Lithuania.

Dalija Gudaitytė is an Associate Professor at the Institute of Educational Studies, Kaunas University of Technology, Lithuania.

Sir Brian Heap CBE, ScD, FRS is former Master of St Edmund's College, Cambridge.

Brigita Janiūnaitė is Professor and Deputy Director for Research at the Institute of Educational Studies, Kaunas University of Technology, Lithuania.

Palmira Jucevičienė is Professor, Head of the Department of Educational Systems and Director of the Institute of Educational Studies at Kaunas University of Technology, Lithuania.

Giedrius Jucevičius is Lecturer at the Institute of Business Strategy, Kaunas University of Technology and the International School of Management at Vilnius University, Lithuania.

Robertas Jucevičius is Professor and Head of the Department of Strategic Management and Director of the Institute of Business Strategy at Kaunas University of Technology, Lithuania.

Monika Kriaučionienė is Lecturer at the Institute of Business Strategy, Kaunas University of Technology, Lithuania.

Irena Leliūgienė is Professor at the Institute of Educational Studies, Kaunas University of Technology, Lithuania.

Daiva Lepaitė is Lecturer at the Institute of Educational Studies, Kaunas University of Technology, Lithuania.

Arūnas Lukoševičius is Professor at the Faculty of Telecommunication and Electronics and Director of the Biomedical Engineering Institute, Kaunas University of Technology, Lithuania.

Terence McLaughlin was Professor of Philosophy of Education at the Institute of Education, University of London and Fellow of St Edmund's College, Cambridge.

Kazimierz Musiał is Lecturer at the Department of Scandinavian Studies, University of Gdansk, Poland.

Slavo Radošević is Professor at the School of Slavonic and East European Studies, University College, London.

Richard Smith is Professor of Education and Director of the Combined Degrees in Arts and Social Sciences at the University of Durham.

Arild Tjeldvoll is Professor of Education at the Institute for Educational Research, University of Oslo, Norway.

Rimantas Vaitkus served as a Vice-minister of the Lithuanian Ministry of Education and Science during 2001–04. He is now Vice-Rector of Mykolas Riomeris University, Vilnius, Lithuania.

Barbara Zamorski works in the School of Education and Lifelong Learning and the Centre for Educational and Staff Development at the University of East Anglia.

Acknowledgements

This book has come together with the support over several years of a number of individuals and institutions to whom we would like to express our sincere appreciation.

The link between Kaunas University of Technology in Lithuania and the Von Hügel Institute at St Edmund's College in the University of Cambridge was supported first by the Open Society Fund Lithuania, the British Embassy in Vilnius and then through the UK Department for International Development/British Council Higher Education Links scheme – and we are grateful to all of these bodies for making it possible for staff of the two institutions to visit each other and develop shared thinking around the themes of this book.

The publication of this volume has been made possible through the generous support of the Lithuanian Ministry for Education and the personal commitment of the former Vice-minister Dr Rimantas Vaitkus, to whom we are especially grateful. The Ministry was one of the sponsors – along with the British Council and other institutions – of two international conferences on higher education held in Vilnius and Kaunas in 2003 and 2004 at which a number of the contributions included here had their first presentation. The Ministry also funded the trip of a number of Lithuanian contributors to the European Conference on Educational Research in Hamburg in 2003 to take part in several symposia specially organized around the themes of the book.

The task of editing (and in some cases translating) this collection of work from different countries has been a substantial one, and the editors could not have managed without the dedicated, untiring and excellent assistance of Victoria McNeile in particular, and the secretarial staff of the Institute of Educational Studies at Kaunas University of Technology.

Finally, we would like to thank the Master and Fellows of St Edmund's College and the Rector and colleagues in Kaunas University of Technology for the warmth of their welcome to international visitors and their support throughout this collaboration.

Introduction

David Bridges and Terence McLaughlin

The focus of this book is on change in higher education in the context of, in particular, the multi-dimensional transition experienced by countries of the former Soviet Union over the last decade and the interconnected phenomena of globalization and the knowledge economy.

These are large themes, and in grappling with them we have perforce been selective. Among 'countries in transition' we have (for reasons relating to the origin of the book) focused on the Baltic State of Lithuania in particular and the countries of Central and Eastern Europe in general. These contexts repay attention in themselves in regard to transitions relating to contemporary universities and societies and also illustrate issues and themes which have wider significance and application. The wider issues and themes chosen for attention in this collection are also inevitably selective, although they embrace matters of central contemporary significance.

In this introduction we will briefly indicate some of the transitions relating to societies and to universities which are the concern of the present collection and will outline the structure and themes of the volume.

Transitions in societies

The first (complex) societal transition which provides the background to many of the following chapters is that which has been experienced over the last decade by countries of the former Soviet Union. These have in a very short period achieved political independence, embraced one form or another of a liberal polity and economy and, most recently, become part of the expanded European Community. These countries are often referred to as 'countries in transition' and this term will be used throughout the present collection. In his chapter in this volume Giedrius Jucevičius discusses whether the dramatic changes affecting these societies are not better expressed in the language of countries in *transformation* rather than merely *transition*. The case which is most frequently referred to in this collection is that of Lithuania, but all the countries of Central and Eastern Europe share to a greater or lesser extent in the political, cultural and economic changes which have taken place over the last fifteen years or so.

The interrelatedness of these changes is manifest, although political, cultural and economic aspects can be distinguished for our present purposes. Politically, these societies have embraced forms of liberal democracy and face the wide range of demands and challenges which arise in relation to the requirements and implications of a democratically elected system of government, including the formation of democratic citizens. Culturally, these societies have had to adjust to a range of changes arising in the post-Soviet era such as the expansion of the domain of personal autonomy and action (in relation, for example, to the expression of previously suppressed religious commitments and to the exercise of individual initiative in many matters), an openness to cultural influences from the West (via, for example, 'liberated' mass media and increased opportunities for travel overseas) and challenges relating to the reassertion and appropriation of cultural identity (in its individual, communal and national aspects) in the new circumstances in which these societies find themselves. Economically, these societies have faced changes of very wide-ranging significance. The societies have experienced the loss of a huge internal market for their traditional products, the liberalization of their economies and the exposure of their businesses to market competitiveness as well as to new freedoms of movement and expression which have themselves opened national businesses to new opportunities and new threats. Though the economic changes indicated here have been especially fast and dramatic in countries of Central and Eastern Europe, more mature market economies like the UK, Australia and the USA are still adjusting to the economic liberalism introduced in the Thatcher/Reagan era. Failing businesses and whole business sectors are allowed to collapse with effects that would have elicited heavy government intervention in a previous era.

The wider context of societal change which is of significance for this collection is provided by the interconnected phenomena of globalization and the knowledge economy. Here we are invited to observe the combined effects of the revolution in communications, which makes it as easy to exchange ideas with a person on the other side of the world as with a person in the next office, and the revolution in the movement of capital and the means of production, which allows global corporations to access raw materials and skills wherever these may be most found at the lowest price and/or highest quality and to deploy these to their benefit and profit. In such an environment, business competitiveness, so the analysis goes, requires that companies are constantly innovating in their products and drawing (in particular) on cutting-edge developments in science and technology to remain at, or to win their way to, the front of the field. The ICT revolution not only supports innovation in what are essentially traditional fields (like motor car design and manufacture or photography) but it opens up whole new possibilities for the production and communication of knowledge. Education becomes linked to the huge resources of media-based industries to become one of the fastest growing *businesses* of the twenty-first century. An economy develops in which (i) all sectors of the economy become increasingly dependent on the sophisticated application of ICT and upon innovative ideas;

(ii) especially significant growth is to be found in sectors like pharmaceuticals and communications, which depend almost entirely on cutting-edge science and technology for their competitiveness; and (iii) knowledge itself becomes a high-value commodity to be packaged, marketed and retailed like any other. For 'countries in transition' these global changes are a special challenge, but they are also shifting the requirements which are placed on different sectors of society – not least among them the higher education institutions – in all countries. 'One point is fairly clear', observed Carnoy and Rhoten. 'If knowledge is fundamental to globalization, globalization should also have profound impact on the transmission of knowledge' (Carnoy and Rhoten 2002: 2).

Transitions in universities

The third set of changes which we are interested in here, and which provide the main focus of the book, are in the universities and the broader higher education system but are driven, at least in part, by the broader societal changes to which we have referred.

It is not just 'countries in transition' which have been experiencing a turmoil of change in universities, though clearly the changes in their own political economies have led to new demands in, for example, the teaching of economics and the requirements for business and management education (see, for example, Giedrius Jucevičius' chapter in this volume). In the UK the application of market principles to universities has led to a range of transitions: a shift of responsibility for the cost of higher education from government to individual students; the assessment of quality in university research and the linking of public funding to demonstrable quality; the assessment of the quality of teaching and the publication of these assessments as a basis for student choice of programme in a higher education market; and the development of more transparent costing of higher education activity as a basis for business-style decisions about which activities are financially viable and sustainable. As Kwiek argued in a keynote address to the European Education Research Association: 'We are facing the simultaneous renegotiation of the postwar social contract concerning the welfare state in Europe and the accompanying renegotiation of a ... modern social pact between the university and the nation state' (Kwiek 2005: 1).

Economic requirements for 'higher level skills' have joined with principles of social inclusion to demand wider participation in higher education. The bringing of major areas of professional education and training (for teachers, professions allied to medicine and social work, for example) into the context of the university has been part of this process. The net effect has been what has been called the 'massification' of higher education on a model more traditionally associated with the United States of America. Some 'countries in transition', like Poland, have been leading the way in this development, though, interestingly, in this case by developing private sector provision of higher education.

With massification has come increasing diversity in the forms of provision of higher education. Bridges has described elsewhere (Bridges 2000) the way in which the traditional defining features of the university have been deconstructed by these developments:

The identity of place has been challenged by the acquisition by some universities of up to twelve or fifteen new institutions (e.g. former teacher training colleges, agricultural colleges, colleges of nursing or art and design) and new sites scattered over a region extending forty or fifty miles from the central institution; by the rapid development by traditional universities of distance or distributed learning systems, and also of franchising, validation and accreditation, which enable a student to study for a degree of University X at a further education college in the region, at a higher education institution overseas or at a computer at home (one US higher education provider operates under the slogan 'Let's get the cost of real estate out of education!', Marchese 1998). In the professional fields in particular the development of work placements, work-based learning, school-based teacher education and clinical attachments have extended the HE learning environment from the university into the workplace. Widespread access to e-mail has rendered the face-to-face contact between student and supervisor in the university, and even visits to the library, in some contexts a rare rather than a routine part of the experience:

> The distinction between 'distance education' and regular instruction – even the relevance of distance and other spatiotemporal markers as the key distinction between different types of teaching or different categories of student – is beginning to disappear.
> (Burbules and Callister 1999: 1)

By contrast, the University of Cambridge still tries to maintain a learning community in which students and academic staff are required to live within a certain distance (three miles in the case of undergraduates and ten miles in the case of graduate students and academic staff) of Great St Mary's Church – a landmark in the centre of Cambridge – and in which eating together in the collegiate environment is still seen as a central part of academic interaction.

The identity of time – the idea of a tightly contained academic year of intense interaction broken by long periods of separation, or even of a day in which teaching is largely confined to a period between 9.00 a.m. and 5.00 p.m. has been challenged by demands for part-time evening courses, short courses, day seminars at the weekend and summer schools as well as the need in, for example, health-related subjects and teacher training for years which match the schedules of hospitals and schools and give time for extended practical experience. The units of study have themselves become fragmented as customers weaned on the McDonald's service culture demand 'bite-sized chunks of learning' and 'just-in-time learning' rather than a commitment to a three-year degree.

The identity of the scholarly community has been extremely difficult to sustain as HE institutions have grown exponentially; have spread, as already indicated, to multiple sites; relied more heavily on part-time and short-term contract staff; and entered into all sorts of partnerships in teaching with practitioners in the workplace. One of the consequences of these developments has been the erosion of the link between research and teaching. For many of those teaching, in particular in professional fields, their practical experience rather than their research and scholarship is the resource which they are seen as bringing to their students.

In any case, contemporary research practice is a globalized practice in which a combination of ICT-based communications and international conferences creates communities of scholars drawn from across the world who can feel a closer identity with each other than they do with colleagues working in the next office. The story of the creation of this publication in the acknowledgements section describes just such a community.

The identity of the student community has similarly been rendered more diffuse as it has become larger and topographically more dispersed and as students arrive on campus (if they come at all) at different times of the day and year, are largely non-resident, represent a wider span of ages and cultural backgrounds than ever before and combine part-time work with study. Students on the same course may never meet each other or will learn about each other only through the 'virtual café' on the university intranet site. The demands arising from some of the economic requirements for knowledge transfer to the business community (on this matter see, for example, the chapter by Arūnas Lukoševičius in this volume) also create a new 'student' community in the form of business practitioners and entrepreneurs and requirements for new relationships and forms of pedagogy.

The identity of the discipline or subject (and of the student with such a subject or discipline) has been eroded by the increasing practice of modularizing the curriculum and presenting students with a 'cafeteria' menu of choice (the 'pick-and-mix' curriculum); by the construction of curriculum around professional fields of practice rather than subjects; and by increasing requirements in the research community for interdisciplinary enquiry. 'Knowledge as we have known it in the academy', announced Griffin, perhaps somewhat over-portentously, 'is coming to an end' (Griffin 1997: 3).

The disintegration and diversity which follow from these and other changes in higher education have led some commentators to write of 'the postmodern university', characterized by Smith and Webster in terms of '*a multiplicity of differences*':

> different academics pursuing different knowledges, different teams of researchers combining and recombining to investigate shifting topics, different sorts of students following different courses, with different modes of study and different concerns among themselves, different employment arrangements for different types of staff – difference everywhere in this the postmodern, flexible, accommodating university.
>
> (Smith and Webster 1997: 104)

But these changes in higher education, as well as sustained and sustaining loyalties to some of the traditional guiding principles of the university and its public responsibilities, are in constant interaction with the wider social changes to which we have referred. This interaction is our particular interest in this collection.

The structure and themes of the volume

This collection is concerned with the interaction between the two sets of transitions which have been indicated above. The volume is divided into six parts.

The first part of the collection contains two chapters which are scene-setting with respect to the collection as a whole. Robert Cowen cautions against any unduly confident assumption that educational principles and practices – including those relating to higher education – can be in any simple way 'compared' with each other across societal contexts and 'transferred' or 'applied' across these contexts. In insisting upon the importance of social contextualization, Cowen identifies 'deductive rationalities' as featuring in a prominent, but flawed, conception of the way in which educational principles and practices are identified and find expression in a particular societal context. In 'deductive rationalities' educational principles and practices are *deduced* from the starting point of an overarching conception of the good prevalent in a particular society (as in Mao's China, Nazi Germany and the USSR). Cowen suggests that the currently internationally dominant discourse of economic globalization ('a new international economic Darwinism') constitutes an overarching conception of the good from which, via a 'deductive rationality', the economically driven conception of the university of the sort indicated above emerges. Cowen invites critical attention to this dominant discourse and the principles and practices of higher education supposedly deduced from it, together with the issues of political positioning and power in which they are implicated. Richard Smith begins his chapter by noting the range of different demands which contemporary societies now make upon universities. He is alert, however, to the thought that universities have aims and purposes which are more central and important than others (summed up in his references to 'the important question of just what a university is for' and to the 'primary responsibilities' of the university). Given that, for Smith, any direct and systematic discussion of the aims and purposes of universities is likely to be couched in the distorting language of instrumental reason, he urges a pragmatic responsiveness on the part of universities to the demands made upon them (not all of which are inappropriate or alien to the tradition of universities) with constant vigilance, solidarity and resistance in the face of the 'absurdities and perversions' perpetrated against 'our best understanding of what a university is'. Smith also draws attention to difficulties arising from the internationalization and globalization of culture for the claim that the contemporary university has a mission with respect to 'national culture'.

The second part of the collection is concerned with the implications for universities of transitions in conceptions of society, captured in concepts such as 'the knowledge society', the 'learning society' and 'the intelligent country'. These are all terms which conceal perhaps as much as they reveal; none of them are unproblematic, and none of the contributors regard them as such. Some contributions more than others, however, make it their business to interrogate the rhetoric. In their chapter Palmira Jucevičienė and Rimantas Vaitkus discuss the 'knowledge society' and the 'knowledge economy' in relation to higher education, with particular reference to 'countries in transition' and to Lithuania. In addition to implications for higher education in general (in which knowledge production in the context of application – 'Mode 2' knowledge – the 'internationalization of knowledge' and the educational implications of 'supercomplexity' are important points of reference) Jucevičienė and Vaitkus analyse the application of these concepts in the context of Lithuania. One of the particular issues which is given attention in this context is the problem (shared with other 'countries in transition') of how to find a remedy for the phenomenon of 'brain drain' arising from the development of the 'knowledge society' and the 'learning economy'.

In the next chapter in this section, Palmira Jucevičienė addresses the multifaceted concept of the 'learning society' and its educational implications, with particular reference to 'countries in transition' and to learning at different levels of society, including 'learning regions'. In the final chapter in this section, Robertas Jucevičius argues that the concept which best captures the kinds of qualities which are necessary for economic success and survival in the 'knowledge economy' is that of 'intelligence', which he argues can be applied at every level up to the level of a country. Since 'intelligence' is properly understood as an advanced intellectual capacity which is only weakly captured in the notion of 'skills', the importance of the role of higher education in its development comes into focus.

The third part of the collection is concerned with universities and economic development. In the first chapter in this section, Flavio Comim analyses various conceptualizations of 'development' and their relationship to education Education in general and higher education in particular is seen as having a constitutive role in relation to the significant recent conceptualization of development which emphasizes the achievement of human functionings and capacities. From the perspective of this conception of development, higher education becomes a central element in the achievement of flourishing for human beings. The two remaining chapters in this section focus attention on the role of the university in relation to regional development. David Bridges considers in his chapter the role of the university in regional economic development with particular reference to his experience of working with higher education, business and regional government and economic agencies in the east of England. In the next chapter, Kazimierz Musiał analyses the role of universities – and, in particular, 'regional universities' – in relation to regional development in the Baltic region.

The fourth part of the collection is concerned with universities and the demands of the economy. In the first chapter in this part, Slavo Radošević and Monika Kriaučionienė explore the role of higher education in relation to 'national systems of innovation' in Central and Eastern Europe, with particular reference to knowledge development, diffusion and utilization. Lithuania is taken as a case study of the themes developed in the chapter. Arūnas Lukoševičius examines the role of universities in 'technology transfer' – the process of joining together the production of knowledge with its application in a business environment – with particular reference to 'countries in transition'. In his chapter, Giedrius Jucevičius discusses the changing requirements in these countries for business management and business education. One of the major themes of the chapter is that cultural perspectives need to be included alongside institutional perspectives in any consideration of these matters, which, in the case of Lithuania, include attitudes to hierarchy, to formal rules and structures and to the relative importance of different kinds of work goals and motivations as well as attention to differences between 'traditional' and 'innovative' parts of society. In the next chapter in this part of the collection, Daiva Lepaitė analyses the nature of 'competences' and the role of higher education in relation to their development. In the final chapter in this part, Arild Tjeldvoll and Auksė Blaženaitė discuss the concept of the 'service university', which is central to the kinds of responsiveness to economic demands which is being urged upon contemporary universities, and they argue that the notion of a 'critical service university' is the most defensible version of this kind of university.

The fifth part of the collection contains chapters which address social, civic and ethical demands which are placed on contemporary universities. In the first chapter in this part, Brigita Janiūnaitė and Dalija Gudaitytė examine the role of higher education as an agent of social innovation, with particular reference to 'countries in transition', and argue that this role should be seen in the context of a continuing emphasis upon the traditionally central role of the university: the achievement of intellectual and personal emancipation. This traditionally central role is seen as contributing in a general way to the needs of social innovation, whilst a specific contribution to these needs can be made by higher education via appropriate forms of professional training, partnership, consultancy and research. In the next chapter, Irena Leliūgienė and Viktorija Baršauskienė discuss the role of the university in relation to community development, with particular reference to some examples of the role played by Kaunas University of Technology in this process. In the next chapter, Vilius Grabauskas illustrates the important contribution of higher education to health policy development in Lithuania. Hanan Alexander, in his chapter, addresses the role which higher education should play in the development of citizens, and argues that an initiation into a study of traditions of thought and practice concerned with 'how one should live' ('education in intelligent spirituality') has a significant role to play in this matter. In the final chapter in this part, Sir Brian Heap argues that whilst advances in science, engineering and technology have been major 'drivers' of economic development in industrialized countries and attract the attention of 'countries in transition', they give rise to matters of ethical content and acceptability and invite the exercise of wisdom. In pursuit of this general theme, a number of issues, including the importance of the significance of rigorously conducted and peer-reviewed science in informing public understanding and policy on such controversial issues as genetically modified crops, stem cell research, and the control of major diseases like HIV/Aids and 'mad cow' disease are brought into focus.

In the final part of the collection, two chapters offer an overall perspective on the discussions in the volume as a whole. Barbara Zamorski considers the future role of universities in relation to 'quality' in the variety of virtual, physical and intellectual environments which characterize the contemporary multi-purpose university, and offers a number of alternatives to the familiar approach to quality assessment via 'audit' which she sees as inadequate in important respects. In the final chapter in this part, Terence McLaughlin offers a number of critical reflections on traditions, transitions and tensions in relation to universities and societies.

The chapters in the volume do not represent a single point of view on the range of matters which are the concern of this collection. If the contributors do not, however, reach a collective conclusion on these questions, we hope to have provided the stimulus and resources for our readers to reach their own.

The origins of the publication: a case of higher education networking

It will be evident already that this book brings some new authors to the attention of an international readership as well as, hopefully, some more familiar ones. It may be helpful to explain briefly how this book came together. This in itself reflects something of the character of contemporary practice in higher education, and in particular the networking which is characteristic of it.

The project had its origins when Jolanta Stankevičiūtė came to St Edmund's College, Cambridge to study Economics as a graduate student. There she met Terence McLaughlin, who was subsequently invited to visit her home university, Kaunas University of Technology in Lithuania. He became a regular visitor to Kaunas where he became a Visiting Professor and for some years taught a course in Philosophy of Education to research students (a number of whom have contributed to this volume). Palmira Jucevičienė (Head of the Institute of Education) and Robertas Jucevičius (Head of the Institute of Business Strategy) at Kaunas University of Technology paid return visits to Cambridge and to St Edmund's as Visiting Fellows. On one of these occasions David Bridges was invited to give some lectures at Kaunas. His visit led to the establishment of a DFiD/British Council supported academic link between Kaunas University of Technology and the Von Hügel Institute, a multi-disciplinary research institute at St Edmund's, of which David Bridges would later become Chair.

The theme of the changing role of higher education emerged as a strong focus of shared interest between the partner institutions and it was the natural choice for collaborative exploration and research. The proposal for a book bringing together contributions from the two institutions and a wider network of colleagues was linked to proposals to make this work the focus of a symposium at the European Education Research Association Conference in Hamburg in 2003, at which a number of papers included here received their first airing, and at a national conference held in the parliament building in Vilnius in 2003 and in 2004. Arild Tjeldvoll, Hanan Alexander (who had also been a Visiting Fellow at St Edmund's), Kazimierz Musiał and Barbara Zamorski all contributed to one or both of these conferences. The remaining contributions are from colleagues in the Von Hügel Institute or professional colleagues of the editors in the UK.

The international publishing world is dominated by voices in particular from the USA, the UK and Australasia and by the agenda which they bring with them. This book seeks to give expression to some new authors from a neglected part of contemporary Europe. It will quickly be evident that these authors draw on much of the same international sources as any other contributor might do, but they bring distinctive perspectives to the material and invite us to greater awareness of, and admiration for, the extraordinary transitions they are managing in a part of the world which is subject not only to the huge general challenges of globalization and its economic implications, but also to the significant distinctive challenges of 'countries in transition'.

References

Bridges, D. (2000) 'Back to the future: the higher education curriculum in the 21st century', *Cambridge Journal of Education*, 30 (1), 37–55.

Burbules, N.C. and Callister, T.A. (1999) 'Universities in transition: the challenge of new technologies', paper presented to the Annual Conference of Cambridge Branch of the Philosophy of Education Society of Great Britain, St Edmund's College, Cambridge, September 1999.

Carnoy, M. and Rhoten, D. (2002) 'What does globalization mean for educational change? A comparative approach', *Comparative Education Review*, 46, 1.

Griffin, A. (1997) 'Knowledge under attack: consumption, diversity and the need for values', in R. Barnett and A. Griffin (eds) *The End of Knowledge in Higher Education*, London: Cassell.

Kwiek, M. (2005) 'Renegotiating the traditional social contract? The university and the state in a global age', an address to the Annual Conference of the European Education Research Association, Dublin, September 2005 (forthcoming in the *European Education Research Journal*).

Marchese, T. (1998) 'Not-so-distant providers', *Bulletin of the American Association for Higher Education*, 50, 3–7.

Smith, A. and Webster, F. (1997) 'Conclusion: an affirming flame', in A. Smith and F. Webster (eds) *The Postmodern University? Contested Visions of Higher Education in Society*, London: London University Press.

Part I

Universities, societies and transitions

Setting the scene

Chapter 1

Comparing and transferring
Visions, politics and universities

Robert Cowen

> What is clear ... is that there are indeed 'circles of the mind': that is, a great deal of borrowing and copying is going on. Governments are looking at what other governments are doing in the evaluation of higher education systems, and through various networks, are establishing contacts, arranging for seminars for policy makers and adapting well or poorly the foreign evaluation policies which interest them. At the moment the metaphors of ideological and actual penetration are those of business, and systems especially information systems, and efficiency. Evaluation and higher educational systems will be 'managed'. It will be interesting and probably disturbing to see the institutional consequences of the management and routinization of creativity.
>
> (Cowen 1996: 3)

Introduction: the 'double problem' of international educational transfer

This chapter tries to say something cautionary about universities, political visions and international educational relations, partly because there are international fashions in university reform. Such fashions are tempting to politicians, who can justify their own views on the need for reform and the solutions they are advocating by claiming to be prepared to 'learn from others'. The phrase, which has an honourable enough history in comparative education, is often a signal that the politician is about to glide past the significance of social contextualization – a mistake which will destroy the benefits claimed for the proposed borrowing.

This sort of political foolishness is not a monopoly of the Americans, who wanted at one point to know 'why Ivan can read and Johnny cannot' and then embraced a model of teaching drawn from the English infant school. Nor is it only a foolishness of the English, who seem to have been convinced for about 100 years that if only they could borrow the German vocational–technical education system, all would become well with the UK economy. Such international errors are widespread in space and in time. The pattern includes the Japanese and Russians who, between the wars, thought that the ideas of John Dewey would give them the kind of educational system they wanted; those Chinese after 1949 who thought that borrowing Soviet educational practices would contribute to the creation of a Chinese socialist society; the Belgians and Brazilians who thought in the 1990s that the English university quality control system would prepare their countries for a globalized world; and those (also in the last decade) who thought that shifting to an American-style competency-based model of teacher education would give them competent teachers.

Overall, in the twentieth century, the theme of comparing and transferring educational principles and practices has been quite visible. For example, in Western Europe in the 1950s there was a 'comprehensive school' movement which involved debate about the utility of Swedish or American models of a unified secondary school for assuring equality of educational opportunity. There were also examples of 'transfer' almost in the literal sense of that word: the exact translation of Soviet text books into Chinese and their importation into the PRC. More generally, the Soviet model of education was also 'exported' to countries in Europe such as Czechoslovakia, East Germany, Latvia, Poland and so on. In the early 1970s, the ideas of the Brazilian educator Paulo Freire were taken up with enthusiasm in the USA, especially by radical students and specialists in adult education. Later in the twentieth century, the neoliberal educational reforms of Australia, New Zealand and the UK proved surprisingly attractive to other nations. All these examples illustrate specific routes of international influence, and mark specific crises which the supposed 'transfer' was supposed to resolve – normally within a naïve (or political) over-confidence that such transfers will work in their new domestic contexts.

This over-confidence (about how easy it is to transfer educational solutions transnationally) is especially irritating because it was about 100 years ago that problems of context and comparing and 'learning from others' were discussed with clarity by Sir Michael Sadler. He gave a classic lecture, asking 'How far may we learn anything of practical value from the study of foreign educational systems?' (Higginson 1979: 48). Sadler offered a very cautious answer to his own question. He emphasized in 1900 how educational systems were deeply rooted in local contexts, reflecting the 'spirit of battles long ago'.

In other words, Sadler's question was how to analyse and how to understand educational 'transfers'. The unanswered question still is how to analyse such transfers. And the question is going to remain how to analyse and understand such 'transfers' because in times of multiple transglobal mobilities and the collapse of some empires and the rise of others, the international transfer of educational ideas and practices is becoming more frequent.

New knowledge structures and processes are developing quickly. These include the flow of information about foreign education, the international, regional and national agencies whose work includes the advocacy of 'good educational practice' implicitly suitable for many places, the foreign experts descending from jet planes, and contract research aimed at specifying solutions to very salient worldwide problems, such as academic freedom, or skill formation, or the retention of minority languages, or lifelong learning. All these processes reconfirm the need to readdress the Sadlerian problematique about the terms on which it is possible to learn from others – noting that some environments are more dangerous than others. Being in a neighbourhood store with a small amount of cash is one definition of a shopping experience. Being in a large supermarket with a high-value credit card (chargeable to your own bank account) redefines the scale and the significance of the shopping act. A refusal to buy anything at all might be a sensible initial position.

Thus this chapter will try to articulate a Cassandra voice on university transfer by using a comparative perspective. Like philosophy, comparative thinking often rearranges a well-known landscape into new topographies and new *Verstehen*; and sometimes it fails to do so. At the core of comparative education there are two extremely intractable problems which the literature has not yet resolved.

The first comparative puzzle is: what are the ways to understand the relationships between societies and educational systems? In other words, how do societal 'pressures' work so that educational institutions and processes take on some of the style and characteristics of the society in which they are located? This can be called the *osmotic problem*. This puzzle has been central to the history of academic comparative education since it took shape in universities from the late nineteenth century.

The second comparative puzzle is the *transfer problem*: how can we manage and understand the deliberate moving of educational ideas and practices across international boundaries? The very modern comparative education defined by Jullien in his text of 1817 (a 'reading of the global' that was encyclopaedist and positivist) was intended to make the international movement of educational systems and educational practices into a 'scientific' activity (Fraser 1964). However, like a weak doctoral candidate, Jullien moved too quickly to thinking of his comparative education in terms of fieldwork possibilities. There are difficulties with this perspective.

Rushing into action with the wrong theory – or no theory at all – can produce disaster. If we cannot understand the *osmotic problem* even in one place, then it is difficult indeed to understand the *transfer problem*, which involves at least two places. When a model of pedagogy, or a curriculum idea or a model of a university or university system is moved across international boundaries, there is a *double* osmotic problem to be understood: the one which happened in the old society and the one which begins to happen in the new. The transfer problem contains osmotic processes and 'the osmotic problem' helps to define the configuration of the transfer problem.

Thus, the two questions (of the relationship of societies to educational systems, and of the movement of educational practices across international boundaries) are tightly related, asking for an intricate double dance of answers, because the two problems interweave theoretically (and practically). Are there no possible simplicities? There are not many. The literature is rather confused.

Perhaps, later, something simple can be said, but let us move through the argument, which is a long one, step by step.

The double problem: classic approaches

How societies affect educational systems – the *osmotic problem* – is a puzzle which it is difficult to sort out because everything can be seen as relevant to everything else. As a matter of common sense, it does seem that history ('battles long ago' in Sadler's phrase), politics, religion, economics and many many other social forces define the 'nature' of societies and the 'nature' of those societies affects the patterns of educational systems. How do you address that nexus? How do you escape from that 'common sense' and this common sense pre-analytical social swamp, in which notions of 'the nature' of social things and 'many, many social forces' splash about? Which vocabularies do you need, which discursive frames?

An early way to talk about 'the osmotic problem' was through the concept of national character (Mallinson 1966). Perhaps indeed the French are or once were logical, perhaps the Germans work hard or used to do so, but the empirical evidence was difficult to assemble and the banalities and obvious crudities of the national character argument meant that it did not live long in the comparative education literature as a major interpretative device. However, it is worth noting that the concept did address the osmotic problem directly. Unfortunately it addressed it badly, trapping itself in a circularity of argument from which there was no elegant intellectual escape.

Another, crisper, way to get at the osmotic problem was proposed by Nicholas Hans, who argued that 'forces and factors' external to educational systems define the styles and some of the specific patterns of those systems. Part of the elegance of the approach was that the list of 'factors' was finite: geographic and economic circumstances, race, language, religions and political principles (Hans 1950). At one time, a particular factor – religion in Thailand, politics in French and post-colonial Vietnam, language in Indonesia – might be especially important in shaping educational provision. Over time and in combination, in Argentina, in Chile, in Ecuador or in Peru, the 'factors' of race, religion and language were important in defining the architectures and cultural modalities of the educational systems of those countries. Hans still offers one of the more coherent approaches in the literature to the osmotic problem.

Nevertheless, there are two important weaknesses in the approach. The first difficulty with the categories – in addition to the obvious points that Hans was politically incorrect on race, casual on gender, and underemphasized the economic factor – is that they provide a reading of the world of educational policy only in very large print, though that large print can be used as a *Gestalt* for understanding the society–education nexus in particular places. The second difficulty is that the factors tell you little about how to transfer educational policies. The 'factors' approach offers only very approximate answers to the *double* osmotic problem which always occurs in international educational transfer. Despite these weaknesses, the work of Hans, firmly rooted in the London culturalist tradition which continued in varied forms for another twenty years (Lauwerys 1965, Holmes and McLean 1989), was not directly attacked and destroyed by critics.

Instead there was a generational shift in attention. In the 1960s there was an enthusiastic search for the modernist academic's equivalent of the Holy Grail: the magical methodological bullet which would make comparative education scientific (Bereday 1964, Holmes 1965, Eckstein and Noah 1969, Noah and Eckstein 1969). That work was much criticized subsequently and it is certainly out of fashion currently.

However, what has never been pointed out is that Brian Holmes offered a *unified* way to see the problem of osmotic translation and the international transfer of educational ideas and practices. In other words, Holmes in his methodological position indirectly addresses the *double* osmotic problem. Certainly his new methodology, the problem-solving approach in comparative education, was directly aimed at creating a science of the international transfer of educational ideas and practices, in the sense that it would reliably predict the results of such transfers (Holmes 1965). But the buried surprise in Holmes' work is that the osmotic problem is defined through the same conceptual apparatus as the transfer problem.

For Holmes, the social context could be split taxonomically into normative, institutional and environmental categories. Change, social contextualization *and* international transfer had to take into account the normative, the institutional and the environmental. The 'normative' was defined by Holmes as a value position held in a society; for example that schools must be secular or religious, or that good knowledge was Platonic or Cartesian, Confucian, Islamic and so on. Given a rapid normative change, institutions have to be adjusted – they were, before the moment of rapid change, linked to old values. In different words, one modality of (the social–educational) osmosis was already in existence; and a new osmosis must now occur. Occasionally a rapid environmental change (such as the discovery of oil) might produce a Holmesian problem, that is, a disequilibrium in norms and in institutional patterns. Obviously, international transfers of educational ideas and practices (which Holmes called 'piecemeal cultural borrowing') would produce such disequilibria.

Thus for Holmes the osmotic problem and the international transfer problem could be handled through the same conceptual apparatus: weighing the significance of norms, institutions and environmental circumstances (to which there was a late addition of the concept of 'Mental States') in particular places. Overall, Holmes constructed a major methodological position which was, in many ways, a life work, drawing particularly on his interest in the philosophy of science and his early background as a physicist. His comparative approach stressed quite delicate Popperian versions of tentative predictability (Holmes 1986). Unfortunately he placed these delicacies on the base of a very mechanistic sociology.

That sociology emphasized re-establishing equilibria in a social universe framed by sociological laws. A social engineer would know those laws and would understand (through what Holmes called his three 'circles' of norms, institutions and environment) enough about social osmosis to construct educational reform – of the right kind with predictable results – through international educational transfer. The strategic characteristic of Holmes' methodological position was that it was a very particular culmination of the technicist position in comparative education; at least until the last decade when the effective and efficient schools movement decided it could do comparative education, when the international agencies grew strident in their abstracted certainties about policies such as lifelong education, and when quality control systems for higher education were on offer in the international marketplace as proven solutions to educational problems.

The difficulties of the general technicist position in comparative education are two – and they are of dramatic contemporary importance both in terms of practical action and in terms of theoretical error. The first flaw is the assumption that *teckne* – here meaning a technical solution to a problem – can be divorced from social context, in the sense that no theory of context is required or that adapting the solution to local context is a job for the locals. This is a typical error of the international agencies. The second flaw (a typical error among academic comparative educationists) is the continuation into the twenty-first century of old epistemic assumptions about social time and social progress: the linearities of time; of piecemeal reform; of correlations and of predictability; of stages in 'development' (for example, in the Third World); of progress; of the gradualness of things. This kind of comparative education is, de facto, a comparative education of liberal states and, in terms of the sociology of knowledge, it is an extremely odd intellectual construction: it is politically blind.

At the same time as much of the classic academic work on the osmotic and transfer problems was being written (between 1945 and 1970), major and very well-publicized examples of non-linearities, of the non-gradualness of things, were available for analysis. These examples contained illustrations of osmotic translation devices of dramatic clarity. There was no serious shortage of information – but the information was not theorized.

Comparing and the osmotic problem: visions, politics and deductive rationalities

The evidence for understanding one version of the osmotic problem was easily available in the cases of Nazi Germany, the USSR of Stalin post-1945, and Mao's China. All three societies constructed *osmotic translations* that carried the 'nature' of the society into the architectures and cultural modalities of the educational system. In all three cases, these were societies of visions. The visions were of a long future, the visions were apocalyptic and their implementation was forceful, literally as well as metaphorically. There was a past to be ideologically destroyed and, with the help of education, a future to be built.

The three examples show *one extreme form* of osmotic translation of the society–education nexus. This form of osmotic translation in these societies I recently termed 'deductive rationalities' (Cowen, 2005).

Deductive rationalities are not, in any pleasing way, rational. They are a very specific social logic and potentially extremely dangerous, because from a chosen starting point which captures an intense belief (the white man's burden; class oppression; the will of Heaven) there can be deduced life rules and life chances and social, economic, political and educational relations. 'Deductive rationalities – it has been suggested – are the peculiar quasi-determinant social logics which follow from mono-optical visions of the social universe. That is, the rest of the social universe is deduced from a major first principle embraced by the State – Nazism, Marxism, Maoism' (Cowen, 2005).

In a state which deliberately organizes itself around a mono-optical vision, two social processes occur rapidly: (a) the expression of deductive rationalities in state discourses; and (b) the definition – through newly invented control agencies – of institutional shapes and cultural and educational practices (including political expectations about the nature of the university). To be dangerous, deductive rationalities require major acts of social invention: ideas and agency are both required.

In education, in Mao's China, in the USSR and in Nazi Germany for example, new social rules were invented and socially enforced. The rules defined, in principle and in practice and often with brutal effects: who could teach; gender and youth roles in the educational system and in extra-curricular activities; what was good knowledge and how that should be examined and transmitted and by whom; the kinds of educational research that were important; and the kind of university needed for that society. The enforcement was through new control agencies invented for the surveillance of education (Cowen and Jones 1991, Fitzpatrick 1970, Grant 1979, Hayhoe 1996, Hayhoe and Bastid 1987, Law 1995, 1996, Price 1977, Ringer 1969, Sunker and Otto 1997, Tomiak 1972).

The cases of Mao's China, Nazi Germany and the USSR alert us to the possibility that other cultural forms of deductive rationalities can be identified, with implications for international educational relations and the international 'transfer' of universities. For example, deductive rationalities can be constructed from a religious principle (such as the particular interpretation of Islam in the Iran of Ayatollah Khomeni) or from the principle of national mobilization (as in Meiji Japan after 1868: 'revere the Emperor, defend the Nation, enrich the Nation') which redefined Japan in the nineteenth century. In other words, deductive rationalities are not only visible in circumstances of totalitarian politics.

Similarly the early (and later) post-1949 relations between China and the USSR alert us to the proposition that deductive rationalities also define what may properly be 'borrowed' from overseas, and what is impure. At first glance it looks as if the Japanese borrowed somewhat eclectically in education after 1868 from the Americans, the Dutch, the French, the Germans and so on. For example, the Japanese modelled their new University of Tokyo on Humboldt's conception of the university, which was already institutionalized in Prussia. That kind of university would clearly be useful for training an excellent Japanese civil service. However, the Japanese were borrowing with precise cultural eclecticism and were removing impurities from the borrowing. As Tanaka has pointed out, the Japanese state did not emphasize the principle of academic freedom which was central to Humboldt's view of the proper relationship between the university and the state (Tanaka 2003).

The transfer problem: world models of the university and changing international educational relations

As hinted in the previous paragraph, the German university system in the nineteenth century was a model for the world of what a good university was like. The German university tradition gave us our idea for most of the twentieth century of 'the Professor' as a scholar of deep and extensive learning, pursuing truth. German notions of meticulous scholarship gave us our conception of a good bibliography, the possibilities of serious 'scientific' research (in all subjects), and clear ideas about the correct hierarchies within the academic profession. From the modern German tradition came the modern version of 'the doctorate' (Walters 1996).

The German university model was internationally influential (Gellert 1993). The conception of the Humboldtian university and the doctorate affected not merely the Nordic countries but even England where, as a matter of international economic and cultural competition, the PhD was slowly introduced into the university system (Simpson 1983). As mentioned above, the German university model was attractive to the Japanese: the University of Tokyo would train modernizing elites for Japan and there would be a special relationship between the Japanese state and the University of Tokyo. There was; and there still is (Passin 1965). And in China notions of the German university were part of a range of educational institutions such as the American college – often a missionary college – and the Confucian tradition of examinations, which shaped the higher education system before 1949 (Hayhoe 1996).

In particular, the German university model influenced the United States (Rohrs 1995). Many young Americans in the nineteenth century, who would be future academics in the United States, studied in Germany. This was true in almost all branches of study, because at that time (the second half of the nineteenth century) Germany was the one place where a major training in how to do research could be gained, and academic standards were very high. This was as true for persons wanting to study history or archaeology as it was for persons wanting to train in chemistry or physics. The Americans took home the concepts of 'the doctorate', the professor who researched, the advanced studies seminar.

At places such as Johns Hopkins and Chicago, the American graduate school and research university was born. The American 'research university' system is now probably the most famous in the world (Clark 1993).

These illustrations of 'world models' of universities highlight two general points: the international transfer of models of the modern university is 'normal'; and views about what is a good 'world model' of a university change. There is a considerable literature on the international influences on the academic profession and on the transfer of university systems (Altbach and Selvarantnam 1989, Ashby 1966, Becker 2004, Castro 1983, Figueiredo 1986, Hayhoe and Bastid 1987, Kim 2001, Rothblatt 1997, Schwartzman 1979, Tanaka 2003).

There is rather less literature on what is a good 'world model' of a university or a university system, though certainly the concept of a 'research university' has been well researched (Clark 1993). However, an important caveat here is that while some of the most famous of American universities are 'research universities' (MIT and Stanford and so on), the American higher educational system, with its traditions of Land-grant colleges, the liberal arts colleges and the community colleges, is complex, institutionally varied and very flexible in its purposes. It is this flexibility and the range of higher education institutions which makes the US pattern of higher education so remarkable. For certain purposes (which probably would include efforts to improve equality of educational opportunity) it is the American higher education system – and not the research university – which would be the 'world model'.

Currently, what are the world models of the university or of university systems that are fit to transfer? And for which purposes and for whose purposes are they 'fit to transfer'? Two of those models are well known and most countries have versions of them Crucially, those two models of the university (which will be called the 'apex' and the 'citational' models of the university) are normally home grown. In more academic language, they have been osmotically shaped over time. It is the third model which is puzzling and which can be used to pull the overall theoretical argument of the chapter together.

Of the existing, institutionalized, models of the world-class university, the classic and famous model is the 'apex university': a university such as Oxford or Cambridge, Harvard or Yale, the *grandes écoles* of France (if we avoid the trap of entanglement with the word 'university'), the University of Tokyo or Seoul National University. Each of these is widely recognized in its own country as being among the best universities there. Normally such universities are very difficult to get into. They take children of talent, often from families of high socio-economic status, and they prepare those children for future elite positions, particularly in politics, law and business, or in the highest branches of the civil service. By and large such universities – however correctly or incorrectly in fact – are seen as confirmatory of existing social, cultural, economic and political patterns.

The second model began to emerge in the last century. It can be called the 'citational university' – that is, one often cited by politicians and the media or the Party as being at the cutting edge of innovation in the natural, social or applied sciences. In some ways, such universities are a twentieth-century version of the nineteenth century American land-grant college movement which 'grew' universities such as Cornell and Wisconsin. Examples of 'citational universities' would be MIT or Novosibirsk, the London School of Economics and Political Science or Imperial College in London (again sliding past the problem of exactly what is locally defined as a university in a particular context). By and large such universities – however correctly or incorrectly in fact – are seen as being aimed at redefining the future through the kind of knowledge they generate.

The international transfer of such universities, or the 'copying' of both of these kinds of universities is a long-standing practice. Most countries have grown their own apex universities and their own citational universities or research institutes – and that includes former colonies in the French and British Empires as well as countries such as Argentina, Brazil and Chile, which have had far longer to live out their own osmotic processes for the definition and indigenization of their own university systems.

It is the third kind of 'world-class university' which begins to consolidate the themes of visions, politics and universities, including their international transfer.

The English have recently invented, in the period 1980 to 2000, a third style of university, one version of 'the entrepreneurial university'. That is, the university system was initially placed by the British state in a condition of financial instability. Thereafter (particularly after 1988) individual universities were expected to seek research funds from outside 'clients'; students suddenly were being called 'customers'; and universities themselves became aware of the need to generate their own income and to be, literally, 'businesslike'.

Increasingly I am inclined to call this English creation the 'managed university'. During the time when the initial vision of the entrepreneurial university was being implemented by specifying the rules of competition which would tell it how entrepreneurial it was being, the controls became cumbersome. There were rules made by a variety of control agencies which defined success: in teaching, published research, contract research, consultancies, doctoral supervision, how to specify the details of an MA course, student satisfaction – almost everything except the professional pleasure quotient (PPQ) of academics working in the system. Crucially, 'educational excellence' was defined by externally stated standards and externally monitored assessment. A new administrative cadre was required inside and outside of the university to monitor, to organize and to manage on the basis of precise information (Bleiklie 1998, Deem 1998). All the rules for academic and teaching performance, for assessment and for monitoring (and thus indirectly for internal university management) are national rules.

In other words, the British state had embraced an ideological position (Barnett 2003) but it had created not a market, but a quasi-market, so tightly defined by national rules of performance that English universities are not, primarily, entrepreneurial institutions. They are *managed* institutions. They are trapped in a local audit culture which publishes a national rank order and the scores of universities based on criteria of locally-measured excellence (Bowden 2000). Instead of having a world-class higher education system which is multi-faceted and which is – as if it were a market – organized around the principle of 'any person, any study', we have a managed university trying to excel on measures of research and teaching excellence defined by agencies strongly influenced by the British state. How was this remarkable contradiction (the parochialization of quality and the routinization of creativity of the university in times of trans-global mobilities) made possible?

Deductive rationalities and transitologies

By the end of the 1970s, it was well known that the UK was in a crisis of late modernity. The Conservative Party said so; and won an election on that basis. Under the remarkable leadership of Mrs Thatcher, the country was made ready for the twenty-first century, which, popular literature and the politicians said, would demand rapid adjustments to global economic competition (Porter 1980, Reich 1991). New flexibilities in the responses of all institutions – educational as well as economic – and a new sense of social responsibility were called for by the new government. Laws were changed, the state shrank, and major reforms were put in place urgently.

In other words, what occurred was a *transitology*: the more or less simultaneous collapse (or destruction) and reconstruction of state apparatuses, socio-economic stratification patterns and political visions of the future, and the deliberate use of the educational system to create that future in a short time period – let us say ten years (Cowen 2000). Like so many transitological moments, the English transitology was mono-optical: the tone was strident, it was asserted that the crisis was massive, and almost all social and educational reforms were deduced from what was called earlier 'a major first principle embraced by the State': here, the market. This mono-thematic view of the world, at the centre of state policies, gave a pattern to the urgent reforms to implement the new political vision.

Deductive rationalities were put in place for education. For example, the state reduced the influence of the universities on teacher education and emphasized practical teaching skills (there were many incompetent teachers, it was said); all young people were brought within a broader examination system that included vocational qualifications that would prepare them for the labour force; a new National Curriculum was defined and was made compulsory in all state schools; new national tests of attainment were used on all children at certain age points; new educational research was called for, which would provide 'robust data' for educational policy decisions; and new national control agencies for education with interesting initials (Ofsted, QAA, HEFCE, TTA) were created. As part of these deductive rationalities, a vision of a market-framed university system was also implemented during the last fifteen years (though, as I argued above, the actual results of the speed and symbolic violence with which the vision was implemented in a context with a stable osmosis – the powerful pre-existing pattern of relations with the state, conceptions of good knowledge, the economy and the university – are odd and are getting odder).

Nevertheless, the quality control procedures in the UK have been of interest to networks of visitors from overseas also interested in 'quality assurance'; and they are not dramatically dissimilar to some of the surveillance systems in place or recently introduced for universities in Australia, Canada, the Netherlands, New Zealand and the United States (Amaral *et al.* 2002, Barrow *et al.* 2003). Equally, the university systems of some of the East Asian countries (for example, Hong Kong, Japan and South Korea) are being subjected to major redefinitions of their relationships with the state, or with the economy, or with parents and students, or in quality assurance mechanisms, or they are being offered the new challenge of 'internationalization' (Enders and Fulton 2002, Kim 2005, Lee and Gopinathan 2003, Yonezawa 2003a, 2003b).

What we are seeing (notably in Europe) is the emergence of strong regional discourses about governance and the regulation of universities and a strong international discourse about internationalization and economic globalization. The available literature is massive and can be traced in recent books by Enders and Fulton (2002) or Barrow *et al.* (2003). The point is not just that there are several similar changes going on in a world characterized by tighter quality control systems for universities, the restructuring of education in Central and Eastern Europe and Russia, and the 'coordination' of education in newly defined regions such as NAFTA and, within the EU, the 'harmonization' of education around principles embraced in Bologna and Prague and so on. It is not merely that the international discourses on education are starting to attract analytical attention from researchers and specialists in comparative education (Beech 2005, Phillips 2003, Phillips and Ochs 2004, Schreiwer 2000, Steiner-Khamsi 2000, 2004).

The point is that the international discourses *are becoming deductive rationalities* which in their 'reading of the global' take as their starting point a mono-optical, intensely held belief in the processes of economic globalization.

The economic reading of this globalized age – whether from the OECD or the World Bank or even from some EU documents – insists on the truth of hypotheses about a shift into an information age (of a certain sort); the importance of knowledge economies; the internationalization and mobility of capital; the international mobility of labour and sites of production; the astonishing new rapidity of technological change and the need for labour forces and for individuals to retrain for different careers several times in a life cycle; and the crucial need for nations to prepare for economic competition on these terms.

The educational discourse which follows from this mono-optical point of departure emphasizes the economic relevance of education (particularly vocational-technical training); shifts the language of the discussion of education to talk about 'skills' (generic, transferable, communicative, team-building, informational and so on) rather than 'knowledge'; and places 'lifelong learning' at the centre of all educational provision, at the very least rhetorically. The university itself is suddenly important. Indeed – inside the world view of such deductive rationalities – the university is at the centre of the knowledge economy and will be at the centre of the distribution of life chances for individuals and survival chances of whole nations.

This new international economic Darwinism repositions all educational institutions (once you step inside the deductive rationality). It repositions the university domestically within the political, economic, social and educational systems; and it repositions the university internationally.

That is, like all good deductive rationalities, it tells you what is pure and what is impure. Thus it defines what kind of university should be 'transferred' (were you looking to transfer a university or a university system). Such a university will probably define its knowledge in terms of a competences and skills discourse, it will be undertaking contract research for money, it will be offering 'useful' courses, it will know the occupations which its graduates entered, and it will have well-monitored information about its market share of international and national students, its consultancy income, and its levels of internationalization. It will have a clear mission statement that will probably say something about transparency, efficiency and a globalized world – the economic one, that is. The ideological signals are in the educational discourse. And the social actor which builds the other half of the deductive rationality is the new believer: any 'nation-state' which embraces the ideology and wants to check on 'progress'.

Conclusion

Thus, currently the international transfer of universities is a most uncertain and dangerous business. The theme is under-theorized in the literature of comparative education, even though the descriptive literature is large. But the problems of constructing such a theory are considerable. As I wrote a few years ago:

> We need a sharper sense of the international, regional, rim and domestic politics which frame transfers and we need an explicit theory of the blockages on the transfer of educational practices. We have – against limiting cases such as cultural imperialism or dependency – tended to assume that transfer with predictable consequences is possible. We may be better off starting with the initial assumption that 'transfer' is not possible, before we revisit examples of success. Of course there is a massive momentum, buttressed by the international agencies and by regional and national aid agencies to press on with a positive agenda.
>
> (Cowen 2002)

However, things are moving along. Beech (2005) in particular has offered an excellent contemporary analysis of some of these processes (with special reference to Latin America and reforms of teacher education).

We also need a much-improved analytical vocabulary to sort out terms such as transfer, borrowing, copying, reproduction, appropriation, international cooperation, imposition, neocolonialism and post-colonialism and so on. On those themes, as indicated earlier, David Phillips, and David Phillips and Kimberley Ochs, and Gita Steiner-Khamsi have done a great deal of work. We also need continued improvements in our theorizations of what Schreiwer called 'world referential models', Phillips saw as 'cross-national policy attraction' and Cowen called 'circles of the mind' and Steiner-Khamsi termed 'the circularities of transfer'. Which university systems are judged to be attractive: why, when, by whom, for which precise purposes, and who influences whom?

Then, when the international 'transfer' has taken place, we need a vastly improved theory of what counts as 'indigenization' or as osmotic absorption. Arguments that newly borrowed educational policies must be 'sensitive to local context' – which is the new academic rhetoric about international and development education in the last five years – do not begin to approach key difficulties: what is 'successful indigenization', who is going to do the indigenization, and who will suffer in the mean time? We also need a sharper sense, within the 'osmotic process', of which things are going to go wrong and why. If you say you want an entrepreneurial university, you should be very careful not to finish up with the horrors of a managed one.

We are also is some danger, perhaps, of missing what is obvious: the almost permanently important, massive political positionings which inform many 'international transfers'. The transfer of educational practices is not merely a technical exercise. When the Japanese 'borrowed' foreign educational ideas and practices heavily after 1868 it was within a clear modernization project, which was radical economically but conservative socially. When the Soviet Union imposed educational ideas and practices within its sphere of political domination in Eastern and Central Europe after 1945 it was within a transformative (Soviet) vision of politics not always warmly appreciated in the countries to which it was applied. Similarly, the educational borrowings of the Brazilian Generals after 1964 were transformative also – but in that instance they were sharply conservative within a particular strategic vision of the geopolitical relations between North and South America.

Currently, what are the political positionings of the big international and regional agencies which construct educational discourses and which are explicitly in the transfer business? International educational transfer is not merely the movement across international borders of a social technology that is supposed to fix something which is broken. It is not merely an interesting and very difficult puzzle for academics who specialize in comparative education. International educational transfer is politics, part of the cultural and economic and political international relations and discourses of the global stage on which power is made visible through each act of advocacy about what to do. Or what not to do.

References

Altbach, P.G. and Selvaratnam, V. (eds) (1989) *From Dependence to Autonomy: the Development of Asian Universities*, Dordrecht: Kluwer Academic Publishers.

Amaral, A., Jones, G.A. and Karseth, B. (2002) *Governing Higher Education: National Perspectives on Institutional Governance*, Dordrecht: Kluwer Academic Publishers.

Ashby, E. (1966) *Universities: British, Indian, African: a Study in the Ecology of Higher Education*, Cambridge, Mass.: Harvard University Press.

Barnett, R. (2003) *Beyond All Reason: Living with Ideology in the University*, Buckingham, Open University Press.

Barrow, C.W., Didou-Aupetit, S. and Mallea, J.R. (2003) *Globalization, Trade Liberalization, and Higher Education in North America: the Emergence of a New Market Under NAFTA*, Dordrecht: Kluwer Academic Publishers.

Becker, R.F.J. (2004) 'The politics of performativity and universities: a comparative analysis between England, The Netherlands, and Germany', unpublished thesis, Institute of Education, University of London.

Beech, J. (2005) 'International agencies, educational discourse, and the reform of teacher education in Argentina and Brazil (1985–2002): a comparative analysis', unpublished thesis, Institute of Education, University of London.

Bereday, G.Z.F. (1964) *Comparative Method in Education*, New York: Holt Rinehart and Winston.

Bleiklie, I. (1998) 'Justifying the evaluative state: new public management ideals in higher education', *European Journal of Education*, 33 (3), 299–316.

Bowden, R. (2000) 'Fantasy higher education: university and college league tables', *Quality in Higher Education*, 6 (1), 41–59.

Castro, C.M. (1983) 'The impact of European and American influences on Brazilian higher education', *European Journal of Education*, 18 (4), 367–75.

Clark, B.R. (ed.) (1993) *The Research Foundations of Graduate Education: Germany, Britain, France, United States, Japan*, Berkeley: University of California Press.

Cowen, R. (ed.) (1996) *The Evaluation of Higher Education Systems: World Yearbook of Education 1996*, London: Kogan Page.

—— (2000) 'Fine-tuning educational earthquakes', in D. Coulby, R. Cowen and C. Jones (eds) *Education in Times of Transition: World Yearbook of Education 2000*, London: Kogan Page.

—— (2002) 'Sketches of a future', in M. Caruso and H.-E. Tenforth (eds) *Internationalisierung: Semantik und Bildungsystem in vergleichender Perspektive*, Peter Lang: Frankfurt-am-Main.

—— (2005) 'Extreme political systems, deductive rationalities and comparative education: education as politics', in D. Halpin and P. Walsh (eds) *Educational Commonplaces: Essays to Honour of Denis Lawton*, London: Institute of Education, University of London.

Cowen, R. and Jones, C. (eds) (1991) *Essays in Honour of J.J. Tomiak*, Institute of Education, University of London: The Department of International and Comparative Education and the Urban Education Research Group.

Deem, R. (1998) '"New managerialism" and higher education: the management of performance and cultures in universities in the United Kingdom', *International Studies in Sociology of Education*, 8 (1), 47–70.

Eckstein, M. and Noah, H. (eds) (1969) *Scientific Investigations in Comparative Education*, London: Collier-Macmillan.

Enders, J. and Fulton, O. (eds) (2002) *Higher Education in a Globalising World: International Trends and Mutual Observations. A Festschrift in Honour of Ulrich Teichler*, Dordrecht: Kluwer Academic Publishers.

Figueiredo, M. (1986) 'Academic freedom and autonomy in the modern Brazilian university – a comparative analysis', unpublished thesis, Institute of Education, University of London.

Fitzpatrick, S. (1970) '*The Commissariat of Enlightenment: Soviet Organization of Education and the Arts Under Lunacharsky, October 1917–1921*, London: Cambridge University Press.

Fraser, S.E. (1964) *Jullien's Plan for Comparative Education 1816–1817*, New York: Teachers College Columbia University.

Gellert, C. (1993) 'The German model of research and advanced education', in B.R. Clark (ed.) *The Research Foundations of Graduate Education: Germany, Britain, France, United States, Japan*, Berkeley: University of California Press.

Grant, N. (1979) *Soviet Education*, 4th edn, Harmondsworth: Penguin.

Hans, N. (1950) *Comparative Education*, London: Routledge and Kegan Paul.

Hayhoe, R. (1996) *China's Universities, 1895–1995: a Century of Cultural Conflict*, New York, London: Garland.

Hayhoe, R. and Bastid, M. (1987) *China's Education and the Industrialized World: Studies in Cultural Transfer*, London: M.E. Sharpe.

Higginson, J.H. (ed.) (1979) *Selections from Michael Sadler: Studies in World Citizenship*, Liverpool: Dejall and Meyorre International Publishers.

Holmes, B. (1965) *Problems in Education: a Comparative Approach*, London: Routledge & Kegan Paul.

—— (1986) 'Paradigm shifts in comparative education', in P.G. Altbach and G.P. Kelly (eds) *New Approaches to Comparative Education*, Chicago: The University of Chicago Press.

Holmes, B. and McLean, M. (1989) *The Curriculum: a Comparative Perspective*, London: Unwin-Hyman.

Kim, T. (2001) *Forming the Academic Profession in East Asia: a Comparative Analysis*, New York & London: Routledge.

—— (2005) 'Old borrowings and new models of the university in East Asia', *Globalization, Societies and Education. Special Issue: Globalization, Changing Nature of the State and Governance in Education*, 3 (2) (in press).

Lauwerys, J.A. (1965) 'General education in a changing world', *International Review of Education*, 11, 385–401.

Law, W. (1995) 'The role of the state in higher education reform: mainland China and Taiwan', *Comparative Education Review*, 39 (3), 322–55.

—— (1996) 'Fortress state, cultural continuities and economic change: higher education in mainland China and Taiwan', *Comparative Education* 32 (3), 377–93.

Lee, M. and Gopinathan, S. (2003) 'Reforming university education in Hong Kong and Singapore', *Higher Education Research and Development*, 22, 167–82.

Mallinson, V. (1966) *An Introduction to the Study of Comparative Education*, London: Heinemann Educational.

Noah, H.J. and Eckstein, M.A. (1969) *Toward a Science of Comparative Education*, New York: Macmillan.

Passin, H. (1965) *Society and Education in Japan*, New York: Columbia University, Teachers College and East-Asian Institute.
Phillips, D. (2003) 'Toward a theory of policy attraction in education', in G. Steiner-Khamsi (ed.) *Lessons from Elsewhere: the Politics of Educational Borrowing and Lending*, New York: Teachers College Press.
Phillips, D. and Ochs, K. (eds) (2004) 'Educational policy borrowing: historical perspectives', *Oxford Studies in Comparative Education, 12 (2)*, Oxford: Symposium Press.
Porter, M.E. (1980) *The Competitive Advantage of Nations*, London: Macmillan.
Price, R.F. (1977) *Marx and Education in Russia and China*, London: Croom Helm.
Reich, R. (1991) *The Work of Nations: a Blueprint for the Future*, New York: Vintage.
Ringer, F.K. (1969) *The Decline of the German Mandarins: the German Academic Community, 1890–1933*, London: Wesleyan University Press.
Rohrs, R. (1995) *The Classical German Concept of the University and its Influence on Higher Education in the United States*, Peter Lang: Frankfurt-am-Main.
Rothblatt, S. (1997) *The Modern University and its Discontents: the Fate of Newman's Legacies in Britain and America*, Cambridge: Cambridge University Press.
Schreiwer, J. (ed.) (2000) *Discourse Formation in Comparative Education*, Frankfurt-am Main: Peter Lang.
Schwartzman, S. (1979) *Formação da Comunidade Científica no Brasil*, São Paulo: Nacional.
Simpson, R. (1983) *How the PhD came to Britain: a Century of Struggle for Postgraduate Education*, Guildford: Society for Research into Higher Education.
Steiner-Khamsi, G. (ed.) (2000) 'Transferring education, displacing reforms', in J. Schreiwer (ed.) *Discourse Formation in Comparative Education*, Frankfurt-am-Main: Peter Lang.
—— (2004) *The Global Politics of Educational Borrowing and Lending*, New York: Teachers College Press.
Sunker, H. and Otto, H.U. (eds) (1997) *Education and Fascism: Political Identity and Social Education in Nazi Germany*, London: The Falmer Press.
Tanaka, M. (2003) 'The transfer of university concepts and practices between Germany, the United States, and Japan: a comparative perspective', unpublished thesis, Institute of Education, University of London.
Tomiak, J.J. (1972) *The Soviet Union*, Newton Abbot: David and Charles.
Walters, G. (ed.) (1996) *The Tasks of Truth: Essays on Karl Jaspers' Idea of the University*, Peter Lang: Frankfurt-am-Main.
Yonezawa, A. (2003a) 'The impact of globalization on higher education governance in Japan', *Journal of Higher Education Research and Development*, 22, 145–54.
—— (2003b) 'Making "world-class universities": Japan's experiment', *Higher Education Management and Policy*, 15, 9–23.

Chapter 2

Conceptions of the university and the demands of contemporary societies

Richard Smith

This chapter makes two apparently contradictory claims: that we need continually to attend to the important question of just what the university is for – a question usually expressed as what its aims and purposes are – and at the same time that there are peculiar dangers in talking about these aims. It argues that under the sway of instrumental reason, the dominant form of thinking in the West, some of the most widely-canvassed aims have a strange way of turning into each other, and that the role of the university in fostering national development is an especially vulnerable aim in this context. The chapter concludes that, rather than engaging in high-level philosophical debate about the aims of the university, we should be pragmatic about the different demands that contemporary societies make of their systems of higher education, while exercising continual vigilance in the face of the absurdities and perversions that politicians, bureaucrats and, of course, academics themselves perpetrate against our best understanding of what a university is: and that our best understanding is often arrived at in contradistinction from these absurdities.

Much is expected of universities of the twenty-first century, in all countries. They are required to respond to a variety of needs and fulfil many sometimes incompatible aims, and this is not simply a matter of external demands but of the multifaceted commitment, rooted in tradition, of universities themselves and of the academic profession. Since I shall be sceptical below of talk about aims, I shall write here of the *responsiveness* of the university. We might distinguish, roughly, five dimensions of responsiveness. First, and perhaps particularly relevant in the context of this book, is the university's responsiveness to its national and cultural setting: its role in forging, consolidating and questioning what it means to be a member of its nation-state. Second, which is by no means the same thing, the university responds to the demands of the national and local economy: traditionally through the supply of a trained and skilled workforce (it should never be forgotten that the universities of Europe originated as professional training schools: as suppliers of doctors, lawyers and priests) and nowadays, increasingly, through what are sometimes called 'third strand' activities involving engagement with business, industry and commerce through consultancy and the development of 'spin-off' companies. Third, the university has an international or global dimension in fostering awareness of issues of justice and sustainability. Its alumni are to be citizens of the planet, in a world of increasing interdependence, particularly in the era of the 'knowledge economy', and not just of a particular country. Fourth – in a somewhat debased version of this global dimension – universities are increasingly ranked in international leaguetables that compare their standing in research and other terms and universities can hardly fail to respond to this. Fifth, there are ideals of education as such (as it has been traditional to put the matter), of the emancipation of the human spirit or the broadening of the individual's horizons: ideals that still exercise their influence if only as a kind of guilty awareness that the other dimensions leave out something important and distinctive.

An excellent example of how the university – especially perhaps the nascent or renascent university – finds itself pulled in all these different directions comes from a recent speech given by Thabo Mbeki, President of South Africa, to the Association of Commonwealth Universities. The theme of his speech is for the need for the revival of the African university to underpin the regeneration of Africa itself.

> Our entire continent remains at risk until the African university, in the context of a continental reawakening, regains its soul ... The new Africa can only be a product of the creative interface between the public, private and civic sector domains. At the centre of this interface is education.[1]

There is a clear instrumental and economic element to this creativity. The system of higher education 'is to supply society with citizens of vision and commitment ... In this context, a university should not be an enclave or an ivory tower whose curricula have little relevance to the society in which it operates'. It should be 'imbued with a commitment to global responsibility'. Africa's universities are to become 'integrated into the international networks that are so critical to success in the knowledge economies in which we now live'. And at the same time of course (that conscientious voice of the fifth dimension) education must be 'a space for unfettered intellectual inquiry', fostering 'the capacity of the human intellect to liberate through questioning and disputation' (ibid.).

Now it would be easy to view this as one more example of a familiar kind of rhetoric. This, however, would be to miss the point, which is that the modern university, of any country in the world, finds itself positioned among just these kinds of different demands, and having to decide where its primary responsibilities lie. I shall suggest that two of these dimensions should give us particular concern, and I shall make a case for regarding these issues as, significantly, a matter of the different *languages* that are available to us for articulating the nature and work of the university.

It will perhaps seem odd that I am sceptical about discussion of aims, since I have more than once (e.g. Blake *et al.* 1998) complained of the paucity of such discussion in a world where more and more it appears that the crucial questions are those concerning means (for instance, how to fund the university, or widen access to it). This is a world where a major European White Paper, 'Teaching and Learning: Towards the Learning Society' (1995: 27) can speak of 'the demise of the major ideological disputes on the objectives of education' as an accomplished fact and contain a section entitled 'The end of debate on educational principles' (ibid.), thus effectively abolishing consideration of aims by *fiat*. We do not seem to have become much clearer about what the university is for in recent years, yet it does seem more and more that there is a case for saying that talk of aims itself brings a number of problems, and it is these that this chapter is in part concerned to highlight. The first point to note is that talk of aims inevitably takes place in a particular kind of language. Discussion of aims or ends invites us to consider the means that lead towards those aims or ends: thus it brings in the language of instrumental reason. It is necessary here to explain what is meant by instrumental or technical (I follow common practice in using these terms interchangeably) reason.[2]

Instrumental reason involves the discovery of the best means for achieving preordained ends: where for instance we determine what is the optimum speed for a car to travel in order to minimize consumption of petrol, or which way of investing our money will give us the best and most secure return. We employ instrumental reason in education in quite straightforward ways when we consider how to retain valued members of staff who might otherwise leave the university, or when we try to work out the least time-consuming way of communicating messages effectively to a large group of students. Here, talk of effectiveness seems entirely appropriate and uncontroversial. Martha Nussbaum puts it aptly: instrumental reason is concerned with 'the management of need and with prediction and control concerning future contingencies' (Nussbaum 1986: 95). It leads us in the direction of developing rules and procedures; it helps us to arrive at general and not just piecemeal solutions: for example, an effective way of communicating messages to one large group of students may work for all such groups. It helps us to achieve a high degree of precision and to construct explanations that help us to refine our rules and procedures still further (cf. Nussbaum 1986: 9–6).

Instrumental reason is of course a wonderful thing. It is perhaps the most valuable expression of the ambition of the Enlightenment to ameliorate the human condition, and without it our lives would be poorer, shorter and more brutish. For instance, it is instrumental reason that a doctor uses to work out the right dosage of a prescription for a particular patient, or a heating engineer to uncover a blockage in the radiator system. The question is simply – or relatively simply – what restores the patient to health or the central heating system to working order. The first example here reminds us, however, that even where it has been most successful, instrumental reason requires the supplement of other forms of thinking. The doctor may reason that a particular dosage of antidepressants will alleviate the patient's anxiety, but still hesitate to prescribe on the grounds that she is dealing merely with symptoms and not with underlying causes. What causes difficulty, for the world of education especially, is that 'the power of "scientific" pictures of practical rationality affects almost every area of human social life, through the influence of the social sciences and the more science-based parts of ethical theory on the formation of public policy' (Nussbaum 1990: 55). The achievements of instrumental reason in the areas to which it is appropriate – in technology (and particularly now information technology), especially and naturally enough for a form of reason also called technical reason – have been so spectacular that its influence and its methods risk expanding into areas where its use is inappropriate or needs to be moderated with other forms of thought.

Critics of the influence of the Enlightenment and the technical and instrumental rationality that it installed as the epitome of human thinking have long argued that the power of instrumental reason to predict and control has, for all its benefits, brought in its train sophisticated forms of manipulation and enslavement. Horkheimer and Adorno wrote in *Dialectic of Enlightenment* (1979: 2) that 'the fully enlightened earth radiates disaster triumphant'. More recently many writers have echoed the criticism in different ways. Following the ground-breaking work of Jean-François Lyotard in *The Postmodern Condition* (1984) it is easy for us to see how new computer technology enables us to store and retrieve enormous amounts of information, thus creating a demand for the supply of such information which in itself places additional demands (on professionals in all spheres of the public services in particular). In this way technical reason both liberates and oppresses. Our fundamental human need to understand and communicate with each other, and our interest in emancipating ourselves from our dependence on the world around us, do not fall within the remit of instrumental reason and require different forms of rationality.

The domination of instrumental reason in education can easily be seen in western countries in the context of schooling, in particular in the insistence that quality in schooling can be measured, bench-marked and raised by the setting of targets. The school curriculum is commonly spoken of, in the UK at least, as something that can be 'delivered', with the implication that, once content is specified, purely instrumental questions can be asked about the best method of delivery. Both in schooling and in higher education one of the surest symptoms of 'instrumental reason syndrome' is the way that talk of effectiveness is everywhere. To be effective is all about means, about reaching goals as cheaply or reliably as possible. It implies agnosticism about whether the goal is worth reaching. Talk of 'effectiveness' and 'efficiency' often hides the fact that no real thought has been given to questions of ends and ultimate aims, or that such questions are assumed to belong to an age now superseded, as in the example from the European White Paper cited above.

There is nothing particularly new in the claim that technical or instrumental reason has come to dominate talk about higher education, as in many other parts of our world. In *The Limits of Competence* (1994: 5, 78), for example, Ronald Barnett writes:

higher education is being locked into a Weberian iron cage of prescriptive rationality, of given ends and of operationalism ... in its various forms – bureaucratic, purposive, strategic and technocratic – instrumental reason so seeps into social institutions and human affairs generally that it becomes the dominant mode of reason.

We learn to speak, that is, a technicized discourse in which some things – competences that can be acquired and listed, for example – can be talked about more readily than others (ideas about the flourishing of the human spirit, for instance, require a very different language). Martin Heidegger (1966: 56) wrote that 'The approaching tide of technological revolution in the atomic age could so captivate, bewitch, dazzle and beguile man that calculative thinking may someday come to be accepted and practiced as the only way of thinking', realizing that technology risked becoming less something that we control than something which controls us. What is true for technology itself is true for the language of technology.

Herbert Kliebard (2004: 34), in the course of making a persuasive case for the importance of studying the history of education, reminds us that certain questions that are typical of current educational debate – questions about the objectives of education, or about what experiences will prepare children for adult life, or about what children's needs are and how schools can help to meet them – are not necessarily the eternal and fundamental questions to ask about education. They, and similar questions about the aims of the university, are the products of a particular time in history, precisely of the time when the technicized language of Fordism, of the drive towards ever greater effectiveness and efficiency, began to assert itself. Kliebard argues that we might profitably abandon rather than continually try, and fail, to answer questions such as these. He suggests that 'The key problem, often, is not to find an answer to a question but to get past it', and quotes John Dewey to the same effect:

> Old ideas give way slowly; for they are more than abstract logical forms and categories. They are habits, predispositions, deeply ingrained attitudes of aversion and preference. Moreover, the conviction persists – though history shows it to be a hallucination – that all the questions that the human mind has asked are questions that can be answered in terms of the alternatives the questions themselves present. But, in fact, intellectual progress usually occurs through sheer abandonment of questions together with both of the alternatives they assume – an abandonment that results from their decreasing vitality and a change of urgent interest. We do not solve them: we get over them.
> (Kliebard 2004: 34)

The stale questions that Kliebard urges us to abandon have new life continually breathed into them by the technology that shapes our thinking. Consider for a moment how the ease with which text can be bullet-pointed facilitates the construction of lists of aims. Here, for instance, are the four main purposes of higher education as expressed by the UK's 1997 Dearing Report of the National Committee of Inquiry into Higher Education (5.11):

- to inspire and enable individuals to develop their capabilities to the highest potential levels throughout life, so that they grow intellectually, are well-equipped for work, can contribute effectively to society and achieve personal fulfilment;
- to increase knowledge and understanding for their own sake and to foster their application to the benefit of the economy and society;
- to serve the needs of an adaptable, sustainable, knowledge-based economy at local, regional and national levels;
- to play a major role in shaping a democratic, civilized, inclusive society.

These 'purposes' are subsumed under an overarching aim, which is 'to enable society to make progress through an understanding of itself and its world: in short, to sustain a learning society'. But the nature of a learning society is made only too clear in the introductory paragraphs of Dearing:

1.1 The purpose of education is life-enhancing: it contributes to the whole quality of life. This recognition of the purpose of higher education in the development of our people, our society, and our economy is central to our vision. In the next century, the economically successful nations will be those which become learning societies: where all are committed, through effective education and training, to lifelong learning.
1.2 So, to be a successful nation in a competitive world, and to maintain a cohesive society and a rich culture, we must invest in education to develop our greatest resource, our people. The challenge to achieve this through the excellence and effectiveness of education is great...

Talk of what is life enhancing turns out to be talk of economic competitiveness and 'effectiveness'. Our people turn out to be a resource ('human resources', Heidegger's *Bestand* or 'standing reserve') to be developed.

I have tried to illustrate here the way in which the different 'aims' of education readily lose their separate identities and, in particular, the language of instrumental reason, being the default language of our time, works subtly to install its own client aims in the place of its rivals. This, I now want to argue, is a particular danger in the case of the aim that the university should contribute to the development of the nation-state. And that aim is not just one among many but has a special and unique status, since the modern idea of the university came into being partly as an institution that instantiates culture, and not just any culture or culture in the abstract, but the culture of the nation-state.

To put a complicated story briefly, German thinkers of the nineteenth century (predominantly Schiller and Humboldt) required an intermediary state between the contingent, teeming world of nature and the austerity of pure reason and found this in the idea of *Bildung* as the cultivation of character through cultural education, and in a conception of the university as the site for such education. Readings (1996: 65) writes:

> The University of Culture, instituted by Humboldt, draws its legitimacy from culture, which names the synthesis of teaching and research, process and product, history and reason, philology and criticism, historical scholarship and aesthetic experience, the institution and the individual. Thus the revelation of the idea of culture and the development of the individual are one. Object and process unite organically, and the place they unite is the University, which thus gives the people an idea of the nation-state to live up to and the nation-state a people capable of living up to that idea.

But if it is national cultural mission that has up to now provided the university with a significant part of its aims and purposes then there is a problem. Put simply, the economic patterns of the twenty-first century mean that culture is now internationalized and subject to the forces of globalization. The process of 'Americanization' that labels 'the generalized imposition of the rule of the cash-nexus in place of the notion of national identity as determinant of all aspects of investment in social life ... implies the end of national culture' (ibid., p. 3). This picture is familiar enough to need little illustration, but it is worth mentioning one particular way in which these forces affect higher education. No university can afford to ignore the league tables that show the international standing of universities across the world. Criteria in such league tables include international recruitment of students, particularly post-graduates, and staff (and of course potential students and staff will increasingly consult these league tables in making their decisions about where to study and work). The result is that the nation-state is no longer the major site at which capital reproduces itself (ibid., p. 13). Hence Readings writes of 'the university in ruins': the university is ruined because it has lost its historical *raison d'être*. It no longer has a role in safeguarding and propagating national culture.

In Readings' account the discourse of 'excellence' comes to replace the ideology of national culture, the University of Excellence (his capitals) being an institution dominated by total quality management and league tables, where academics have become human resources and students customers. What I want to add to Readings' account, however, is an argument to the effect that it is precisely because the idea that the university should contribute to the development of the nation-state has become untenable and unstable that it turns into, rather than simply being replaced by, the idea of excellence in the sense above. Or, to put it slightly differently, excellence as a matter of doing better than our rivals in the international league tables etc., *is what national culture has turned into*. Naturally, standing in such tables is not seen as a good purely in itself: the thought that it means more funding for research, and more overseas students paying substantial fees for their study in the prestigious university, tends to lie behind it. And the shift from Culture to Excellence is greatly facilitated by the difficulty experienced at all levels in the world of policy making and of educational administration in speaking any language other than that of instrumental reason.

If my surmise here is correct then 'countries in transition', to use a phrase from elsewhere in this book, have every reason to be cautious in thinking of national development as an aim of the university, if such development is seen in cultural terms. Far better, perhaps, to argue frankly in terms of creating jobs and serving the economy and training professionals, of countering the threat to the West's relative standard of living by the burgeoning economies of the Far East and, increasingly, of India. At least that way of putting it tends to remind us – by default – that there might be something more to higher education. As we have seen above, grander aims have a worrying way of turning into more mundane and instrumental objectives while pretending that they are still being respected. It is not so much that national development and *Bildung* are absurd ideals: rather that we should exercise scepticism towards their endless tendency, in our time of late or postmodernity, to turn into something else.

However, let us not talk of the postmodern university, for this only gives ammunition to those who control its sources of funding (a postmodern university might be supposed – absurdly – to be one where 'anything goes', and thus to have abandoned its standards; or it might be suspected of being one where people were having *fun*). Still, the idea of 'the aims of the university' does look rather like one of those 'grand narratives', incredulity towards which is often held to be a central feature of postmodernism (cf. Lyotard 1979). And it may be that in our concern for the university and its values we do better to attend to the local issues, the unspectacular daily business of committees and bureaucrats, the 'little stories' that gradually bring into being a university of one sort rather than another. To finish, then, an example, a *petit récit* – such a small thing, perhaps beneath notice, or a harbinger, perhaps, if allowed to go unremarked. The Arts Faculty of one UK university has recently circulated the following guidelines to its constituent departments:[3]

> All teaching that raises issues which are likely to cause offence to some/be subject to ethical concern, must have ethical approval from the Departmental Teaching and Learning Committee. It is anticipated that this may cover such topics as race, slavery, witchcraft, abortion, euthanasia, many gender issues etc.
> The Teaching and Learning Committee must satisfy themselves that
> – the subject is academically appropriate
> – appropriate balance is maintained in delivery and discussion
> – appropriate notice is given to students
>
> Teaching is broadly defined to include lectures, seminars (including those presented by students), tutorials, essay topics, examination questions etc.
> *The Times Higher Education Supplement* (2004: 2–3)

As one academic of the university concerned commented: 'There goes my teaching. It's hard to be balanced about the Holocaust.' Taken literally, these guidelines would mean that all teaching would have to be determined, in advance, in some detail. A seminar discussion on relativism, for instance, might involve a student asking whether there are not some things that are absolutely and unconditionally wrong: the sexual abuse of children, for instance. At this point the teacher who has not sought ethical approval will presumably have to terminate the seminar. All spontaneity is ruled out by the clause that appropriate notice should be given to students. In any case, ought not some students, holding particular opinions, to be offended or caused 'ethical concern'? It may offend a creationist or a racist to discover that some people think their views are complete rubbish (rather than to be met with the anodyne response that there is no doubt something to be said for such views, and something to be said against them) but perhaps they ought to be thus offended. The guidelines would of course have stopped Socrates in his tracks.

Examples like this provide fruitful ways of developing, or recovering, our sense of what the university is for. It is less that we compare the guidelines above with an established set of aims for higher education and find them wanting: more that our idea of the university, none the worse for not being explicitly articulated, evolves in ever-changing ways in response to what we know to be nonsense. We thus attend to the question of just what the university is for, what values should underpin and inform it, without talking of aims in any thoroughgoing or programmatic way. The work that needs to be done here is as much political – a matter of politics on both the small and large scale, and of solidarity and resistance – as it is theoretical. Which is a lesson that many 'nations in transition' have taught the rest of us, to our gratitude.

Notes

1 All quotations are from the version of the speech in *The Times Higher Education Supplement*, 12 November 2004: 12.
2 The following paragraphs owe something to chapter 3 of N. Blake *et al.* (1998).
3 As reported in *The Times Higher Education Supplement*, 17 November 2004: 2–3.

References

Barnett, R. (1994) *The Limits of Competence*, Buckingham: Open University Press.
Blake, N., Smith, R. and Standish, P. (1998) *The Universities We Need: Higher Education after Dearing*, London: Kogan Page.
European White Paper (1995) 'Teaching and learning: towards the learning society', Brussels: European Commission. Available at: europa.eu.int/comm/education/doc/official/keydoc/lb-en.pdf (accessed 6 March 2005).
Heidegger, M. (1966) *Discourse on Thinking*, trans. Anderson and Freund, New York: Harper & Row.
Horkheimer, M. and Adorno, T. (1979) *Dialectic of Enlightenment*, trans. John Cumming, London: Verso.

Kliebard, H. (2004) 'Wozu Geschichte der Pädagogik?' ['What is the purpose of pedagogy?'], *Zeitschrift für Pädagogische Historiographie*, 10, 2.

Lyotard, J.-F. (1984) *The Postmodern Condition*, trans. B. Massumi, Manchester: Manchester University Press.

National Committee of Inquiry into Higher Education (The Dearing Report) (1997), London: Her Majesty's Stationery Office.

Nussbaum, M. (1986) *The Fragility of Goodness*, Cambridge: Cambridge University Press.

—— (1990) *Love's Knowledge: Essays on Philosophy and Literature*, Oxford: Oxford University Press.

Readings, B. (1996) *The University in Ruins*, Cambridge, Massachusetts: Harvard University Press.

Part II

Universities and transitions in conceptions of society

Chapter 3

The development of higher education for the knowledge society and the knowledge economy

Palmira Jucevičienė and Rimantas Vaitkus

The beginning of the present century is characterized by the competition that is taking place among the various states who are on their way to becoming 'knowledge economies'. Whilst the concept of a 'knowledge economy' stands in need of further analysis, it is already quite obvious that the economic success of these states will directly depend upon the production, distribution and use of knowledge and information. The importance of the role of higher education in relation to these aspects of understanding and capacity is greater than ever (on these matters see, for example, the contribution of Comim to this volume). 'Countries in transition' are trying to catch up with western countries, who have enjoyed a head start in becoming knowledge economies.

How realistic are the possibilities of 'countries in transition' 'catching up' in this way? It is well known that the knowledge economy is accompanied by contemporary processes of globalization which create mega-level opportunities for the development of this kind of economy in a particular country. At the same time, globalization can cause multiple challenges to many small countries with newly emerged market economies. Robertson (2000) notes that entire nations, especially small states and 'countries in transition', have to learn new attitudes and patterns of behaviour in the context of globalization.

The small 'countries in transition', such as the Baltic States, face a particular need to make an intelligent use of the opportunities made possible by globalization whilst at the same time facing up to the various challenges which are posed by globalization to their national identity and resources.

What do these countries have to learn to become successful knowledge economies? In general, they must realize their potential to be treated as partners rather than 'third world' countries by their global counterparts, and take their place on the international and global stage. However, they must also take steps to avoid an excessive drain of their newly acquired human potential away from themselves to the globalized environment (as in the widely recognized phenomenon of 'brain drain').

Most authors see higher education as a central resource for the development of knowledge economies. Higher education in general and universities in particular are, after all, knowledge- and competence-producing institutions.

Further, the work of universities has always had a 'global' dimension and this has been on the rise since the end of the last century (Rothblatt 2000) with the increasing communication and diffusion of academic information and knowledge (Soete 2001).

Many western researchers have offered analyses of the role of higher education in general and universities in particular in relation to the facilitation of the knowledge society and economy (Clark 1995, 1998, Scott 1995, 1997, 1998, 2000, Barnett 1994, 2000, Bridges 2000). 'Countries in transition' are particularly concerned with the reform of higher education (Jucevičienė 1999, 2000, Poškienė 2002, Kraujutaitytė 2002, Grabauskas and Šveikauskas 2000). Prominent questions relating to proposals for reform include: What are the features and qualities of higher education that correspond to European and global trends in higher education, meet the country's demand for modern educational achievements, and reflect and foster its national culture at the same time as enabling its researchers to effectively participate in the international academic community?

The essential features and qualities of higher education which are needed if a 'country in transition' is to develop successfully into a knowledge economy tend not to be brought into clear focus. This matter is the concern of the present chapter.

The present discussion focuses on Lithuania – a small country with 3.4 million inhabitants. Lithuania has a successful track record of transition, as marked by its admission to membership in the EU in 2004 and its achievement of one of the world's fastest growing economies (9.1 per cent GDP growth in 2003).

The chapter consists of three sections. In the first section, we will try to outline the features of higher education which enable a 'country in transition' to enter the race towards the knowledge economy in partnership with developed countries. In the second section, we will examine the qualities in Lithuanian higher education under reform which particularly relate to the promotion of a knowledge economy. In the third section, we examine a paradox arising from the improvement of Lithuanian higher education in the ways we indicate: the phenomenon of 'brain drain' from Lithuania. In this third section we refer to the results of a pilot survey carried out by one of the authors of this chapter. At the end of this section of the chapter, we will discuss how higher education in Lithuania can inhibit the phenomenon of 'brain drain', thereby enabling the country to participate effectively in globalization without diluting its national identity and economic interests.

Features of higher education relevant to the development of the knowledge economy

A core insight valued by the present authors is contained in Delanty's (2001) observations presented in his book *Challenging Knowledge: The University in the Knowledge Society*.

> [Although] ... the university is losing its role as the site of knowledge production, it is still one of the most important producers of knowledge, ... but ... it is not the main user of knowledge. (...) The knowledge society refers to a situation in which knowledge is being used to produce knowledge and the conditions of knowledge production are no longer controlled by the mode of knowledge itself. (...) Cognitive processes not only produce knowledge as content, but also give rise to new cognitive structures and identities...
>
> (Delanty 2001: 152)

The suggestion here is that the social space for knowledge production is expanding. The growing importance of *praxis*, and implicit knowledge made explicit as knowledge-in-use, is emphasized.

Any university which seeks to play a significant role in the knowledge economy and to have an impact on the development of the knowledge society has to attend to three kinds of new interconnecting relationships: between higher education and society, between disciplines taught and researched in higher education, and between higher education and the state.

New links between higher education and society

More than a decade ago, Barnett (1990) wrote about the reality of a changing relationship between higher education and society. This topic has been addressed by more and more authors who focus on the changing role of universities vis à vis society, driven by the need for higher education to adapt to social change and to be more responsive to the needs of society. In this, higher education must accept that it has no monopoly of expertise, but has to take part in a wide *public discourse* (Delanty 2001: 8).

A new model of knowledge creation, described as Mode 2 by Gibbons, is particularly relevant to the reality of contemporary human life and to the new kinds of relationship between higher education and society. The distinction between these differing modes of knowledge production can be described roughly in this way:

> **Mode 1.** The complex of ideas, methods, values and norms that has grown up to control the diffusion of the Newtonian model of science to more and more fields of enquiry and ensure its compliance with what is considered sound scientific practice.
> **Mode 2.** Knowledge production carried out in the context of application and marked by its: transdisciplinarity; heterogeneity; organizational heterarchy and transience; social accountability and reflexivity; and quality control which emphasizes context- and use-dependence. It results from the parallel expansion of knowledge producers and users in society.
>
> (Gibbons *et al.* 1995: 167)

The differences between Mode 1 and Mode 2 (Gibbons 1998) are elaborated in more detail by Klimašauskienė *et al.* (2003).

Mode 2 knowledge production expresses a basic shift in understanding about the creation of knowledge. Whilst we are not implying that Mode 2 forms of knowledge production have replaced Mode 1 forms, or are appropriate in every domain of knowledge, we nevertheless consider that universities, in 'countries in transition' and beyond, need to be more open to the demands of Mode 2.

A new learning concept in knowledge creation, supported by the action science theories of Argyris and his colleagues (1985), requires application in universities in 'countries in transition' and more widely.

The training of researchers of a traditional kind no longer has pride of place in a university. Gibbons and colleagues refer to professionals of outstanding competence as *symbolic analysts*: people who work with symbols, concepts, theories, models and data, and configure them into new combinations (Gibbons *et al.* 1995: 84).

The ability of higher education to produce many highly competent professionals, especially *knowledge workers*, is central to its ability to be responsive to society's contemporary needs. Such a demand calls for a mass and diversified system of higher education with a reformed structure as well as a new approach to study programmes.

Professional competence requirements posed by the knowledge economy require the emergence of competence-based programmes, where the notion of a 'competence' is understood in a broad and not a narrow way (see the chapter by Lepaitė in this volume). These programmes stress the ability of the person to act professionally in practical situations by implementing original cognitive structures and deploying appropriate personal and social qualities. The implementation of a competence-based study programmes system does not, however, mean that all the programmes are necessarily oriented solely to the highest competence level. The higher education system has to educate many professionals with varying levels of competence, although there is, of course, a special need for knowledge workers at the highest level.

All of the aforementioned are indications of the some of the considerations which universities must bear in mind if they are to become effective sources for the development of the knowledge economy and society.

However, in the case of 'countries in transition', the factors mentioned above are not sufficient. The opening up of higher education should also mean making public use of its international experience and opportunities. In the case of 'countries in transition', the internationalization of higher education itself is of crucial importance, as these countries have for almost half a century been separated from the West by the 'iron curtain'. Van der Wende (1997: 19) perceives this internationalization as 'any systematic, sustained effort aimed at making higher education (more) responsive to the requirements and challenges related to the globalization of societies, economy and labour markets'. For most countries, and especially the Central and Eastern European states, it means the introduction of a common degree system, the introduction of multicultural and European dimensions in study programmes, an increase in teacher and student mobility and other developments.

However, we consider that one of the most important factors needed in relation to the internationalization of higher education in the transition countries is *knowledge internationalization*, and, in particular a synergy of distinct Eastern and Western European knowledge (Jucevičienė 2000).

New links between disciplines taught and researched in higher education

According to Barnett (2000), the activities of individuals and organizations are growing in their complexity. They are based not only on the knowledge created by academics, but also on the knowledge that comes from practice. Barnett (2000: 6) refers to this situation as involving *supercomplexity*. This notion is exemplified in the contemporary work of the medical doctor who is faced with a plethora of choices in relation to information and to theoretical frames of evaluation, not merely concerning his or her strictly medical tasks but also in relation to managerial, legal and ethical matters. Medical doctors are working not only in the situation of *complexity*, but also in that of *supercomplexity* (Barnett 2000).

Knowledge workers today will typically perform in situations of *supercomplexity*. Therefore, if higher education seeks to serve the knowledge society and contribute to its development, it has to ensure communication between disciplines, since single disciplines can no longer encompass all the demands of supercomplexity. All this has implications for the internal structure of universities (Delanty 2001: 8).

These changes involve the idea of *multiversity*, where multidisciplinarity is achieved by emphasizing the links between the departments and researchers from different disciplines through common work on multidisciplinary research and study projects and the analysis of supercomplex situations in consultation with professionals engaged in these situations.

Changing relations between higher education and the state

Increasingly, the state acts as a regulator in relation to the performance of universities, especially in 'countries in transition'.

States understandably seek to develop the knowledge economy and to mobilize all their resources, including higher education, in support of this development. Economic policy therefore influences policy in relation to higher education. However, it is widely known that university autonomy and academic freedom are not only important principles worthy of respect but also important conditions for ensuring critical knowledge creation and the ability of higher education to make its distinctive contribution to the development of the knowledge economy and the knowledge society. External regulatory mechanisms in relation to universities are therefore doubly problematic. The challenge is to strike the right balance between, on the one hand, the regulation of institutions of higher education, especially in the course of the reform of higher education, and on the other hand, appropriate and necessary forms of institutional autonomy. An open dialogue between society and the university on these matters is called for.

Features of Lithuanian higher education as a knowledge economy development facilitator

In order to explore the current status of the reformed Lithuanian higher education system as a facilitator of knowledge economy development, we offer here a brief general review of the current state of development of the system, with reference to the factors which have been singled out in the first part of the chapter.

Links between higher education and society

With regard to the orientation and responsiveness of higher education to society, relevant discussions have been taking place in Lithuania among the academic community and practitioners. Mode 1 knowledge creation retains pride of place in universities, and many academics lack appreciation and skill in relation to Mode 2. However, there are signs that this situation is gradually changing. Questions which require sustained attention here include: What is the more detailed nature and defensibility of the distinction between Mode 1 and Mode 2 knowledge production, and what is the legitimate scope of application of each? How can the forms of understanding and commitment needed in relation to the development of Mode 2 best be brought about? What managerial implications follow, for higher education and business, from the aspiration to promote Mode 2? The increasing openness of universities to society, industrial enterprises and business organizations is an important aspect of the promotion of Mode 2 knowledge production. An important corollary of these developments is that it will be necessary for Mode 2 knowledge production to be legitimated in academia and to be reflected in the evaluation of the research and publications of academics.

Higher education cannot ignore realities in the social context in which it is located. The proportion of students in Lithuania in the age group 19–24 who are in higher education is steadily increasing (34.1 per cent in 2001, 39.9 per cent in 2002, 48.4 per cent in 2003). An obvious question which arises, given limited financing for higher education (4.4 per cent of the national budget in 2001 and less than in most developed countries), is whether this expansion (which includes increasing numbers of higher education colleges springing from technical schools) can be achieved without loss of quality.

An increased number of students is, of course, only one of the features of mass higher education, properly understood. Important structural and educational changes are involved (Schuller 1995) which are especially complex in 'countries in transition' (Gudaitytė and Juzevičienė 2000) (see also the chapter by Musiał in this volume).

With regard to structural changes, in Lithuania a binary higher education system exists. During the last ten years a number of colleges have been transformed into universities. A unified structure of higher education is lacking: the development of colleges, for example, is not coordinated with the development of universities. This does not seem to be a very coherent policy if higher education is to maximize its potential to contribute to the development of the knowledge society and the knowledge economy in Lithuania. The current system of Bachelor's, Master's and Doctoral degrees was introduced in 1991.

With regard to educational changes, most of the universities in Lithuania offer academic programmes, whilst colleges offer professional programmes. Kaunas University of Technology is the only university to offer a competence-based programme (in teacher education). The competence-based programmes maintain a sufficient level of fundamental knowledge whilst at the same time enabling the would-be professional to gain practical experience in a course of study which emphasizes practical skills (which cannot, of course, be divorced from values and attitudes). Such programmes, which demand a high level of judgement and professional insight to implement effectively, play a key part in regional development. Programmes of this kind should be introduced in universities as well as colleges and a process of 'pedagogization' should be implemented across the higher education sector to enable staff to create and implement these courses in an appropriate way.

Links between disciplines taught and researched in higher education

Research in most universities in Lithuania has been located within familiar academic disciplines. Often there is more communication and cooperation between the same disciplines across different universities nationally and internationally than there is between different disciplines in the same university. There is, however, an increase in multidisciplinary research projects and this gives rise to some optimism in relation to the establishment of the kinds of appropriate interdisciplinary links which we outlined above and the emergence of the multiversity paradigm.

Multidisciplinary study programmes tend to be rare and there is as yet little formal provision for them.

It may well be that special action is needed to stimulate the right kind of interdisciplinary and multidisciplinary work within universities, given the inertia that is associated with the well-established disciplinary paradigm. 'Of the right kind' is an important qualification here: interdisciplinary and multi-disciplinary are not panaceas per se but must satisfy criteria of coherence and appropriateness.

Links between higher education and the state

Since 1990 systematic and effective attempts have been made to reform Lithuanian higher education. The state has a strong influence on higher education and the significance of this influence for higher education reform in a 'country in transition' cannot be underestimated. A legislative basis for higher education has been created. A modern system of degrees and a modular credit system has been introduced. Most study programmes have successfully passed national accreditation, in some cases involving international experts. A Lithuanian centre for quality assessment in higher education has been set up which organizes expert assessment (peer review) of work in universities, accumulates and publishes information about its quality, and offers suggestions for improvement. This centre also disseminates information, stimulates consultation and makes recommendations relating to the recognition of qualifications.

Qualities of higher education as a facilitator of knowledge economy development in the context of Lithuanian higher education reform

As can be seen from the discussion in the last section, all the features of higher education as a facilitator of knowledge economy development have, to a lesser or a greater degree, found a response in Lithuanian higher education reform. The move to a mass higher education system which occurred during the last couple of years is impressive, but, as we have noted, this move gives rise to concerns about issues of quality.

Systematic efforts at the level of higher education management should be made to enable appropriately placed university teachers to acquire a new pedagogical competence in relation to the creation and implementation of competence-based programmes. Moreover, a system of Accreditation of Prior Learning should be created on a national level, and the preparation of symbolic analysts in various study fields should be developed. The improvement of higher education in Lithuania requires an increased level of financial support, which currently falls short of western norms. The greater openness of higher education to society, especially business organizations and industrial enterprises, should be encouraged. The value of knowledge created according to Mode 2 should be legitimated in many areas of study and this should be reflected in the evaluation of the work of researchers and their publications.

Of course, a mutual agreement between the state and university concerning the boundaries of university autonomy should be reached. Then, more opportunities for flexibility would be welcome in individualizing study programmes and innovating their contents. Legislation on joint degrees as well as on Accreditation of Prior Learning should be created.

In spite of the fact that the number of multidisciplinary research projects and programmes is increasing, this process should be encouraged by a systematic introduction of the multiversity conception. The internationalization of Lithuanian higher education is developing rapidly, but there is a lack of balance in the process of mobility: there are relatively large numbers of students and teachers who study and teach in western countries, whereas only a very small number of foreign academics, especially students, come to Lithuania. Efforts should be made to ensure a greater equilibrium in this matter.

A paradox of first successes: 'brain drain' – the phenomenon and its causes

What kind of paradox is generated by a 'brain drain'?

Lithuanian higher education nurtures and generates capacities and qualities in its graduates that stand comparison with those achieved by graduates from overseas, and therefore many able and committed students are attracted by excellent opportunities for employment outside Lithuania.

As a result, Lithuania may encounter a paradoxical situation, when the higher quality of university education creates a more intense process of 'brain drain'. The economic costs of this phenomenon could be higher than the profit of western business investment to Lithuania, thereby resulting in a net loss to the country. In this way, a small 'country in transition' can lose its resources, eventually become unable to join globalization processes under the conditions of partnership, and be non-competitive in the market of the knowledge economy. This is quite a serious problem for Lithuania which requires investigation. In order to look more closely at the reasons for the 'brain drain' phenomenon in relation to Lithuania and to identify strategies to combat it we refer to research by Jucevičienė et al. (2002), '"Brain drain" and its reflection on Lithuanian intellectual capital: pilot research'.

The research analyses the nature and causes of 'brain drain' in Lithuania, via an appropriate research methodology and instruments, and provides policy advice to overcome the problems identified.

The survey encompassed forty respondents. A standard respondent was relatively young, around the age of thirty, single, without children, a university graduate (usually at postgraduate level), who had lived abroad for approximately four years, working in the field of their specialism for three years in the USA or in northern Europe.

The methodology of the study was designed to enable measurement of the relative advantages of foreign and domestic environments as judged by the respondents, based on their competences and their perceptions of the 'good life'.

The respondents' perceptions of the 'good life' were dominated by economic and self-actualization factors such as development and choice opportunities relating to jobs, opportunities for the implementation of independent thinking and for the achievement of financial sufficiency. Socio-cultural factors, such as the nature of the local environment and of participation in cultural life, were seen as being of relatively less importance. With regard to their work, the respondents also tended to prefer to act in an established system rather than to shape it.

The respondents with a PhD shared many of the above characteristics, but placed more importance on such workplace-related factors as the availability of equipment and resources (including resources for further study) and the appropriateness of their work for the level of qualification which they held. Most of the respondents indicated that their competences and qualifications played a role in their decision to work outside Lithuania.

An area of concern for Lithuania was that the advantages offered by the foreign environment were emphasized by the respondents, more than the drawbacks of remaining in Lithuania: this potentially limits the effectiveness of any policy measures which Lithuania might contemplate to retain its talented graduates. Further, the 'domestic' socio-cultural advantages of remaining in Lithuania that respondents acknowledged, were not rated as highly as 'foreign advantages' related to economic and workplace factors.

The research has confirmed the hypothesis that it is easier for a country such as Lithuania to keep intellectual capital at home than to retrieve it once it has departed. Although the respondents were in principle willing to maintain ties with their homeland and did not deny the possibility of returning in due course, their salary expectations on return are inflated and in some cases unrealistic.

In the light of this study it would appear that the most rational course of action on the part of Lithuania in relation to the phenomenon of 'brain drain' is for the country to adopt the policy of creating the conditions and incentives to keep its intellectual capital, in the form of its talented graduates, at home, whilst making the best use of ties with its emigrant intellectual capital.

Despite the fact that the research did not address the connection between the quality of higher education and the phenomenon of 'brain drain', interviews with other 'brain drain' subjects suggest that this connection is a real one.

A country such as Lithuania seems therefore to face a dilemma. Should it invest its resources in the search for better quality in higher education, viewing it as a strategic means of pursuing the knowledge economy, whilst thereby running the risk of contributing to the phenomenon of 'brain drain'? Or should other strategic means to combat 'brain drain' be adopted? Since the role of higher education as a tool in the development of the knowledge economy seems to be an inescapable one, how is the phenomenon of 'brain drain' to be addressed?

Addressing 'brain drain'

In order to implement strategies to encourage talented individuals to remain in Lithuania and exploit possibilities for keeping in contact with, and exploiting the talent of, those who leave to work abroad, policies at the state level, supported by managerial, material and financial resources, are necessary.

In this discussion, we limit ourselves to highlighting a particular potential feature of higher education which may help to address the problem of 'brain drain'. This feature can be described as involving a structured *network of professionals*, which can be initiated, created and maintained by a university or college so that it can establish a partnership with its alumni and other contacts. The purpose of this network and partnership would be to disseminate innovation and strategies for the solution of problems encountered in the development of the knowledge economy. Students at all levels should be included in such networks. Partnership networks are important features of the knowledge economy and agents of its development, ensuring the existence of learning communities. Such networks constitute important psychological and organizational antidotes to the 'brain drain' phenomenon in helping Lithuanians overseas to keep in touch with, to relate to, and to establish bonds of solidarity with, professionals in their own country. Professionals who leave Lithuania to live and work abroad may therefore continue networking with professionals in their country of origin and thereby create real possibilities not only to participate in the processes of the knowledge society and knowledge economy which are taking place in their own country, but also to enrich these processes with western experience. This does not mean, therefore, that such networks must have a narrowly national or local character, or be closed to internationalization.

It should be noted that Cheng (2001) sees the role of the university as an initiator, creator and supporter of networks of this kind as one of the major tasks for the universities of the future, involving a paradigm shift in higher education. We agree with this perspective and consider this task as a major future priority for universities, requiring further investigation and research.

References

Argyris, Ch., Putnam, R. and McLain Smith, D. (1985) *Action Science*, San Francisco: Jossey-Bass Publishers.

Barnett, R. (1990) *The Idea of Open Education*, Buckingham: SRHE & Open University Press.

—— (1994) *The Limits of Competence: Knowledge, Higher Education and Society*, Buckingham, Bristol: SRHE & Open University Press.

—— (2000) *Realizing the University: in an Age of Supercomplexity*, Buckingham, Philadelphia: SRHE & Open University Press.

Bridges, D. (2000) 'Back to the future: the higher education curriculum in the 21st century', *Cambridge Journal of Education*, 30 (1), 37–55.

Cheng, Y.Ch. (2001) 'Paradigm shift in higher education: globalization, localization, and individualization', paper presented at Kenya Ford Foundation Conference on Innovations in African Higher Education, Kenya, October.

Clark, B.R. (1995) *Perspectives of Higher Education*, Los Angeles: University of California Press.

—— (1998) *Creating Entrepreneurial Universities*, Oxford: Pergamon.

Delanty, G. (2001) *Challenging Knowledge: The University in the Knowledge Society*, Buckingham, Philadelphia: SRHE & Open University Press.

Gibbons, M. (1998) 'Higher education relevance in the 21st century', in K. Kriščiūnas and L. Rinkevičius (eds) *Aukčtojo mokslo, technologijų plėtros ir inovacijų politika*: *Compendium*, Kaunas: Technologija.

Gibbons, M., Limoges, C., Nowotny, H., Schwartzman, S., Scott, P. and Trow, M. (1995) *The New Production of Knowledge: the dynamics of science and research in contemporary societies*, London: Sage.

Grabauskas, V. and Šveikauskas, V. (2000) 'The pedagogical system of the public health bachelor studies and their characteristics in the interaction context of essential traditional and modern features of higher education', *Socialiniai mokslai*, 3 (24), 129–46.

Gudaitytė, D. and Jucevičienė, P. (2000) 'The essence of the process of the massification of higher education: the paradigm and characteristics', *Socialiniai mokslai*, 3 (24), 112–22.

Jucevičienė, P. (1999) 'Universities on the way to the world-wide academic community: the problems of the development of critical thinking and research skills', paper presented at international conference 'The Role of Social Sciences in the Development of Education, Business and Government Entering the 21st Century', Kaunas, April/May 1999.

—— (2000) 'New generation of researchers in education in Lithuania', in Ch. Day and D. van Veen (eds) *Educational Research in Europe: Yearbook 2000*, Louvain: Garant.

Jucevičienė, P., Viržintaitė, R. and Jucevičius, G. (2002) '"Brain drain" and its reflection on Lithuanian intellectual capital: pilot research report', unpublished manuscript, Kaunas University of Technology.

Klimašauskienė, R., Janiūnaitė, B. and Chreptavičienė, V. (2003) 'Problematic aspects of knowledge production in higher education, dissemination and conversion into innovation', *Socialiniai mokslai*, 1 (38), 15–23.

Kraujutaitytė, L. (2002) 'Value system of democratic higher education', *Socialiniai mokslai*, 4 (36), 28–38.

Poškienė, A. (2002) 'Critical pedagogy and language learning/teaching in the context of university change', in R. Gerd-Bodo, I. Musteikienė and P. Jucevičienė (eds) *Towards the Learning Society: Educational Issues*, Frankfurt-am-Main: Peter Lang.

Robertson, D. (2000) 'Students as consumers: the individualization of competitive advantage', in P. Scott (ed.) *Higher Education Re-formed*, London and New York: Falmer Press.

Rothblatt, S. (2000) 'A Connecticut Yankee?', in P. Scott (ed.) *Higher Education Re-formed*, London and New York: Falmer Press.

Schuller, T. (ed.) (1995) *The Changing University?*, Buckingham, Philadelphia: SRHE & Open University Press.

Scott, P. (1995) *The Meanings of Mass Higher Education*, Buckingham: Open University Press.

—— (1997) 'The crisis of knowledge and the massification of higher education', in R. Barnett and A. Griffin (eds) *The End of Knowledge in Higher Education*, GB: Redwood Books.

—— (1998) *The Globalization of Higher Education*, Buckingham: Open University Press.

—— (ed.) (2000) *Higher Education Re-formed*, London and New York: Falmer Press.

Soete, L. (2001) 'The New Economy: a European perspective', in D. Archibugi and B.-Å. Lundvall (eds) *The Globalizing Learning Economy*, Oxford: University Press.

Van der Wende, M. (1997) 'Missing links: the relationship between national policies for internationalization and those for higher education in general', in *National Policies for Internationalization of Higher Education in Europe*, Stockholm: National Agency for Higher Education.

Chapter 4

The role of the university in the development of the learning society

Palmira Jucevičienė

Since its emergence, the idea of the 'learning society' has been associated with the recognition that societies are changing and that appropriate responses to these changes are needed. The concept of a 'learning society' is not, of course, a straightforward one, and several different versions of the concept can be discerned. One prominent general difficulty is a tendency, in discussions of the concept, to imply that learning per se is a good thing. In a full discussion of the concept of the learning society (and for that matter the learning organization, learning university, etc.) attention is needed to the question: learning *what?* Learning can be superficial, irrelevant or harmful. Certain *kinds of learning* are assumed in the following discussion and although these forms are not articulated in detail here, they require detailed articulation in a fuller account.

The concept of the 'learning society' has been particularly embraced by educationalists, although it has also claimed the attention of specialists in management (especially by those concerned with 'knowledge management' – 'a set of management activities aimed at designing and influencing processes of knowledge creation and integration including processes of sharing knowledge' (Foss and Mahnke 2003: 78)) – and by sociologists. It is widely argued that the task of bringing about the 'learning society' is not an easy one. According to Barnett (1997), 'the learning society' is more an aspiration than a reality. While the author of this chapter agrees with Barnett that 'the learning society' has not yet been fully achieved in any context, she disagrees with Barnett's claim that such a society will never be realized. The opportunities for learning, especially in the information society, are huge and one is inclined to believe that the learning society will be achieved in a number of countries.

Whilst the idea of 'the learning society' originated in, and has been most fully pursued in the context of, western societies, the post-Soviet 'countries in transition' can also legitimately aspire to implement the concept. The concept cannot, however, be uncritically transplanted from one context to another without careful attention to the specific features and needs of 'countries in transition'.

This chapter offers an exploration of the notion of the 'learning society' and its underlying theoretical basis and practical implications, with particular reference to the context of 'societies in transition' and to the role which higher education must play in the implementation of the idea of the 'learning society' in these contexts.

The nature and significance of the learning society

Educational perspectives on the learning society

As noted by Merricks (2001), the idea of the learning society, which features prominently in the area of educational research and practice, developed from the concept of lifelong learning (LLL) for individuals, the theoretical basis of which was developed by Schön (1971) about three decades ago. The implementation of LLL requires the provision of conditions for education which apply to the whole of society. Is a society where most of its members are learning *ipso facto* a learning society? Coffield (2000), before presenting the findings from the Economic and Social Research Council's (ESRC) programme of research into the learning society, offered a critical analysis of the concept of a learning society. Based on a review of research, Coffield suggested ten models or fragments of a learning society, involving the following dimensions:

- '*skills growth*' – continuous skills improvement seen as essential for increasing competitiveness;
- '*personal development*' – the involvement of individuals in various forms of learning with the aim of helping them to achieve self-fulfilment;
- '*social learning*' – learning seen as a social rather than an individual process involving cooperation and competition, a relationship with a social context and outcomes which constitute forms of social capital;
- '*a learning market*' – market forces seen as operating in education as well as in business;
- '*local learning societies*' – features ascribed to the learning society seen as operating in local and regional contexts rather than in society in general. This is the core idea in Longworth's (2000) book *Making Lifelong Learning Work: Learning Cities for a Learning Century*;
- '*social control*' – forms of social control seen as necessary to ensure that no people are left 'outside learning';
- '*self-evaluation*' – continuous and systematic assessment of a country's lifelong learning achievements seen as necessary (e.g. by publishing annual 'state of the nation' reports on lifelong learning);
- '*centrality of learning*' – *learning* and *learners* seen as requiring emphasis in all educational plans and strategies;
- '*a reformed system of education*' – the national educational systems seen as needing reform (e.g. by developing a national credit framework and exploring formal and informal learning at work so as to create opportunities for relating academic and vocational learning);

- *'structural change'* – the three systems – education, training and employment – seen as requiring structural change in order to produce an integrated system.

Certainly, these ten fragments do not encompass all views of the learning society. Coffield is right to insist, along with Young (1998), that the concept of the learning society is contested and that a variety of notions of the learning society are in play, determined by different conceptions of society held by their proponents.

Young (1998) suggested another classification of ideas about the learning society consisting of several key models: the *schooling* model is based on high participation in full-time post-compulsory education; the *credentialist* model emphasizes enabling the majority of citizens to acquire the qualifications needed for work and to further develop them in the course of life; the *access* model emphasizes self-directed learning everywhere and at any time (with particular significance given to e-learning), and the *connective* model is based on the reconceptualization of academic and vocational curricula, learning and qualifications, and the relations between learning and production.

Based on an interpretation of Coffield's ideas, the latter connective model is presented in Jarvis' (2001) book *The Age of Learning: Education and Knowledge Society* as the *reflexive* model, especially emphasizing the development of the capacity to learn. In this context, capacity is regarded as a major feature of all social relations: personal, organizational and societal (Young *et al.* 1997).

As one can see from the ten fragments of the learning society highlighted by Coffield (2000) and from the work of Young and his co-authors, the authors of the ESRC Programme of research into the learning society view a learning society as a society which arranges its education, including education conducted in collaboration with businesses and other organizations, in order to provide educational conditions for all its members' lifelong and life-wide learning for employment as well as for democracy, participation, self-fulfilment and citizenship.

As Jarvis (2001: 61) points out, most definitions of the learning society 'acknowledge a conflict between economic and democratic imperatives'. According to Jarvis, this conflict goes deeper than economics and politics: the learning society 'raises issues of a philosophical kind, especially about the nature of learning and knowledge, as well as about the identity and autonomy of learners' (ibid., p. 61). Referring to the ideas on the development of the learning society which are outlined in the works of Hutchins (1968), Husén (1974) and Boshier (1980), Jarvis discerned three models of the learning society (*cultural, technological* and *democratic*) based on particular philosophical outlooks.

The first, Hutchin's *cultural* model, characterized the learning society by reference to particular *values* relating to learning and the nature of the person, relating to the notion of the liberally educated, rational, autonomous individual. In the second, *technological* model which is also called *futurological* (Jarvis 2001:

63), Husén (1974) also invokes the notion of the *self-directed* learner, arguing that such learners must first of all learn how to learn, and then continue learning to achieve necessary competences in relation to the community, business organizations and society in general. The third – Boshier's *democracy/ participation/ citizenship* – model, is related to Mill's conception of democratic society (Mill 1954). The emphasis of this model is on liberal ideas, including respect for the individual, who must have a voice in society, including in any policy decisions. Since 'learning employees' are the basis for the development of the learning organization, in the course of adopting the features of the learning organization business organizations may be acting as powerful agents of democracy because employees and organizations are significant interest groups able to influence political decisions at the level of society. Thus, through learning individuals and learning organizations which develop under their influence, not only the development of the learning society, but also its democratization and liberalization are stimulated by business organizations. It might be objected that this is true only if the organizations in question are not inimical to liberal democratic values: however, if these organizations are learning organizations, or aspiring to develop into them, they must already contain democratic features, since such features are part of 'learning organizations' properly understood.

Managerial perspectives on the learning society

These perspectives emphasize the importance of organizational learning (Elkjaer 2003) and the influence of organizations and the environment on learning, whilst at the same time not denying the significance of the individual, especially the leader, for organizational learning (Argyris and Schön 1978, 1996, Duncan and Weiss 1979, Miller 1996, Vera and Crossan 2003). Organizational learning emerges when individual and group learning is institutionalized by the organization, i.e. knowledge created during learning in action is embedded in routines, systems, structures and culture. Continuous learning by employees, and learning at the organizational level, are united in the notion of the learning organization (Senge 1990, Pedler *et al.* 1991). Nonaka and Takeuchi (1995) developed a theory of becoming a 'knowledge-creating company', in this way defining the *knowledge organization*.

A special role in learning organizations is assigned to organizational learning based on member interaction, which is illuminated by the notion of *communities of practice* (Wenger 1998, Plaskoff 2003) and their related networks (Wijk *et al.* 2003). Child and Rodrigues (2003) argue that organizational learning can influence *social identity* and vice versa.

Compared to the educational perspective, the managerial view expands understanding of the learning society by adding organizational learning as a creation of shared knowledge taking place at different levels of organizations and society. Whilst both perspectives acknowledge the importance of social learning theory, the educational perspective stresses the significance of individual learning in whatever context it is taking place and the managerial perspective stresses the importance of networking and organizational learning.

Sociological perspectives on the learning society

What can be meant by learning at the level of society? Barnett's suggestion is that 'society can learn about itself' (Barnett 1997: 159). Learning at the level of society implies that even dominating perspectives and ideologies 'can be placed and kept under critical surveillance', and thereby *a critical society* can be developed. In this process the appropriate participation of academics and the existence of 'a high general level of education, a full flow of information and democratic structures' in society (ibid., p. 160) is required.

The notion of the learning society: educational, managerial and sociological perspectives combined

Integrating the educational, managerial and sociological perspectives on the learning society, it can be argued that from a systematic point of view a *learning society* can be regarded as learning at the three interrelated levels – individual, (formal and non-formal) organizational and societal (involving networking between citizens and civic and business institutions and bodies of different kinds).

Review of policies and practices of the development of learning societies

Experience of the developed countries

The implementation of the ideas of the learning society must inevitably be analysed in the context of the implementation of the lifelong learning concept. Longworth assigns special importance to the Delors' (1996) Report on Education for the 21st Century, *Learning: The Treasure Within*. The important European Commission White Paper on education and training *Teaching and Learning – Towards the Learning Society* (European Commission 1996) specified the following aims (ibid., p. 52): to encourage the acquisition of new knowledge; bring schools and the business closer together; combat exclusion; develop proficiency in three Community languages; and treat capital investment and investment in training on an equal basis.

The documents mentioned above emphasize individual learning and the creation of educational conditions for it. Both Dunne, who reflected on the Delors' Report (Dunne 1999), and Smith, who commented on the European White Paper and on the American initiatives *A Nation at Risk* and *America 2000* (Smith 2000), noted that these concepts were developed in a spirit of economic competitiveness. Dunne's insightful question is pertinent: 'to what extent should considerations of economic productivity outweigh all others in the promotion of a learning society for the future?' (Dunne 1999: 17).

The studies of the implementation of the EU policy on the development of learning societies suggest certain positive developments in providing citizens with educational opportunities which have an impact on the economy, e.g. in relation to higher employment rates (Sellin 1999: 28), However, it is doubted whether efforts to promote learning societies have any impact on those who already have relatively good education and whether these efforts will reduce the gap between those with the best and those with the poorest education (European Commission 2001). It was noted that, despite the policy of bringing closer together general and vocational education tracks, a gap between them remains (Sellin 2000). Although EU member countries are moving forward in joining different societal, business and education forces for developing the European accreditation of the non-formal learning system outlined in the White Paper, one can notice different traditions and practices in this area related to at least five country groups (Bjønåvold 2000). At the same time, it can be noticed that all EU countries have a strong interest in lifelong learning. They accept it as a policy priority for national economic and, increasingly, social well-being (Leney *et al.* 2000).

Countries which are worth discussing in relation to the development of the learning society are Japan and the UK. A number of authors (Trivellato 1997, quoted in Keep and Rainbird 2002, Longworth 2000, Jelenc 1999, Okamoto 1994) point out that Japan's societal organization, cultural and historical inheritances, and labour and market characteristics enable this country already to have some features of the learning society which are manifested at various levels, not only that of individual learning.

The UK has also set a goal at the national level to develop a learning society at all levels – individual, organizational, regional and national (National Committee of Enquiry into Higher Education 1997). To achieve this, various means have been adopted. In response to the Green Paper 'The Learning Age' (The Stationery Office 1998) and the White Paper 'Learning to Succeed' (Department for Education and Employment 1999), the vision of the learning society was disseminated and special bodies were established at the national and regional level (e.g. Learning and Skills Council, Higher Education Funding Council for England, University for Industry, etc.), which are actively working in their respective areas. However, according to Keep and Rainbird (2002), referring to the research conducted by Green (1998), Coffield (1997a, 1997b), McGivney (1997), Keep and Mayhew (1996) for the Economic and Social Research Council's (ESRC) 'Learning Society' Programme, 'the UK has a long way to go before it becomes a learning society' (Keep and Rainbird 2002: 81). British researchers pointed out a number of structural and cultural characteristics suggesting 'that the UK offers an environment that may be relatively hostile to the swift and easy development of high levels of organizational learning' (ibid.).

Developing the learning society is problematic if certain inequalities remain in education, for example, due to social backgrounds (Aldrich 2002, referring to the UK example, where, according to Bauman (1998), the gap between the rich and poor is constantly increasing). It is important to attend to the socially excluded (Jarvis 2001: 202).

The path of post-Soviet 'countries in transition'

The development of the learning society and its relationship with lifelong learning is of special interest in 'countries in transition', whose citizens have rather high, although usually specialized, education, but have spent a relatively long time under authoritarian closed regimes. A number of post-Soviet countries (Poland, Latvia, Lithuania, Estonia, Slovenia) can be usefully discussed here.

Lithuania has adopted at the national level the strategy for the development of the information society. However, no official position has been expressed at the national level regarding the development of the learning society, although two ministries – Ministry of Education and Science and Ministry of Social Care and Labour – have approved a common Strategy for Ensuring Lifelong Learning (Švietimo aprūpinimo centras 2004). This document contains all the attributes of LLL but does not mention either organizational learning, or learning on the societal level. The document 'Guidelines for Education' (Švietimo kaitos fondas 2002), which reflects the political accord on the development of education in Lithuania up to 2020, emphasizes that education is a force which modernizes society and is an inseparable part of national culture. The key purpose of education is seen as providing individuals with the basis for mature autonomous life, helping them to engage in the lifelong development of their capabilities, and developing their community spirit and ability to combine their aims with those of the civic society, in this way laying the foundation for the autonomous and creative life of the nation. It is emphasized that Lithuanian education will fulfil its societal obligations only if its evolution is faster than that of society.

A similar inattention to the notions of the learning society and the knowledge society is discernible in initiatives in relation to lifelong learning in countries such as Poland (Elsner 2000, Cimdiņš 2000).

In 1998 'Learning Estonia' was presented as one of four scenarios for developing Estonian education up to 2010 (Loogma *et al.* 1998), involving the notion of the learning society, including lifelong learning and partnership networks which are capable of implementing organizational and societal learning. However, one of the deficiencies in this initiative was that there was no clear strategy for adult education or for long-term partnerships with enterprises or municipalities (Talvi and Jõgi 2000: 102).

In his work 'Slovenia – The Learning Country', Jelenc (1999) argues that 'the creation of a national policy and associated strategy is not possible without State support and approval, but, on the other hand, it should be initiated from the professional side' (Jelenc 1999: 51). The author points out that many projects are under way. In the course of preparation for the development of the learning country, some unfavourable circumstances were also taken into account. They include the still-existing 'strong school' tradition (authoritarian pedagogy) and significant economic problems caused by the situation of the 'country in transition'. According to Jelenc, although Slovenian people have good working habits, 'they need stimulating circumstances and opportunities to promote learning; they must be pushed and challenged to start learning' (ibid., p. 51). In addition, appropriate attitudes towards lifelong learning in schools and in society as a whole do not prevail, and the notion of organizational learning and learning at the societal level are not clearly brought into focus.

Common problems and their solutions in the developed countries and 'countries in transition'

Summarizing the situation of the developed countries and the 'countries in transition' in the context of the development of learning societies, it should be noted that almost all of them have the same problem – incomplete understanding of the learning society at the level of political will.

Other obstacles in the development of learning societies include the role of the social forces of global capitalism (Jarvis 2001) and the need to go beyond merely utopian visions (Ranson 1994) to identify strategies for development. In our study 'The Bottom-Up Strategy for the Development of Learning Society in a "Country in Transition" and the Particularities of its Implementation' (Jucevičienė *et al.* 2003) we showed that in countries where there is a lack of understanding of the learning society at a macro level it is advisable to implement regional strategies, i.e. to develop specific learning regions, cities, towns, villages, etc. – the structures for which the *communities of practice* methodology is more relevant, though not to the exclusion of macro-level considerations. In the development of the learning region (Longworth 2000, 2003), learning at the individual, organizational and 'semi-societal', i.e. regional level, is pursued. The next strategic step in the development of learning regions is the development of the learning-in-partnership networks, in this way promoting the learning society at societal level.

A special role in the learning society, and especially in the development of regions, is played by higher education, particularly by modern universities (Delanty 2001, Longworth and Davies 1996). It is to the nature of this role that we now turn.

The potential of universities in the development of the learning society

The role and possibilities of universities in the development of the learning society have been widely discussed (Barnett 1997, 2000, Bowden and Marton 1998, Delanty 2001, Scott 2000a, 2000b, Rothblatt 2000, Duke 2002, Waterhouse 2000, Robertson 2000). A number of ideas and doubts have been expressed about how universities could and should contribute to these processes. This section of the chapter is devoted to defining the potential which the university must possess to be able to influence in a fundamental way the development of the learning society.

The role of the university in the development of the learning society is inseparable from its role in the development of the knowledge society.

The key feature and strength of the university, even a traditional one, is its experience of organizational learning. Organizational learning and organizational knowledge are two interrelated components of the learning community phenomenon (Vera and Crossan 2003).

According to Bowden and Marton (1998), the creation of knowledge takes place not only when a scholar makes a discovery during his/her research, but also when the knowledge is shared on the collective level. This discussion inevitably takes place at the organizational (at least, the university departmental) learning level, whereas the new knowledge legitimized by the academic community inevitably becomes their collective (organizational) understanding of the matters at stake. So, in this respect the community of scholars at a research university is acting as a learning organization.

University as a knowledge organization

What should a modern university be like in order to be 'an example of open-mindedness for society' (Rothblatt 2000: 5), and, more specifically, for the emerging knowledge and learning society? What should it be like to act as a constructive critic of society (Barnett 1997), a developer of individual and organizational learning competence, an involver of individuals and organizations into learning at individual and organizational level, a creator of the learning partnership networks ensuring societal learning?

Foremost, it has to be a *multiversity*, simultaneously performing many functions which converge into three major objectives for the university: (1) research, (2) studies, and (3) community service. The university involvement in *supercomplexity* is discussed by Barnett (2000). Barnett makes a number of claims relating to each of the three major objectives for universities mentioned above: (1) as a producer of knowledge the university also produces new frameworks of understanding; (2) as a teacher of students the university has to prepare students so that they have 'human qualities capable of withstanding a world of supercomplexity' (ibid., p. 116); (3) as a contributor of community service the university has to play a civic and enlightenment role in helping society to live in conditions of supercomplexity (Bowden and Marton 1998).

All three objectives overlap to the extent that the university is related to knowledge in a special way. In earlier times the university had a monopoly of knowledge production. In the emerging knowledge society, where, along with the traditional Mode 1 of knowledge production, Mode 2 knowledge production has emerged, thereby demonopolizing knowledge production (Gibbons *et al.*

1994), the university is maintaining its monopoly in a special space which is between the level of knowledge production and the level of knowledge utilization by social actors (Delanty 2001).

The university plays a special role of *reflexive* knowledge communication, aimed at producing new cognitive structures as cultural models, because in the university the following necessary features of reflexivity as cognitive transformation are united: the university is an expert institution (Giddens 1990, 1991) and a critical force in society (Beck *et al.* 1994). The work of the university is not confined to its own institutional space and it involves interaction with many social actors.

This special role of the university enables it to develop the learning society on a societal level, involving not only the development of learning partnership networking techniques, but, more importantly, collective learning as transformation of cultural models. For example, in developing the 'learning city' the university helps to establish partnership networks among various social actors, not only by teaching them techniques of cooperation, but also by promoting attitudes towards greater social awareness and responsibility.

University as an institution of learning

The role of the university in educating professionals and other members of the knowledge and learning society calls for special discussion. For students the university should be a key institution for bringing into being a learning society in its fullest sense: (a) students have to be exposed to multiple discourses extending beyond the academic to those which relate to practical knowledge necessary for society and requiring public discussion within society; (b) students should be enabled to develop a broader understanding within their knowledge field, and to consider the potential impact of this intellectual field on the other knowledge fields and on practice (Bowden and Marton 1998).

A difficult necessary transition is from the educational paradigm of *teaching* to *learning* under conditions of mass higher education, and the creation of learning environments which students can accept as their own (Jucevičienė and Tautkevičienė 2003).

The work of the university teacher has a paradoxical character. On the one hand, due to mass higher education, the intellectual abilities of the 'average' student are diminishing and the number of non-traditional students is increasing, but on the other hand, students need increasingly complex knowledge, knowledge requirements for professionals are growing, and students need the skills of the *learning society* member. Meeting these challenges by the university requires not only professionally trained teachers, but also researchers capable of and having the necessary conditions for realizing four forms of scholarship as engagement in producing knowledge (Bowden and Marton 1998: 10): (1) *discovery* (engagement in original research); (2) *integration* ('stepping back from one's investigation, looking for connections; interpreting, fitting one's own research, or the research of others, into large intellectual patterns'); (3) application; and (4) teaching. Hence, to influence the development of the learning society in many ways, a university has to be the *learning university in the sense that it is open to learning the sorts of things outlined above.*

The specific role of universities in the development of learning regions

Without repeating the key features of the *learning university*, in this section I will discuss the specific role of the university in developing its region into a learning region.

A university of average size (not a mega-university) will probably not be able to *fundamentally* influence the development of the learning society in its country. At the same time, such a university can be a *key* agent in stimulating its region's development into a learning region. First of all, through its 'voice' in the region it can be an initiator of the development of the learning region, making the 'first move' (Longworth 2000). It is now widely argued (Duke 2002, Delanty 2001, Scott 2000b) that universities which focus on regional and local community development do not diminish their international prestige, but through a relatively quick achievement of recognized results and the realization of a broader range of the possibilities of a modern university, achieve a higher recognition both in their country and internationally. However, different opinions emerge about the possibilities and intentions of the traditional and new universities (or *regional universities*, as they are called in some countries) to participate in regional development. It is believed that elite universities will confine themselves to delegating the relations with the local community to their continuing learning departments, thereby relegating such relations to second-class status (Jarvis 2001: 128). The possibilities of the new universities are doubted by those who value highly the mission of the university in the development of a learning society but question whether such universities are capable of providing reflexive capacity for the local community.

Real-life examples can help to dissipate the doubts of both camps. For example, in the UK, which has set a regional mission for higher education in 2001 (HEFCE 2001), there are nine regional higher education consortia. One of them, including various universities and colleges, has among its members the University of Cambridge, which directly participates in the development of the learning region in various ways. Consortia and other associations based on *networking* easily achieve synergy (see the contribution by Bridges in this volume).

The networking experience of universities can not only result in the synergetic influence of higher education institutions on the region, but also helps to resolve the issues of human resources which are crucial for the development of the learning region. First, through its networks the university can invite professionals important for the region to teach, conduct research and work as experts (in the region or virtually). 'So we may see universities in Cape Town,

Auckland or Sydney in merger–alliance with universities in America, Europe, China or Japan' (Robertson 2000: 86). Second, the university can use its networks with social partners in the region to involve its students in intellectual and practical activities important for their education. This would help not only to educate better professionals, but also to 'settle' them in the region, enabling them to contribute to the region's social capital by remaining in these networks, even when they physically leave. Also, the university can use its intellectual and social capital by participating in other regional networks aimed at dealing with regional problems, in this way stimulating *collective learning and understanding*. The UK universities together with regional development agencies help to implement innovations, provide targeted training in higher-level skills, contribute to social inclusion, help attract inward investment, contribute to the strategic thinking and expertise in the region (HEFCE 2001). (On this see the contribution by Bridges in this volume.)

Many universities have expertise enabling them to offer consultations to the region as it develops into a learning region. For example, the city administrations of Paramatta and Penrith (Western Sydney locality) invited the local university to assist the process of becoming learning cities (Duke 2002: 50).

The universities operating in 'countries in transition' play an especially important role in the development of learning regions, and through them, in the development of the learning society. In addition to theoretical and practical problems related to the development of the learning society which are common for all countries, there are some specific difficulties observed only in post-Soviet countries. The key problem is lack of democratic thinking and the residue of Soviet thinking, which are especially problematic. (On these matters see, for example, the contribution by Janiūnaitė and Gudaitytė in this volume.) The fact that these residues still remain and are not easily overcome can be explained by complexity theory (Davies 2000).

It is unlikely that post-Soviet countries will soon achieve collective competence at the political level which will lead to political decisions to develop a learning society that is not 'empty of meaning' (Duke 2002: 50). This competence is likely to be developed sooner at the regional level, because the regions deal with more local problems, involving in their solution a smaller circle of social actors. These processes can be *fundamentally* influenced by the regional university/universities. (On the regional significance of universities in the Baltic region see the chapter by Musiał in this volume.)

The discussion on the specific role of the university in regional development and some activities of the *learning university* can be illustrated by the case study of Kaunas University of Technology (KTU), which is participating in developing the second-largest Lithuanian city, Kaunas, into a learning city. Discussing this case study in full would take a separate article. Here it should be noted that after KTU initiated the development of Kaunas into a learning city in 2001, the local government included this goal into their strategy and is successfully implementing it. At the same time, KTU is conducting research on the development of the learning city which has been recognized as a priority research area by the National Research Foundation. Kaunas University of Technology is sharing its theoretical knowledge and practical experience with other Lithuanian cities: three other cities followed the example of Kaunas and embarked on a journey towards becoming learning cities.

Summarizing the discussion, it should be noted that the *learning society* is a rather complex, multidisciplinary construct. The full meaning of this construct is revealed not only by analysing individual and organizational learning, but also by exploring learning of these two types in the milieu of the learning organization, learning region (also, city, town, village) and the whole of society. The features of the development of a learning society can be noticed in different countries, including some 'countries in transition'. These features are more visible not at the level of the whole of society, but at the lower levels – those of the learning city, learning organization and learning individual. A greater contribution to the development of these features by universities as institutions with *critical thinking* potential allows one to hope that the learning society is not an unreachable ideal. In the 'countries in transition', universities should play an essential role in the development of the learning society at the above-mentioned levels and in the above-mentioned ways.

References

Aldrich, R. (2002) *A Century of Education*, New York: Routledge/Falmer.
Argyris, C. and Schön, D.A. (1978; 2nd edn 1996) *Organizational Learning II: Theory, Method, and Practice*, Reading: Addison–Wesley.
Barnett, R. (1997) *Higher Education: a Critical Business*, Buckingham: The Society for Research into Higher Education & Open University Press.
—— (2000) 'Reconfiguring the University', in P. Scott (ed.) *Higher Education Reformed*, London and New York: Falmer Press.
Bauman, Z. (1998) *Work, Consumerism and the New Poor*, Buckingham: Open University Press.
Beck, U., Giddens, A. and Lasch, S. (1994) *Reflexive Modernization*, Cambridge: Polity.
Bjørnåvold, J. (2000) *Making Learning Visible: Identification, Assessment and Recognition of Non-formal Learning in Europe*, Thessaloniki: CEDEFOP – European Centre for the Development of Vocational Training.
Boshier, R. (ed.) (1980) *Towards a Learning Society: New Zealand Adult Education in Transition*, Vancouver: Learning Press.
Bowden, J. and Marton, F. (1998) *The University of Learning: Beyond Quality and Competence in Higher Education*, London: Kogan Page.
Child, J. and Rodrigues, S. (2003) 'Social identity and organizational learning', in M. Easterby-Smith and M.A. Lyles (eds) *The Blackwell Handbook of Organizational Learning and Knowledge Management*, USA: Blackwell Publishing Ltd.
Cimdiņš, P. (2000) 'Higher education in Latvia – a strategy for 2010', *Humanities and Social Sciences Latvia*, 2 (27), 4–14.
Coffield, F. (1997a) 'Nine learning fallacies and their replacement by a national strategy for lifelong learning', in F. Coffield (ed.) *A National Strategy for Lifelong Learning*, Newcastle: University of Newcastle.

—— (1997b) 'A tale of three pigs: building the learning society with straw', in F. Coffield (ed.) *A National Strategy for Lifelong Learning*, Newcastle: University of Newcastle.

—— (ed.) (2000) *Different Visions of a Learning Society: Research Findings*, vol. 1, Great Britain: The Policy Press.

Davies, L. (2000*)* 'Chaos and complexity in the study of school management', in R. Alexander, M. Osborn and D. Phillips (eds) *Policy, Professionals and Development*, vol. 2, Oxford: Symposium Books.

Delanty, G. (2001) *Challenging Knowledge: the University in the Knowledge Society*, Buckingham: SRHE and Open University Press.

Delors, J. (1996) 'Learning: the treasure within', Report on Education for the 21st Century, Paris: UNESCO.

Department for Education and Employment (1999) *Learning to Succeed: a New Framework for Post-16 Learning*, Cm 4392 UK.

Duke, Ch. (2002) *Managing the Learning University*, Buckingham: SRHE and Open University Press.

Duncan, R. and Weiss, A. (1979) 'Organizational learning: implications for organizational design', in B. Staw (ed.) *Research in Organizational Behavior*, Greenwich, CT: JAI Press.

Dunne, E. (1999) 'Change in higher education: a learning society and the role of core skills', in E. Dunne (ed.) *The Learning Society: International Perspectives on Core Skills in Higher Education*, London: Kogan Page.

Elkjaer, B. (2003) 'Social learning theory: learning as participation in social processes', in M. Easterby-Smith and M.A. Lyles (eds) *The Blackwell Handbook of Organizational Learning and Knowledge Management*, USA: Blackwell Publishing Ltd.

Elsner, D. (2000) 'Reflection on megatrends in education from a Polish perspective', in T. Mebrahtu, M. Crossley and D. Johnson (eds) *Globalization, Educational Transformation and Societies in Transition*, Oxford: Symposium Books.

European Commission (1996) 'Teaching and learning – towards the learning society', White Paper on education and training, Luxembourg: Office for Official Publications of the European Communities.

—— (2001) 'National actions to implement lifelong learning in Europe', Belgium: CEDEFOP, EURODICE.

Foss, N.J. and Mahnke, V. (2003) 'Knowledge management: what can organizational economics contribute?', in M. Easterby-Smith and M.A. Lyles (eds) *The Blackwell Handbook of Organizational Learning and Knowledge Management*, USA: Blackwell Publishing Ltd.

Gibbons, M., Limoges, C., Nowotny, H., Schwartzman, S., Scott, P. and Trow, M. (1994) *The New Production of Knowledge*, London: Sage.

Giddens, A. (1990) *The Consequences of Modernity*, Cambridge: Polity.

—— (1991) *Modernity and Self-Identity: Self and Society in the Late Modern Age*, Cambridge: Polity.

Green, A. (1998) 'Core skills, key skills and general culture: in search of the common foundation in vocational education', *Evaluation and Research in Education*, 12 (1), 23–43.

HEFCE (Higher Education Funding Council for England) (2001) 'Higher education and the regions: HEFCE policy statement', UK.

Husén, T. (1974) *The Learning Society*, London: Methuen.

Hutchins, R.M. (1968) *The Learning Society*, Harmondsworth: Penguin.
Jarvis, P. (ed.) (2001) *The Age of Learning: Education and the Knowledge Society*, London: Kogan Page.
Jelenc, Z. (1999) '"Slovenia – the learning country": how to reach the pre-set strategic goal', in E. Dunne (ed.) *The Learning Society: International Perspectives on Core Skills in Higher Education*, London: Kogan Page.
Jucevičienė, P. and Tautkevičienė, G. (2003) *Academic Library as a Learning Environment: How Do Students Perceive It?*, Leeds: University of Leeds. Online. Available at: www.leeds.ac.uk/educol/documents/00003274.htm (accessed 10 November 2004).
Jucevičienė, P., Bagdonas, A. and Jucevičius, G. (2003) 'The bottom-up strategy for the development of learning society in a "country in transition" and the particularities of its implementation', *Socialiniai mokslai*, 3 (40), 104–11.
Keep, E. and Mayhew, K. (1996) 'Towards a learning society – definition and measurement', *Policy Studies*, 17 (13), 215–31.
Keep, E. and Rainbird, H. (2002) 'Towards the learning organization?', in F. Reeve, M. Cartwright and R. Edwards (eds) *Supporting Lifelong Learning: Organizing Learning*, vol. 2, London and New York: The Open University.
Leney, T., Green, A. and Wolf, A. (2000) 'European trends in the development of vocational education and training systems and provision', in B. Sellin (ed.) *European Trends in the Development of Occupations and Qualifications: Finding of Research, Studies and Analyses for Policy and Practice*, reference document, vol. 2, Thessaloniki: CEDEFOP.
Longworth, N. (2000) *Making Lifelong Learning Work: Learning Cities for a Learning Century*, London: Kogan Page.
—— (2003) *Lifelong Learning in Action: Transforming Education in the 21st Century*, London: Kogan Page.
Longworth, N. and Davies, W.K. (1996) *Lifelong Learning: New Visions, New Implications, New Roles – for Industry, Government, Education and the Community for the 21st Century*, London: Kogan Page.
Loogma, K., Ruubel, R., Ruus, V., Sarv, E.S. and Vilu, R. (1998) 'Estonia's education scenarios 2015', in K. Loogma and E.S. Sarv (eds) *Eesti Ühiskond Ja Haridus*, Tallinn: Trükk As Rebelis.
McGivney, V. (1997) 'Adult participation in learning: can we change the pattern?', in F. Coffield (ed.) *A National Strategy for Lifelong Learning*, Newcastle: University of Newcastle.
Merricks, L. (2001) 'The emerging idea', in P. Jarvis (ed.) *The Age of Learning: education and the knowledge society*, London: Kogan Page.
Mill, J.S. (1954), cited in P. Jarvis (ed.) (2001) *The Age of Learning: Education and the Knowledge Society*, London: Kogan Page.
Miller, D. (1996) 'A preliminary typology of organizational learning: synthesizing the literature', *Journal of Management*, 22, 485–505.
National Committee of Enquiry into Higher Education (1997) *Higher Education in the Learning Society*, London: HMSO (The Dearing Report).
Nonaka, I. and Takeuchi, H. (1995) *The Knowledge-Creating Company*, Oxford: University Press.
Okamoto, K. (1994) *Education Policy Analysis*, Paris: OECD.
Pedler, M., Burgoyne, J. and Boydell, T. (1991) *The Learning Company*, England: McGraw-Hill Book Company Europe.

Plaskoff, J. (2003) 'Intersubjectivity and community building: learning to learn organizationally', in M. Easterby-Smith and M.A. Lyles (eds) *The Blackwell Handbook of Organizational Learning and Knowledge Management*, USA: Blackwell Publishing Ltd.
Ranson, S. (1994) *Towards the Learning Society*, London: Cassell.
Robertson, D. (2000) 'Students as consumers: the individualization of competitive advantage', in P. Scott (ed.) *Higher Education Re-formed*, London and New York: Falmer Press.
Rothblatt, S. (2000) 'A Connecticut Yankee? An unlikely historical scenario', in P. Scott (ed.) *Higher Education Re-formed*, London and New York: Falmer Press.
Schön, D. (1971) *Beyond the Stable State: Public and Private Learning in a Changing Society*, New York: Norton.
Scott, P. (2000a) 'A tale of three revolutions? Science, society and the university', in P. Scott (ed.) *Higher Education Re-formed*, London and New York: Falmer Press.
—— (ed.) (2000b) *Higher Education Re-formed*, London and New York: Falmer Press.
Sellin, B. (ed.) (1999) *European Trends in the Development of Occupations and Qualifications: Finding of Research, Studies and Analyses for Policy and Practice*, reference document, vol. 1, Thessaloniki: CEDEFOP.
—— (ed.) (2000) *European trends in the development of occupations and qualifications: finding of research, studies and analyses for policy and practice*, reference document, vol. 2, Thessaloniki: CEDEFOP.
Senge, P. (1990) *The Fifth Discipline: the Art and Practice of the Learning Organization*, New York: Doubleday Currency.
Smith, R. (2000) 'Democratic education and learning society', in F. Crawley, P. Smeyers and P. Standish (eds) *Universities Remembering Europe: Nations, Culture and Higher Education*, Oxford: Berghahn Books.
Švietimo aprūpinimo centras (2004) *Mokymosi visą gyvenimą užtikrinimo strategija* [Strategy for Ensuring Lifelong Learning], Vilnius.
Švietimo kaitos fondas (2002) *Lietuvos švietimo plėtotės strateginės nuostatos, Švietimo gairės: 2003–2012 metai: projektas* [Guidelines for Education: 2003–2012], Vilnius: Švietimo kaitos fondas.
Talvi, M. and Jõgi, L. (2000) 'Estonia in the grip of change: the role of education for adults in the transition', in T. Mebrahtu, M. Crossley and D. Johnson (eds) *Globalization, Educational Transformation and Societies in Transition*, Oxford: Symposium Books.
The Stationery Office (1998) *The Learning Age: renaissance for a New Britain*, Cm 3790 UK.
Trivellato, P. (1997) 'Japan as a learning society – an overall view by a European sociologist', in F. Coffield (ed.) *A National Strategy for Lifelong Learning*, Newcastle: University of Newcastle.
Vera, D. and Crossan, M. (2003) 'Organizational learning and knowledge management: toward an integrative framework', in M. Easterby-Smith and M.A. Lyles (eds) *The Blackwell Handbook of Organizational Learning and Knowledge Management*, USA: Blackwell Publishing Ltd.
Waterhouse, R. (2000) 'The distributed university', in P. Scott (ed.) *Higher Education Re-formed*, London and New York: Falmer Press.
Wenger, E. (1998) *Communities of Practice: Learning, Meaning, and Identity*, Cambridge: Cambridge University Press.

Wijk, R.V., Van Den Bosch, F.A.J. and Volberda, H.W. (2003) 'Knowledge and networks', in M. Easterby-Smith and M.A. Lyles (eds) *The Blackwell Handbook of Organizational Learning and Knowledge Management*, USA: Blackwell Publishing Ltd.

Young, M.F.D. (1998) *The Curriculum of the Future*, London: Falmer Press.

Young, M., Spours, K., Howieson, C. and Raffe, D. (1997) 'Unifying academic and vocational learning and the idea of a learning society', *The Journal of Education Policy*, 12 (6), 527–37.

Chapter 5

The concept of the 'intelligent country'

Robertas Jucevičius

Introduction

This chapter starts with the concept of a knowledge economy and asks: what are the characteristics of an organization, a region, a country which will allow it to compete successfully in such an economy? It considers such concepts as 'knowledge management', 'the learning organization' and 'the learning region', but goes on to argue that these characteristics are best captured in qualities which might be referred to as the 'intelligence' of an organization or economic unit and in the idea of 'the intelligent country'.

The knowledge economy

The term '*the knowledge economy*' is used in the literature to refer to a number of different things:

- a particular subset of business which is focused on informatics, telecommunications and perhaps pharmaceuticals;
- an 'informational economy' in which 'the productivity and competitiveness of units or agents ... depend on their capacity to generate, process, and apply efficiently knowledge-based information' (Castells 2000: 77). Such economies are (importantly) global and networked;
- all parts of the economy which draw upon – or ought increasingly to be drawing upon – the higher level skills necessary for the generation and use of new knowledge.

It is especially the second sense of the term – an 'informational economy' – which is being applied here (but see also Cowey 2000). In such an economy the acquisition and use of knowledge requires access to and the ability to use information and communication technologies on a different scale and complexity than ever before. It also requires an effective education system which provides opportunities for lifelong learning; new approaches to innovation which bring together researchers, entrepreneurs and policy makers; and an economic and institutional framework which supports the use of knowledge to provide new and competitive products, services, social initiatives and methods for all social actors. The need to base the support and management of developmental processes on intellectual capacity is changing our understanding of the essence of management and leading to its convergence with the field of education. Organizational learning is becoming the primary function of management. It comes from understanding that contemporary management requires, above all, the leadership of organizational learning, transformation and performance (Underwood 2001). Researchers from many different fields of social science are making an attempt to understand the complexity of the new phenomenon and to develop effective mechanisms to deal with it (Stacey *et al.* 2000, Komninos 2002, Underwood 2002a, etc.). I shall be drawing here from, in particular, recent work in management and organizational science to offer a view of these mechanisms.

If structures, governance and management processes are not properly aligned to support a knowledge culture, any investment in building intellectual capital will be of little value. It is not merely a matter of having and training up the skills (or more particularly the higher-level skills) required for a knowledge economy: success in the knowledge economy requires new agility in the use of these resources; a different level of engagement with innovative ideas; a long-term commitment to innovation as a continuing process; new relationships between research, product development, marketing, production and distribution – and all of this in a global market. These requirements demand new concepts of value creation in the business community as well as new expectations of higher education as a source not just of the innovative technology which can contribute to competitiveness but also of the social and managerial processes of the new economic order.

Kim and Mauborgne (1999) call this 'value innovation'. Value innovation means finding new and more efficient ways to achieve targeted goals and to enrich stakeholders by combining existing and new knowledge about environment, technologies, interest groups, values, approaches and attributes of value. The concept of value innovation could be compared to the concept of hyper-competition that requires the ability of business to combine different and sometimes even contradicting features of the product or service. It also requires the ability of businesses to regard their customers as individuals even if they supply their products or services to a mass market. Value innovation requires a different set of interdisciplinary knowledge than a more specialized and narrowly targeted orientation. In a knowledge economy the ability of individuals, organizations and the state as a whole to deal with the complexity is becoming an important competence. One of the most complicated problems for organizations employing such a concept is how to combine two complementary competences: a very specialized knowledge in a particular field and an ability to see a complex picture composed of the elements from different fields of knowledge. This is due to the fact that this kind of innovation needs more synthesis rather than analytical skills. There is also a challenge for higher education and other institutions involved in the development of competence in value innovation. Playing a part in global networks and virtual organizations requires an understanding of all the social interplays of such a system. This comes into direct contradiction with the recent trends (driven by the perceived short-term interests of businesses) towards more narrowly specialized education and training

'Intelligence' – and the intelligent country

There are already in the management literature a number of different concepts which attempt to capture the conditions for success in a knowledge economy, or the characteristics required of successful organizations, institutions or economic entities. These include: 'information society' (Radovan 2003, Grippenberg et al. 2004), 'knowledge management' (Davenport et al. 1992), 'knowing organization' (Choo 1998, Rowley 2000, Stankevičiūtė and Jucevičius 2003), 'learning organization' (Senge 1990) and 'learning regions' (Arbonies and Moso 2002). In fact all of these, even if they do have application to a knowledge economy, have their limitations.

The concept of an 'information society' is mainly related to the use of information as a key asset. The problem with this concept is that individuals and organizations are becoming overcrowded with information that is not always of much use. IT tools have only a limited capacity to manage the information and, more particularly, to transform it into understanding. The gap between information and understanding is wide and full of complexities.

'Knowledge management' mainly deals with handling internal organizational knowledge, i.e. transforming implicit knowledge into explicit knowledge and storing, disseminating and using it. However, it is not easy to find cases where both internal and external knowledge are taken into account when developing knowledge management concepts and tools. The next step beyond the concept of knowledge management is the concept of the 'knowing organization' proposed by Choo (1998). He advocates use of internal knowledge management tools by organizations for gaining awareness about what is happening in the environment and making sense of it. However, the main emphasis is still on internal issues.

The concepts of 'learning region' and 'learning organization' are based on two cornerstones: creating tools and preconditions for individual and organizational learning and developing learning partnerships and networks. Such qualities of organizations and other social systems are of crucial importance in the knowledge economy. However, although they serve as an efficient tool for the achievement of developmental objectives, they lack the content for such development.

The socio-economic environment is increasingly defined and described in terms of information. Managers, specialists and business leaders are being overwhelmed by facts and data. Often they are confronted with conflicting information and, instead of acting, they become paralysed. While external data storage capacity and data transmission speed have both increased dramatically over the past decades, the data storage capacity and data transmission speed of the human mind have stayed the same. In this situation people are making bad decisions and judgements simply because of inability to cope with data overload. The most advanced organizations understand that the key to success in today's environment lies not so much in knowledge as in 'intelligence'.

'Intelligence' combines many of the most important features of the other concepts which I have referred to. It is at the heart of a systemic and continuous process at both strategic and operational levels dealing with the collection, *interpretation* and sharing of market-related, political, technological and social information in order to assure developmental processes. Also, it is the art of monitoring weak signals which tells us whether the social system (institution, organization, region, etc.) is on the right track or not.

The fundamental difference between intelligent and traditional organizations lies, however, in their time perspective. Traditional ones are focused on the present and have only a very limited perspective on the future. They start acting just after something happens and the signals from the market become clear for all players. In the mean time, intelligent organizations are trying to catch weak signals that indicate trends and possible changes. They begin to prepare themselves to be ready to act when the time comes. This allows them to acquire a competitive advantage. For example, it was not so difficult to forecast the decline of high-tech industry at the very beginning of this century if one understood the reason why the stock value of such companies had been overestimated. The textile industry is facing really big problems all around Europe because of globalization and pressure from Asian producers. Even if many companies are going to be closed, some of them are nevertheless expanding and expect to have a bright future. This is because they understood well the new rules of the game, anticipated the challenges which were going to come and took steps to adjust their products and production in ways which kept them competitive.

The same principles apply not just to a business or an organization but also to states, especially when we try to answer the question: why do some nations advance and prosper, and what are their prospects for the future? If we look at the success stories of the most dynamic European countries in the last ten to fifteen years – countries like Ireland, the UK, Finland, Sweden, Denmark – one can recognize the similarities between the developmental patterns of these countries. The rise (or recovery) of the national economy in all these countries has been based on the creation and use of productive knowledge. They show that capacity to generate intellectual capital – knowledge, information, intellectual property together with experience and the *ability to use them* in the most efficient way – is probably the most important precondition of success in the knowledge age. This capacity to discern a changing environment at an early stage, anticipate its significance and adjust, ahead of the field, to its new requirements could be called the *intelligence* of the state or an organization.

The concept of intelligence, as applied here, extends beyond management practices and economics. It sees the world as a shifting variety of social systems and each system as a communication network with its own 'personality' and culture, interacting in a variety of ways and exercising its intelligence function in the service of its goals (Dedijer 1993). Understanding how to develop an intelligent institution – business, public or voluntary sector organization, or indeed a university – is becoming one of the priorities for researchers in many fields of the social sciences. Most attention has so far been paid to this concept in the business world (Bernhardt 1994, Ettore 1995, Fuld 1985, 1995, Sutton 1998, Underwood 2002b). The authors focus mainly on issues of business intelligence or competitor intelligence, trying to develop tools and approaches which will allow a company to preserve its competitiveness. Dedijer (1993), Jequeir and Dedijer (1987), De Luca (1988), Toffler (1991), Raymond et al. (2001) and others stress the technological and social aspects of intelligence. Beal (2000), Choo (1998) and Friedman et al. (1997) focus on organizational learning as the key characteristic of intelligence in an organizational setting. My own experience in developing intelligent as well as learning organizations/regions in Lithuania confirms that both qualities are interrelated. Both require not just individual knowledge but also organizational knowledge and well-developed internal and external networks and supporting infrastructure. Organizational intelligence refers therefore to much more than just intellectually competent individuals. Moreover, this notion of organizational intelligence can be applied at every level, from the small business to the community, region or even country.

Afele (2003), for example, considers smart communities and networks of individuals and organizations as social intelligence tools for a country's development. I will try do develop these approaches later, when talking about the components of the intelligent country or region.

Intelligence as interpreted information

There is, however, a second application of the notion of intelligence in this context which we should observe, because this too has an important role to play in a knowledge economy and in the process of adaptation to its demands. 'Intelligence' is used, in some languages at least,[1] to describe not only features of the flexibility, responsiveness, agility, rationality or good sense of people's behaviour, but also the information, data and analysis which can inform judgement and decision-making, as for example in the term 'labour market intelligence'. It is perhaps an almost definitional truism that a knowledge economy will place a very high premium on 'intelligence' in this sense, though, as I have noted, decisions have often to be made in the absence of perfect intelligence, and one of the indicators of the intelligent actor is his or her capacity to make successful judgements on the basis of limited information.

Business competitiveness in the global knowledge economy places an extra premium upon intelligence of a number of kinds. The requirement for knowledge about the policy, intentions or behaviours of governments, national and international interest groups and institutions implies *political intelligence*. In the case of latecomer countries from, for example, the former Soviet Union, this particular aspect is of crucial importance. Problems posed by fluctuating financial markets or unstable political conditions create the need for *economic intelligence*. Keeping track of innovative efforts and new discoveries requires *scientific and technological intelligence*. Monitoring competitors' positioning and knowledge of customers and suppliers translates into *market or business intelligence*. Learning to cope in an international market with property rights, norms and international regulations concerning investment, taxes, etc., requires high-quality *legal intelligence*. Managing the recruitment, development and use of high-level skills in an era of high mobility and keeping up with the fast development of information technologies requires a much more dynamic *educational intelligence*.

This kind of intelligence needs to be distinguished from data or information. Data by itself is inert, useless. It is only when it is (selectively) brought to our attention, analysed and interpreted that it starts to carry meaning and the kind of understanding that can inform policy and action.

Herring (1998) suggests three critical qualities that are required in turning mere data into the kind of intelligence that can inform action: knowledge about the subject being analysed; clarity of thought, describing how the analysis was actually conducted; judgement – the ability to arrive at the right conclusion. Herring suggests that the first two can be taught, but the third is a quality you have to find in a good intelligence analyst. Not all people possess this capability: nor has it been adequately developed by the traditional curriculum of the business school.

I have considered in the two preceding sections two applications of the concept of intelligence. The first is intelligence in the sense of intellectual agility, a capability to discern changing requirements and to adjust to them, to make judgements in the absence of sufficient information and to make sense of overwhelming quantities of information. The second is intelligence in the sense of the knowledge and understanding to which this capability is applied. More particularly, as a condition of success within a knowledge economy, this is intelligence about technological change, the business environment and the social and political environment which provide the context for business. Further, I have stressed that this latter understanding is not just a matter of having all sorts of information, but also of being able to make sense of it, to interpret it for the purposes for which you intend to use it – which is where the two notions of intelligence join up. (On the significance of these capacities for the forms of 'competence' – especially 'holistic competence' – needed in a knowledge economy see the chapter by Lepaite in this volume.)

In the next section I am going to explore a little further the application of this understanding of intelligence in the idea of an intelligent country.

The intelligent country

Underdevelopment of the kind experienced by countries which have emerged from the former Soviet Union is as much a state of mind as a consequence of environmental, social or technical impoverishment. This is not to deny that prolonged underdevelopment eventually leads to a deterioration of the environment, wastage of natural resources and a destruction of social integrity. However, the worst symptom of underdevelopment is the chronic inability of underdeveloped countries to cope with internal change. This is especially clear for countries with underdeveloped systems of education.

Many of the less developed countries do not know where they are going, or where they wish to go, let alone how they will get there. They vacillate in their acceptance of their cultural base, because it does not appear to fit with the norms of other, successful societies. They ignore or even suppress key information. The tools for development which are chosen are drawn from the slogans and ideologies of countries with vastly different social and political histories, which have themselves discarded them a decade before. Too often it is assumed that tools which bring prosperity to other societies will succeed in a very different environment. The disparity in social structures, cultures and values, and ultimate goals is often ignored. Even when these tools and the economic objectives are compatible, they are not recognized as such by the underdeveloped mentalities which have deployed them. Sometimes, however, the situation is the opposite: the 'uniqueness' of a single country is overestimated and efforts are concentrated on creating 'unique' tools for such country or organization.

Less developed countries tend to lack knowledge – intelligence – about themselves, their friends and their competitors and about the technological, social and economic environment in which they have to compete. Very often developed countries and even multinational companies know more about these countries than the countries themselves. Given that negotiating power is largely determined by the knowledge possessed, it is not surprising that the poorer and less developed countries continue to be exploited by the rich. The less the developing countries know about a foreign investor's mindset, track record, investment policy or strategic intention, the more disadvantaged they are when it comes to rescheduling debt payments or negotiating royalties, licences or preferential trade agreements.

A good example of the lack of political, business and social intelligence was the privatization of the oil refinery industry in Lithuania. The whole industry was sold to the American company Williams International for almost nothing, and with responsibility left to the Lithuanian state to compensate for the possible financial losses of the company. The state failed to retain even a right to participate in decision-making in the company. The main reason for this particular mode of privatization was to prevent the Russians controlling the oil pipeline in Lithuania. The result of this privatization was that hundreds of millions of US dollars were paid to the Williams International 'investors'; none of the expected reconstruction took place and the company ended up anyway in the hands of the Russian oil company Yukos. Americans, not Lithuanians, sold it to the Russians and reaped the financial rewards. As a result, not only the oil refinery, but also the whole infrastructure of the oil industry in Lithuania came under the control of a Russian company. The country has, as a result, become dependent on Russian energy policy. The reason for this was, quite simply, the lack of intelligence on the part of governmental bodies in understanding the mindset and strategy of a particular foreign investor. A number of similar examples from most newly independent countries could be presented.

We can, as in this example, observe the lack of intelligence in a country and its consequences, but what does an intelligent country look like? An intelligent country can be described as one in which the organized intellectual ability of the state enables it to perceive emerging changes in the social, political and economic environment, as well as their reasons and effects, and to use this understanding in the interests of its development. Such a country possesses effective mechanisms for creating new knowledge and competence and for integrating new knowledge with the intellectual capital of individuals, organizations and institutions. Finally, it is capable of making and implementing decisions to achieve its goals by exploiting resources of all kinds in the most efficient way. These capacities are the focus of organizational subsystems which are discussed more fully in the literature on innovation systems and on management (see, for example, Choo 1998, Stacey *et al.* 2000).

Three *core components* of the intelligent country or region may be distinguished.

First, *smart communities* serving as the heart of innovations in which government, business and residents understand the potential of knowledge and ICT and make a conscious decision to use that knowledge and technology to transform life and work in their region in a significant way. Probably the most commonly spread forms of such communities are knowledge-based business clusters, science and technology parks, and business innovation centres. All these forms have the potential to become a smart community, even if they are not yet. The main precondition for that is the existence of a real community of people, scientists and producers operating in an environment within which social relations transform scientific knowledge into new products and where a constant renewal of production processes and exchanges take place.

The second component of the intelligent region or country is the existence of the *virtual space for innovation* that combines knowledge management tools with ICT. This space may also be called the virtual innovation system. Komninos (2002) distinguishes two dimensions of such a space or system: the knowledge management technologies and the information system for the online operation of knowledge and innovation functions. This dimension includes the technologies and methods for innovation that make up a part of the main innovation process and also the rules and conventions which support them, maintained by institutions that manage knowledge and technology flows.

The third component of the intelligent country (region) is the processes of connecting the smart communities, representing the real innovation systems, with the virtual space for innovation. It involves the development of processes, methods and technologies which support the complexity of human interactions and the creativity of human thought in handling unexpected circumstances that do not follow rules and in resolving unknown problems.

The role of information technologies in the development of intelligent organizations, regions or countries is crucial. Such technologies allow them not just to operate in a virtual environment, but also to create virtual innovation environments. One of the key factors for success in today's environment is the ability to use worldwide resources faster than competitors use them and in a smarter way. At a practical level the extension of access to broadband services is becoming a necessary condition for the effective sharing of intelligence, for global collaborative working and, hence, for international competitiveness. Digital regions or cities are not necessarily intelligent, but intelligent ones always have a rich supply of digital elements. The reason for that is the nature of international competition, which requires the ability to work in global networks and partnerships.

Employing 'intelligence' in the sense that has been elaborated here allows countries, regions and organizations to shift competition to cooperation and to draw on the resources of all involved parties. This is extremely important for countries (regions) with limited resources and also for poorer countries struggling to lift themselves from the vicious circle of underdevelopment, ignorance and modern forms of colonial exploitation.

Higher education: learning for intelligent organizations

In the course of this discussion I have referred to the requirement of the knowledge economy for a number of qualities of mind which are captured in the notion of intelligence, whether this is applied to the individual or to a larger or smaller form of social organization. These qualities include: anticipation; judgement; 'flexible executive processes'; 'meta-cognitive understanding' and social and contextual awareness (see especially Cronin 1993). When we begin to assemble these qualities, it quickly becomes clear that we are dealing with advanced intellectual capacity of a kind which is perhaps only weakly captured in the discourse of higher-level 'skills'. The requirement of the knowledge economy is for the exercise of what are really some sophisticated intellectual capacities of a kind especially associated with the academic training provided in universities. Moreover, these qualities are not only cultivated in the fields which are most obviously linked to the new economy, such as technology, computer science and biological science. The study of philosophy might plausibly contribute as much or more to the clarity of mind about logical processes which are called for, or to meta-cognitive understanding; the study of palaeontology might contribute to the ability to construct plausible explanations from the thinnest of data; the study of modern history to the ability to abstract a meaningful narrative from an overabundance of data.

Further, if this is the sort of capability that we want to cultivate for intelligent functioning within a knowledge economy, we might also caution against the reduction of the higher education curriculum to a set of highly specialized or very narrowly defined vocational skills. The knowledge economy, according to the analysis provided here, requires something rather more sophisticated. The intelligent organization and, by extension, the intelligent country, needs to be populated by a citizenry which can bring to its technological, business, social and political functions both the sort of intellectual agility captured in the primary notion of intelligence and the contextually sensitive knowledge and understanding which is captured in its secondary meaning.

It is also interesting to note that even such esoteric intellectual activities as these operate in a global academic space in which everyday academic practice involves international interdisciplinary teams and networks; ICT storage and retrieval of data from different sources across the world; global conversations through e-mail and the web; and global competition to be first with a new discovery or breakthrough in understanding. As a consequence, the same kind of 'intelligence' which, I have argued here, is necessary for national success in the knowledge economy, is also required *(a fortiori* perhaps) in an academic organization that is to be successful in the academic subset of such an economy. The intelligent university, as a form of social organization, is at the heart of the intelligent country, conceived of on a larger scale as another social organization.

Note

1 While the English word '*intelligence*' can be broad or narrow according to British or American usage, the French word '*intelligence*' refers almost exclusively to the psychological intelligence of an individual, not to the information-gathering and digestion activities of a government agency or industrial firm. In Spanish the word '*intelligentsia*' is associated with individual, institutional and social groups intelligence (Cubillo 1993). In many other languages, such as Lithuanian, there is no special word which connotes intelligence activities carried out by organizations. Lithuanian '*inteligencija*' is usually understood as a quality of an individual – his education, culture and sense (Jucevičenė 1999). In Latin '*intellegentia*' means knowledge, ability to understand and foresight.

References

Afele, J.S.C. (2003) *Digital Bridges: Development Countries in the Knowledge Economy*, Hershey: Idea Group Publishing.

Arbonies, A.L. and Moso, M. (2002) 'Basque country: the knowledge cluster', *Journal of Knowledge Management*, 6 (4), 347–55.

Beal, R.M. (2000) 'Competing effectively: environmental scanning, competitive strategy, and organizational performance in small manufacturing firms', *Journal of Small Business Management*, January, 27–47.

Bernhardt, D.C. (1994) 'I want it fast, factual, actionable: tailoring competitive intelligence to executives needs', *Long-Range Planning*, 21 (1), 12–24.
Castells, M. (2000) *The Rise of the Network Society*, 2nd edn, Oxford: Blackwell.
Choo, C.W. (1998) *The Knowing Organization*, Oxford University Press.
Cowey, M. (2000) 'Knowledge management – fact or fad?', *New Zealand Management*, 47, 54–5.
Cronin, B. (1993) 'What is social about social intelligence?', in B. Cronin (ed.) *Information, Development and Social Intelligence*, Los Angeles, CA: Taylor Graham.
Cubillo, J. (1993) 'Techno-economic intelligence (INTEL): what's in it for developing countries?', in B. Cronin (ed.) *Information, Development and Social Intelligence*, Los Angeles, CA: Taylor Graham.
Davenport, T.H., Eccles, R.G. and Prusak, L. (1992) 'Information politics', *Sloan Management Review*, 34 (1), 53–63.
Dedijer, S. (1993) 'Development and management by intelligence: Japan', in B. Cronin (ed.) *Information, Development and Social Intelligence*, Los Angeles, CA: Taylor Graham.
De Luca, J.V. (1988) 'Shedding light on the rising sun', *International Journal of Intelligence and Counterintelligence*, 2 (1), 1–20.
Ettore, B. (1995) 'Managing competitive intelligence', *Management Review*, 20 (4), 15–19.
Friedman, G., Friedman, M., Chapman, C. and Baker, J. (1997) *The Intelligence Edge: How to Profit in the Information Age*, New York: Crown.
Fuld, L.M. (1985) *Competitor Intelligence: How To Get It, How To Use It*, New York: John Wiley & Sons.
—— (1995) *The New Competitor Intelligence: How To Get It, How To Use It*, New York: John Wiley & Sons.
Grippenberg, P., Skogseid, I., Botto, F., Silli, A. and Tuunainen, V.K. (2004) 'Entering the European information society: four rural development projects', *Information Society*, 20 (1), 3–14.
Herring, J.P. (1998) 'What is intelligence analysis?', *Competitive Intelligence Magazine*, 1 (2), 13–16.
Jequeir, N. and Dedijer, S. (1987) 'Information, knowledge and intelligence: a general overview', in S. Dedijer and N. Jequier (eds) *Intelligence for Economic Development: an Inquiry into the Role of the Knowledge Industry*, Oxford: Berg.
Jucevičienė, P. (1999) '*Intelligence* termino sąvokinė erdvė ir jos atspindžio lietuviškoje socialinių mokslų terminijoje problemos' ['The concept of *intelligence* and the problems of reflecting it in the Lithuanian terminology of social sciences'], *Socialiniai mokslai*, 3 (20), 7–21.
Kim, W.C. and Mauborgne, R. (1999) 'Strategy, value innovation, and the knowledge economy', *Sloan Management Review*, 40 (3), 41–55.
Komninos, N. (2002) *Intelligent Cities*, London and New York: Spon Press.
Radovan, M. 'The information society: a sketch for portrait', paper presented at the 25th International Conference on Information Technology Interfaces (ITI), Cavtat, Croatia, June 2003.
Raymond, L., Julien, P.A. and Ramangalahy, C. (2001) 'Technological scanning by small Canadian manufacturers', *Journal of Small Business Management*, 39 (2), 123–38.
Rowley, J. (2000) 'From learning organization to knowledge entrepreneur', *Journal of Knowledge*, 4, 7–15.

Senge, P.M. (1990) *The Fifth Discipline: the Art and Practice of the Learning Organization*, New York: Doubleday Currency.

Stacey, R.D., Griffin, D. and Shaw, P. (2000) *Complexity and Management: Fad or Radical Challenge to System Thinking?*, London and New York: Routledge.

Stankevičiūtė, J. and Jucevičius, R. (2003) 'Theoretical interpretation of knowledge and its implications for knowledge management activities'. *Socialiniai mokslai*, 5 (31), 41–51.

Sutton, H. (1998) *Competitor Intelligence*, New York: SCIP Conference.

Toffler, A. (1991) *Power Shift: knowledge, wealth and violence at the age of the 21st century*, New York: Bantam Books.

Underwood, J.D. (2001) *Thriving in E-Chaos*, Roseville, CA: Prima Publishing.

—— (2002a) *Complexity and Paradox*, Oxford: Capstone.

—— (2002b) *Competitive Intelligence*, Oxford: Capstone.

Part III

Universities and economic development

Chapter 6

Concepts of development
The role of education

Flavio Comim

Introduction

A general examination of the recent history of development economics suggests that approximately every ten years a new conceptual framework becomes popular in the academic and political agenda. From the early concepts of development based on aggregate economic growth, back in the 1950s, to the most recent formulations of human development, concerned with capabilities and sustainable development, it is possible to clearly identify 'shifting fashions' in the conceptualization of development. These fashions are more than an arbitrary change in concepts; they reflect an evolving debate about the appropriateness of a set of principles used to make sense of the links between, on the one hand, complex social phenomena, such as the market, the government and population demographics, and, on the other hand, ways in which different societies are able to structure their production sectors and distribute the generated income. Moreover, this evolution goes well beyond a set of social and economic principles, since it also involves particular conceptions about the purpose of development. When contextualized into a historical perspective, it is possible to see how many concepts of development have been shaped by the particular historical circumstances in which they were formulated. These different concepts of development also seem to present distinct views about the links between development and achievement of quality of life (seen as the main aim of development). A simple stylized-fact version of this recent evolution of development concepts can be classified into: (1) income-centred approaches, and (2) human development approaches. This division characterizes a historical tension concerning the impact of growth on well-being and has important consequences for understanding the role of education and higher education in development.

Early formulations of development were characterized by a search for increasing economic growth under circumstances shaped by the aftermath of the Second World War in Europe and in the USA. As put by Sen (1988: 12), 'It was, therefore, entirely natural that the early writings in development economics, when it emerged as a subject on its own after the Second World War, concentrated to a great extent on ways of achieving economic growth, and in particular increasing the gross national product (GNP) and total employment.' More recently, when those affluent societies have achieved high aggregated standards of living, attention has shifted towards the use of resources for the production of direct constituents of well-being. In addition, early unidimensional perspectives exclusively based on income have been replaced by multidimensional views of well-being, where education appears prominently as an important element of quality of life.

Within a historical perspective of development, it is possible to argue that one major factor that has progressively become increasingly dominant in the discussions of development is the role of education. In the development debate, education went from early neglect to centre stage. It is indeed possible to go even further to argue that a proper understanding of current trends in development is not possible without a proper account of the role of education in the promotion of human flourishing. In other words, understanding the role of education is a *sine qua non* condition for understanding development.

Given this context, the objective of this chapter is to analyse the role of education in the evolution of development economics. The text is written for a non-economist audience, avoiding undue technical information. The argument is not intended to be comprehensive but simply to introduce to non-economists some historical trends and recent key issues debated in development economics that should be of concern to those interested in the role of education in the promotion of human development. The chapter is divided into three parts. The first part reviews briefly early theories of growth, showing the scant importance originally given to the role of education in the promotion of development. The second part analyses the contemporary view of education within a human development perspective, showing its links with the capability approach. The last part suggests a set of issues that should be addressed in exploring the potential of education and higher education in fostering human flourishing.

This chapter aims to demonstrate how the evolution of development economics has been shaped by the increasing role given to education in explaining the mechanisms of development. It calls attention to a different set of challenges lying ahead for the role of education in the promotion of human development.

Theories of growth: the instrumental value of education

The history of development theories in the twentieth century was shaped by the development of the early incursions into the terrain of economic growth. The view of development based on economic growth could also be called the 'income-centred approach' to development. It could be said, following, for example, Rostow (1990), Sen (1970), Henry Wan (1971) and Solow (1996) that the evolution of growth theories can be classified into three periods, namely (1) Pioneering of Growth Theory, 1936–57; (2) Old Neoclassical Growth Theory, 1956–66; (3) Old Keynesian Growth Theory, 1956–70; and (4) New Growth

Theory, 1986–2000. To some extent, the dates are arbitrary; they merely refer to the years when some of the most important contributions were presented. Similarly, the categories are arbitrary; they merely purport to represent along broad lines taxonomic differences already present in the growth literature. It is important to note that not all growth theories had the same impact in the academic and political world. A brief account of the evolution of these growth theories, as the main understanding behind a 'conglomerative view of development' (*Human Development Report* 1997), reveals the instrumental value given to education in later stages of this progression.

During the Pioneering period, defined by the contributions of Harrod (1939) and Domar (1946), no reference was made to education as an element for the promotion of economic growth. The underlying assumption of the so-called Harrod–Domar model was that a dynamic equilibrium between savings and investment was all that was needed for achieving economic growth. Thus, they were simply integrating Keynesian macroeconomic analysis into concerns about steady-state growth. It is interesting to note that Harrod argued that a steady-state growth would be achieved only if the growth rate determined by population growth and technical progress was equal to the 'warranted rate of growth' (that was a function of the saving rate and desired capital/product quotient). For Harrod, there was no reason for the equality between rates to hold. Similarly, Domar pointed out a chronic tendency to underinvestment which would prevent the same equality from holding. This model specification led Harrod and Domar to predict the instability of growth in capitalist economies and any concern with education was absent from their models. There was no explicit reference to education in the Harrod–Domar growth equation, but it is possible to speculate that the effects of education on population growth and technical progress would be meaningful, if they were considered.

The Old Neoclassical Growth period, defined by the contributions of Solow (1956) and Swan (1956), was characterized by the use of the neoclassical production function in growth theories. Because no reference was made to any form of knowledge, beyond the technology incorporated into physical capital, the production function assumed constant returns to scale, diminishing returns to each input, and non-zero elasticity of substitution between the inputs. As discussed below, most of these factors were affected by the introduction of education in economic growth models. The dynamics of the Solow–Swan model were determined by exogenous elements, namely, the rate of population growth and the changes in the level of technology, represented by shifts of the production function. The assumption of continuous substitution possibilities between inputs guaranteed that the capital/labour rate would adjust to satisfy the steady-state condition. This adjustment with equilibrium opposes Harrod's and Domar's predictions of growth instability. Yet, they are similar in their lack of interest in exploring the role of education in the promotion of economic growth and development.

The Old Keynesian Growth Theory period, defined by the contributions of Nicholas Kaldor (1957, 1960) and Joan Robinson (1956, 1962), meant a revival of the Keynesian ideas in the economic growth literature. Whereas Kaldor, through a series of six papers between 1954 and 1962, emphasized macroeconomic aspects of growth, Robinson stressed the choice of techniques and methodological aspects of growth theories. Kaldor's growth theories consisted of (1) a saving function, including a distribution theory of profit and wage shares that replaced the marginal productivity theory of distribution; (2) a theory of full employment, assuming firms with price-making power; and (3) a technical progress function, where the rate of growth of per capita output was an increasing function of the rate of growth of per capita capital. This last element of Kaldor's theories is relevant for understanding the role of knowledge and education in society, because current technology could then be seen as a function of past technological development. By doing so, an element of *path-dependence* was also introduced and a door for later considerations of the role of education was open. Both Kaldor and Robinson criticized the neoclassical theory of distribution and stressed in their models that investment determined savings. This was also relevant for understanding the future role for education in explaining development. If education might be causally related to investment and investment to growth, then this inversion of logic (between savings and investment) might give a causal role to education. But this would only be considered much later in the twentieth century.

Closer to the end of the century, the New Growth Theory period, beginning with the work of Paul Romer (1986) and Robert Lucas (1988), was based on models with spillovers of knowledge across producers and external benefits of human capital, which implied increasing returns to investment in a broad class of capital goods. By then, the theories of human capital, originally formulated by Schultz (1961) and Becker (1964), found their way into the explanation of economic growth and then into the development agenda. The theory of human capital, in simple words, argues that an investment in education is equivalent to an investment in physical capital. But it comes with an important difference: whereas the future returns to a machine are subject to depreciation and decreasing returns, the future returns to an educated individual are expected to increase with time. We then say that education has increasing returns. The theories of human capital have considered that human capital can be 'general', when it affects the overall productivity of an individual, such as one's level of literacy, numeracy, etc., or 'specific', when it refers to specific skills within a certain job description, such as acquaintance with a certain procedure inside a firm or a particular network of contacts. As argued by Johnes (1993: 6), 'The theory of human capital has greatly improved our understanding of the role played by education in the economy.'

Subsequently, R&D theories were incorporated into these growth models in order to explain technological advances and imperfect competition. Diffusion of technology models provided results similar to the ones presented by the Solow–Swan model. However, it must be emphasized that the key element that underlies New Growth Theories is the open acknowledgement of the role of education in the promotion of economic growth and development. This can be seen in the emphasis on increasing returns to capital in these theories. Because education and R&D were included as explanatory causes of technology, these theories are also known as endogenous growth theories.

The general mechanism through which education was to influence growth, and then development, would be by productivity increases and the generation of externalities. Higher levels of education would be conducive to higher levels of marginal product in the economy and this would be conducive to further gains in productivity in a knowledge economy. This would be associated with higher wage levels and the start of a virtuous circle in the economy, with higher levels of education and investment. Within this framework, the role of education in the development agenda is almost exclusively *instrumental*. Education is related to human capital and human capital promotes growth, which in turn fosters development. This means that no intrinsic value is attached to education. Growth theorists would not claim that growth is development, but that growth is the main *means* for achieving development. This argument is based on the idea that most desirable features of development, such as health, literacy, low levels of mortality, etc., are associated with economic growth. It is interesting to remark that much emphasis has been given in these R&D theories to the development of higher education.

Much has been said on the links between growth and development. One problem is the measurement of economic growth by per capita GDP. First of all, it is hard to argue that only the monetary aspects should matter in assessing development, in particular in rural areas. In developing countries, underreporting of income is common. Also, measuring GDP does not say much about how income is distributed in society. And distribution is an important factor of development. Moreover, so-called 'trickle down' effects, reporting the impact of aggregate growth on the income of the poor, have not been historically robust. The Kuznets processes, referring to a trend in increasing income inequality at early stages of development followed by a decrease at later stages (in the shape of an inverted U) have also not proved to be robust, meaning that income inequality in the world has not decreased (Ray 1998) (for more on the analysis of inequality and an alternative view, see Sala-i-Martin 2002). The standard belief in the impact of growth in generating development has been eroding for a long time, and different development theories have been elaborated as a result of extensive criticism of economic growth as a sufficient way of achieving development.

A good (and recent) practical illustration of this critique of the impact of growth on development can be seen in the 2004 *World Development Report*, where it is argued that growth is not enough to reach all the Millennium Development Goals, in particular the education goals. For instance, it is argued that 'If the economic growth projected for Africa doubles, the region will reach the income poverty goal – but still fall short of the health and education goals' (World Development Report 2004: 2). This broad recognition of the ineffectiveness of growth in promoting some important constituents of well-being has been present in the development debate for at least thirty-five years. Many critiques of the role of growth in promoting development have flourished in the last decades. These critiques opened the door for a more serious discussion of the role of education in development. Much more could be said on the evolution of the economics of education and its influence on growth theories and on the evolution of new development paradigms (see Teixeira 2000 as a useful reference on this topic).

To sum up, it could be said that early concepts of development, based exclusively on the promotion of economic growth, were not particularly attentive to education as a factor important for the flourishing of societies. Later, endogenous growth theories, influenced by the concept of human capital, allowed an instrumental role to education in the promotion of growth – and then development. Nevertheless, in the 'income-centred' approach to development the causal and conceptual structure of the growth–development link remained the same. At no time was the constitutive value of education considered. To a certain extent, this concept of development based on economic growth continues to be sponsored in many countries by their governments. It goes beyond a simple prioritization of growth as the main political aim of a society. It has a bearing on the way in which well-being (and education as one of its main elements) is assessed under this paradigm. In short, it could be argued that in development models focused on economic growth, educational development policies tend to be:

1 instrumental: they are important only as means of achieving economic growth;
2 focused on the formation of a specialized labour force to provide for the needs of the markets;
3 gender-insensitive: since well-being is assessed as GDP per capita;
4 focused on the promotion of 'efficiency teaching', motivating teachers to prepare their students in the format of 'teach to the test'.

Not all policies exhibit these features, but, more often than not, promotion of aggregate economic growth is insensitive to particular educational issues since it assumes that investment in education is only important as a means to achieve further growth. In what follows, we briefly describe the role of education in one of the development paradigms that arose as a result of extensive critiques of the growth approach to development.

Human development: the constitutive value of education

The problem with early theories of development centred on the promotion of economic growth was their high level of under-specification of the mechanisms through which well-being could be achieved. The initial shift from the income-centred approach to human development started back in the 1970s when concerns about the distribution of income were expressed by the World Bank. Emphasis was then given to the direct provision of public services as complementary strategies in improving the well-being of larger shares of the world population. The Basic Needs approach was created. Its starting point was that economic growth was not enough to reduce poverty. Education, as other fundamental dimensions of individuals' well-being, was dependent on public provision (Fukuda-Parr 2002). There is some controversy in the literature about the importance of 'participation' in the constitution of the Basic Needs approach, but it seems fair to conclude that a certain concern with institutional settings and communitarian participation was indeed part of this approach in its latest formulations. The approach has been extensively criticized for excessive concern with the provision of public goods and services, rather than with the provision of choices to people. This discussion has stimulated a subsequent emphasis on 'participatory approaches' as means of promoting development. This is an important issue, as argued below, that will inform current debates on the role of education as an element of human development.

Whatever might be the correct interpretation of the role of 'participatory principles' in the formulation of many different versions of the Basic Needs approach, it appears that the approach was able to: (1) go beyond income as the main aim of development, (2) be multidimensional in scope, (3) overcome the limitations of the income-centred approach by putting forward policies for different sectors, (4) direct attention to international development problems at larger scale, and (5) put forward a notion of well-being that was considerably comprehensive, involving aspects of security and institutional stability. Education is considered by the Basic Needs approach as a constitutive aspect of development, worth pursuing for its own sake. Emphasis was given to the provision of materials in the government-led task of supplying individuals with social services.

The Basic Needs approach has heavily influenced much of the work that followed later. The Participatory approach, including 'participatory studies' and 'voices-of-the-poor', benefited from the intellectual climate provided by Basic Needs. As shown by Robb (1999), the universe of participatory assessments, including for instance, PPAs (Participatory Poverty Assessments), RRAs (Rapid Rural Appraisals), BAs (Beneficiary Assessments) and PRAs (Participatory Rural Appraisals), has deepened our understanding of poverty by providing insights into the nature of many developing aspects such as: a) vulnerability, b) gender issues, c) crime and violence, d) seasonality, e) powerlessness, f) social exclusion, g) ethnicity. Participatory studies are based on a variety of flexible methods that aim to communicate the experiences of individuals as defined by themselves, rather than using a predetermined set of questions. The Participatory approach to a certain extent complemented the Basic Needs approach, but it placed much less emphasis on the role of government. The role of civil society was stressed much more in participatory studies. PPAs put forward a way of thinking about development that involved operation in a very decentralized and diverse fashion. Formulation and implementation of educational policies, for instance, should, according to PPAs, reflect the local specificities of communities.

One problem of the Participatory approach is that assessment is subjective, based on the opinions of individuals. Also, one would expect that education, understood much more broadly than simply schooling, would constitute a fundamental element to enable participation, but in the fashion in which it has been formulated by PPAs, the emphasis continued to be on livelihoods. Education levels were seen for their constitutive value, but PPAs were still dominated by appraisals of the links between education and livelihoods. Therefore, particular educational policies were usually associated with strategies for reducing the (economic) vulnerability of the poor. Now, it must be said that PPAs are still widely popular in development discourse and that their important contribution to the development of bottom-up, grass-root conceptualizations of development cannot be underestimated.

Reference to both Basic Needs and Participatory approaches provides a suitable context for addressing the main concept of development discussed here, namely, the concept of human development – as shaped by the influence of the Capability Approach. The expression 'human development' was coined by Ul Haq back in the 1990s, as a way of articulating those dimensions of development that could not be reduced to economic aspects. At the same time this approach was 'adopted' by the United Nations Development Programme (UNDP), which started to publish annual 'Human Development Reports'. The main premise of the human development approach to development was the aim to enlarge people's choices within a context in which people were treated as ends in themselves and not as means to achieve, for instance, more economic growth. This concept was already present in early formulations of the Basic Needs approach but it was further justified with sophisticated philosophical arguments provided by Amartya Sen's Capability Approach (CA). Sen was influenced by John Rawls' conception of education in shaping a contractualist view of liberal societies, in which, following Rawls (1971: 101), 'the value of education should not be assessed only in terms of economic efficiency and social welfare. Equally if not more important is the role of education in enabling a person to enjoy the culture of his society and take part in its affairs, and in this way to provide for each individual a secure sense of his own worth.'

The CA is a framework for evaluating and assessing social arrangements, standards of living, inequality, poverty, justice, quality of life and well-being. It is not meant to be a substantive theory to explain these issues. Rather, the main purpose of the approach is to enlarge *informational spaces* in normative assessments. Thus, in comparison to other ethical approaches, the CA would include in its informational space not only opulence, utilities, primary goods, rights, but also functionings (beings and doings) and capabilities. Simply put, the valuational exercise required by the CA consists in the identification and weighting of valuable things that people are able to be or to do. This valuational exercise is able to bring forth the different layers of complexity intrinsic to the role of education as an element of human flourishing.

Indeed, the elaboration of a broader informational space is not the only important element in the CA. This space is shaped by *autonomous actions* and it is this feature that gives the name to the approach. Capabilities are more than simply a compilation of functionings. They should reflect in different degrees a person's *freedom* to live in a way that he or she would like. As Sen (1999: 53) puts it, 'The people have to be seen, in this perspective, as being actively involved – given the opportunity – in *shaping their own* destiny, and not just as passive recipients of the fruits of cunning development programs' [emphasis added]. Being an autonomous agent should have intrinsic value and should be constitutive of a person's being. This means that not only achieved functionings are valuable but also individuals' capability to choose and discriminate among possible livings. It would be simple to argue that this emphasis on freedom or capability reflects the agency aspect of a person; however, it is not just any increase in autonomy and choice that counts: the only changes that count are those that produce an expansion of *valuable choices*.

The implications for understanding the role of education in development are dramatic. First, education is seen as a valuable functioning, something that is worth pursuing for its own sake. Second, education is important within a context of 'freedom in being educated'. This means that *freedom*, understood as availability of valuable choices, as part of the process of education, should be translated into real options for individuals to pursue different forms of valuable expansion of their capabilities. Third, education should count for its potential to promote autonomy (the agency aspect of a person). To a certain extent, education becomes a central capability to be developed by an individual, not because it is closer to a human right that should come with a universal provision, but because the meaning of education and *people's ability to develop their capacities* have a high intersection.

In particular, higher education becomes a central element in the flourishing of human beings. Within this context, the pursuit of 'high quality learning experiences' does not reflect the expectations of employers and professional bodies about 'high standards' and value-for-money teaching practices (Middlehurst 1999), but a search for flexible learning strategies where teaching methods, resources and support structures aim to develop the human capabilities of the students (for more on 'flexible learning' see Thomas 1995). As Nussbaum (2004) has observed, education, in particular in its dimension of moral knowledge, is important for the institutional and developmental constitution of laws in society. In their turn, laws influence the multiple ways in which evaluative beliefs are formed in society and how social patterns of evaluation of development are shaped. Higher education can play an important part in this development.

The CA, seen as the most influential philosophical basis for the human development approach, puts education at the centre stage. No development can be achieved without education. The difference from the income-centred approach to development is remarkable. Having said that, it is important to acknowledge that according to the CA, education has both (1) an intrinsic value, and (2) an instrumental value. This means that education is also relevant as a means of pursuing further economic growth but should not be exclusively valued for that. As Rawls (1971: 107) argues, 'resources for education are not to be allotted solely or necessarily mainly according to their return as estimated in productive trained abilities, but also according to their worth in enriching the personal and social life of citizens, including here the less favoured'. According to Sen (1999), a confusion should be avoided between investing in education because it will enhance economic growth and investing in education because it is intrinsically important. For him, the first alternative involves a confusion between the 'means and ends' of development. Unterhalter (2005) has called attention to the fact that education should not be seen as equivalent to schooling and that:

> Sen's exposition of capability thus elides different meanings and connotations of education and schooling – namely aims, processes and outcomes. Why these elisions are not immediately apparent or confusing in his work is because of his common assumption in all discussion that education is linked either through correlation or cause with freedom and that everything that happens in schools is education valorized in this way. Ideally this would be so. But a great virtue of Sen's work is that it is not a mere exercise in 'ideal theory', but seeks to give guidance for action in the actual, unjust world we inhabit. In this world some forms of education do not enhance freedom, or may do so only partially and in contradictory ways.
>
> Unterhalter (2005: 5–6)

Human development, so formulated, encompasses educational strategies that comprise a notion of 'equality in the space of education' and 'education conducive to autonomous behaviour'. Among a wide range of inequalities, it must be noted that gender discrimination is one of the most perverse sources of inequality among human beings. The use of the CA allows the development of 'women-centred teaching, learning and assessment mechanisms' as part of the formulation of educational strategies in higher education. They comprise changes in institutional provision, course structure and content (Wisker 1996) that are consistent with the promotion of human development in a more egalitarian fashion. From this perspective, investment in higher education is not a step towards improvement of productivity and better income distribution, but an action towards fostering higher autonomous citizens who will be able to decide more intelligently on the alternative lifestyles that they could have.

Another important feature of the CA, with consequences for the role of education in human development, is its acknowledgement of a 'pervasive human diversity' in the characterization of individuals. Sen (1992: xi, 117) qualifies this feature as an 'empirical fact' and uses it to de-emphasize the importance of resources in the assessment of the capability that a person enjoys. There are many sources of diversity among human beings, from which Sen (1999: 70–1) identifies as the most important those concerning: (1) personal heterogeneities; (2) environmental diversities; (3) variations in the social climate; (4) differences in relational perspectives, and (5) distribution within the family

These differences will shape the degree of variations in the conversion of resources into educational capabilities. Consequently, because individuals are diverse, their educational capabilities cannot be measured uniquely in terms of the resources that they have available: also to be taken into account is what they are capable of doing and being with these resources. It is important to note that in Nussbaum's (2000) version of the CA, education is related to a wide range of capabilities associated with a 'truly human way' of flourishing. It is interesting to see the wide implications of the 'senses, imagination and thought' dimensions of capabilities, defined by Nussbaum as:

> Being able to use the senses, to imagine, think, and reason – and to do these things in a 'truly human' way, a way informed and cultivated by an adequate education, including, but by no means limited to, literacy and basic mathematical and scientific training. Being able to use imagination and thought in connection with experiencing and producing self-expressive works and events of one's own choice, religious, literary, musical, and so forth. Being able to use one's mind in ways protected by guarantees of freedom of expression with respect to both political and artistic speech, and freedom of religious exercise. Being able to search for the ultimate meaning of life in one's own way. Being able to have pleasurable experiences, and to avoid non-necessary pain.
>
> Nussbaum (2000: 78)

This conceptual exploration of the impact of capabilities related to education reveals how central education is currently considered within a human development perspective in shaping people's overall capability sets. Moreover, the impact of education is not only related to the capabilities of 'senses, imagination and thought', as a superficial reading of Nussbaum (2000) might suggest, but it is also present in the capabilities of 'practical reason', 'affiliation' and 'control over one's environment'. Thus, education and its influence on the constitution of autonomous human beings came to be considered the main engine of development.

Investment in primary education becomes a necessary but not a sufficient condition for the achievement of human development, given that important functionings and capabilities can be achieved only as part of individuals' further pursuit of higher education. For instance, it is difficult to see how individuals, who have only the benefit of primary education, are free to enhance their capabilities of social inclusion, information and participation in contemporary knowledge societies. Thus, investment in primary education should be seen as a step towards the flourishing of a human being in terms of her/his potentialities. It must be noted that much of the current emphasis on basic education services (see e.g. chapter 7, World Development Report 2004) is still in primary education. This is important as a necessary, but not as a sufficient, condition for the flourishing of human beings. Consequently, the issue of privatization of higher education in developing countries and payment of tuition fees in developed countries should be seen within a broader context: as a relevant strategy in the promotion of human development where access to higher education is not a luxury but a basic capability to be encouraged.

To sum up, the CA's emphasis on the constitutive role of education can seem a long way from early growth theories, but, within a historical perspective, it could also be interpreted as part of an evolving debate about the weak impact of growth in the promotion of human well-being. Indeed, many important hurdles remain to be overcome in exploring the full potential of the role of education in development economics. In particular, the role of higher education should be seen as an essential part of the promotion of human flourishing. In what follows, some of these issues are outlined for further discussion.

Exploring the full potential of education: remaining issues

The argument developed so far can be summarized into two points: (1) the evolution of development theories has been accompanied by an increasing conceptual importance given to education as a development factor, and (2) the role of education has evolved from instrumental to constitutive. These trends did not take place in a linear manner, nor can they be descriptively applied to all distinct shades and approaches used in development. But they constitute a remarkable 'stylized fact', revealing the characterization of the role of education in the history of development economics and human development.

The challenges lying ahead for promoting education to the centre stage of the development process are considerable. The mere recognition of their central importance does not necessarily imply that educational processes are less problematic or easier to achieve: quite the opposite. 'Education' as the central capability to be developed gives rise to a new set of issues, among which the following can be emphasized:

1 Targeting: educational services too often fail poor people. As argued by the World Development Report (2004: 111), education systems face a wide range of problems such as 'unaffordable access, dysfunctional schools, low technical quality, low client responsiveness, and stagnant productivity'. Public provision has often failed to provide universal education and private provision seems to be unequally and unfairly distributed among individuals. There are considerable challenges ahead regarding 'assessment systems' and 'school autonomy'. The simple provision of primary and secondary

education continues to be a hurdle for many developing countries. For more developed countries, the main hurdle is about quality education and the difficulties of motivating socially excluded groups into higher levels of education. This takes us to the second issue.

2   If capabilities represent the autonomy, the choice, of individuals to decide over 'beings and doings', what is there to do when people do not wish to study further? Should we consider education a universal value and make it a compulsory 'functioning'? This seems to be at odds with the *bottom-up* nature of the concept of human development. Alternatively, should we simply respect peoples' views and leave them leading lives in which many of them are 'trapped'? Here, more understanding of the classical problem of 'adaptive preferences' could be helpful. The solution to this challenge remains elusive.

3   If education and schooling are not synonymous, how should educational strategies be pursued? In order to improve the efficiency and targeting of public spending, monitoring systems have been introduced. However, by teaching students 'to the test', the new educational schemes often push students into a linear form of learning. Moreover, targets have been defined in quantitative terms, and policy goals, such as the MDGs (Millennium Development Goals), emphasize the relevance of achieving primary school targets all over the world. Yet, what 'functionings and capabilities' are available today to people with only primary school? How ambitious is this target in comparison to what is required for flourishing human beings? The disregard for qualitative targets in the definition of development goals could prove detrimental to the success of educational policies.

4   Not much work has been done on the links between technological development and equality in educational capabilities. With the global increase in capital intensity of investments and fast technological advances, many individuals in the labour force have become redundant in the international division of labour. Provision of education capabilities is justified from a human development perspective for its intrinsic benefits. But if the full potential of these benefits is not realized because current productive structures are becoming increasingly capital intensive, how can the natural divide in society between the haves and the have-nots be prevented? The task of having in place production patterns with social equity would face the problem of encouraging the creation and preservation of technologies that are labour intensive.

5   The human development perspective highlights the notions of 'choice' and 'freedom' as the most important 'requirements' for individuals to achieve 'autonomy'. But the road to autonomy is more complex than one might imagine. Those individuals without autonomy may, as it has been suggested by Freire ([1970] 1993: 46–7), 'totally lack confidence in themselves' and try to achieve autonomy by simply resembling their bosses. The emotional dependence and alienation that follows from the state of deprivation might

prevent people from achieving 'true critical reflection' and autonomy. The links between capabilities and what Freire called *conscientização* have not been established. Human development without individuals engaging in critical reflection about their situation, leading to their action, seems to be an incomplete approach.

6 The growing emphasis on the enhancement of education functionings and capabilities as an essential element for human development highlights the importance of further attention to higher education as the main engine of this process. Primary education should be contextualized within strategies for providing individuals with full access to conditions for critical reasoning and freedom of choice in egalitarian contexts. Higher education has a very important instrumental role in the advancement of R&D and a crucial intrinsic role in the promotion of liberal versions of humanistic education. This intrinsic role seems elusive in the development agenda when great emphasis is still given to the promotion of primary education without due concern about how different levels of education are linked to each other.

Recent concepts of development, such as those based on the notions of 'sustainability' and 'social capital' raise additional sets of issues. Yet, it may be argued that they corroborate the point made here about the increasing importance of the role of education for human development, rather than offering a different view about the role of education. For instance, when discussing topics such as 'sustainable development' or 'sustainable consumption' the whole burden of the argument seems to be based on a behavioural change of society/individuals that depends on 'awareness' and provision of information and environmental education. Education and educational values are also crucial for understanding the links between ecosystems and human well-being (Alcamo *et al.* 2003). Similarly, the social capital approach to development has widely explored the links between education and valuable social features, such as trust, reciprocity and cooperation in society. In particular, the 'cognitive' dimension of social capital seems to be related to features of educational systems (for more see Uphoff 1999). More could be made of these illustrations if the scope of the chapter permitted; the burden of the argument, however, as developed in this chapter, is on the transition between income-centred approaches to human development and approaches as conceptual foundations of development.

To conclude, a brief analysis of the evolution of the most relevant conceptual shift in the recent history of development, spanning the last decades, shows that there has been a 'revolution' in the way that education (in particular, higher education) is understood, currently being seen as the foundation of autonomous behaviour and flourishing of human beings. A set of challenges, that have been very succinctly discussed above, remain to be solved. What is now clear is that the paths for pursuing educational and developmental strategies have been transformed into a single road by current development thinking.

Acknowledgements

I am very grateful to Angels Varea for her helpful and useful comments and to David Bridges and Terence McLaughlin for their stimulating suggestions.

References

Alcamo, J. et al. (2003) *Ecosystems and Human Well-Being*, London: Island Press.
Becker, G. (1964) *Human Capital*, New York: Columbia University Press.
Domar, E. (1946) 'Capital expansion, rate of growth, and employment', *Econometrica*, 14, 137–47.
Freire, P. ([1970] 1993) *The Pedagogy of the Oppressed*, London: Penguin.
Fukuda-Parr, S. (2002) *Readings in Human Development*, Oxford: Oxford University Press.
Harrod, R. (1939) 'An essay in dynamic theory', *Economic Journal*, 49, 14–33.
Human Development Report (1997), UNDP.
Johnes, G. (1993) *The Economics of Education*, London: Macmillan.
Kaldor, N. (1957) 'A model of economic growth', *Economic Journal*, 67 (268), 591–624.
—— (1960) *Essays on Value and Distribution*, London: Duckworth.
Lucas, R. (1988) 'On the mechanisms of economic development', *Journal of Monetary Economics*, 22 (1), 3–42.
Middlehurst, R. (1999) 'Quality and standards', in H. Fry, S. Ketteridge and S. Marshall (eds) *A Handbook for Teaching and Learning in Higher Education*, London: Kogan Page.
Nussbaum, M. (2000) *Women and Human Development*, Cambridge: Cambridge University Press.
—— (2004) *Hiding from Humanity: Disgust, Shame and the Law*, Princeton: Princeton University Press.
Rawls, J. (1971) *A Theory of Justice*, Cambridge: Harvard University Press.
Ray, D. (1998) *Development Economics*, Princeton: Princeton University Press.
Robb, C. (1999) *Can the Poor Influence Policy? Participatory Poverty Assessments in the Developing World*, Washington: The World Bank.
Robinson, J. (1956) *The Accumulation of Capital*, London: Macmillan.
—— (1962) 'A model of accumulation', in *Essays in the Theory of Economic Growth*, London: Macmillan.
Romer, P. (1986) 'Increasing returns and long-run growth', *Journal of Political Economy*, 94 (5), 1002–37.
Rostow, W. (1990) *Theorists of Economic Growth from David Hume to the Present*, Oxford: Oxford University Press.
Sala-i-Martin, J. (2002) 'The world distribution of income'. Online. Available at: www.nber.org/papers/w8933 (accessed 9 January 2005).
Schultz, T. (1961) 'Investment in human capital', *American Economic Review*, 51, 1–17.
Sen, A. (1970) *Growth Economics: Selected Readings*, Harmondsworth: Penguin.
—— (1988) 'The concept of development', in H. Chenery and T.N. Srinivasan (eds) *Handbook of Development Economics*, vol. 1, Amsterdam North-Holland.
—— (1992) *Inequality Re-examined*, Oxford: Oxford University Press.
—— (1999) *Development as Freedom*, Oxford: Oxford University Press.

Solow, R. (1956) 'A contribution to the theory of economic growth', *Quarterly Journal of Economics*, 70 (1), 65–94.
—— (1996) 'Growth theory', in D. Greenaway, M. Bleaney and I. Stewart (eds) *A Guide to Modern Economics*, London and New York: Routledge.
Swan, T. (1956) 'Economic growth and capital accumulation', *Economic Record*, 32, 334–61.
Teixeira, P. (2000) 'A portrait of the economics of education, 1960–1997', in R. Backhouse and J. Biddle (eds) *Toward a History of Applied Economics*, Durham: Duke University Press.
Thomas, D. (1995) 'Learning to be flexible', in D. Thomas (ed.) *Flexible Learning Strategies in Higher and Further Education*, London: Cassell Education.
Unterhalter, E. (2005) 'The capability approach and gendered education: Some issues of operationalization in the context of the HIV/AIDS epidemic in South Africa', mimeo.
Uphoff, N. (1999) 'Understanding social capital: learning from the analysis and experience of participation', in P. Dasgupta and I. Serageldin (eds) *Social Capital: a Multifaceted Perspective*, Washington: The World Bank.
Wan, H. (1971) *Economic Growth*, New York: Harcourt Brace.
Wisker, G. (1996) *Empowering Women in Higher Education*, London: Kogan Page.
World Development Report (2004) *Making Services Work for Poor People*, Oxford: Oxford University Press.

Chapter 7

The role of the university in regional economic development

David Bridges

Introduction[1]

At the Lisbon European Council held in March 2000 the Heads of State and Government acknowledged that 'the European Union is confronted with a quantum shift resulting from globalization and the challenges of a new knowledge-driven economy' and set the Union a major strategic goal for 2010 'to become the most competitive and dynamic knowledge-based economy in the world, capable of sustainable economic growth with more and better jobs and greater social cohesion'. It stressed that this would require not only a 'radical transformation of the European economy', but also a 'challenging program for the modernization of social welfare and education systems' (European Council 2000: 2). Never before had the European Council acknowledged to this extent the role played by education, training and research systems in the economic and social strategy and the future of the Union.

There is clearly a contribution to be made to this agenda from all sections of the educational community, but since the 1990s there has been increasing realization of the pivotal role of higher education[2] as the source of both the high-level skills and the innovative ideas which are going to contribute to international competitiveness in the knowledge economy and, more broadly, to national and regional prosperity. The European Commission was quick to apply the themes of the Lisbon Presidency Conclusions to the sphere of higher education and its policy document 'The Role of Universities in the Europe of Knowledge' (Commission of the European Communities 2003) is a continuing focus for consultation and action across the community. Kitagawa describes how 'since the mid 1990s, especially, there has been a growing convergence between the agencies with responsibility for territorial development and those in charge of the management of higher education' (Kitagawa 2003: 12. See also OECD/IMHE 1999).

In the UK, the Department for Education and Employment declared in 1997 that: 'Investing in learning in the twenty-first century is the equivalent of investment in the machinery and technical innovation that was essential to the first great industrial revolution. Then it was physical capital; now it is human capital'

(Department for Education and Employment 1997: 5). In 2002 the UK government produced a report signed by three Secretaries of State which opened with the declaration: 'In an increasingly knowledge-driven global economy invention and innovation are critical to Britain's long-term competitiveness. This requires a virtuous circle of innovation: from the very best research in science, engineering and technology in universities and science labs to the successful exploitation of new ideas, new science and new technologies by businesses' (DTI, HM Treasury and DfES 2002: I. See also the DfES 2003 White Paper on *The Future of Higher Education* and the 2003 *Final Report of the Lambert Review of Business–University Collaboration*, Lambert 2003, to which I shall refer at a number of points in this chapter).

I do not propose in this chapter either to amplify or to examine these policies or the analysis which underpins them, or to challenge the expectation that universities should contribute to economic development. Rather, I shall explore some of the ways in which these aspirations can be turned into practice. My question is: how can we most fully realize the economic benefit of the activities of universities and their contribution to business competitiveness?

In attempting to answer this question I shall draw on some experience of working with higher education, business and regional government and economic agencies in the East of England. This is one of nine regions of England, but nevertheless an economic unity with a population of 5.3 million and a GDP per capita of €18,806, so it stands comparison with many of the current member states of the European Community. I have to acknowledge that this experience is recent, largely unresearched and minimally evaluated. But then, the field is a relatively new one, and most people working in it are borrowing ideas and practice from each other in response to somewhat precipitous government demands for new initiatives and without much of an evidential base as to the longer-term values or hazards of what they are doing.

So what can universities do in order to contribute more effectively to regional economic development? I shall organize my response to this question under six headings:

- Universities as hubs of economic activity;
- Developing a regional collaborative infrastructure;
- Applying teaching capacity to business development;
- Applying research capacity to business development;
- Business spin-offs from higher education intellectual property.

Universities as hubs of economic activity

It is perhaps useful to start off with a reminder of the economic significance of a university which is simply carrying out its traditional function(s) without any explicit attempt to contribute to economic development as such. A UK government report estimated that, nationally, universities generated directly and indirectly over £34.8 billion of output and over 562,000 full-time equivalent jobs throughout the economy (DfES 2003). With a total income of £12.8 billion, higher education is a bigger industry than advertising or air transport. It is on a par with aerospace and is not too far behind legal activities in its importance to the economy.[3]

The point is that, independently of what precisely they are teaching or researching, universities bring all sorts of economic and other benefits to the places in or near which they are located. Most obviously, universities provide jobs. In the East of England they are among the largest employers in the region. The University of East Anglia, which is one of the smaller universities, with about 11,000 students, employs over 500 academic and 2,000 other staff. Even in a small country like Lithuania there are some 11,000 academics and about 35,000–40,000 in other roles, employed in higher education. These are, in turn, purchasing goods and services in the local economy and generating more jobs through this economic activity. The universities themselves effectively support a whole supply chain of business activity – for stationery, for communications, computing and other technical equipment, for food for canteens and restaurants. Most significantly in the East of England, the expansion of higher education has resulted in ambitious building programmes. The Estates Department of Cambridge University alone was in 2003–04 managing some £750 million (€1.125 million) worth of building projects. Much of this expenditure trickles down to local businesses. Students as well as staff spend money in local shops, bars, restaurants, hairdressers. Local taxi drivers can see between 50 and 100 per cent increase in business during university term time. Many local people supplement other forms of income by letting rooms to students and staff.

Of course, the benefits of a university to its locality are typically much wider. The university often has extension programmes, public lectures, concerts, theatre and other events which are accessible to local people. In the UK higher education sporting facilities are now commonly developed by universities in collaboration with the local community and for joint use. University staff and students make an important contribution to local voluntary organizations, to political activity, to the institutions of civil society. A recent survey by Cambridge University indicated that 7,741 staff and students contributed 202,412 hours of voluntary activity in community-focused organizations in 2003–04 (University of Cambridge 2004).

It is not surprising therefore that, in the UK, cities and counties which have not hitherto had a university located within them have been competing fiercely to get one or to grow one from their existing, for example, further education institutions.

The first thing to note is that none of this economic activity has anything to do with the business orientation (or otherwise) of the university. Whether it is teaching Greek philosophy or chemical engineering, medieval poetry or business management, the economic activity and benefits are the same. They arise simply because a lot of government and private expenditure, a lot of jobs and a lot of demand for goods and services are concentrated in a particular locality.

The second thing to note, though I shall need to qualify this, is that this activity is in itself not producing a net national profit – since it is essentially redistributing money contributed from within the national economy (via taxes or private contributions). Essentially, the university functions as a mechanism for the locational distribution of economic (and other) benefit. Thus, a government looking to inject some economic regeneration into a region might see the location of a new university in that region as a contribution to this regeneration – hence the competition between localities to become the site for the development of higher education.

There is, however, net national benefit from such investment to the extent that the programmes offered by the universities contribute to providing the higher-level skilled labour force which the local and national economy requires as a direct or indirect condition of its growth.[4]

The second qualification to the suggestion that the traditional activity of a university has only a locational impact on the economy, rather than a net national benefit, is that things change at the point at which a university begins to attract international customers or sponsors for its teaching or research. In the East of England, for example, the University of Luton – a small university of 7,000 students with a very limited research base and a strong community focus – includes in that number some 2,000 students from outside the European Community (1,000 of them from China). These students typically pay higher fees than the universities are allowed to charge UK or EC students – and this is all a net in-flow into the national economy. 'The Global Market in Higher Education' (as it is referred to in the title of a 2001 publication by Mazzarol and Soutar) is expanding on a trajectory set to grow from an estimated 1.8 million students in 2000 to 2.8 million in 2010 and 4.9 million by 2025 (Mazzarol and Soutar 2001: 22). By this time it is anticipated that some 849,000 students from China and 501,000 from India will be studying abroad. It is interesting to consider whether, for example, 'countries in transition' will be able to gear themselves up to participate as providers in this rapidly expanding market or whether they are going to become not only, as they fear, net exporters of graduates but also of undergraduates (see the chapter by Jucevičienė and Vaitkus in this volume). There are clearly serious economic threats as well as opportunities for such countries in this global market.

Third, even if a university simply focuses on its traditional roles without any specific attempts to address the needs of business, it can still act as a magnet to inward business investment – from overseas as well as internally. This is especially the case, as in the East of England, where universities enjoy a cosmopolitan population. Foreign businesses are attracted to locations which are accepting of people of different cultures and ethnicity and where they can meet people who speak their own language and understand something of where they come from. They are attracted, too, by the potential supply of higher-level skills and by the cultural and social environment which a university helps to create. The East of England Inward Investment Agency, which was established to attract businesses to the region, routinely includes a visit to the local university as part of the package which it arranges for business people who are considering such a location. A new scheme in the region arranges to provide international students in the region's universities with a voluntary work placement in a local business which is interested in exporting to their country of origin. The student acquires some useful work experience in a UK business environment and offers to that business insights into the culture and practices of the country in which it is seeking to operate.

So, the point is that universities have an economic impact and an economic benefit, even when they are not trying to do so directly but are focusing on more traditional educational and research roles. They can enhance this economic benefit to the extent that they become entrepreneurial in marketing their (traditional) teaching and research services internationally.

However, governments are looking for something more innovative, more dynamic and more pro-active from their universities – and it is to these kinds of activities that I shall now turn.

Developing a regional collaborative infrastructure

Goddard and Chatterton presented a keynote paper to a UNESCO-sponsored International Congress on 'Universities and regional development in the knowledge society', in which they explained:

> Within advanced economies, there is a growing concern that teaching and research in universities should be directed towards specific economic and social objectives. Nowhere is this 'demand for specificity' more clear than in the field of regional development. Whilst they are located 'in' regions, universities are being asked by a new set of regional actors and agencies to make an active contribution to the development 'of' these regions.
> (Goddard and Chatterton 2001: 9. See also on this Charles 2001 and Florida 1995)

The context from which I write[5] is itself illuminating of this thinking and of the new regional geographies of economic development. I am employed as Executive Director of the Association of Universities in the East of England (AUEE) – a membership organization which brings together seven universities which have their main campuses in the region (Anglia Polytechnic University, Cambridge University, Cranfield University, University of East Anglia, University of Essex, University of Hertfordshire, University of Luton) and one other with a major campus in the region (De Montfort University); four smaller monotechnic higher education institutions (the Royal Veterinary College, Writtle College of Agriculture, Norwich School of Art and Design and

Homerton School of Health Studies) and the Open University, a national distance-learning institution which has in fact the largest student body in our region. There are about 125,000 students studying on programmes at these institutions. Each of the English regions has a similar Association. They were established with some initial support from the Higher Education Funding Council for England (HEFCE) expressly as an enabling mechanism for regional collaboration on such policy issues as widening participation in higher education and the development of a more effective higher education/business interface – and they receive substantial funds from government via HEFCE for projects in support of these policies.[6]

From the universities' point of view, however, the collaboration provides a mechanism for the articulation of a strong higher education voice with new regional institutions which include: the Government Office for the East of England (GO-East); the East of England Development Agency (EEDA) and the East of England Regional Assembly, as well as regional planning bodies, for example, for the National Health Service, which is a very important contractor for education and training from many of our members. In terms of economic development, the most significant body is the East of England Development Agency. This is tasked with developing a regional economic strategy (East of England Development Agency 2001 and see www.eeda.org.uk); it has capital as well as recurrent funding to help establish, for example, science parks and business incubation centres (including some on university campuses); and it has a large network of regional groupings including the Regional Skills and Competitiveness Partnership and the East of England Science and Industry Council, on which AUEE is represented.

One particularly important development out of this collaboration which is especially relevant to the theme of this chapter is a HEFCE-funded project originally called i10 (www.i10.org.uk). This project is led by Cambridge University and involves all the higher education institutions in the region as partners, and was established in particular to help create an infrastructure across the region for higher education/business interaction. This infrastructure has included a pattern of collaborative working between business development officers in all our HEIs; web-based data bases of higher education expertise and facilities; sector-based higher education/business clubs, and indeed many of the activities described below under more specific headings. It at least begins to address the problem of the confusion which business people (and others) face when seeking advice, assistance or service from a university: where do you go? to whom do you speak? do they have anyone who knows about my kind of business? what will it cost? if this university can't do it, is there another nearby that can?

All of these were questions which, until recently, hardly anyone inside a university could answer. Through the i10 collaboration, business people should now be able to identify a point of contact in every university who can also steer them not only to the resources available in their own university but also to those available elsewhere. Most other academics, it must be acknowledged, remain in profound ignorance as to what riches lie a little further down the corridor.

Applying teaching capacity to support business development

In the period of the Thatcher/Major administration in the UK, Conservative Party policies required that public institutions such as universities should be subjected to the 'discipline' of the marketplace. In the case of higher education the market was constructed around the idea that students were the purchasers and universities the providers of higher education. Measures were taken to put the purchasing power in the hands of students (and tie university finance for teaching to the successful recruitment of students) and to ensure that students had information available from independent sources about, for example, teaching quality to help them make informed choices.

One of the problems about a higher education market constructed in this way, however, is that, unless student choice is itself guided by an informed appraisal of the labour market requirements of business[7] (which for the most part it clearly is not) and motivated by a desire to find a place in this labour market (a motivation which appears to gain purchase long after course choices have been made in most cases), it generates a mismatch between the supply side of graduate talent from the universities and the demand side from business.

In many ways the educational and training needs of employers are best addressed through opportunities presented to people who are already in employment, rather than by trying to guess employers' future requirements for graduates, who are as likely to go off to another part of the country or another part of the world as to stay in the neighbourhood of any particular university. Our own approach to the task of applying teaching capacity to support business development has therefore focused on the local delivery to people in work of relatively small packages of training closely focused on current needs. Universities have been working with (on the whole) local employers to find out what their needs are and to 'package' often quite short selections from existing programmes to meet these needs on a timetable and at a place convenient to them. In one case this has taken the form of some fairly elementary book-keeping and accountancy for local shop-keepers; in another language and cultural training for exporting businesses. Slightly less specifically, some of our universities have helped to establish sector-based business clubs which combine a bit of a social programme with updates on research and developments which relate directly to their field. The i10 Project is developing what employers have asked for as a 'navigable map' to help them to find their way into the multitude of modules and programmes and courses on offer in our region's universities. Most recently the Careers Advisory Services of all the region's universities have combined to form GradsEast – a web-based system aimed at enabling employers to identify potential graduate employees from all the universities in the region.

At the margins of our teaching programmes, therefore, we have been developing an approach to our 'offer' to business which is based on market research into their requirements, which is thus much more closely related to their defined needs, which is delivered in forms which make it accessible to employees in work and which, in some cases at least, is paid for directly by employers rather than by students.

One recent development takes this principle further into the mainstream of university development. The UK government has recently introduced a new two-year programme leading to the award of a Foundation Degree. Indeed in 2003–04 the only additional student numbers available for the growing higher education sector were for students enrolled on such degrees. The main features of these degrees are that:

- they have to address the needs of business sectors identified by the Regional Development Agency as priorities for the region;
- they have to be clearly vocationally orientated;
- they have to be designed and delivered in partnership with local employers;
- they have to include a substantial component of work-based learning;
- they are taught ('delivered') not just in the traditional universities, but in further education colleges which have validation or accreditation arrangements for the award of degrees with a neighbouring university.

Pilots of these programmes produced mixed evidence of their success (see, for example, Zamorski 2002), but it is, in truth, too early to judge. I refer to them here as a clear example of an attempt, at least, to link the teaching in our universities much more closely to the identified needs of employers in sectors which, themselves, have been selected as key sectors for regional economic development. It remains to be seen how either students or employers will rate them in comparison with the more traditional academic offerings of universities.

Applying research capacity to support business development

Retrospective and prospective analysis of the conditions for business success indicates that businesses need constantly to be improving their products and services through the application of the latest research, or at least that they need to be 'fast followers' in such application. Even major corporations with their own research facilities will be scouring the research conferences for relevant ideas and findings from the university community. In the UK and elsewhere governments are encouraging closer partnerships between higher education and business, with a view to more fluent application of higher education research into the business community.

There are a number of different mechanisms for such partnerships. Many of them are very informal and largely serendipitous. It has been suggested that most knowledge transfer happens on two legs, i.e. when university graduates take up posts in the business sector. The manufacturers of Kettles Crisps in Norwich were able to triple the life of their cooking oil by adding a chemical component suggested by the Chemistry Department of the University of East Anglia. This happened because the Managing Director was a former student of the department and remembered a lecturer who was doing some work on enzymes which just might be relevant. Accounts of the 'Cambridge Phenomenon' – the great expansion of high-tech businesses around the University of Cambridge through the last decades of the twentieth century – are riddled with stories of chance conversations at the school gates, in the pub and in the squash club. One group in Norwich has tried artificially to replicate this process by convening social evenings which bring together academics and the business community in a local pub. Slightly more formally, colleagues have found that events (often including a meal) which bring together academics and business people around more sharply focused themes which relate to a particular business sector and have a clear relevance to both are an effective way of building relationships. Matthew Bullock, one of the founding figures in the development of the network of high-tech businesses around Cambridge and Chair of the i10 consortium, speaks of bringing academics and business people together in 'dances'. i10 Group has arranged 'speed dating' sessions between academics and business people in search not of romance but of synergy between research and business development. This language indicates that the process of bringing academics and business people together is a social process with large elements of chance – and not something which can be overmanaged and contrived.

Larger companies are used to contracting with known university departments for specific research, though the scale of such contracting in the UK is still relatively small compared with, e.g. the USA. Smaller firms tend not to think in these terms[8] or don't know where to go even if they are interested. Brokerage schemes – intermediaries from, for example, university Business Development Offices or from the national Small Business Service – can assist in identifying needs and matching supply with demand. Thus far, however, these operate on a rather limited scale. It takes a lot of time (which many business people are reluctant to spend) to sit down with businesses and work out with them what kind of research might be relevant and useful and to match any such requirements with the research capacity of universities (whose staff may in any case be more interested in a research agenda of their own). The kind of brokerage indicated here is in fact very skilful. It requires negotiation between two different cultures and perhaps a measure of change in both of them. There are not so many people with competence in the languages of the two cultures and the skills involved in bringing people from them together. We need more initiatives focused on building this capacity. In any case this involves an investment of time which will rarely cover its costs, so it will have to rely to some extent on government subsidy. There is increasing recognition that the limited resources available have to be carefully targeted on the areas of higher education and business where there is perhaps a greater readiness to engage with each other, rather than on attempts to change sectors where there is very little interest.

One initiative in the UK which seems to have been warmly appreciated on all sides is what, until recently, was called the Teaching Company Scheme and is now Knowledge Transfer Partnerships. The essential features of this scheme are as follows:

- a postgraduate researcher is attached to a company for three years to work on a piece of research which that company has identified;
- as part of the package the company and the researcher have continuing access to the research expertise of the university department from which the researcher has come;
- the researcher receives a salary – and the university department also receives a payment;
- the costs are shared by the company and a government grant.

In the initial stages the universities in the East of England have received a grant from the Regional Development Agency to help get this programme established, but once universities have enough of these projects under way, the income they receive for each placement will be sufficient to make the brokerage of new projects self-financing.

A limitation of this scheme is that it requires a more substantial commitment over a longer period of time than small and medium-sized enterprises are, on the whole, prepared to make. As a result we have developed in the East of England a slimmed-down and more flexible scheme tailored more closely to the requirements of small and medium-sized enterprises.

Business start-ups and spin-offs[9] from higher education intellectual property

The 'intellectual capital' of universities can, as I have illustrated, be applied to business development in businesses which are already established, but there is, too, the interesting prospect of new businesses being established out of promising new ideas and products – and this is something which bodies such as the Regional Development Agency have been keen to encourage. It is very easy to underestimate, however, the long distance between (a) someone having a bright idea or producing a few grams of something which clearly has exciting business potential and (b) there being a functioning company which is making money out of this idea or product. A lot of the initiatives in which we are engaged in the region are focused on enabling this process. They include:

- sorting out intellectual property rights, e.g. between individual researchers, their department and their university (the European Commission acknowledges that 'A major obstacle to better application of university research results is the way intellectual property issues are handled in Europe', and it contrasts these with the facilitative 'Bayh–Dole' Law in the United States – (see Commission of the European Communities 2003: par. 5.1.3);

- developing understanding of and specialist assistance with the process of patenting;
- developing practices which provide those with what they think is an idea with the commercial potential to get some early appraisal and advice;
- developing Business Incubation Centres (now in nearly all our universities) which can provide a supportive environment with professional advice on, for example, business planning, legal matters, accountancy;
- establishing a Proof of Concept fund to subsidize the early testing of an idea or product with a view to establishing its viability;
- establishing government-sponsored schemes to assist new businesses with finance through the early stages of business start-ups;
- developing an infrastructure of venture capitalists interested in investing in new companies.

These last three initiatives are focused on business start-ups of all kinds and not just those emanating from universities, but they provide, nevertheless, part of a wide infrastructure of support which is now available to academics with bright ideas with some commercial potential. I should also emphasize that we are, so far, looking at a relatively limited scale of development. In 2002 a total of 158 business spin-offs from university research were created in the UK. Indeed, the Lambert Report in the UK concluded that: 'there has been too much emphasis on developing university spin-outs, a good number of which may not prove to be sustainable, and not enough on licensing technology to industry' (Lambert 2003: 5).

Key issues

I have tried to describe some of the different ways in which universities can and do contribute to economic and business development nationally, regionally and in their particular locality. There is, of course, nothing new in the idea that university teaching or research might contribute to business development. In engineering in particular there is a long tradition of applied research in higher education that has been commissioned by or taken up by engineering companies. Part of the rationale for company sponsorship of undergraduates in universities (though this has always been on a very limited scale in the UK) has been based on those companies' expectations that the training they receive will, at a future date, be used to the benefit of the company.

What is new is the priority which government has been giving to the development of higher education/business collaboration, the variety of initiatives aimed at encouraging such partnership and the programmatic way in which it features, for example, in the economic strategies of Regional Development Agencies and indeed in the strategic plans of universities.

Many UK universities created Technology Transfer or Business Development offices only in the late 1990s; the Lambert Report reckoned that by 2003 there were, on average, about six staff employed in this role per higher education institution, though most of these were on fixed-term contracts because of uncertainty about the longer-term funding arrangements. There is, however, very little systematic evaluation of these developments, and such as there is has often been demanded by government before the initiatives have really had a chance to demonstrate in any mature way their actual effects. I think there are, however, some key messages emerging from our early experience, and also some important issues which it raises. These relate, in particular, to access (to the intellectual capital of universities); the demand for such access from businesses (or the absence of such demand); the key role of brokerage; and the need for what might be described as process support. I shall expand briefly on each of these themes.

Access

The problem is not, on the whole, that academics want to keep their knowledge to themselves. Indeed one of the problems for those in universities responsible for its commercial exploitation is to prevent academics giving it away too freely. It is rather that the established channels for access to higher education knowledge (registration as an undergraduate student on a three-year course or as a research student for a PhD or attendance at international research conferences) are not routes that are readily available to or suitable for businesses with, perhaps, very specific requirements. Similarly, if a business has such specific requirements, then it is not easy for it to know whom to approach or even which university to go to. Even when it gets the answer to these questions there have been few well-developed structures for handling such enquiries, though an early priority for Business Development Officers has been to put such structures in place.

Demand

Is it there? Do businesses want the services that universities can offer? And if not, what can government or other agencies do to generate this demand? The Lambert Report was quite blunt about this:

> The biggest single challenge when it comes to encouraging the growth of business–university collaboration lies in boosting the demand from business, rather than in increasing the supply of products and services from universities. Academic researchers are working much harder than in the past to reach out to business. Will companies respond to the opportunities?
> (Lambert 2003: 1.12)

This problem is not unique to the UK. According to a European Community Innovation Survey 'Less than 5% of innovative companies considered information from government or private non-profit research institutes, and from universities or other higher education establishments, as being a very important source of information' (Commission of the European Communities 2003: 7).

Brokerage

I have already stressed the importance of this role for bringing universities and businesses together – or at least for building channels of communication between the two around research, training and other potential forms of collaboration. It seems to me to be key to building these collaborations, especially in the early stages of this development. If neither higher education nor business is currently giving a high priority to liaison with the other, or neither feels it has the time to explore possibilities, and if there are problems of linguistic and/or cultural difference, then there is an important role for a third party with the dedicated function of finding the shared interest and opportunity around which both can see advantage. In the UK we are building such brokerage roles outwards from the universities through Business Development offices (variously named), which typically recruit people with business experience, and inwards from the business and business support community, through, in particular, Business Link and the Small Business Service. There are still dysfunctions between the two; both are in any case thin on the ground; and Business Link and the Small Business Service have themselves been slow to engage fully with the university sector; but their activity seems to me to be crucial to the building of the higher education/business partnership.

Process support

The points I made about bringing a good idea or product to market have application across this field. All forms of 'transfer' of knowledge (the government's expression, not one a seasoned pedagogue would choose) require an extended support for processes which can mean a lot of retailoring, repackaging (retail metaphors abound here) or re-presentation of teaching or research if these are to meet the needs of a business community, as well as market research aimed at identifying their real requirements. These processes require knowledge and skills that are not commonly available in universities. The Lambert report acknowledges:

> Technology transfer is difficult and requires a wide and specialist set of skills. So it is hardly surprising that some universities have problems building professional offices on their own. Protecting and managing intellectual property requires specific legal knowledge. Licensing needs a combination of market awareness, subject specific knowledge, marketing and negotiating skills. Spin out creation requires entrepreneurship skills, links with business angels and venture capitalists, business planning, management and

company formation expertise. These skills are difficult to find in a small group of people and expensive to buy in.

(Lambert 2003: 4.32)

Some issues

My initial question was: 'what can universities do in order to contribute more effectively to regional economic development and, more specifically to business competitiveness?' and I have tried to answer this directly with, in particular, reference to the recent experience of universities in the East of England. But of course the question begs or ignores a number of others. Let me in conclusion raise just two of these.

First, there are two policies in the UK (and perhaps elsewhere) which tend to get muddled together in these discussions. One policy is to do with drawing on the intellectual capital which lies in universities, with a view to rendering business more competitive. A second policy is to do with developing a 'third stream' of funding for higher education, derived from the supplying of services to the business community and running alongside the funding that universities already receive from the Higher Education Funding Council for teaching and for research. These two policy objectives appear to have a very convenient symmetry, but the Director of Technology Licensing at Massachusetts Institute of Technology pointed out in a public lecture in Cambridge that this was a misleading picture. In the USA knowledge transfer between higher education and business is seen primarily as part of the public service function of a university, rather than as a means of raising income for the university. She warned that universities would be lucky to make as much as 2 per cent of their income from this activity. Happily, this is a view endorsed in the UK in the recently published Lambert Report: 'Public funding for basic research, and for the development of technology transfer offices, is intended to benefit the economy as a whole rather than to create significant sources of new revenue for the universities' (Lambert 2003: 4).

The experience I have outlined illustrates again and again the huge amount of work which is required to bring any results in these collaborations. Very little of the work in which we have been involved in our region would have been viable if we had assessed the likely returns against the investment of time and effort, and without the benefit of government subsidy for, in particular, the start-up costs. It seems evident to me that the potential benefit to business from knowledge transfer from our universities will be severely reduced if, from an early stage, this activity is expected to be conducted on the basis of cost recovery – and much of it may require continuing financial support from government (and of course the tax revenue it derives from the business community) if it is to be sustained.

Second, those engaged in or advocating the kind of activity I have described in this chapter invite a raft of accusations of the kind that this represents a distortion, a betrayal, a prostitution, perhaps, of the properly educational mission of a university. Instead of learning for its own sake, we are offering the commodification of knowledge. Instead of the disinterested pursuit of truth, we offer the utilitarian pursuit of commercially viable products and processes. Instead of the moral discipline of study and scholarship we offer the service university as a retail outlet for 'off the shelf learning packages' and 'bite-sized chunks of learning'!

I have more than a little sympathy for these charges and I do think that universities need to be careful, in developing a relationship with the business community, not to cheapen (in the cultural sense) what they have to offer. Universities are a significant point of reference for those wishing to know about and understand things, precisely because of the systematic and sustained way in which learning and enquiry are pursued in their precincts; precisely because of the academic discipline which is imposed on those seeking to learn and those developing enquiry through scholarship and research; and precisely because they are communities in which academic virtue, in the form of requirements about honesty, authenticity, humility, care and thoroughness, is cultivated and demanded. If universities start to abandon these principles in the interests of the business or any other exploitation of their work, then they will quickly lose the characteristics which make them worth approaching in the first place.

On the other hand, universities have a responsibility to place knowledge in the public arena – and the factory, office, farm or port is just as much a public arena (in some ways more so) than that rather exotic research conference in Honolulu or Aix-en-Provence. And universities have also a teaching function which might reasonably be deemed to require the exercise of at least some ingenuity and imagination in the interests of the communication of the university's knowledge to an interested community of learners, whether these be a bunch of undergraduates in jeans or a bunch of business people in suits.

Better still, since I have already indicated my discontent with a model of the relationship between higher education and business as a one-way 'transmission' or 'transfer of knowledge', it seems to me that many of those who do actually work in this field quickly realize that engaging with the business community as a teacher or researcher is a two-way learning process from which the academic can gain as much as his or her business colleague. Principles of management, environmental protection, health care or glass construction get challenged or amplified by hard cases from people's direct experience; new angles on research questions and new approaches to the enquiry itself arise in their application in live contexts; assumptions which have gone unchallenged in the academy or the research conference suddenly look less secure in the working environment or when confronted with the solidly grounded experience of a class of entrepreneurs. Higher education/business engagement might, in other words, be viewed not just as another burden on an already over-stretched academic community, but as something which might present to that community just the sort of cut and thrust of argument and challenge to established assumptions on which academics themselves are supposed to thrive.

Notes

1 This chapter is based on a lecture given at the International Conference *Lithuanian Higher Education: Diagnoses and Prognoses* at the Lithuanian Parliament, Kaunas, 11 December 2003, an earlier version of which was published in *Socialiniai Mokslai* (Bridges 2004).
2 In this chapter I shall use 'higher education' and 'universities' interchangeably and intend it to include all forms of higher education provision, though some parts of the discussion apply more especially to higher education institutions with a distinctive research role.
3 A detailed case for the economic importance of universities is made in a Universities UK Report available at www.universitiesuk.ac.uk/bookshop/downloads/economic impact.pdf.
4 A direct contribution might be, for example, the education of a software engineer who goes on to sell his or her software overseas, or a chemical engineer who manages to cut the costs of a significant production process. An indirect contribution might be, for example, the training of a health worker or a teacher who provides essential services for the good functioning of the community and helps to make it an attractive environment for business location or development.
5 The regional context from which I write is the East of England – one of the nine government regions of England identified under the Blair administration as the focus for economic development and possibly increasingly devolved governmental functions. The East of England includes six English counties (Norfolk, Suffolk, Cambridgeshire, Essex, Hertfordshire and Bedfordshire) and a mainly low-lying area of just over 19,000 square kilometres. It has a population of nearly 5.5 million, of whom 2.7 million are employed in 350,000 businesses. It has a €115 billion economy; a GDP per capita of €18,806 and is third in the UK in terms of Gross Domestic Product though only average in Europe. (Source: East of England Development Agency 2001.)
6 There are similar associations in each of the nine English regions, though they operate in slightly different ways which reflect their histories and the constituencies they serve. There is a useful thumbnail sketch of the nine associations in Kitagawa 2003 – as well as a substantial and interesting discussion of many of the issues dealt with much more briefly in this chapter. More information about AUEE can be found at www.auee.ac.uk – as also can links to other regional associations.
7 In fact it is extraordinarily difficult to obtain usable information about the employment requirements of business – especially if you are looking for information about what these requirements might be in four to five years' time. Small and medium-sized enterprises in particular find it difficult to predict what staff they will be looking for in twelve months' time, or indeed, whether, at that interval of time, they will be recruiting or laying off.
8 Some official reports have raised questions about the capacity of British managers to absorb science and innovation into their operations. A benchmarking study by the OECD, for example, highlights 'the issue of the educational profile of top managers in UK-owned firms, who have rarely been trained as scientists in contrast with US executives, who have often both a PhD and a Master of Business Administration, or with their French counterparts' (OECD 2002).
9 Hague and Oakley distinguish spin-offs and start-ups as follows: 'Spin-offs are firms created to allow universities to exploit intellectual property arising from academic research . . . Start-ups are firms created to apply more general knowledge and expertise' (Hague and Oakley 2000: 5). I am not sure that this distinction can be rigidly maintained or is widely observed.

References

Bridges, D. (2004) 'Higher education and economic development', *Socialiniai Mokslai*, 2 (44), 7–16.

Charles, D.R. (2001) 'Universities and regions: an international perspective', *Proceedings of the International Congress on Universities and Regional Development in the Knowledge Society*, Polytechnic University of Barcelona.

Commission of the European Communities (2003) *Education and Training 2010: the Success of the Lisbon Strategy Depends on Urgent Reforms*, COM (2003) 685 Final, Brussels.

Department for Education and Employment (1997) *Excellence in Schools*, London, HMSO.

Department for Education and Science (2003) *The Future of Higher Education*, London: DfES.

Department for Trade and Industry, HM Treasury and Department for Education and Skills (2002) *Investing in Innovation: a Strategy for Science, Engineering and Technology*, London: HM Treasury (also available online at: www.hm-treasury.gov.uk).

East of England Development Agency (2001) *East of England 2010: the Regional Economic Strategy*, Cambridge: EEDA (also available online at: www.eeda.org.uk).

European Council (2000) *Lisbon European Council Presidency Conclusions*. Online. Available at: europa.eu.int/comm/off/index (accessed 10 December 2004).

Florida, M. (1995) 'Towards the learning region', *Futures*, 27, 527–36.

Goddard, J. and Chatterton, P. (2001) 'The response of HEIs to regional needs', *Proceedings of the International Congress on Universities and Regional Development in the Knowledge Society*, Polytechnic University of Barcelona.

Hague, D. and Oakley, K. (2000) *Spin-offs and Start-ups in UK Universities*, London: Committee of Vice Chancellors and Principals.

Kitagawa, F. (2003) 'Universities and the regional advantage in the knowledge economy: markets, governance and networks as developing in the English regions', unpublished thesis, University of Birmingham.

Lambert, R. (2003) *Lambert Review of Business – University Collaboration: Final Report*, Norwich: HMSO (also available online at: www.lambertreview.orit.uk).

Mazzarol, T. and Soutar, G.N. (2001) *The Global Market for Higher Education*, Cheltenham, UK and Northampton, MA: Edward Elgar.

OECD (2002) *Benchmarking Industry–Science Relationships*, Paris: OECD.

OECD/IMHE (1999) *The Response of Higher Education Institutions to Regional Needs*, Paris.

University of Cambridge (2004) *University of Cambridge Community Engagement Summary 2003–4*, University of Cambridge Corporate Liaison Office (mimeo)

Zamorski, B. (2002) *Foundation Degree Evaluation Report: Evaluation of the Anglia Polytechnic University, University of Essex and University of East Anglia Foundation Degree Consortium*, Norwich: University of East Anglia (also available online at: www.auee.ac.uk, under publications).

Chapter 8

Regional universities in the Baltic Sea region

Higher education and regional development

Kazimierz Musiał

Introduction

Some of the most vigorous debates about the role of universities in regional and national development have taken place in the advanced industrial countries – in the United States (University of California 1993, Ward 2002), Great Britain (Chatterton 1998, DfEE 1998, Robson *et al.* 1997, Bobe 2002) and Australia (Duke 2000 and 2002) to take just a few examples. However, the Global University Network for Innovation has argued that the role of universities in economic development and regeneration is relevant for rich and relatively poor countries alike (GUNI 2004). In the Baltic region, it is an agenda which is taken very seriously both by countries like Sweden and Finland, which have long experience in research-based innovation and economic growth (and in the case of the Helsinki region perhaps the most successful experience in Europe) and also in countries like Poland, Lithuania, Latvia and Estonia, which have only recently emerged from a Soviet-style economy.

There have, of course, been strong financial considerations to prompt universities throughout Europe towards a refocusing on *regional* economic agenda. In many cases the new emphasis on a regional role is a response to the reduction of resources coming from national government and an attempt to tap into alternative sources of income. In some countries there has been a deliberate decision by national governments to channel funds to regional administrations or agencies which have then been able to use them as an incentive to university engagement with the regional agenda. In the European Community other, for example structural, funds have been targeted at regions, and more agile, regionally orientated universities have been able to benefit from local partnership programmes supported by these funds. Quite naturally this availability of locally based funds may lead to more of the kind of service orientation discussed by Tjeldvoll and Blaženaitė elsewhere in this volume, but it also allows for diversifying the income sources and thus makes the financial basis of the university more sustainable.

Decision makers such as university rectors and other statutory bodies of higher education institutions are faced with a number of different choices which can be made with respect to the strategic development and management of their institutions. They have been caught, in particular, between two competing major trends unfolding in the environs of their institutions – globalization and regionalization. Sometimes these processes are regarded as two sides of the same coin or as an unavoidable action and reaction. Globalization has been seen as leading to fragmentation, plurality or even chaos or, as an opposite force, leading to a market-driven uniformity, homogeneity and standardization (Delanty 2001: 116). As such, globalization has been a stronger aspiration in some universities, while in others it has been counterbalanced by the opposite tendency to 'go regional' and seek the support of the safe and natural surroundings of the closest locality. Perhaps the major strategic decision facing any university is whether to seek a future primarily as an institution deeply embedded in its local community; as a 'regional university' with outreach to and engagement with a wider region (of the sub-national kind favoured in the policies of the European Community); as a national institution; or, in the case of a favoured minority, as a global player marked, probably, by the international excellence of its research as well as its teaching.

This chapter examines some of these different allegiances and identities and, with particular reference to the Baltic region, some of the different ways in which universities operate with them. Before turning to this, however, it is perhaps worth making one or two points about higher education in the Baltic region, since this is not necessarily well known to international readers.

The Baltic Sea regional context

The Baltic Sea region has been conceptualized as a testing ground for a peaceful political, social and economic transformation in Europe after the fall of the Iron Curtain. The recognition of its possible regional dimension within the EU has come together with the 'discovery' of the Baltic Sea cross-border region as both an action unit and an action space (cf. Henningsen 2002: 7). From being regarded as a litmus test with respect to peaceful policy making and conflict resolution in the post-Cold War Europe in the beginning of the 1990s (Genscher 1999), since the second half of the 1990s the region has also functioned as a laboratory for unparalleled systemic transition in other dimensions.

Among the issues deserving attention are the reforms of higher education systems. These take a variety of forms as a result of the national, ethnic, economic and cultural variations in this area. The earlier differences between the Soviet-dominated group of countries and the group of countries belonging to the West may sometimes still be felt. While these differences render attempts at a broad generalization difficult, the existing diversity must not necessarily be seen to have negative consequences. It provides for a diversity of economic resource and capacity. Many poorer regional actors have been able to learn from their more developed neighbours and have received support from them. Within diversity, new networks and communicative systems have encouraged the development of cross-regional partnerships at all levels.

One of the most profound problems existing in the part of the region formerly dominated by the Soviet Union is public understanding of the role of universities in society. It still seems to suffer under the long-lasting systemic division into three sectors: universities (teaching), Academies of Science (research) and R&D institutes (development). Continuation of this system after 1989 has led to universities losing the academic status associated with serious research engagement, R&D institutes producing 'non-applicable applied research' and the Academies losing contact with the younger generation of scholars (Karczewski 1995: 38). As could be witnessed in Poland in 2004, the legacy of a centralized system of R&D institutes still poses a problem. It makes it difficult to react quickly to the needs of the knowledge-based economy, and the institutes do not deliver the advanced, research-based, high technologies so badly needed by the transforming economy (Gazeta Wyborcza 2004). The lack of reform of the system has also negative consequences for the quality of research delivered by the universities and leads to insufficient and inefficient financing of the whole higher education sector (Kwiek 2001, 2003).

Undoubtedly, the system of innovation based on the Soviet-style R&D institutes and a unified division of educational and research institutions is not a solution that the Baltic Sea region as a whole can usefully contribute to the European Research Area. Nevertheless, Poland and other countries of the former Soviet bloc may be able to show how to respond efficiently to the challenges of the market and of globalization as they impact on higher education (Scott 2003: 305). In Poland, for instance, the massification of higher education has happened mainly thanks to the growth in the private university sector. Starting from scratch in 1990, there were fifty-six private higher education institutions registered in 1994; eighty in 1995; 116 in 1996; 146 in 1997; and 221 in 2001. In terms of enrolment the growth of the sector was from some 50,000 students in 1994 to about 510,000 students in 2001, which in that year accounted for about half of the total HE student population in Poland. The sheer increase in numbers of students in the private sector boosted the scholarization rate from 12.9 to 43.6 (gross) and from 9.8 to 32.7 (net), in the period between 1990 and 2001 (Kwiek 2004). The question of quality assurance and accreditation was one of the first to be answered and this has been done more or less satisfactorily. The system is guaranteed by three accreditation institutions that came into existence along with the growing number of private institutions and new degree programmes that they offered. The University Accreditation Commission, based on an agreement of all eighteen state universities, the Rectors Conference Accreditation Commission, including institutions of technical and vocational higher education, and finally the State Accreditation Committee, provide for a thorough and fairly strict accreditation procedure encompassing all institutions of higher education in Poland. Failing to meet the accreditation criteria leads to closing down of the given institute, regardless of its ownership status.

The systemic changes in Polish higher education are worth observing, but the region can also demonstrate a number of different models of regional success which may be of importance for the whole of Europe. To this category belongs experimentation with 'the regional university' – and it is to this concept and its realization that I shall now turn.

The regional university as a concept

We have already begun to see that there are a number of different ways in which a university may be defined or perceived as a 'regional' university. This may reflect no more than the fact that it is perhaps the only such institution located in a particular region. It may make a statement about its particular foundation and the public and private agencies which established it and hence developed a sense of ownership (as, for instance, is the case of the Vidzeme University College in Latvia). It may reflect a particular cultural affinity (as with, for example, the University of Catalonia). It may reflect its own mission and its view of the constituencies which it seeks primarily to serve – and this may in turn lead to its identification with economic development within a particular region. It may be a statement about its academic culture (perhaps allied to locally applied research and to close links with employers in the provision of work-based as well as more traditionally academic education and training). Although the concept of a regional university is relatively widespread, the manifold interpretation and often ambiguous use of this term makes its analysis difficult.

One of the other questions for a 'regional' university is to do with what the university identifies as its region. Charles, who studied the reshaping of the regional role of UK universities, observed that the university is embedded in many different types of 'community': some local, some global, some overlapping and interacting, some barely recognizing each other. Charles (2003: 13–14) identifies four criteria for determining how universities define their local community:

- the relationship between an institution and its physical surroundings as influenced by the historical and institutional context;
- the different scales by which attributes or impacts of the university should be measured or assessed;
- the different geographic scale or territory over which the university provides different types of 'local' service;
- the perceptions held by the institution and its management of the local community, which is identified in institutional missions.

According to some scholars, in particular in the German-speaking countries, the concept of a regional university has the negative connotation of being a provincial, i.e. more or less unsophisticated, institution, and for that reason it is being avoided as a term by some university managers (Teichler 1994: 62–3). In the 1990s that was the reason why it was suggested that a regional university might remain an analytical category but would be problematic as a rhetorical concept to be used in policy fora. However, the regional development policies unfolding in Finland and Sweden since the early 1990s, and in other countries of the Baltic Sea region later in the decade, go some way to contradict this view. Especially in the Finnish debate, the regional universities were explicitly and positively identified as key actors in the Centre of Expertise Programme introduced by the Finnish government in its Regional Development Act in 1994. Similarly, in Sweden the term 'regional university' has been used without any negative connotation attached to it. Analyses of regional universities in this country focus rather on the ability of such institutions to meet the dual task of establishing a traditional academic reputation *and* active participation in regional development processes (Westlund 2003).

The relatively positive connotation of the adjective 'regional' in the name of some universities in the Baltic Sea region notwithstanding, the term causes some problems as an analytical unit. The regional borders are often arbitrary and do not coincide with individual definitions and perceptions. The processes of administrative reforms created new regions which had no real historical or cultural identity. As the administrative divisions were in many cases paired with the regional development plans which featured an academic centre, some universities became 'regional' by decree rather than out of their own choice.

To make matters more complicated, with the growing trend towards greater autonomy of regions as subunits of current nation-states on the one hand, and the cross-border regions becoming supranational entities in Europe on the other, it often remains unclear whether the reference 'regional' is made to the subregion or some cross-border regions, like Pomerania, Nemunas, or even supranational structures like 'the Baltic region'.

Regionalism, nationalism and internationalism

Jürgen Enders from the Centre for Higher Education Policy Studies at the University of Twente wrote in his paper on the relationship between higher education, internationalization and the nation-state that higher education is still predominantly shaped at a national level and this has many consequences for the links the university develops. Nevertheless, Enders mentions activities under the heading 'internationalization' as a burgeoning challenge to the predominance of the nation-state. This process is claimed to change the conception of social, economic and cultural roles of higher education and their configuration in national systems of higher education (Enders 2004: 361).

When discussing the way in which the universities function today, Enders sees internationalization as a universal trend in higher education. This may be a correct assumption, but for smaller regional universities regionalization is just as important. Also, authors who see globalization as the most influential societal phenomenon affecting the university point to the necessity of preserving national or regional variations in the future. Fred Halliday, for instance, who explored the potential of the 'international university', noted that globalization has already managed to produce new elites, a 'cosmocracy' of people who are mobile as between countries and cultures. Nevertheless, the universities of the future should not become homogenized and should remain like restaurants that have distinctive cuisines, 'more or less connected to national origins, invented or real' (Halliday 1999: 101).

There is, however, synergy to be found in combining some of these different identities. One of the contributions which a university can make to its local or regional community is to lift it out of parochialism by bringing into it the broader perspectives of a cosmopolitan staff and student population, to join local conversations with national and international ones, to reach out to major national and international corporations (and provide a magnet to inward investment) as well as supporting local business development. The regional university serves its region badly in economic and cultural terms if it only recycles the cultural capital that is already available in the region.

In the countries around the Baltic Sea the regional higher education institutions react in very different ways to the globalization and the regionalization taking place in their environment. The big universities located in the capital cities mostly remain a good source of student 'cosmocracy', with a global rather than regional frame of mind. In the institutions of higher education located outside of the capitals an interesting transformation can be observed. In the subregions, especially in Sweden and Finland, the universities pay greater attention to the needs of their localities.

In the following sections, two possible patterns of identification of such regional institutions will be demonstrated. In the first, the regional affiliation of the university is taken as being with the local administrative subunit of the nation. The second pattern is characteristic of institutions that choose a supranational or cross-border region as their primary area of identification. In conclusion, a third pattern of multiple regional identification is mentioned as a possible future trend that combines the subregional, national and panregional frameworks.

Regional universities as identified with subunits of the nation

This pattern of identification relates to the role played by the universities on the micro level in their subnational localities. Focusing on a region below the nation results in the question how the university is able to meet the challenges and fulfil its mission in a more concrete way, for example, by increasing the innovativeness of regional economies. The local impact of the university might in this case be measured by investigating how the university manages to contribute to local development and innovation strategies, or how it interacts with industry and the government or local administration. These kind of considerations have been represented in studies of regional innovation systems (Cooke *et al.* 1997) and have supported the idea of an entrepreneurial university. In 1996 Sverker Sörlin illustrated this trend with very convincing examples from Sweden, the most convincing being the pattern of relationship between Sörlin's home institution, the University of Umeå, and its sparsely populated locality in northern Sweden (Sörlin 1996). In smaller regional communities the university was often the largest single employer in a town or region but there were other ways too in which it was naturally identified as a driving force behind economic as well as cultural development. Indeed, even cursory analysis of the unemployment rate in regions in which a university is based might lead to the conclusion that the importance of the university for regional development must be immense.

In the Baltic Sea region in general, with its transition status in the economic, political and social sense, universities have, from an early stage, played a very important role in the development of regions. In many cases regional innovation strategies were drafted collaboratively between the university and the local administration and some universities explicitly showed links with the closest locality in their mission statements. Universities located in Turku, Joensuu and Oulu in Finland, Kaunas in Lithuania, Linköping and Umeå in Sweden and Gdansk in Poland are good examples of this sort of relationship. In this way they showed the university's commitment to addressing the educational and research needs of potential students and the public in the local community. Their primary identification is with the subregion in which they reside. They participate in regional development projects there and are regarded as motors for regional development.

From a historical perspective the Nordic countries were the first in the Baltic Sea region to recognize the value of a regional development policy built around cooperation with the local, 'regional' university. Finland was perhaps the most successful, as it led the way by emphasizing a new, expertise-based regional policy. Reforms in higher education were integrally linked with regional development processes in the 1990s. The reforms were based on a strategy which had three components: a framework provided by central government, university evaluation reports and local development strategies. A closer look at the University of Oulu reveals how these components were interconnected. First, the strategic plans of the government and the Ministry of Education provided a conscious 'regionalization' framework. Second, the university carried out its individual institutional evaluation against the criteria embedded in this framework, which aimed at the identification of its strong and weak disciplines. Finally, the business strategy of the Oulu region was consulted when the university senate enacted the first overall university strategy plan in 1994 (Lajunen, Aaltonen and Koivunen 1999). Similar developments could be observed in Jyväskyla, Joensuu and Turku (Vartiainen and Viiri 2002, Kettunen 2004, Lönnberg and Puukka 2001) to mention just some of the more outstanding examples. The general conclusion was that 'even by being passively present, the university makes its presence felt' (Lajunen, Aaltonen and Koivunen 1999: 82, but see also Bridges in this volume).

The optimism of the 1990s about the impact of universities on regional development has been less evident in the first years of the twenty-first century. In

Sweden, for instance, two reports from the Swedish Institute for Studies of Education and Research about the regional impact of higher education institutions (Sandström *et al.* 2003 and Westlund 2003) have mostly confirmed the pessimistic analyses that were made a few years earlier. In 2000 Sverker Sörlin and Gunnar Törnqvist delivered a study of the importance of the university for the economic development of Sweden and its welfare. They pointed, among other things, to the weak theoretical and empirical evidence behind the belief in the importance of the university for local development. Sverker Sörlin had to reevaluate his individual case studies from the 1990s and concluded that the successful experience of one university with its own community can not necessarily be expected to bring about the same effects at another location (Sörlin and Törnqvist 2000: 110).

The supranational Baltic Sea region as an action space for the university

Apart from the universities that focus on regional activities of the first kind which I have identified, i.e. where region is a subset of the national, there are also universities that transgress the boundary of their close locality without at the same time becoming cosmopolitan. They address a larger region than their closest community and they define it in a more arbitrary manner. Their region is the area of their scholarly interest and the area which they want to serve. These universities are no longer regional in the narrow sense of their closest locality but they have, for example, made either a part or the whole Baltic Sea region their space of reference. The most explicit cases where this phenomenon can be observed are Södertörn University College, located south of Stockholm, in Sweden and Øresund University, located in the cross-border region consisting of South-western Sweden and the greater Copenhagen area in Denmark.

Adopting the perspective of the whole Baltic Sea region or some of its cross-border areas leads to a macro-scale regional affiliation. Here we can observe that both the virtual and physical mobility of academics have created a new type of transnational community or, to use the terminology of Manuel Castells, a network where universities serve as the nodes and hubs and academics carry knowledge between these points in the network. The role of academia, traditionally associated with generating and processing knowledge, now appears to have expanded as never before, and cultural norms and patterns transferred by mobile scholars are increasingly important by-products of academic activity.

At the level of a given university, incorporation of the supranational perspective into university activity may seem to be an example of increasing globalization. Globalization involves institutions in creating networks, regardless of national affinity and disregarding the distance. Such universities look beyond the immediate gains their localities have in terms of innovation and growth, and think long term and organize resources not solely relying on the state where they reside. This strategy has long been practised by the big universities.

Yet, the choice made by some regional universities to identify with a larger community rather than with the nearest locality may be seen as a pragmatic step taken in order to meet the demands of students. Both students and university managers are well aware of the conditions and trends in the labour market, where international mobility has become a keyword. With EU enlargement, and with the free flow of labour becoming a norm within the next few years, tailoring courses and strategies to the demands of new types of clients and stakeholders will also become a requirement for success.

In the Baltic Sea region a good example of this pattern is Södertörn University College with its Baltic and East European Graduate School. According to its own description, despite offering a number of disciplines across the whole academic field, Södertörn University College has two main profiles, 'Humanities and Social Science, with great breadth and a special interest in Eastern and Central European issues' (*About Södertörns högskola*, 20 November 2004). Indeed, the very epitome of this supranational orientation can be witnessed at the graduate level. In the late 1990s a decision was made to provide a learning environment for graduates from the Baltic Sea region and Eastern Europe. In 2000 the school started operating in cooperation with Stockholm University and other Swedish universities under the name of the Baltic and East European Graduate School. Financing for the school comes from a grant from the Foundation for Baltic and East European Studies (Östersjöstiftelsen), which was originally established by the Swedish government in 1994 (Henningsen 1999).

Another example of a supranational university structure in the Baltic Sea area is Öresund University located in the Öresund region. For the broad European public it is particularly interesting as an experiment in linking the transformation of cross-border regions with the enhancement of economic innovation. Öresund University is a primary example of a cross-border higher education institution which, due to its structure based on cooperation of several universities over the national borders of two countries, can be called a 'network university'. This appellation owes much to the fact that the term 'university' covers here a formal collaboration between eleven higher education establishments in Öresund. The individual institutions serve here as nodal points of the network, but it is in their totality that they generate the added value with respect to increasing social capital, aggregation of research capacity and improving study opportunities for students. The network was created as a 'learning cluster' comprising the higher education institutions in Copenhagen, Roskilde, Lund and Malmö in the second half of the 1990s. It is based on regular student exchange programmes, organizing common study programmes and bridging the institutional distance between the Danish and Swedish systems of higher education. The relevant educational fields are expected to develop bottom-up, as a response to regional specialization. The regional labour markets in Copenhagen and the region of Scania are expected to become the immediate beneficiaries of the initiative in the long run. The strategy is to provide an infrastructure for integration (OECD 2001: 74).

Undoubtedly, Öresund University has both a unifying function across the area over which it extends and contributes to building regional identity. Created in an attempt to revive the stagnating economies of the regions on both sides of the Sund, separating Denmark from Sweden, the Čresund region exploits the potential of the 'learning region'. In this way it links networking among universities with the carefully designed political and administrative structure of the cross-border region in Öresund. Apart from some spectacular Finnish localities, such as Oulu, where Nokia and other high-tech industries caused the rejuvenation and rediscovery of the remote northern European periphery, the development of the Öresund region has to be regarded as one of the more original European experiments in networking among universities in a close locality. It is also the most successful exemplification of the developing knowledge-based society in the Baltic Sea countries – and the universities are at the heart of the process.

Multiple regional identification patterns

Apart from the two models of the regional university described above (the first identified with a local region which is a subset of the country and the second with a wider region which crosses national frontiers), it is also possible to observe the emergence of a multiple identification pattern in some regional universities – of interaction between the subregional and panregional orientation within one institution. It is characterized by a dual or multiple orientation of a given institution towards its closest locality, as well as towards other possible regional communities that the university perceives as its region. Such an understanding of regional agenda transgresses the close regional and national boundaries and opens up the opportunity for institutionalizing multiple regional communities.

Multiplication of the target regions that are important for the university takes place because of the frameworks provided by the national governments or other founding bodies. For instance, the university might be focusing on its closest locality when potential undergraduate and graduate students are addressed. However, attracting postgraduate students will demand a different definition of the potential region. In a similar manner, the university research agendas may be defined. If the research is to serve primarily the local community through creating innovation and employment, the focal point will be on the local community of up to fifty kilometres radius from the institution. At the same time, if the university wants to win research contracts that require wider cooperation and networking, the area of reference will be very different – nationwide or even global. The discussions concerning the Development Contract for the University of Aarhus in Denmark bear witness to this tendency in defining a university's locality. The evolving multiple-institutional identity is characterized by the strategic overlapping of local and regional interests with international and global strategies. Interestingly, the currently valid development contract of the Aarhus University does not mention the national dimension at all, while defining two categories of near and farther regional locality as its action space (University of Aarhus 2000).

The trend to conceptualize the region as both the close and the remote locality stems from the functional approach to the alliances into which a university enters, both to prove its relevance and to remain competitive. In the long run such behaviour will have a bearing on how universities look at their role in the regional or local development. On the one hand it seems plausible that the triple helix model may well lead to a rediscovery and redefinition of the regional agenda. It is also possible that the entrepreneurial paradigm may force the universities to look for the most suitable partners elsewhere than in the closest community. This process may intensify with the networking that has become a required condition of funding within the European Union. Such developments would fit well with the European Research Area and the European Area of Higher Education, as this kind of institution must necessarily be built on networks broader than the states. The Baltic Sea states and their regional universities are building experience which will equip them to rise to this challenge both to the reach of their work and to their very identities.

References

About Södertörns högskola. Online. Available at: webappo.sh.se/ (accessed 20 November 2004).
Bobe, M. (2002) 'The University of Warwick and its region: deepening the engagement', *Industry and Higher Education*, 16 (2), 91–6.
Charles, D. (2003) 'Universities and territorial development: reshaping the regional role of English universities', *Local Economy*, 18 (1), 7–20.
Chatterton, P. (1998) 'The university and the community: an exploration of the cultural impacts of universities and students on community', unpublished thesis, University of Bristol.
Cooke, P., Uranga, M.G. and Etxebarria, G. (1997) 'Regional innovation systems: institutional and organizational dimensions', *Research Policy*, 26 (4), 475–91.
Delanty, G. (2001) *Challenging Knowledge: the University in the Knowledge Society*, Buckingham: The Society for Research into Higher Education & Open University Press.
DfEE (1998) *Universities and Regional Development*, Newcastle School of Management, Department for Education and Employment.
Duke, C. (2000) 'Regional partnership – building a learning region', *Perspectives*, 4 (3), 61–7.
—— (2002) *Managing the Learning University*, Buckingham: The Society for Research into Higher Education & Open University Press.
Enders, J. (2004) 'Higher education, internationalization, and the nation-state: recent developments and challenges to governance theory', *Higher Education*, 47, 361–82.
Gazeta Wyborcza (2004) 'Zjechać z bocznego toru' ['Getting on track'], *Gazeta Wyborcza*, 8 November, 32.
Genscher, H.D. (1999) 'The future development in the Baltic Sea area: a litmus test for European politics', *Nordeuropaforum*, 2 (99), 99–106.

GUNI (2004) *Global University Network for Innovation Newsletter*, 2004–03. Online. Available at: 213.27.152.26/guni1_en_print.htm (accessed 20 November 2004).
Halliday, F. (1999) 'The chimera of the "international university"', *International Affairs*, 75 (1), 99–120.
Henningsen, B. (1999) 'Das Projekt Södertörn. Bemerkungen zur Wissenschaftspolitik in Nordeuropa' ['The Project Södertörn. Comments on the scientific policy in Northern Europe'], in R. vom Bruch (ed.) *Jahrbuch für Universitätsgeschichte*, 2, 219–24.
—— (ed.) (2002) *Towards a Knowledge-based Society in the Baltic Sea Region*, Berlin: Berlin Verlag Arno Spitz GmbH.
Karczewski, W.A. (1995) 'The values and the limits of mutuality: is there a common agenda in the Central and Eastern European countries for the transformation of their higher education and research systems?', in *Western Paradigms and Eastern Agenda: a Reassessment*, Vienna: Institute for Human Sciences.
Kettunen, J. (2004) 'The strategic evaluation of regional development in higher education', *Assessment and Evaluation in Higher Education*, 29 (3), 357–68.
Kwiek, M. (2001) 'Social and cultural dimensions of the transformation of higher education in Central and Eastern Europe', *Higher Education in Europe*, 26 (3), 399–410.
—— (2003) 'Academe in transition: transformations in the Polish academic profession', *Higher Education*, 45, 455–76.
—— (2004) 'The international attractiveness of the academic profession in Europe: the case of Poland', in J. Enders and E. de Weert (eds) *The International Attractiveness of the Academic Profession*, Frankfurt-am-Main: Gewenkschaft Erziehung und Wissenschaft (GEW).
Lajunen, L.H.J., Aaltonen, M. and Koivunen, S. (1999) 'How a regional university can both survive and develop in a rapidly changing operational and economic environment: the case of the University of Oulu', *Higher Education in Europe*, 24 (1), 81–9.
Lönnberg, H. and Puukka, J. (2001) 'The University and its region: the case of the University of Turku', *Higher Education in Europe*, 26 (3), 315–20.
OECD (2001) *Cities and Regions in the New Learning Economy*, Paris: OECD.
Robson, B. et al. (1997) *Higher Education and Regions*, Report 9, The National Committee of Inquiry into Higher Education, London: HMSO.
Sandström, U., Abdallah, L. and Hällsten, M. (2003) 'Forskningsfinansiering genom regional samverkan' ['Financing research through regional cooperation'], Working paper 2003, 22, Stockholm: Institutet för studier av utbildning och forskning.
Scott, P. (2003) 'Challenges to academic values and the organization of academic work in a time of globalization', *Higher Education in Europe*, 28 (3), 295–306.
Sörlin, S. (1996) *Universiteten som drivkrafter. Globaliseringen, kunskapspolitik och den nya intellektuella geografin*, Stockholm: SNS Förlag.
Sörlin, S. and Törnqvist, G. (2000) *Kunskap för välstånd, Universiteten och omvandlingen av Sverige*, Stockholm: SNS Förlag.
Teichler, U. (1994) 'Regionsuniversitäten – Situation und Perspektiven in den neunziger Jahren' ['Region-based universities – situation and perspectives in the 1990s'], in P. Kellermann (ed.) *Regionsuniversitäten: ein transnationaler Polylog zur Bestimmung der Spannung zwischen hochschulischen Funktionen und Standortbedingungen*, Klagenfurt: Kärntner Druck- und Verlagsgesellschaft.
University of Aarhus (2000) *Udviklingskontrakt 2000–2003*. Online. Available at: www.au.dk/da/rammer/udv-2000.htm (accessed 5 December 2004).

University of California (1993) *USC and the Community*, Office of University Public Relations.

Vartiainen, P. and Viiri, A. (2002) 'Universities and their local partners: the case of the University of Joensuu, Finland', *Industry and Higher Education*, 16 (2), 83–9.

Ward, D. (2002) *The University in Partnership with Wisconsin: Building on a Tradition of Excellence*, Madison: University of Wisconsin-Madison.

Westlund, H. (2003) 'Regionala effekter av högre utbildning, högskolor och universitet. En kunskapsöversikt' ['Regional impact of higher education, colleges and universities. A knowledge overview'], Working paper 2003·28, Östersund: Institutet för tillväxtpolitiska studier and Stockholm: Institutet för studier av utbildning och forskning.

Part IV

Universities and the demands of the economy

Chapter 9

The role of higher education in national innovation systems in Central and Eastern Europe

Slavo Radošević and Monika Kriaučioniené

Introduction

Central and East European countries (CEECs), including Lithuania, have joined the EU in the hope that this will accelerate their growth, improve security and welfare through higher income per capita and enable them to catch up with more developed countries. If these aspirations are to be realized, then politicians and professionals in these countries need to understand the drivers of economic growth and social development.

Economists agree that factor expansion (i.e. growth in employment, population and capital), is secondary to increased productivity as a source of growth. When trying to understand the determinants of productivity, however, the literature suggests several proximate causes of growth: increased capital intensity, human capital, technological change, and competition (OECD 2003). A key problem is whether it is appropriate to consider each of these components as separate factors, as their contributions are closely interrelated. We have seen a failure of academic research to understand sources of growth because it has treated individual determinants of growth as 'stocks' (Easterly 2002) rather than as parts of interrelated systems.

The literature on national systems of innovation is still undeveloped, but a promising, newly emerging area of research considers growth as a process creating complementarities between different social subsystems (businesses infrastructure, science, government, etc.). Interaction between these subsystems involves extensive active learning and synergies, which, in successful cases, lead to robust national systems of innovation. Countries successful in this respect demonstrate complementarities between institutional and technical change rather than an abundance of a single growth factor. Variations in rates of growth could therefore be ascribed less to the proportions of individual growth factors and more to differences in national systems of innovation (Freeman 2002).

The type, style and intensity of interactions among different socio-economic subsystems are defined by the social, institutional and economic context of the national innovation system. Among the key conditions for a successful national innovation system are interactive learning among agents and the cultivation of knowledge-intense activities within the economy (Kriaučionienė 2002). Institutions of higher education contribute significantly to knowledge-development activities and to the creation of conditions enabling knowledge diffusion and innovation within the economy.

In this chapter we take an *innovation systems* perspective on growth as the conceptual framework from which to explore the role of higher education systems in the countries of CEE. Our interest in higher education systems originates from the assumption that growth in the twenty-first century will be based on different requirements from those of the past (Freeman 2002, Radošević 1999). Sources of growth within developed economies are in innovation, knowledge, and in the capacity to integrate ICT into business and social processes, and these will increasingly be based on a developed university system. Nelson (2004b) argues that advanced formal training and a strong science base has become a substantial basis for 'learning by doing'. In addition, 'a university-mediated trans-national conduit of learning will be of particularly great importance during the twenty-first century for countries seeking to catch up' (ibid., p. 7). Nelson (2004a) argues that a strong science base significantly reduces the importance of seeking apprenticeship training overseas or tutelage by foreign industrial experts.

The requirement for a scientific basis for industry and the changing character of manufacturing embodying ICT-based services both increase the importance of higher education in national systems of innovation. In the field of life sciences, over 90 per cent of US businesses today have some type of relationship with a university, over 50 per cent of faculty members have consulted for industry, while about one-quarter of faculty members at major US universities have received support for research from industry (Blumenthal 2003). These indicators suggest that some changes in the 'regime of growth' have already been in operation in economies at the frontiers of technology.

As technological change becomes driven by a variety of knowledge sources, a technologically based ability to compete becomes increasingly systemic, i.e. shared across connected networks. Hence, despite the increasing importance of universities in a regime of growth based on knowledge economies, pouring money into the higher education system is not the only issue. As Nelson (2004b) argues, building new institutions or adapting old ones to new purposes may be the most difficult part of the catch-up process. There are two particularly complex aspects of institutional change that are necessary to ensure the effective role of higher education in national, twenty-first century systems of innovation.

First, as pointed by Nelson (2004b), the key challenge for universities and public research institutes is that of bridging between two governance regimes – public and private. Historical experience shows that maintaining a balance between basic science on the one hand and close links to the user community on the other is essential for the effective contribution of universities and public research institutes to the economy. However, these systems operate with different objectives and with different rules of governance. The management of the relationship between the two is a complex process which requires sophisticated skills that are not widely developed (see Bridges in this volume). An assessment of the effects of the US Bayh–Dole Act, that pushed universities to patent their inventions, shows that there are limits to the extent to which academic science can and should be driven into a mode of commercial knowledge production (Mowery *et al*. 2001, Mowery and Ziedonis 2002, Stankiewicz 1986).

Second, CEE universities, in particular, have to embrace new functions in addition to their traditional teaching role. The new growth regime of the knowledge-based economy requires universities to balance their functions of teaching (knowledge diffusion), research (knowledge generation) and the commercialization of their R&D and consultancy (knowledge utilization). However, given that there are limits to the extent to which academic science can be driven into commercial and technological modes, and given the differences in the governance regimes of the three functions, the challenge for universities is not trivial (Stankiewicz 1986). The special tailoring needed for the institutional aspects of this catching up requires new organizational models. As the CEECs' disappointing experience of copying organizations such as science parks suggests, the differences in functions and forms between leading economies and those catching up are too large to be bridged by exact copying. This only achieves surrogate modernization and does not promote transformation towards a knowledge-based economy.

In exploring the role of universities in CEECs (and in Lithuania in particular) in the transformation of their national systems of innovation, we are specifically interested in discovering, first, the current state of transformation or the emergence of market-based national systems of innovation in CEECs. Second, we are considering the current state of transformation of universities in CEECs from the perspective of systems of innovation. Third, we ask what are the developments that would be needed for universities to contribute to knowledge-based growth in CEECs. In finding the answers to these questions we have developed some arguments that should further our understanding of these issues.

First, we show that there is a gap between the value-chain logic of the emerging systems of innovation in CEECs and the fragmented integration of universities in CEECs into a national system of innovation and international science networks. This gap explains why policy initiatives in the CEECs to enhance academy and industry links during the last ten to fifteen years have such meagre results.

Then we show that the new functions of universities, in terms of knowledge services provision and increased involvement in contract R&D, have operated mainly as a substitute for the undeveloped sector of knowledge-intensive business services. Although this provides universities with cash, this type of involvement of universities does not develop their knowledge-utilization function and creates problems of organizational coherence.

Finally, we show that pressures on universities in all CEECs to pursue their teaching function through large increases in the number of students participating in higher education puts their knowledge-generation and knowledge-utilization functions under strain. This, coupled with limited budgets, has probably resulted in the declining quality of teaching and has endangered the balance between the universities' three functions. All this suggests that universities in CEECs are not yet able to be key drivers and promoters of linkages in national innovation systems. However, individual success stories do suggest that in some countries, including Lithuania, we may see the emergence of universities as important drivers of such systems in the near future.

In section two we explore the role of CEECs' universities in national systems of innovation through several types of data. Section three analyses the Lithuanian higher education system and its transformation towards meeting the requirements of the knowledge-based economy. Our conclusions bring the Lithuanian picture into comparative perspective and draw policy implications.

The higher education system as a building block of national innovation systems in Central and Eastern Europe

During the 1990s, the economic growth of CEECs was based on reallocation and non-investment-based productivity improvements (see Havrylyshyn 2001, Fischer, Sahay and Vegh 1998, Berg *et al.* 1999). Growth was not based on local knowledge and R&D (Radošević and Auriol 1999). Reallocation from industry to services, from domestic to foreign businesses, and from large to small businesses was accompanied by productivity improvements through better organization, lay-offs, and creating value through closer links with markets and users. However, these sources of growth are coming to an end in several CEE economies and there are signs that countries may be facing structural barriers to growth, which is now dependent on the accumulation of physical capital as well as capital of more intangible kinds.

In the 1990s, Central and Eastern Europe became a global production locality in several sectors such as automotive and electronics. The integration of CEECs, through foreign direct investment and subcontracting networks, has led to highly productive plants and it has had significant positive effects. Foreign direct investment has been the main vehicle of restructuring and productivity growth (Damijan and Rojec 2004). However, the indirect effects of foreign direct investment, or spillovers from this investment, are mainly vertical: that is, they operate along the supply chain, while any horizontal spillovers are either absent or negative (Smarzynska-Javorcki 2004, Damijan *et al.* 2003). These econometric results have been confirmed by large sample surveys (Majcen *et al.* 2004). Foreign direct investment is strongly present in high- and medium-high-tech industries but in the low value-added segments of these industries. Damijan and Rojec (2004) show that the growth of total factor productivity in these industries in Central Europe is not necessarily related to this foreign investment. Their conclusion is that catching up via foreign direct investment is going on mostly in industries at the lower end of technological intensity. These results are

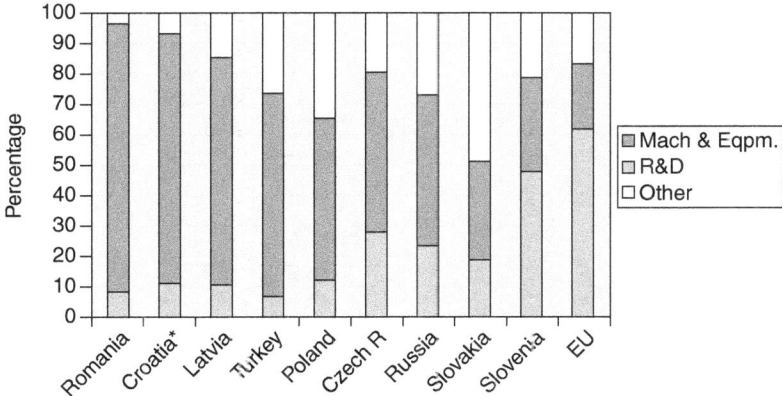

Figure 9.1 Innovation expenditures in manufacturing, by economic activity (sources: For Russia, Poland, Turkey and Romania: R&D and innovation statistics in candidate countries and the Russian Federation, Data 1996–97, EC, Theme 9, R&D, Eurostat 2000. For Slovakia: Slovak Statistical Office. For Turkey: Turkish Statistics Institute. For Slovenia: Statistical Office, Rapid Report No. 307/2002. For Latvia: Latvian Statistics, Innovation Survey Results 2003. For EU: (2000) Statistics of Innovation in Europe, Eurostat, Luxembourg. For Croatia: National Innovation Survey (preliminary data) 2004).

Note
Mach & Eqpm – Machinery and equipment.

compatible with data from innovation surveys which show that innovation in CEE is mainly about new machinery and equipment (Figure 9.1).

Growth and recovery have not been accompanied by a growth of demand for R&D and local technology (Radošević 2004). However, it seems that there has been increasing demand for knowledge-intensive business services. Balaz (2004) shows a growth of knowledge-intensive businesses in Central European countries with high levels of output elasticity. Results for EU economies show that there is strong correlation between growth in the communication services purchased by industry and the business services purchased by the same industries. However, for Central European countries these correlation coefficients are much lower than in the EU-15, which suggests that the development of business services was not primarily driven by the development of communication services. Balaz (2004) concludes that it was change in the system environment, rather than technological changes, which promoted the spread of these industries in Hungary, the Czech Republic and Slovakia.

The results of both Damijan and Rojec (2004) and Balaz (2004) are comparable to those of Table 9.1, an analysis of which shows two things. First, a similar

Table 9.1 High-tech and medium-high-tech manufacturing and knowledge-intensive services (KIS) in EU-15 and in new member states and candidate countries

		Share of employment (%)		Annual average growth rate of employment (%) 2000–03			
		High, Med-high-tech manufacturing	KIS	High-tech KIS	Financial KIS	Market KIS	Other KIS
	Slovenia	8.94	24.19				
	Czech Republic	8.71	24.47				
	Hungary	8.27	27.95				
	Slovakia	8.00	24.16				
	Romania	5.32	13.02				
	Bulgaria	4.66	22.05				
	Estonia	3.35	31.61	−5.76	1.31	12.79	6.86
	Lithuania	3.03	24.22	−10.46	−4.51	9.30	−5.14
	Latvia	1.85	23.97	−2.73	−3.28	8.44	1.17
				−3.79	5.10	8.40	−0.39
	Slovakia			2.39	−4.56	8.35	0.26
	Bulgaria			1.65	−5.32	8.24	2.44
	Hungary			2.00	0.05	5.10	1.74
	Slovenia			1.70	0.95	1.85	0.20
	Czech Republic			1.63	2.17	−2.52	0.52
	Latvia						
CEE-9	Average	5.79	23.96	−1.49	−0.90	6.66	0.85
	St dev	2.58	4.69	4.25	3.44	4.29	2.94
EU-15	Average	5.72	34.35	2.21	−0.14	3.93	2.44
	St dev	2.29	7.57	2.85	2.46	2.36	1.29

Source: Eurostat, Statistics in Focus, S&T, 10/2004.

Notes
CEE – Central and East European Countries.
EU-15 – The original 15 member countries of the European Union.

proportion of employment in high- and medium-high-tech manufacturing in CEE and the EU-15 is not accompanied by a similar proportion of employment in knowledge-intensive services. Second, employment growth in knowledge-intensive services in CEECs is mainly located in the sector of market services, while the high-tech sector records either low or negative employment rates.

Figures 9.2 and 9.3 further confirm this pattern. We tested for EU-25 relationships between employment in medium-high tech manufacturing and high-tech services (x-axis) with the share of working age population with third level education (y-axis). While this relationship, although insignificant, is positive for EU-15, it is negative for new member states, i.e. high-tech employment is inversely related to educational endowment.

These results suggest, first, that there is a very limited demand for R&D and local technology and technology-related services in CEECs. Growth has been driven by foreign direct investment and physical investment with a limited intangible component. These drivers of growth have enabled quick productivity improvements, but by themselves do not ensure long-term growth or convergence to EU income levels. Second, university education in the population does not seem to relate to employment in technology-intensive manufacturing and services. This points to a mismatch between potential capacities and outcomes. In order to achieve convergence, the national innovation capacity of the CEECs will have to be improved, and, in particular, the demand for technology (see Radošević 2004).

This brings us to the issue of a national system of innovation and the role of the higher education sector. Further growth of CEECs is increasingly dependent on the accumulation of technology and on the quality of 'narrow' national systems of innovation, i.e. on the quality of R&D and the educational infrastructure.[1]

CEECs are faced with the challenge of how to develop their knowledge-based economy, in which universities should play a pivotal role. A national system of innovation will remain the key basis of growth in a globalized economy. Moreover, local systems of innovation are essential if CEECs are to avoid the pitfalls of open and integrated but stagnant economies.

The emerging systems of innovation in CEE operate along value chains and are focused on enterprise and its suppliers and buyers (Majcen et al. 2004). This pattern originates from the logic of globalization and is exacerbated in CEECs, which tend to be strongly dependent on foreign direct investment. In that respect, national systems of innovation in CEE exist only in organizational, not in functional terms. As these economies are becoming increasingly integrated into the global economy as markets and production locations, they are becoming technologically integrated, mainly through foreign investment and subcontracting. This makes their 'narrow' national systems of innovation increasingly irrelevant, and poses a challenge for these economies in terms of how to integrate flows of knowledge, within value chains, into local networks.

Universities are important organizations in these processes and will have to

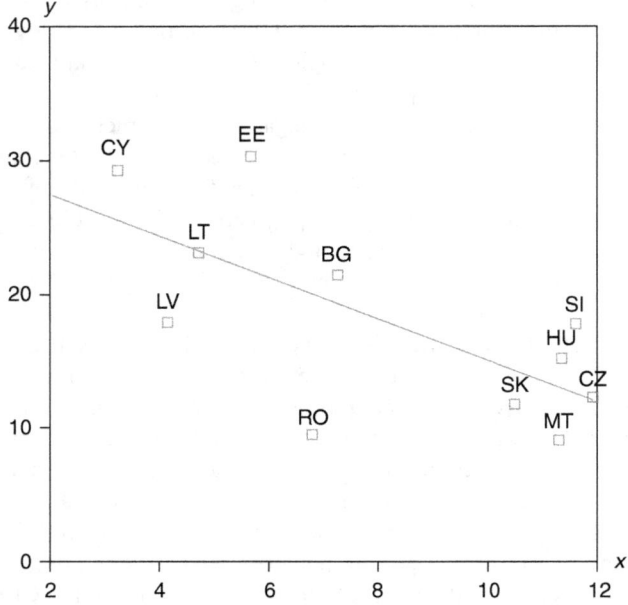

Figure 9.2

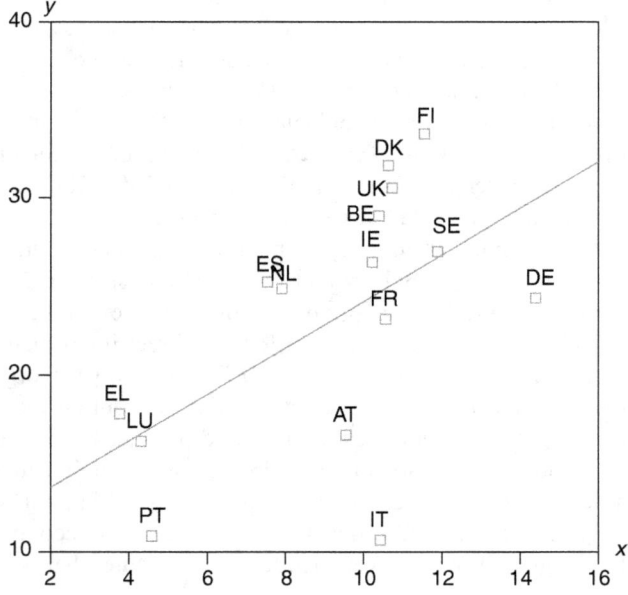

Figure 9.3

play an increasingly important role as nodes in knowledge flows. We now explore whether universities are able to meet these challenges.

Functional transformation of universities in CEE

CEE universities will have to modernize in order to contribute to catching-up processes. An important part of their modernization is focused on balancing or rebalancing relationships between their three key functions: knowledge diffusion, knowledge generation and knowledge utilization. Historical experience suggests that when universities have seen themselves simply as scientific bodies linked to the broader scientific community but isolated from the user community, or when they pursued short-run practical interests, they have not been a productive part of innovation systems (Nelson 2004a). It is only when they managed to operate between these two extremes that they have acted effectively as one of the drivers of systems of innovation.

The knowledge-generation function of CEE universities

Historically, the majority of CEE universities were predominantly teaching institutions (Radošević and Auriol 1999). However, the implosion of R&D, which has been accompanied by the strong erosion of industrial R&D institutes, the closure or downsizing of Academies of Science and budget cuts, have reshaped R&D systems in these countries. Today R&D plays a dominant role in the higher education system. Table 9.2 shows that in these respects Baltic economies' R&D systems have undergone the biggest changes as former Soviet era industrial R&D institutes were closed down. It also shows that R&D personnel in higher education in CEECs play a larger part than in the EU-15. The Czech Republic, Slovenia and Romania, however, have retained relatively large

---

Figures 9.2 and 9.3 The relationship between employment in medium-high-tech manufacturing and high-tech services and share of working age population with third level education in new member states and in EU-15 (source: European Innovation Scoreboard 2004).

Notes
A – Austria; B – Belgium; BG – Bulgaria; CZ – Czech Republic; D – Germany; DK – Denmark; E – Spain; EE – Estonia; EL – Greece; F – France; FIN – Finland; HU – Hungary; I – Italy; IRL – Ireland; LT – Lithuania; LV – Latvia; NL – Netherlands; P – Portugal; RO – Romania; S – Sweden; SL – Slovenia; SK – Slovakia; UK – United Kingdom.
Figure 9.2:
y axis: share of working age population with third level education in the new EU member states.
x axis: share of employment in medium-high-tech manufacturing and high-tech services in the new EU member states.
Figure 9.3:
y axis: share of working age population with third level education in 15 EU member states (old EU).
x axis: share of employment in medium-high-tech manufacturing and high-tech services in 15 EU member states (old EU).

Table 9.2 Share of R&D personnel by institutional sectors, 2001 (based on full-time equivalent)

	BES (%)	GOV (%)	HES (%)
European Union (15)	55	14	30
ACC (2000)	28	28	44
Estonia	16	19	62
Latvia	5	39	55
Lithuania	25	20	55
Poland (2000)	24	24	53
Slovakia	33	28	40
Hungary	30	34	37
Czech Republic	46	30	23
Slovenia	50	28	20
Bulgaria	13	70	17
Romania	61	26	13

Source: Eurostat (2003).

Notes
BES – Business enterprise sector.
GOV – Government sector.
HES – Higher education sector.
ACC – Accessing European Countries.

numbers of R&D personnel in the business enterprise sector. This has led to some differences in the profile of national systems of innovation among CEECs between those that are oriented towards the higher education system and those that are oriented towards the business enterprise sector.[2] Slovakia and Hungary represent intermediate cases where all three institutional sectors are present to similar degrees.

A high proportion of R&D personnel in the higher education sector should not be interpreted as a sign of its dynamism, but rather as the reliance of research personnel on a system that has teaching as its core source of income. Overall, the R&D intensity of CEECs expressed as a share of R&D personnel in its labour force is 62 per cent of the EU-15 level (Table 9.3). Estonia is the only Central and East European country where the proportion of R&D personnel at universities is above the EU-15 average (0.52 per cent). A relatively high share of 55 per cent of R&D personnel working in the Lithuanian higher education sector represents only 0.22 per cent of the labour force, or less than half of the EU-15 share, and three times lower than in top CEE countries. Slovenia is the only CEE country where the R&D intensity in terms of personnel is at the EU-15 average. A common feature of all CEECs, except Bulgaria, is the comparatively small role of the government R&D sector.

However, the escape into the higher education sector by a comparatively large number of personnel has not been followed by a rush of R&D funding into

Table 9.3 R&D personnel as percentage of labour force, by institutional sectors in 2000

	BES	GOV	HES	All
EU-15	0.65	0.18	0.52	1.37
ACC	0.20	0.18	0.46	0.84
Estonia	0.14	0.17	0.67	0.98
Hungary	0.20	0.28	0.64	1.11
Poland	0.14	0.13	0.46	0.73
Slovenia	0.54	0.35	0.46	1.36
Slovakia	0.25	0.18	0.43	0.86
Latvia	0.15	0.12	0.42	0.69
Czech Republic	0.39	0.23	0.30	0.93
Lithuania	0.02	0.12	0.22	0.36
Bulgaria	0.06	0.32	0.09	0.48
Romania	0.24	0.08	0.06	0.39

Source: Eurostat EU Structural Indicators 2004.

Notes
ACC – Accessing European Countries.
BES – Business enterprise sector.
GOV – Government sector.
HES – Higher education sector.

the higher education R&D system (Table 9.4). In most CEE countries, the larger share of R&D funding is spent in the business sector. This may be expected, given the relatively higher capital intensity of R&D in the business sector and the academic orientation of R&D in higher education. A reorientation of R&D into academic science also meant reorientation towards a cheaper and more labour-intensive type of science.

Data suggest that universities in CEE have embraced research more as a result of the crisis-driven restructuring of the R&D system rather than as a new area of activity with great opportunities. They are places with the greatest concentration of R&D personnel, but with the exception of Estonia and possibly Slovenia – which both invest in higher education R&D above 0.25 per cent of GDP – CEE universities are locations where a mainly theoretical type of academic research can be undertaken. This seriously undermines opportunities for fulfilling the knowledge-generation function of universities, which would require modern instrumentation and capital-intensive equipment. In Romania, Bulgaria and Slovakia, R&D expenditure at universities is so marginal that it is very difficult to talk about the knowledge-generation function of the university sector. However, our aggregate picture most likely contains a variety of disparate individual cases where some universities have managed to maintain or enhance R&D capacities. These are the universities that have managed to get plugged into the EU and other international scientific networks through which some of these problems could be alleviated.

Table 9.4 R&D expenditure as a percentage of GDP, by institutional sectors in 2001

	BES	GOV	HES
EU-15	1.30	0.25	0.41
ACC	0.39	0.24	0.20
Estonia	0.15	0.15	0.35
Slovenia	0.86	0.39	0.25
Lithuania	0.13	0.25	0.22
Poland	0.25	0.23	0.22
Czech Republic	0.80	0.34	0.19
Hungary	0.36	0.21	0.19
Latvia	0.19	0.11	0.18
Slovakia	0.44	0.16	0.06
Bulgaria	0.11	0.36	0.05
Romania	0.26	0.07	0.04

Source: Eurostat (2003).

Notes
ACC – Accessing European Countries.
BES – Business enterprise sector.
GOV – Government sector.
HES – Higher education sector.

Knowledge-diffusion function of CEE universities

Unlike the research function of the CEE universities, which suffers from a gap between its nominal capacities and actual investment, the teaching function has enjoyed a real stimulus through the rapidly expanding demand for higher education. A key driver to this is the significantly reduced risk of unemployment among those graduating at tertiary level. As Eurostat (2003) data show, unemployment rates for those educated at tertiary level are similar in the EU-15 and in the CEECs – both are standing at 3 per cent. For example, among CEECs, unemployment rates for the tertiary educated (2001) varied between 1 per cent (Czech Republic) and 6 per cent (Bulgaria), while rates for non-tertiary educated varied between 6 per cent (Hungary) and 22 per cent (Poland). In EU-15 countries, however, unemployment rates for the non-tertiary educated are much lower, ranging from 3 per cent (Netherlands, Luxembourg) to 13 per cent (France).

A high demand for tertiary education resulted in very high annual increases in the numbers of graduates in CEECs when compared to the EU-15 (Table 9.5). In all CEECs, annual rates of growth are from two to up to ten times higher than in the EU-15. In terms of the number of graduates per 1,000 population of this age group, half of the CEECs are at or above EU levels.

This demand-induced explosion in the higher education system has resulted in some deterioration in the quality of teaching. In addition, demand has become

Table 9.5 Relative number of graduates and annual changes (AAGR)*[a]

	Total graduates		In science			In engineering, manufacturing and construction	
	AAGR 1998–2001	Per 1,000 population aged 20–29	AAGR 1998–2001		Per 1,000 population aged 20–29	AAGR 1998–2001	Per 1,000 population aged 20–29
EU-15	2.5	40.4	5.4		4.5	1.9	5.9
ACC	19.5	55.3	42.3		2.3	7.3	4.9
Czech Republic	12.5	25.9			2.7		3.0
Estonia	10.0	39.9	28.1		2.4	31.9	4.8
Latvia	24.8	62.6	32.9		3.2	−3.0	4.4
Lithuania	12.7	51.5	18.0		2.5	13.2	10.6
Hungary*	15.0	36.1	−16.6		0.9	−0.9	3.6
Poland	23.6	74.3	83.8		2.6	9.8	5.1
Slovenia	7.1	40.0	−1.8		1.5	2.3	6.6
Slovakia	14.6	29.4	23.6		2.6	21.6	5.0
Bulgaria	4.3	43.7	10.8		1.8	10.7	6.6
Romania	4.0	22.7	2.0		1.3	4.9	4.2

Source: Eurostat 2003.

Notes
ACC – Accessing European Countries.
* 1998–2000.
[a] Average annual growth rate.

skewed towards areas of immediate demand, mainly around social sciences (economics, management, accounting and marketing). Demand for engineering, manufacturing and construction-related degrees has been stronger than for science degrees. On average, the rate of increase of science graduates has been very high, but there are big differences among the CEECs in this respect, as some countries have recorded negative rates. The rate of increase in engineering graduates was the lowest, but the relative levels are still significantly higher than for science degrees. However, much higher numbers of graduates from non-science and technology degrees show that, broadly speaking, demand for tertiary education in CEECs has become skewed towards these areas. This structure of demand explains the big rise in the number of private universities, which are better able to cater for demand in non-S&T (science and technology) areas. A shift in teaching towards these areas is also compatible with the tendency of research at universities to move to theoretical areas that do not require modern instrumentation and expensive scientific equipment.

The knowledge-utilization function of CEE universities

Knowledge utilization refers to the actual utilization of knowledge acquired or developed in universities within the innovation process, i.e. in commercialization. This is a relatively new function of universities in most of the CEE countries, which have entered into this area of activity driven by the need to earn additional income in conditions of falling public budgets. During the 1990s, this type of activity was officially encouraged and promoted through different schemes that funded so-called 'bridging institutions' (science parks, innovation centres, spin-off companies, etc.).

The assumption was that, during the socialist era, the R&D system had accumulated knowledge that could be commercialized in new market conditions. As a result, universities encouraged the formation of spin-off businesses in the hope that this might buffer budgetary shortfalls. In addition, a policy focus on linkages through high-tech SMEs was seen as a solution to a lack of demand for R&D from industry. In general, the results of these policies have been rather meagre (Webster 1996). However, if universities are to become important agents in a knowledge-based economy it is necessary that they develop this function. Unfortunately, there is no data that monitors this type of activity at national level and hence our analysis is inevitably unsystematic and based on our knowledge of country situations and through personal involvement in programmes of technical assistance.

We believe that the reason for the still very modest improvements of universities in mastering this function lies in a mistaken understanding of what constitutes 'objects' or 'outputs' of university research. Pavitt (1991) has shown that the key contribution of academic science was not only in direct information (i.e. publications) but in knowledge of instrumentation, research methodologies and informal transfers. Mowery *et al.* (2001, 2002) argue that patents and exclusive licences are not always the best approach to maximize the results of public R&D investments. Channels through which businesses benefit from university research are publications, conferences, informal information channels and consulting. In his analysis of academic entrepreneurship Stankiewicz (1986) developed a threefold taxonomy of academy–industry engagement modes.

- *Consultancy and R&D contracting mode (CC)* sells problem-solving capabilities; performs specific technical functions based on its special skills and/or access to unique equipment; and develops client-specific applications on its unique equipment and undertakes R&D contracts.
- *Product-oriented mode (PO)* In this mode, new technology-based businesses are organized around a new product, and its manufacturing and marketing. This type is the most widely studied and analysed and university industry linkages are primarily perceived through this mode of work.
- *Technology assessment mode (TA)* In this mode the university deals with technologies that are already commercialized (through spin-off companies, licensing, joint ventures or other types of alliances with industry). Activities include the establishment of intellectual property rights, the identification or even creation of markets for technological assets, and in some cases development of the technology to the point where the market value is optimal. The US Bayh–Dole Act enables universities to develop knowledge-utilization functions primarily through this mode of work, i.e. by establishing patenting and licensing activities (Mowery et al. 2001, Mowery and Ziedonis 2002).

In CEE, academy–industry linkages have been primarily encouraged through the expectation that universities will either sell their new products through university-sponsored spin-off companies or that they will sell knowledge by patenting and licensing it to commercial organizations. Within this product-oriented mode perspective it is expected that the university will generate knowledge that will be *directly* used in the innovation process.

These expectations contradict empirical evidence from CEE innovation surveys, which show that universities are marginal to industry as a direct source of information for innovation. In that respect, the results of CEE innovation surveys are no different from results for other countries, including the EU-15 (Table 9.6).

However, it seems that universities are much more important as an indirect source of information for innovation (Pavitt 1991). In terms of the Stankiewicz (1986) taxonomy, universities are the most effective in consultancy and R&D contracting mode *selling* problem-solving capabilities. This function is quite complementary to their role in informal knowledge transfer through professional networks. It is true that fundamental research in biomedicine and genetics has produced directly commercially relevant results. It is also true that software can be commercialized within or in relationship with universities. However, this

Table 9.6 Ranking of sources of information by importance for enterprises

	Enterprise	Competitors	Value chain	Professional networks	External knowledge organizations
EU – CIS3	1	2	3	4	5
Latvia (1996–98)	1	3	2	4	5
Slovenia (1999–2000)	1	2	4	3	5
Czech Republic (1999–2001)	1	3	2	4	5
Slovak Republic (1999)	2	1	3	4	5
Turkey (1995–97)	1	4	2	3	5
Lithuania (1997–98)	1	4	3	2	5

Source: *R&D and innovation statistics in candidate countries and the Russian Federation 1990–99* (Eurostat), for Czech Republic – Czech Statistical Office, for Latvia and Lithuania – national statistical offices, for Croatia – National Innovation Survey, 2004.

Notes
External knowledge organizations: average importance for universities, consultants and R&D institutes.
Value chain: average importance between clients and suppliers.
Professional networks: average importance of professional conferences, meetings, fairs, exhibitions and electronic networks.

reasoning should not be extended to the entire spectrum of science and technology, as the proximity of academic science to commercial application varies greatly.

The contribution of CEE universities to national innovation systems is much greater through the consulting and contracting than the product-oriented mode. Their most important contribution is through the development of high-level problem-solving skills (Pavitt 1991). As the science base becomes essential background knowledge for all sectors, the universities' role in generating high-level PhDs becomes an essential precondition for industrial research. If we take this broader notion of 'utilization' of knowledge, then CEE universities still have to make large strides towards this objective. Unsystematic evidence in CEECs indicates that the consultancy and R&D contracting mode is the major part of universities' 'utilization' of knowledge activities. We do not know to what extent these are standardized knowledge-intensive services and to what extent these are services which closely rely on the results of academic research. Case-study evidence would suggest that, in this respect, universities in CEE are substituting for the still undeveloped sector of knowledge-intensive services. Universities are complementing extra-mural business R&D institutes in CEE which de facto operate as knowledge-intensive service providers. Often the informal character of this activity, which is undertaken by individual academics, and the lack of institutional involvement, makes it difficult to assess the scale and scope of this substituting function.

In an ideal model, the three functions of universities would reinforce each other. We would argue that, contrary to this, we observe substituting effects instead of complementarities between individual functions. As a result, universities are not operating as dynamic nodes in national systems of innovation in CEE. Evidence suggests that this trend is not unique to the CEECs. According to Geuna (1997), many universities are driven by budget cuts to do routine contract research for industry which neither leads to high publications (and spillovers) nor lays a basis for long-term fundamental innovations. The empirical evidence shows that this is the case for the CEECs' economies where the highly developed higher education and R&D sector faces the challenge of economic survival. It is reorienting itself to market-led activities, which in many cases are more routine and are application- rather than R&D-oriented. In summary, substitutive effects between different knowledge functions dominate over synergy effects.

The changing functions of universities in Lithuania and their role in a national innovation system

Lithuania is a very interesting and relevant case for understanding the role of the higher education system in a national innovation system in CEE. It has the highest number of graduates in science and technology per 1,000 population of the respective age group among the CEECs (Table 9.7). This is striking, given its income per capita. In addition, its relative expenditure on tertiary education is at the top of this group (Table 9.8). However, its high ranking on the higher education side is not accompanied by a high ranking on the demand side. Data on investments in lifelong learning show that Lithuania ranks very low, which

Table 9.7 Tertiary graduates in science and technology per 1,000 of population aged 20–29 years, 2002 (*2001)

Lithuania	14.6
EU-15*	11.9
Bulgaria	11.7
Slovenia	9.5
Iceland	9.2
Latvia	8.1
Poland	8.1
Slovakia	7.8
Portugal	7.4
Estonia	6.6
Romania	5.8
Czech R	5.7
Hungary	4.8
Cyprus*	3.7
Malta*	2.7

Source: Eurostat (2003).

primarily reflects low investment by enterprises in the training of its labour force (Table 9.9).

Table 9.10 also confirms that the supply side is relatively better developed than the demand side, but it also shows that the weakest part of the Lithuanian innovation system is its linkages, or lack of them. On the demand side, business-level technology absorption is unusually highly ranked (score 5.3). However, we should bear in mind that this is explained by the nature of the competitive advantages of Lithuanian businesses, which are in activities based on labour costs rather than in unique products and processes (score 3.2). In that context, a very low level of staff training, which is indicated in Table 9.10, can only be partly attributed to the inactivity of companies and much more to the fact that, given their competitive advantages, they do not necessarily need to improve staff training.

On the supply side, the availability of specialized research and training services is ranked the lowest (4.3). This suggests that indeed Lithuania does not have the developed sector of knowledge-intensive services that would be needed. The university sector in some respects substitutes for this lack through individual scientists and engineers whose availability is ranked very high (5.4). In that respect, the issue may not be so much 'linkage failure' which would follow from a direct reading of these data, but mainly 'agent failure'. By this we mean the absence of specialized research and training-services organizations on the supply side. On the demand side, we mean very weak demand from industry for R&D services, which is the result of competitive advantages based on standardized technologies and labour costs rather than on unique products and processes. In that respect, very weak linkages (average score 3) are the consequence rather than the cause of the problem. The brain drain problem, which is ranked by the lowest mark (2.8), is the outcome of the weak demand for highly skilled scientists and engineers. The absence of a local constituency for innovation (i.e. enterprises that would base their competitive advantage on

Table 9.8 Public expenditure on tertiary level education (% of GDP)

Lithuania	1.3
Turkey	1.2
Poland	1.1
Hungary	1.1
EU-15	1.1
Estonia	1.1
Latvia	0.9
Slovakia	0.8
Romania	0.8
Czech R	0.8
Bulgaria	0.6

Source: Eurostat (2003).

Table 9.9 Lifelong learning: percentage of working age population participating in education and training

Slovenia	15.1
EU-15	9.7
Latvia	8.1
Estonia	6.2
Hungary	6.0
Czech R	5.4
Poland	5.0
Slovakia	4.8
Lithuania	4.5
Bulgaria	1.4
Romania	1.3

Source: Eurostat (2003).

intellectual property) may also explain the very low ranking of Lithuania in terms of weak intellectual property protection (score 3.4).

The weak demand for complex technical activities is also confirmed by data from the Lithuanian innovation survey. The higher education system is ranked as the least important major source of information for innovation. In that respect, Lithuania complies with a pattern which has been recorded in other CEE and EU-15 countries (see Table 9.2). A weak demand for scientific knowledge from companies is restricted by the dominance of routine, low-tech activities in businesses whose competitive advantage lies in labour costs (Table 9.11). This explains why the Lithuanian business sector employs only 5.3 per cent of the total R&D personnel in the country and only 1.7 per cent of the scientists.

Although higher education establishments are not the major source of information for innovative enterprise activities, they have closer links to industry than state R&D establishments (Figure 9.4). This may suggest that higher education institutions are more successful in creating links with industry than 'pure' R&D institutions.

However, even with weak links and weak direct impact on innovation generation, the higher education sector in Lithuania, as well other CEE countries, remains the most important sector in terms of R&D employment (see Table 9.2). Its role as the most important employer is accompanied by an equally important role as a performer of R&D. Higher education in Lithuania performs 58.17 per cent of the overall R&D in the country (see Table 9.11). However, 79 per cent of this R&D is funded by government, 7.4 per cent by business and 5.6 per cent by foreign funds.

Table 9.11 shows a few important features of the role of the Lithuanian higher education system as part of the national innovation system. First, higher education is not very internationalized and attracts only 21 per cent of the overall foreign funds. In that respect, the business enterprise sector and

Table 9.10 Assessment of supply, demand and linkages in the Lithuanian education system

	Score	Rank	Standard deviation
Tertiary enrolment in 2000	52.48	23	–
Availability of scientists and engineers	5.4	28	1.1
Quality of maths and science education	5.2	23	1.2
Quality of public schools	4.7	36	1.4
Quality of scientific research institutions	4.3	38	1.3
Local availability of specialized research and training services	4.3	42	1.1
Quality of educational system	4.2	33	1.3
Quality of education infrastructure – average	**4.7**	**33**	**1.2**
Intellectual property protection	3.4	59	1.3
University/industry research collaboration	3.3	47	1.4
Brain drain	2.8	69	1.3
Linkages – average	**3.0**	**58**	**1.3**
Business-level technology absorption	5.3	25	0.9
Company spending on R&D	3.5	40	1.3
Capacity for innovation	3.5	40	1.1
Extent of staff training	3.4	67	1.4
Nature of competitive advantage	3.2	47	1.4
Demand for human capital – average	**4.0**	**44**	**1.2**

Source: Based on *The Global Competitiveness Report 2003–04*, World Economic Forum, New York: Oxford University Press.

Note
A higher ranking means a better position of the country on a scale 1–7. In the case of brain drain, a low average mark denotes the existence of a brain drain problem.

government research institutes are doing much better. Second, the contract R&D relationships between business and higher education are, in general, more important for business as it spends 23.2 per cent of its R&D funds on contracts with universities. However, this relationship plays a relatively minor role in the Lithuanian higher education system as its funding from business amounts to only 7.4 per cent of its total funds. Overall, data on R&D between the higher education system and the business enterprise sector suggest that knowledge linkages are only moderately developed.

In Lithuania, as in other CEE countries, universities were the main agents anticipating the establishment of innovation relay centres, business incubators, science and technology parks and other special establishments. Today there are ten university science centres in Lithuania, aimed at connecting scientific knowledge to technological business needs. Universities, together with the Ministry of Economy, are founders of five existing technology parks and one technological business incubator, and are taking part in their development. Their effectiveness, however, is limited by the current state of demand for R&D. Crucial constraints

Table 9.11 Sources of R&D funding and performance by institutional sectors in Lithuania 2003 (%)

Sources of funding	Performers of R&D			
	Total	HES	GOV	BES
Total	100.0	52.6	26.4	21.0
GOV	100.0	63.4	33.4	3.1
BES	100.0	23.2	8.7	68.1
HES	100.0	99.4	0.6	0.0
PNP	100.0	50.0	50.0	0.0
ABR	100.0	21.2	23.9	55.0

Sources of funding	Performers of R&D			
	Total	HES	GOV	BES
Total	100.0	100.0	100.0	100.0
GOV	64.6	77.9	81.6	9.6
BES	16.7	7.4	5.5	54.2
HES	4.8	9.0	0.1	0.0
PNP	0.1	0.1	0.2	0.0
ABR	13.8	5.6	12.5	36.2

Source: Statistics Lithuania.

Notes
GOV – Government sector.
BES – Business enterprise sector.
HES – Higher education sector.
PNP – Public non-profit.
ABR – Abroad.

are not in linkage failures but in the low demand by enterprises or problems at the universities in generating relevant R&D services, i.e. 'agent failure' (compare Bridges' comments on demand-side failure in the UK in his chapter in this collection).

The education and business training market in Lithuania is dominated by higher education institutions and its establishments. In this respect, as we argued above, universities operate as a substitute for an undeveloped knowledge-intensive services sector. Universities with business and economy studies have also developed business-oriented consulting centres, etc. They are actively seeking to commercialize R&D results, especially in high-tech industries. These activities result in spin-offs and R&D/industry partnerships in such high-tech sectors as laser technologies, biotechnologies, information technology applications. However, because of the strong market orientation of this work, it does not lead to a sufficient level of scientific or applied achievements to generate new knowledge in forms of patents or scientific publications. The universities in

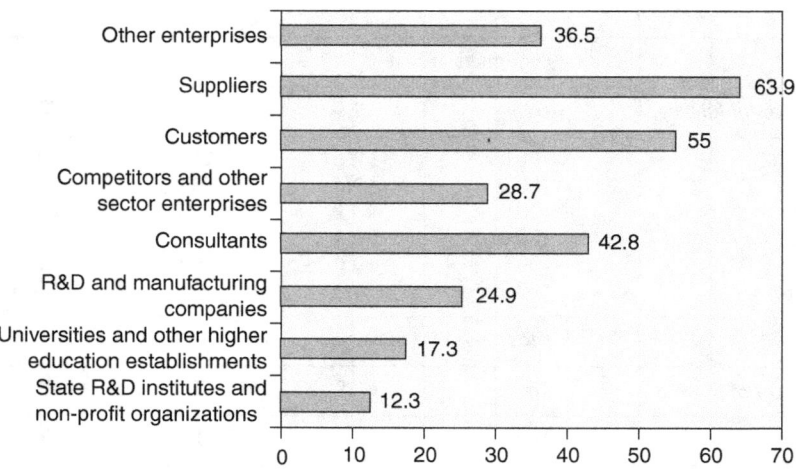

Figure 9.4 Partners of innovative activities in Lithuanian enterprises (%) (source: Community Innovation Survey III, Statistics Lithuania (2002)).

CEECs face a challenge of too strong a market orientation, which hinders their scientific performance. In this respect, the Lithuanian case confirms our proposition from section two, that the substitutive effects between different knowledge functions of the universities dominate over the synergy effects.

The case of the largest technological university in the Baltic States, Kaunas University of Technology (KTU), illustrates this situation well. In 2003, income from services delivered comprised 26 per cent of the university's total revenues, which shows that its activities are oriented not only to the functions defined and financed by the state (state budget assignments made up 48.37 per cent of the university's total income), but to market needs as well. R&D activities are even more strongly oriented to business needs than is the university as a whole. Business funding is the second most important source after state budget assignments and state institutions, and comprises 37 per cent of the university's total R&D funding (Kaunas University of Technology 2004). However, this results in weak scientific and inventive performance, which follows the tendency of the whole of Lithuania: patenting activities here have declined by 37 per cent in the last decade and the number of its scientific publications has been one of the poorest in Europe.

In summary, the Lithuanian higher education system has embraced knowledge utilization as a new function, which is important in a knowledge-based economy. However, its knowledge-generation function is still underdeveloped and it seems that there are problems in generating synergies between teaching, R&D and contract services. The case of Lithuania confirms Nelson's (2004b) proposition that building new institutions, or adapting old ones to new purposes, may be the most difficult part of the catch-up process.

Conclusions

In order to catch up with the EU-15, CEECs will have to establish higher education institutions as one of the major drivers of their national innovation system. This will require the higher education system to embrace all three knowledge functions: knowledge generation, diffusion and utilization. By using a national innovation system perspective, we analysed where CEECs, and Lithuania in particular, stand in this process. Our conclusions are inevitably very tentative due to a lack of comprehensive data and case evidence regarding this issue. Hence, they should be treated as tentative propositions for a possible future research project.

First, R&D systems in most CEECs have become oriented towards the higher education system. From a long-term perspective this should be considered as a positive development, as it will enhance the role of universities as knowledge generators as well as knowledge diffusers. In the short term, this reorientation has been driven by the lack of demand for R&D in the business enterprise sector, by reductions in public R&D funding, and by large increases in the number of students and hence, increased demand for teaching. The issue is whether this trend could be turned into an advantage for universities and an opportunity for national economies.

Second, systems of innovation in CEE have been emerging around international value chains, which are major sources of productivity improvements in economies that are, in general, highly dependent on foreign direct investment. The logic of growth for a national innovation system poses problems for universities whose links with domestic or foreign enterprises are undeveloped and fragmented. Nevertheless, universities have been able to develop new functions, such as the commercialization of their knowledge, and to gain access to foreign R&D funding. However, limited R&D demand from local enterprises, and its 'downstream' character, seriously restricts the nature of the universities' links with industry. As a result, orientation towards commercialization activities has not enhanced the knowledge-generation function of the higher education system. In addition, the lowering of teaching quality because of huge increases in the number of students has further undermined the link between teaching and R&D as well as between teaching and cooperation with enterprises. Instead of generating complementarities, the expansion of functions has undermined the coherence of universities, i.e. the synergies existing between different functions.

Third, these problems are not unique to CEE but are different in degree because of the gap between the higher education system's capacities and outcomes. In order to embrace new functions, higher education has to operate in two governance regimes. This hybrid form is inherently difficult to manage and there is a built-in tendency to go for 'pure' solutions. However, public and private dimensions of knowledge generation, diffusion and utilization are embedded in the very nature of knowledge, and organizational solutions will have to take this into account. Demand pressures on universities in all CEECs to pursue their teaching function through greatly increased numbers of students make it more difficult for them to embrace knowledge-generation and knowledge-utilization functions. This, coupled with limited budgets, has probably resulted in a declining quality of teaching and has endangered the balance between the three functions of universities. All this suggests that universities in CEECs are not yet key drivers and promoters of linkages in national innovation systems.

Finally, it is likely that we are observing a very turbulent transition process in which it is difficult to capture an accurate picture. Individual success stories do suggest that in some countries, including Lithuania, we may see the emergence of universities as important drivers of national systems of innovations in the near future. These universities will be integrated internationally and nationally and will embrace opportunities provided by EU-wide reforms of the education market (notably through the Bologna process). This is a great opportunity for the CEECs, as all successful cases of catch-up have involved considerable cross-border flows of people. Universities will play an increasingly important role in this international market.

Notes

1 The national innovation system in the 'narrow' sense is defined as organizations and institutions which are directly involved in knowledge creation and innovation development activities – R&D – and higher education institutions, technical labs, etc. In the broad sense, a national innovation system encompasses all institutions that influence interactive learning, knowledge and innovation development (see Freeman 2002).
2 We should bear in mind that the business enterprise sector in CEECs is dominated by a high share of extra-mural R&D organizations that operate as independent R&D companies offering a variety of R&D and technical services rather than being in-house R&D departments of industrial enterprises.

References

Balaz, V. (2004) 'Knowledge intensive business service in transition economies', *The Service Industries Journal*, 24 (4), 83–100.

Berg, A., Borensztein, E., Sahay, R. and Zettelmeyer, J. (1999) 'The evolution of output in transition economies – explaining the differences', IMF Working Paper WP/99/73, Washington: International Monetary Fund.

Blumenthal, D. (2003) 'Academic–industrial relationship in the life sciences', *New England Journal of Medicine*, 349 (25), 2452–7.

Damijan, P.J., Knell, M., Majcen, B. and Rojec, M. (2003) 'The role of FDI, R&D accumulation and trade in transferring technology to transition countries: evidence from business panel data for eight transition countries', *Economic Systems*, 27, 189–204.

Damijan, P.J. and Rojec, M. (2004) 'Foreign direct investment and the catching up process in new EU member states: is there flying geese pattern?', WIIW Research Report No. 310, Vienna: Vienna Institute for International Economic Studies.

Easterly, W. (2002) *The Elusive Quest for Growth: Economists' Adventures and Misadventures in the Tropics*, Cambridge, MA: The MIT Press.

Eurostat (2003) 'Catching up with the EU? Comparing highly qualified human resources in the EU and the Acceding Countries', *Statistics in Focus*, Theme 9, 9/2003.

Fischer, S., Sahay, R. and Vegh, C. (1998) 'From transition tc market – evidence and growth prospects', IMF Working Paper, WP/98/52, Washington: International Monetary Fund.

Freeman, C. (2002) 'Continental, national and sub national innovation systems – complementarity and economic growth', *Research Policy*, 31, 191–211.

Geuna, A. (1997) 'Allocation of funds and research output the case of UK universities', *Revue d'Economie Industrielle*, 79, 143–63.

Havrylyshyn, O. (2001) 'Recovery and growth in transition: a decade of evidence', IMF Staff Papers. Vol. 48, Special Issue, Washington: International Monetary Fund. Available online at: www.imf.org/external/pubs/ft/staffp/2001/04/pdf/havrylys.pdf (accessed 1 December 2004).

Kaunas University of Technology (2004) Kaunas University of Technology Activity Report 2003. Online. Available at: www.ktu.lt/lt/scriptas1.asp?meniu=virsus2_1.html&pirmas=ktu/ktu_menu.html&antras=ataskaita/atask.html (accessed 1 December 2004).

Kriaučionienė, M. (2002) 'National innovation system: methodology of development', unpublished thesis, Kaunas University of Technology.

Majcen, B., Radošević, S. and Rojec, M. (2004) 'Strategic control and productivity growth of foreign subsidiaries in Central European economies', paper prepared within the EU project 'Productivity Gap'. Online. Available at: www.iwh-halle.de/projects/productivity-gap/ (accessed 1 December 2004).

Mowery, D.C., Nelson, R.R., Sampat, B.N. and Ziedonis, A.A. (2001) 'The growth of patenting and licensing by U.S. universities: an assessment of the effects of the Bayh–Dole Act of 1980, *Research Policy*, 30 (1), 99–119.

Mowery, D.C. and Ziedonis, A.A. (2002) 'Academic patent quality and quantity before and after the Bayh–Dole Act in the United States', *Research Policy*, 31 (3), 399–418.

Nelson, R.R. (2004a) 'The changing institutional requirements for technological and economic catch-up', paper presented at DRUID's Summer Development Conference, Elsinore, 2004.

—— (2004b) *The Changing Institutional Requirements for Technological and Economic Catch-up*, New York: Columbia University.

OECD (2003) *Science, Technology and Industry Outlook*, Paris: OECD.

Pavitt, K. (1991) 'What makes basic research economically useful?', *Research Policy*, 20 (2), 109–19.

Radošević, S. (1999) *International Technology Transfer and 'Catch Up' in Economic Development*, Cheltenham: Edward Elgar.

—— (2004) 'A Two-Tier or Multi-Tier Europe?: Assessing the innovation capacities of Central and East European countries in the enlarged EU', *Journal of Common Market Studies*, 42 (3), 641–66.

Radošević, S. and Auriol, L. (1999) 'Patterns of restructuring in research, development and innovation activities in Central and Eastern European countries: analysis based on S&T indicators, *Research Policy*, 28, 351–76.

Smarzynska-Javorcki, B. (2004) 'Does foreign direct investment increase the productivity of domestic firms? In search of spillovers through backward linkages', *American Economic Review*, 94 (3), 605–27.

Stankiewicz, R. (1986) *Academics and Entrepreneurs: Developing University–Industry Relations*, London: Francis Pinter Publishers.

Webster, A. (ed.) (1996) *Building New Bases for Innovation: the Transformation of the R&D System in Post-socialist States*, Cambridge: Anglia Polytechnic University.

Chapter 10

Bridging knowledge and economy
Technology transfer and higher education

Arūnas Lukoševičius

Introduction

A number of contributions to this volume draw attention to the increasing volume of analysis and policy documents which point to the importance of knowledge-based innovation to business competitiveness in what is identified as 'a knowledge economy' (see especially Bridges above), though the people who continue to clear our blocked drains, care for our elderly and clean the houses of 'money rich, time poor' software designers and financial executives may feel with some reason that they occupy a different economic space. Setting aside such reservations, however, it is clear that in such an economy joining together the production of knowledge with its application in a business environment – or *technology transfer* as it is most widely referred to – becomes a general necessity. Such transfer takes place between the research and development arms of business itself and between publicly and privately funded research institutes and business, but in this context it is more particularly technology transfer between higher education and business which is the focus of this chapter. In the 'countries in transition' this is especially important, because in these countries, as Radošević and Kriaučioniené have indicated in their contribution to this volume, it is in the universities that most of the research capability is concentrated.

Technology transfer is a social transaction which takes its form from different social contexts and cultural traditions. It is possible to distinguish two major attitudes and cultures of technology transfer: American and European. Historically, the United States of America is known for the promotion of an entrepreneurial spirit. Typical of this is the technology-licensing process in the USA, which acquired its present form after the passage of the Bayh–Dole Technology Transfer Act of 1980 (Coupe 2003). This defined the rules for the commercial use of knowledge generated by government-funded research (mainly provided by universities).[1] The Massachusetts Institute of Technology, one of the leading generators of new technologies, has practised technology transfer since the early twentieth century.

In the US (for example in Oregon state), the definition of technology transfer has a clear element of trade

Technology transfer means any activity that is intended to lead to the sale, license, assignment or other grant of a right to use specified intellectual property assets developed, owned or controlled by a higher education institution. Intellectual property assets include, but are not limited to, any right, title or interest arising out of a patent, copyright, trade secret, trademark or other analogous proprietary right.

(Enroled Senate Bill 102, 2001: 1)

This can be formulated more briefly: technology transfer is a relationship between two entities with the intent of capitalizing on research for commercial purposes. The commercial aspect of technology transfer is evident in the two basic ways by which high technologies are defined and evaluated in the USA. These are either the percentage of scientific and technical employment in a particular industry compared with all industries (workforce measure), or the research and development dollars spent as a percentage of total sales, which is a measure of research intensity (research expenditures intensity measure). This means that research, technologies and 'technology transfer' are mostly driven by inherently strong market processes. The permanent strength of those processes constitutes a vehicle and common motivator for technology transfer. This is the force of the American technology transfer paradigm, which partly explains the leading role of the US in many fields of technological and economic development.[2]

In European universities, technology transfer activity is at a different stage of development. A diversity of university systems, a fundamentally heterogeneous cultural landscape and a varied technological and economic base pose entirely different challenges for technology transfer (Caracostas and Muldur 1998, Caloghirou *et al.* 2001, Commission of the European Communities 1996). In many parts of Europe the public service tradition of the university and commitment to the free availability of research findings runs counter to new demands for the commercial exploitation of university-generated knowledge and many European university communities have a culture which is better characterized in terms of hostility to business entrepreneurship than amicable alliance with such activity. Unsurprisingly also, there is not the same tradition that has been established in the United States of reference by business to universities for the solution of business problems (Abramson *et al.* 1997). However, if Europe is to withstand global economic competition in which technologies play an increasingly important role, then some of these traditional attitudes may need to change. Europe – and *a fortiori* the 'countries in transition' – now needs to enter into a new model of technology transfer.

'Countries in transition', those newcomers to the European Union, are facing especially big challenges in what is referred to as a 'triple transition' which involves (i) transition from status as part of the former Soviet empire to an autonomous nation-state operating with a liberal economy; (ii) adjustment to the new economic environment of the European Community; and (iii) adjustment to the practices and challenges of a global economy, which are challenging enough to much more sophisticated and robust economies. The development of technology transfer seems to be an especially pressing requirement in those countries that are forced to look for all possible resources of economic survival in the newly experienced conditions of global, European and regional competition.

The new geopolitical situation and coordinated activities of the enlarged European Union naturally open new development opportunities in the field of technology transfer. Europe, with its deeply rooted multidisciplinary science traditions and diversity of research institutions, will look to capitalize on its assets to create competitive advantage. It needs to consider technology transfer carefully, including the American model and those ideas coming from new European Union members. In newcomer countries, there are more diversified technology transfer processes, many of them already verified by real, sometimes unusual situations. In other words, 'transition countries' are kinds of laboratories for intense technology transfer theory and practice trials The severe shortages and financial cutbacks typical in those countries further motivate universities to use technology transfer as a supplementary source of necessary income.

Technology transfer is a real and very complicated issue for analysis, which attracts lots of attention all over the world. Between 1975 and 1999, at least 579 technology transfer books and monographs were produced (not counting thousands of journal articles). An excellent review, synthesis and critique of the voluminous, multidisciplinary literature on technology transfer has recently appeared (Bozeman 2000). In this chapter I limit myself to the discussion of only four issues, which are considered in the context of transition processes in the economy and higher education:

Positive and controversial sides of technology transfer in the triple transition environment

The triple transition process mentioned above highlights both the positive and the more controversial sides of technology transfer. There is openness of scientific discovery yet restriction in licences and patents; conflict over public and private intellectual property ownership; delay in scientific publication due to non-disclosure agreements; confrontation between a curiosity-driven scientific culture and market-driven utilitarianism and entrepreneurship; increased industrial challenge on the one hand but the distortion of scientific structures for short-term industrial gain on the other. Further issues for analysis include the balance to be created in national and international technology transfer between countries that are donors and countries that are recipients. There is a new division of roles in the global map of technologies.

The generation and transfer of knowledge

The harmonization of the two missions of higher education – the generation of technological knowledge and technology transfer – should be reconsidered from the point of view of the requirements for technology transfer. The emerging importance of a technology-transfer paradigm is gradually changing even the classic division of research from that of basic and applied research to the Mode 1, or 'free', and Mode 2, or 'ordered', research (Gibbons *et al.* 1995). The question remains as to which one is more suitable for long- and short-term technology transfer. Careful harmonization between free and industry-oriented research is therefore needed and appropriate instruments and motivations require to be developed on both the higher education and industry sides.

'Countries in transition' have a specific legacy of technological knowledge, which has been generated in closed, plan-oriented societies. Its content, therefore, is sometimes unexpected yet interesting and complementary to the western one. However, it is in the form of tacit knowledge, difficult to transfer. By contributing to contemporary converging technologies (Nordmann 2004, Roco and Bainbridge 2002), there is a chance for 'transition countries' to leap-frog into the competitive technology market and find niches in a diversified multidisciplinary frontline. HE should educate both good generalists and creative specialists who are able to generate global knowledge and create a technologically oriented entrepreneurial spirit.

Technology transfer: policies and the role of government

Technology transfer during transition is a highly dynamic process as higher education and industry are both undergoing rapid change. This is simultaneously a challenge and an opportunity. There is a search for effective technology transfer policies that will create favourable channels for technology transfer, motivate recipients and encourage permanent demand. Since an entrepreneurial culture is in the early stages of development, there are expectations that government will take a pro-active role. Possibilities exist for state institutions to provide radical or incremental change strategies to initiate iterative learning processes of technology transfer, and to adapt and adopt best foreign practice.

The bridging role of higher education in technology transfer

Universities have an important role at the heart of society in anticipating and leading positive changes, particularly in the field of technology. Universities have the responsibility to contribute insights into the consumption and market-driven development of technologies (Jones-Evans and Kloftsen 1998). They also have to humanize them and create a favourable environment for research. Creating general public acceptance of research and development is among higher education's most important responsibilities.

Universities have many assets including: active and motivated students; research and teaching staff; research facilities; spin-offs and technological centres; and growing technological clusters in their environs.

These topics are discussed below in more detail from the perspective of higher education. A comparison of Western and Eastern European experiences in technology transfer will help to outline the incremental western style of technology transfer development, and the more radical attempts and related problems in the 'countries in transition'. Particular attention is paid to the peculiarities of technology transfer in the dynamic situation that transition is. We try to answer the question, 'Is it possible to find the most effective contribution from higher education to all systems of technology transfer?'

Positive and controversial sides of technology transfer in the triple transition environment

Since the main renewable resource for further economic development remains knowledge (Commission of the European Communities 1996, Etzkowitz and Leydesdorff 1999, Archibugi and Lundvall 2002), we are in transition from earlier forms of capitalism (in which machinery, plant and raw materials were the primary focus of investment) to a knowledge society in which the investment, as the title suggests, is in knowledge and skills (Drucker 1998). Technology transfer is the final stage of the knowledge capitalization process. It is interesting to note that the importance of knowledge and its close links with the economy and society implies a new political formulation – the knowledge society – which de facto has gained recognition in many countries, including those in transition. In economic terms technology transfer is one of the most important tools for the increase of competitiveness on a global, regional and national scale (OECD 1992).

The European Union – recently enlarged and facing global competition – is putting this tool at the heart of policy (Caracostas and Muldur 1998, Commission of the European Communities 2002, 2003a). In these documents one can find proposals on how to turn European diversity into strength by innovation and technology transfer.

Post-Soviet countries and former Eastern bloc countries were previously considered as the main military competitors of western countries because of their economic and scientific resources and high-level R&D investments. This legacy can be converted to a national system of innovation and socially oriented technologies. The constructive role of technology transfer and commercialization processes, along with the promotion of technological entrepreneurship, will play a fostering role in the socio-economic renaissance of Eastern Europe and Russia (National Research Council and Russian Academy of Sciences 1998, Egorov and Carayannis 1999, Hobrough 2004).

'Countries in transition' predominantly have small, open economies and a prevailing small and medium-sized enterprise structure, in which technology transfer is an opportunity (Mayer and Blaas 2002, Jones-Evans and Pandya 1996). A good experience has evidently been gained through Finnish technology policy, which is analysed in the context of the institutional integration of the science and technology system – the Triple Helix thesis (Leydesdorff and Etzkowitz 1998, Kaukonen and Nieminen 1999). The strategy of technology transfer is considered as a possible solution to the economic plight of developing nations (Lado and Vozikis 1996).

Countries that have recently entered the European Union have special hopes for science and technology development and for their commercialization and economical impact (Dyker and Radosevic 1999). In Lithuania particularly, a non-governmental knowledge and economy association was established and a special agreement on the development of the knowledge economy was signed by all the major political parties. A special White Paper was also published on Lithuanian Science and Technology in 2002. Unfortunately those activities have proved to be more rhetorical and inspirational in character than substantial and practical.

The controversial aspects of technology transfer are mainly caused by the confrontation of two cultures in higher education and, more specifically, the research community: one is scientific, discipline oriented and seeks high-level recognition in academic society, and the other pragmatic, utilitarian, market-driven and seeks commercial benefit. In 'transition countries' the gap between the two cultures is especially wide for several reasons (Commission of the European Communities 2003b, Daines 1996). This is primarily because science and technological developments have for many years been oriented to the so-called 'plan based' economy characterized by the implementation of top-down decisions concerning both fundamental and applied science, with a particular emphasis on defence applications. A linear model of innovations was employed consisting of consecutive actions: fundamental science, applied research, implementation to industry, and – at the very end – the market. A lot of technology transfer failures were caused by the neglect of market needs at each step and the lack of feedback and iterations closely related to the consumers and users of technologies (Egorov and Carayannis 1999). This also is reflected in the recent rather low ranking of high and medium-high technologies in Lithuania.[3]

The confrontation of two cultures (both in transition) has reciprocal effects. This is a chance to influence positive change, but it is not an easy task. The gap between cultures makes it difficult to separate the transfer object from its author (Bozeman 2000). Consequently the author rather than the created technology 'spins off' from the university to industry or abroad. On the other hand, confrontation forces universities and industry to discuss and find new ways of cooperative collaboration. Different models of collaboration have been proposed: the development of a market orientation in universities (Buchbinder 1993), support for university–industry cooperation by the EU (Caloghirou et al. 2001), sending educators into industry (Conway 2002), practising entrepreneurship by technology transfer in universities (Stephan 2001), and the follow-up and benchmarking of technology transfer (Tornatzky 2001). The problem is to keep a balance between the ways that industry and universities influence each other. If industry is too influential this will distort university research, forcing it to adopt a short-term perspective; if universities are too strong, their influence can shift industry's attention from market needs and cause business failure.

The actual form of implementation of technology transfer depends on prevailing (sometimes competing) technology transfer paradigms. Bozeman describes three such paradigms which have had different kinds of influence during particular historical periods and across countries: market failure, mission and a cooperative technology paradigm (Bozeman 2000). From those three, the mission paradigm best describes the present situation in 'transition countries'. Unfortunately the authorized programmatic mission of agencies is still rather formal, and political documents and legislation have limited force, remaining rather in the form of paper declarations. But positive change could be expected by entrenching the powerful market failure paradigm with cooperative technology paradigm elements.

Countries that are newcomers to the family of western countries already well established in the global technology market are looking for niches in this market. Seeking equal partnership status, they aspire to create technologies, wanting to be at least partly donors and not just recipients of technology transfer. The situation of a country that is a recipient of foreign technologies is not a stable one, since investment (being extremely mobile in the global village) can be temporary, lasting only until another recipient country will offer slightly lower costs for a labour force or facilities. Another reason to seek the status of technology donor lies in the technical complexity and economic cost of configuring globally generated knowledge for a particular local application (Gibbons *et al.* 1995). Without the ambition to create technologies, a country can find it hard to absorb and adopt new technologies and will have problems with their use.

The requirements of organizations concerned with the commercial exploitation of research clash with the norms which for many years have been at the heart of the scientific community. In his 1942 essay 'The Normative Structure of Science', Merton identified four norms characteristic of the practice of science. These include universalism (founded on the idea that current and future research is based on the discoveries of scientific predecessors); communism (if scientific knowledge is collective property, then it cannot be private property); disinterestedness in foregoing personal gain (scientists' behaviour may be distorted by the demands of private contracts or financial gain); and organized scepticism (an agreement by the research institution that to delay publication can compromise the quality of research). Unfortunately, technology transfer in all countries, including those in transition, has the potential to violate each of Merton's four norms, and it is a key issue for knowledge transfer managers in universities to reconcile their requirements with the expectation that knowledge can be used to contribute to economic competitiveness.

The generation of knowledge for the purposes of technology transfer

The generation and dissemination of knowledge is an inherent mission of universities, but technology transfer requires specific knowledge directed towards commercialization. Knowledge transfer and technology transfer are related, since technology is attached to knowledge about how to use and implement technology.

Universities themselves illustrate two contrasting paradigms: the university as a detached sanctuary of science, and the university as a market-oriented enterprise (Buchbinder 1993, Daines 1996). The mission, management and consequently the knowledge generated by these two kinds will differ (OECD 1999). The arguments of the classical universities are also classical: science must be free, independent, driven by research logic and curiosity, while the arguments of the entrepreneur universities focus on industry, economy and society and the suitability of specialists for performing applied and practical work. If we take into account a new classification of science by Gibbons et al. (1995) in which there is no innate division between fundamental science and applied science, both paradigms seems to be equally important and valuable. In real life both types of universities present arguments which favour their own kind of activity in their competition for government funding.

The generation of scientific knowledge for technology transfer, or just for practical application, is one of the main outcomes (besides educating students) of university activity, and the focus of considerable interest in many countries (Gorman 2002, Klauss 2000). Indicators such as the numbers of patents and licences issued by higher education institutions feature increasingly as measures of their success (Coupe 2003). It should be noted here that in 'transition countries' there is no real intellectual property protection and this is a serious obstacle in technology transfer. Particularly in Lithuania, national patents are too weak to provide legal protection for commercially valuable technologies. Patenting in Europe, or in other countries, is hardly affordable for under-financed research institutions. The number of patents has therefore dropped dramatically. In the Soviet era, one Lithuanian university, Kaunas University of Technology, was registering more than 300 Soviet patents annually. Nowadays this university registers ten to twenty national patents per year and few European ones. At the same time, a lot of large foreign companies are patenting their own technologies and brand names in Lithuania.

The problem here is also one of low demand from industry, which is also in transition. Industrial managers try to use old knowledge or tacit knowledge by employing the necessary specialist rather than purchasing a licence for a patent. In many cases, companies are using their own knowledge or simplified understanding, or are working under the technological guidance of foreign companies. This of course makes the 'technological pull' from industries and companies low, and at the same time suppresses the motivation to generate national knowledge for technology transfer. One of the indicators of such a situation is the low level of investment in research by companies.

On the universities' side, there are also specific problems of proper knowledge and technology generation, including the ageing of staff, limited knowledge of industrial problems by educators, under-financing of research and a lack of a general entrepreneurial spirit (Conway 2002, Commission of the European Communities 2003b).

Technology transfer policies and the role of government

Technology transfer objects require favourable transfer media, demand and recipients. Creating these is an issue of transfer policy. Technology transfer policies are discussed in numerous articles and documents (Bozeman 2000, Sayetat 1993, Geroski 2000, McBrierty 1993, Stephan 2001, Commission of the European Communities 2000).

Taking a broader view, technology transfer is the process by which existing knowledge, facilities or capabilities developed under governmental R&D funding are utilized to fulfil public and private needs (Rip et al. 1996, Schmiemann and Durvy 2003). This definition involves government as an agent in technology transfer. 'Countries in transition' put their hopes more on government-supported technology transfer than on university–industry relationships based on pure commercial interest. The role of government is therefore more pronounced. Indicators of such a pro-active governmental role are: a consolidated state order placed on universities requiring technological knowledge and technology transfer; the co-financing by government of corporate university–industry research; the setting of national priorities or targets for research and development; support for technological incubators, science parks and centres; and the implementation of an adequate system of research assessment and evaluation of results (Koschatzky 2002).

Governments in 'transition countries' with many economic problems to solve usually pay insufficient attention to technology transfer. Reasons include a lack of tradition, limited common understanding of the importance of technologies, and an underestimation of technological impact on the competitiveness and economic welfare of the country. A permanently changing political situation, rather weak young parties and a lack of continuity and stability in policy programmes are also reasons for the limited influence of government.

Another problem for governments in 'transition counties' is that, in previous decades, the main industrial agents had been large state-owned companies, governed by strict top-down orders. The management of those companies by the state was therefore comparatively simple. Also in the West in the 1960s and 1970s, large companies dominated the economy.

Since then, the trend has started to reverse. The number of business owners in OECD countries increased from twenty-nine million to forty-five million between 1972 and 1998. In 'transition countries', this process started in 1991 and now the majority of products and services are generated by small and medium-size enterprises (SMEs). The 'Charter for Small Enterprises', adopted on 13 June 2000 by the General Affairs Council, was endorsed at the Feira European Council on 19–20 June 2000. Strengthening the technological capacity of small enterprises was among the main topics discussed.

Because of the problems mentioned, Lithuania is making its first steps in shaping a technology transfer policy and the entrepreneurial management of innovations. In Table 10.1 the figures show that the role of research institutions in technology transfer is low and this is associated both with donor and recipient problems. (In recent years, the situation has been improving, but an extensive survey has not yet been undertaken.) Higher education and research institutions are not ready to meet companies' needs, since technological problems are usually small-scale, not well specified, diversified, and related to hidden commercial interests. For their part, firms which are recipients of technology try to solve problems without investment: they usually have no resources for research and technology development, being concerned mainly about survival in the market. Many technology-oriented companies are in joint enterprises with foreign companies, the suppliers of the technologies needed. Therefore more than one-fifth of new technologies are acquired from foreign parent companies or by international cooperation with specialists.

Governments, especially those in transition, find it hard to create suitable environments for technology transfer for SMEs. In this situation, universities should rise to the challenge to facilitate technology transfer structures for trading university–company transactions and for cooperative agreements.

The bridging role of higher education in technology transfer: a summary

There are several practical reasons for universities to take the lead in creating an environment to foster dialogue and create bridging links with industry and

Table 10.1 Ways of developing technological innovations in 1999

Method	Percentage
Acquired by licences	9.9
Together with foreign specialists	23.0
Together with other enterprises	9.1
Together with research institutions	3.7
On their own	54.3

Source: Lithuanian Science and Technology White Paper 2002.

Note
The data is from the Lithuanian Department of Statistics; about 500 firms were surveyed.

government. First, in Lithuania, 96 per cent of total R&D manpower and 99.6 per cent of scientists with a PhD are employed at state research and higher education institutions. In 1999 the R&D sector employed 15,296 people. Calculated in man-days, the total R&D manpower per 1,000 inhabitants was 3.5 (the average in EU countries is 4.2). This is a relatively high number. However, only several per cent of scientists are working in industry, in comparison, for example, with Germany, where about 62 per cent of researchers are employed in industry (*Lithuanian Science and Technology White Paper* 2002). In other words, if Lithuanian industry is to be research-led, then that leadership must come from the country's universities. The same principle will apply to a greater or lesser degree to most 'countries in transition'. (For more detail on the distribution of research personnel between higher education and business see the chapter by Radošević and Kriaučionienė in this volume.)

Second, governments have no financial instruments sufficiently powerful to foster technology transfer. Lithuania spends US$17 per capita for R&D (compared with the USA, for example, which spends 681). The contribution of private enterprise to R&D is only 14.7 per cent, compared with about 70 per cent in western countries. On the other hand, fifteen state universities with about 100,000 students is a powerful base for development.

Third, enterprises in Lithuania are predominantly small and medium size (99.4 per cent of all enterprises) and in 2003 they generated 68.2 per cent of General Domestic Product (GDP). Enterprises differ greatly in their technological level and motivation for technology transfer as well as in the goods and services produced. Higher education institutions, with their potentially wide social and geographical reach, are therefore the most suitable platform for collaboration.

There are other, more general, reasons for university leadership, which arise from European goals of knowledge-based economy development. The capacity to change and adapt to economic change is crucial for competitiveness, and higher education has a historic mission here. Every radical transformation needs either very strong political will (this way, unfortunately, ends in failure if not supported by other, bottom-up means) or a special environment – creative, dynamic, reproductive. A 'country in transition' has no stable industry at which higher education can target its developed technologies. Industry is highly influenced by the triple transition processes mentioned above and is changing rapidly and radically. Higher education institutions therefore have a strong mission to forecast dynamic transitional changes in knowledge generation, marketing and technology transfer. The paradigm of a so-called service university (a university serving the needs of society and industry) is not directly applicable because of transition. Universities are expected to take the ideological leadership in re-engineering the economy and not merely be concerned with responsive technology transfer to a predefined industry. In that respect, the mission of a university can be formulated as a bridging between present transition and future development. (For complexities related to this mission in Lithuania and in the countries of Central and Eastern Europe more generally see the chapter by Radošević and Kriaučionienė in this volume.)

The strongest resource of higher education is its students, with their guarantee of reproducible knowledge, dynamism, high motivation, sustainability and continuity. A noticeable generational change in ways of thinking and an emerging entrepreneurial spirit positively influence all spheres of university life, including technology transfer. Because of the difficult economic situation, many students are self-supporting through employment in state and private enterprises. By studying in the university and at the same time tackling technological problems in real life, they are naturally bridging higher education and industry.

In the context of insufficient protection of intellectual property (which is the case in 'transition countries'), authors of bright technological ideas often go outside the university in order to establish their own business and continue with the commercial exploitation of the technology. For the university, this is a kind of brain drain (on the phenomenon of brain drain in Lithuania see the chapter by Jucevičienė and Vaitkus in this volume). An even more painful brain drain is when authors and their created technologies leave the country. To counter this problem, really effective technology transfer, licensing and patenting policies are needed inside the country.

Because of transition, companies and enterprises are 'boiling' – rearranging their activities, changing management, location and legal statuses, and creating dynamic clusters in order to survive and take the most secure and profitable position in the market and institutional environment. Universities – centres of technological intelligence – have the chance to be the centres of these naturally emerging clusters. Technology centres, parks, incubators and spin-off companies around universities become a kind of technological bridging cluster, permanently fed by university specialists.

One of the important bridging missions of higher education is international technology transfer. The mobility of students and staff, international programmes and projects, naturally facilitates the dissemination of technological ideas. Sometimes technologies are transferred and applied by means of consortium agreements between partners of international EUREKA, Framework COST projects.

'Countries in transition' are at the meeting point of very intense market influences and consumption-driven behaviour (Coppola 2001, Lukoševičius 2002). This raises the question of the significance of a humanization of technologies, promoting controlled development instead of depraving, demand-based consumerism. Defining the social and human needs of a country is another important role of the university/government consortium. Bridging between the 'wild' and 'uncontrolled' development of technologies and the human needs of society is a difficult one, but it is one on which a university, with its multidisciplinary resources across the humanities and social sciences as well as natural sciences and technology, and its tradition of open debate, is perhaps uniquely placed to take a lead.

Of course, the everyday problems facing higher education institutions in 'transition countries' are too pressing to leave much space for the contemplation of bridging missions in technology transfer. But the importance of technology for the competitiveness of the country is too great for it to be neglected.

Notes

1 The Bayh–Dole Act of 1980 and the Stevenson–Wydler Act of 1980 laid the groundwork for the process, and the 1986 Federal Technology Transfer Act opened the doors to research and development partnerships between federal labs and US industry. Subsequent legislation and Executive Orders have broadened their scope.
2 In 1997, for example, US high-technology industrial production was nearly half as great as Japan, and nearly six times as great as Germany or China – its three closest competitors (National Science Board 2000).
3 Industrial production in Lithuania in 2000 (production sold) as per industry and industry ranked according to the level of technology (OECD definition): share of high-technology industries – 4.9 per cent, medium–high-tech industries – 11.0 per cent (including chemicals 6.0 per cent), medium–low-tech industries – 27.8 per cent, low-tech industries – 56.3 per cent (including manufacture of food products and beverages 23.4 per cent) (Industry 2000).

References

Abramson, H.N., Encarna-Cao J., Reid, P.P. and Schmoch, U. (eds) (1997) *Technology Transfer Systems in the United States and Germany: Lessons and Perspectives*, Washington, D.C.: National Academy of Engineering.
Archibugi, D. and Lundvall, B.A. (2002) *The Globalizing Learning Economy*, Oxford: Oxford University Press.
Bozeman, B. (2000) 'Technology transfer and public policy: a review of research and theory', *Research Policy*, 29, 627–55.
Buchbinder, H. (1993) 'The market oriented university and the changing role of knowledge', *Higher Education*, 26, 331–625.
Caloghirou, Y., Tsakanikas, A and Vonortas, N.S. (2001) 'University–industry co-operation in the context of the European Framework Programmes', *The Journal of Technology Transfer*, 26 (1–2), 153–61.
Caracostas, P. and Muldur, U. (1998) *Bringing Together Research, Innovation and Society in Europe: a European Vision of Research and Innovation Policies for the 21st Century*, Brussels: European Commission, DGXII.
Commission of the European Communities (1996) 'Green Paper on Innovation', Luxembourg.
—— (2000) *Innovation Policy in a Knowledge Based Economy*, Luxembourg: Commission of the European Communities.
—— (2002) *Industrial Policy in an Enlarged Europe*, Communication from the Commission to the Council, the European Parliament, the Economic and Social Committee and the Committee of the Regions, Brussels.
—— (2003a) *Innovation Policy: Updating the Union's Approach in the Context of the Lisbon Strategy 2003*, Communication from the Commission to the Council, the European Parliament, the Economic and Social Committee and the Committee of the Regions, Brussels.

—— (2003b) *Entrepreneurship in Europe: Green Paper of Commission of the European Communities*, Brussels.
Conway, C. (2002) *Welcome to the Real World: Educators in Industry*, VIETA: Southern Growth Policies Board. Online. Available at: www.southern.org/pubs/realworld.pdf (accessed 26 November 2004).
Coppola, B.P. (2001) 'The technology transfer dilemma: Preserving morally responsible education in a utilitarian entrepreneurial academic culture', *HYLE International Journal for Philosophy of Chemistry (special issue on Ethics of Chemistry)*, 2 (7), 155–67.
Coupe, T. (2003) 'Science is golden: academic R&D and university patents', *The Journal of Technology Transfer*, 28 (1), 31–46.
Daines, G.P. (1996) *The Role of Technology Transfer in University Development: implications and disadvantages of traditional paradigms vs. academic entrepreneurship*. Online. Available at: www.celcee.edu/publications/digest/Dig98-9.html (accessed 26 November 2004).
Drucker, P. (1998) 'From capitalism to knowledge society', in D. Neef (ed.) *The Knowledge Economy*, Wedburn, MA: Butterworth.
Dyker, D.A. and Radosevic, S. (1999) *Building the Knowledge-based Economy in Countries in Transition – From Concepts to Policies*, Brighton: University of Sussex Falmer. Online. Available at: www.sussex.ac.uk/spru/ (accessed 26 November 2004).
Egorov, I. and Carayannis, E.G. (1999) 'Transforming the post-soviet research systems through incubating technological entrepreneurship', *The Journal of Technology Transfer*, 24 (2–3), 159–72.
Enroled Senate Bill 102 (2001) 'An act relating to higher education technology transfer account', 71st Oregon Legislative Assembly. Available at: pub.das.state.or.us/LEG_BILLS/PDFs_2001/ESB102.pdf (accessed 20 March 2005).
Etzkowitz, H. and Leydesdorff, L. (1999) 'The future location of research and technology transfer', *The Journal of Technology Transfer*, 24 (2–3), 111–23.
Geroski, P.A. (2000) 'Models of technology diffusion', *Research Policy*, 29, 603–25.
Gibbons, M., Limoges, C., Nowotny, H., Schwartzman, S., Scott, P. and Trow, M. (1995) *The New Production of Knowledge: the Dynamics of Science and Research in Contemporary Societies*, London: Sage.
Gorman, M.E. (2002) 'Types of knowledge and their roles in technology transfer', *The Journal of Technology Transfer*, 27 (3), 219–31.
Hobrough, J. (2004) 'Modelling higher education in Eastern and Central Europe since *perestroika*: the application of dynamic concept analysis', *Industry and Higher Education*, 18 (4), 267–77.
Jones-Evans, D. and Kloftsen, M. (1998) 'Role of the university in the technology transfer process', *Science and Public Policy*, 25 (6), 373–81.
Jones-Evans, D. and Pandya, D. (1996) 'Universities and enterprise development on the periphery of Europe', *Academy of Entrepreneurship Journal, European Edition*, 2 (1), 21–43.
Kaukonen, E. and Nieminen, M. (1999) 'Modelling the Triple Helix from a small country perspective: the case of Finland', *The Journal of Technology Transfer*, 24 (2–3), 173–83.
Klauss, R. (2000) 'Technology transfer in education – application to developing countries', *The Journal of Technology Transfer*, 25 (3), 277–87.
Koschatzky, K. (2002) 'Networking and knowledge transfer between research and indus-

try in transition countries: empirical evidence from the Slovenian innovation system', *The Journal of Technology Transfer*, 27 (1), 27–38.
Lado, A.A. and Vozikis, G.S. (1996) 'Transfer of technology to promote entrepreneurship in developing countries: an integration and proposed framework', *Entrepreneurship Theory and Practice*, 21 (2), 55–72.
Leydesdorff, L. and Etzkowitz, H. (1998) 'Triple helix of innovation', *Science and Public Policy*, 25, 6.
Lithuanian Science and Technology White Paper (2002), Vilnius: Justitia.
Lukoševičius, A. (2002) 'Mokslo, technologijų ir inovacijų plėtra visuomenės gerovei' ['Development of science, technologies and innovation for society's welfare'], *Mokslas, technologija ir visuomenė: harmoningosios raidos paieškos*, Kaunas: Technologija.
McBrierty, V. (1993) 'The university–industry interface: from the lab to the market', *Higher Education Management*, 5 (1), 75–94.
Mayer, S. and Blaas, W. (2002) 'Technology transfer: an opportunity for small open economies', *The Journal of Technology Transfer*, 27 (3), 275–89.
National Research Council and Russian Academy of Sciences: Committee on Utilization of Technologies Developed at Russian Research and Educational Institutions (1998) *Technology Commercialization: Russian Challenges, American Lessons*, Washington, D.C.: National Academy Press.
Nordmann, A. (2004) (rapporteur) *Converging Technologies: Shaping the Future of European Societies (HLEG, Forsighting the New Technology Wave)*, VIETA: European Communities. Online. Available at: europa.eu.int/comm/research/conferences/2004/ntw/pdf/final_report_en.pdf (accessed 28 May 2005).
OECD (1992) *Technology and Economy: the key relationships*, Paris.
—— (1999) *Science, Technology, Industry: University Research in Transition*, Paris.
Rip, A., Misa, Th.J., Schot, J. and Freeman, C. (1996) *Managing Technology in Society: the Approach of Constructive Technology Assessment*, London: Continuum International Publishing Group.
Roco, M.C. and Bainbridge, W.S. (eds) (2002) *Converging Technologies for Improving Human Performance*, Arlington, Virginia: Nanotechnology, Biotechnology, Information Technology and Cognitive Science. Online. Available at: www.wtec.org/ConvergingTechnologies/Report/NBIC_report.pdf (accessed 26 November 2004).
Sayetat, F. (1993) 'Strategies for promoting technology transfer', *Higher Education Management*, 5 (1), 49–53.
Schmiemann, M. and Durvy, J.N. (2003) 'New approaches to technology transfer from publicly funded research', *The Journal of Technology Transfer*, 28 (1), 9–15.
Stephan, P.E. (2001) 'Educational implications of university–industry technology transfer', *The Journal of Technology Transfer*, 26 (2), 199–205.
Tornatzky, L.G. (2001) 'Benchmarking university–industry technology transfer: a six year retrospective', *The Journal of Technology Transfer*, 26 (3), 269–77.

Chapter 11

The changing requirements for business management and business education in the 'countries in transition'
Combining cultural and institutional perspectives

Giedrius Jucevičius

Transition and transformation: brief insights into the concepts

In this chapter I refer to the passage from central planning to a market economy as a *transition*. The transition from a centrally planned to a market economy is characterized by the change of the institutions that govern the economic activities of multiple agents (Meyer 2000). Thus, the Central and Eastern European countries, eight of which have recently entered the EU, are legitimately referred to as 'transition economies'. The new EU member states, as the most successful of the post-Soviet states, are, however, already widely recognized as functioning market economies that have (formally, at least) completed this institutional passage, so the term *transition* may need some redefinition.

The new EU member states from Central and Baltic Europe are joining the category of 'latecomers in the global economy' (Storper *et al.* 1998), as a group of countries in an intermediate position between the developed and developing worlds. Until recently, such countries as Ireland, Greece and South-east Asian 'tiger' states fell into this academic category. The Central and Baltic European countries have become active players in the global competition arena, yet find themselves in unequal competing positions with the developing world. They have established a basic physical infrastructure, educational institutions and the elements of an innovation system, but lack the consolidated production structures, social capital, industrial culture and some essential organizational capabilities (Storper *et al.* 1998). In particular, the new EU member states fall short in terms of the soft aspects that underlie the newly established hard or formal institutions. Murrel (2003) notes that the main challenge associated with post-Soviet transition was that the central planning system had radically different institutions from those encountered in market economies, and that these had lasting effects on people's value systems and patterns of behaviour. As latecomers in the globalized economy, the new EU member states maintain a degree of their post-Soviet character at various levels of governance.

Some authors (Whitley 1999, Storper *et al.* 1998) claim that the complex process of transition from a centrally planned economy may produce multiple forms of market economies. In this case, the term *transformation* better describes the diversity of possible outcomes (Melnikas 2002, but see also on this notion of transformation Porter 1990, Drucker 1994, Hall and Soskice 2001, Richardson 1994, Ravallion 1994 and Downes 1996). Given the prevailing complexity of interacting forces, transformation best reflects the nature of the shift that is taking place not only in post-Soviet Central and Eastern Europe but also in the developed world. The interaction of a globalized environment, the prevalence of Anglo-Saxon neoliberal concepts of governance, and the phenomenon of transformation raise a fundamental question as to the direction and model by which countries evolve worldwide. This question is raised in various disciplines of the social sciences, such as political economy, management and organization theory and economic sociology. Is a convergence towards one model for managing economic activities in sight at organizational and state levels? Or is the coexistence of various economic governance patterns, embedded in different value systems and patterns of actor behaviour, to continue well into the future?

Today, especially in Europe, an approach which recognizes a diversity of approaches to capitalism (Hall and Soskice 2001) is gaining new currency. This approach claims the existence of at least two institutional systems of capitalist market economies: liberal (e.g. Anglo-Saxon) and coordinated (e.g. German, Scandinavian). These coexist and evolve in their own ways without clear signs of convergence. They consist of at least four institutional elements: corporate governance structures, industrial relations, inter-company relations in technology transfer, and business education and vocational training systems (Hall and Soskice 2001, Whitley 1999). This last element determines the pattern of competences that employees and managers possess once they enter their national work organizations. Liberal market economies (for example, in the USA) tend to produce generalist management competences (e.g. American MBA programmes), while the coordinated capitalist systems (those in continental Western Europe, especially Germanic ones) equip their organizations with technically specialized competences at all organizational levels (for example, in the German Fachhochschule).

The pattern of business education and vocational training systems does not emerge in some kind of institutional vacuum, but is closely related to the institutional elements previously mentioned. This is the principle of institutional complementarities (Hall and Soskice 2001). Particular outcomes can be related to their context. In liberal market economies, the short-term capital markets, deregulated labour markets with their low-cost hiring and firing, and competition-based setting of product standards contribute to the overall dynamism of the business environment. There are incentives for managers and employees to acquire the generalist competences that would enhance their marketability and interorganizational mobility. The coordinated capitalist systems, however, rely on the availability of relatively cheap long-term capital via the well-developed banking sector, the strong role of industrial associations and cooperative behaviour in setting product standards, cooperative labour relations, and long-term organizational commitments. These form the background to company and industry investment in the technically specialized skills of employees.

The institutional differences between the western market economies reinforce different patterns of innovation and competitive advantage. On the one hand, the generalist competences of managers and employees favour so-called radical innovations characterized by essential product or process improvements. These focus on new, fast-growing industries (for example, biotechnology, pharmaceuticals, medical engineering, information technologies, semiconductors, telecommunications, etc.). The specialized competences, however, contribute to the incremental innovations that maintain a competitive edge in traditional industries. They build upon existing competences, making continuous improvements in product quality, costs and customer relationships (for example, in civil and mechanical engineering, transport, machinery and machine tools, and materials processing). The analysis carried out by Hall and Soskice (2001) reveals that, in the context of globalization, each of these systems follows its own paths of change, which are embedded in their distinct institutional frameworks. Only recently has the German system of management education started introducing the American-style MBA programmes, while American or British managers are preoccupied with improving their vocational training programmes and the specialized skills of employees.

The theoretical framework constructed by Hall and Soskice (2001) mainly concerns the Anglo-Germanic comparison, but does not fully encompass some capitalist institutional systems, such as those of France or Japan, which have (to some degree) hierarchically controlled structures. These systems are also undergoing evolution, so that, for example, the elitist French education system is gravitating towards more democratic forms of governance, while Japanese *keiretsu* moves towards greater openness to market forces. A report on research into vocational training in Europe (European Centre for the Development of Vocational Training 2001) shows that all EU-15 countries (except the Netherlands) tend to decentralize the financing of vocational training programmes. All except the UK, which already has a high proportion of private involvement, are moving from predominantly public to private financing. The widely acclaimed German system is often blamed for equipping its labour with skills better fitted to the traditional 'Taylorist' factories than for the knowledge economy, and so is also faced with the challenge of transformation (Buck 2002).

What are the implications of all this for an analysis of the transformation phenomenon of post-Soviet Central and Eastern European countries (CEECs)? Just as developed countries show the global nature of transformation through processes such as the growth of the knowledge economy, so (it is reasonable to believe) the 'new' countries will develop their own distinct models of business organization and institutional frameworks. These would be based on their specific cultural and institutional context, but at the same time would also be successful in the globalized environment.

The post-Soviet transition economies may be a valuable laboratory for researching the global transformation phenomenon, because the change in these countries has been very dramatic and is less distorted by a previously existing institutional infrastructure.[1] The analysis of industrial policies in Western and Eastern European countries by Žeruolis and Jucevičius (2003) has shown that the policy transformation on either side is not as different in substance as might appear at first sight. It is somewhat paradoxical that the principles of a 'Taylorist' or rational bureaucratic model of administration have been to a large extent implemented in Soviet enterprises (Jaffee 2001) and are still highly influential in the manufacturing systems of Western Europe (for example, France or Germany), not to mention the public administration sector (Hancke 2001, Lawrence and Edwards 2000). Dismantling the 'Taylorist' structures in business, education and public administration is only one of the challenges uniting old and new Europe in their quest for global competitiveness.

The cultural and institutional context of transformation and its implications for business management

The transformation environment and its implications for business management and education may be analysed from various angles. This short chapter mainly relies on the findings of doctoral research carried out in the Baltic state of Lithuania. This is an example of a relatively successful 'country in transition' that has completed major market reforms and become a member of the EU. As a 'latecomer in the global economy' (Jucevičius 2004) it still faces numerous challenges, as described above. The doctoral dissertation sought to disentangle the cultural and institutional factors that underlie emerging management systems in a transition environment and to combine them in an integrated theoretical framework.

There is one paradox or dilemma inherent to any transformation environment. The newly emerging forms of economic organization (business organizations or institutions) can no longer rely on the old value system, but, at the same time, no structural change can happen without the necessary cultural support. This 'chicken and egg' dilemma cannot be resolved, for, according to Handy (1999), dilemmas can only be managed. It does not, however, rule out the necessity of evaluating this relationship and its potential conflicts and synergies.

There is a growing consensus that the traditional cultural and institutional methodologies formulated by Western European or American authors cannot sufficiently capture the complexities of the transformation environment (O'Reilly 1996, Wilkinson 1996). The culturalists (Hofstede 1980, 1991, 2001,

Laurent 1983, 1986) are usually criticized for their static approach to culture, i.e. they claim the stability of collective mental maps over time, which may not be true in an environment characterized by radical structural changes. For their part, the institutionalists (Maurice, Sellier and Silvestre 1982, Whitley 1992, Hall and Soskice 2001) tend to rely on historically evolved institutional structures of large developed states to rationalize the institutional environment. Again, this makes their approach alone insufficient to explain the complexities of transformation, especially in Eastern European countries. Both major approaches need to be combined to provide better insights into the complexities of the business environment and to look for proper educational and managerial solutions.

So what is the 'cultural soil' for emerging management structures? What are the directions of change in the institutional environment that will have a direct effect on businesses? What are the challenges for business education in managing the cultural and institutional complexities of the transformation environment? These are the questions that will be briefly addressed in the following sections.

Cultural specifics of the transformation environment

To identify the cultural background of Lithuania as a country undergoing economic transformation, two major methodologies have been combined: the Hofstede (1980, 1991, 2001) methodology of cultural dimensions and the Trompenaars (1984, 1993) methodology of cultural dilemmas. The former enjoys enduring recognition in the academic world because of its extensive empirical basis (it covers over 116,000 respondents in seventy-two countries) and its conceptual conciseness (it compares cultures on the basis of only five empirically derived cultural dimensions). The latter methodology is more popular among business practitioners for, although it also relies on the survey method, it is more qualitative in nature. Whereas Hofstede presents culture as the differentiating factor across nations (a functionalist approach to culture), Trompenaars perceives culture as a dynamic, learning environment of managing the dilemmas of opposite values (such as individualism and communitarianism) to create wealth. Each approach has its pros and cons, which have been widely discussed in the academic literature (Cooper 1982, McSweeney 2002a, 2002b, Holden 2002) and by the authors themselves (Hampden-Turner and Trompenaars 1997, Hofstede 1996). The two methodologies were combined in order to address the specific objectives of research in the transition environment. The survey, which was carried out in Lithuania and took place in several stages from 2000 to 2004, covered 5,311 respondents from various demographic groups and organizations.

It has revealed and structured the overall cultural complexity and paradoxes of the transformation environment.

Approach to hierarchy

The standard respondent shows an expressed need for clearly defined hierarchical responsibilities, while a bottom–top initiative is considered by subordinates as a potential source of danger and instability. The respondents tend to prefer the parental decision-making style (i.e. 'we discussed with you – I have decided'). It is the power to make decisions, rather than higher technical competence, that is considered to characterize a good manager. The employees consider good working relations with their direct superior as an important workplace guarantee. This preference for a hierarchical relationship may stem from the lack of democratic tradition in economic governance and the overall search for stability in a volatile transformation environment. Looking specifically at the Lithuanian case, the roots of such an approach may also be traced as deep as the society's Catholic and rural elements. It is also important to note the general element of mistrust in relationships with authority that is rooted in the tradition of alienated elites.

Approach to formal rules and structures

The relationship with rules is probably the most controversial one. People do show a need for clearly defined responsibilities and instructions, and have a cautious approach to free competition, which, in their opinion, might do more harm than good. All this, according to Hofstede (2001), implies a high degree of uncertainty avoidance. It is important to note the paradox of this cultural dimension, which is particularly noticeable in the transformation environment: despite the general need for structured situations and for organizational rules, these can easily be broken with a pragmatic end in mind. Although Hofstede explains this by the emotional (rather than practical) nature of a need for rules in a high uncertainty avoidance cultural environment, breaking the rules in the post-Soviet context was often a matter of survival. The traditions of the rule of law in some of these countries are only beginning to emerge.

Hofstede claims that the approach to hierarchy (or power distance) and approach to rules (or uncertainty avoidance) are the two dimensions that shape the nature and structure of national work organizations. The research by different authors (Kruzela 1995, Hofstede 2001, Kolman et al. 2003, Nasierowski and Mikula 1998, Varga 1986, Mockaitis 2002) confirms the overall trends of high power distance and high uncertainty avoidance in most Central and East European countries, just as in the South European countries (France, Italy, Spain, Greece, Portugal). Without disregarding the actual cultural differences among different states, such trends indicate widespread cultural support for the bureaucratic or Taylorist forms of governance. Is this all happening in the context of the emerging knowledge economy and flattening knowledge organizations? Paradoxically, though perhaps not surprisingly, various authors notice the persisting spread and even some renaissance of a Taylorist organization in the region (Bučiūnienė 1995, Lawrence and Edwards 2000, Marcinkevičiūtė 2003).

Approach to the work goals: a split between micro- and macro-space

The cultural approach to evaluating work goals in the transition environment is probably the most controversial one. The respondents show very contradictory results as far as the preference for social or professional goals in the work environment (Hofstedian masculinity–femininity) is concerned. On the macro or organizational level, the respondents aspire for a non-competitive environment, while on the micro or personal level they show a clear preference for performance-based motivation schemes (i.e. competition). On the organizational level they wish for cooperative colleagues, while emphasizing career progress on the personal level. On the macro level, the respondents claim the need for a socially oriented role for firms (i.e. profit should not be firms' only objective), while on the micro or individual level, the emphasis on individual economic work goals strongly prevails.

Some authors relate this duality to the legacy of the Soviet system. An example would be the imposed standards of 'double morale', i.e. the inconsistency between publicly declared goals and real interests or, to put it another way, socialist ideals versus individual power aspirations. The research by Jucevičius (1995) has revealed the existence of a 'double life syndrome' in Lithuanian organizations. The respondents in this research have admitted a split between their publicly declared and privately held values, and acknowledge that it still impacts on their patterns of behaviour. As far as the work goals research is concerned, this macro–micro split may be due not so much to moral issues, but to an inadequate understanding of the market economy environment. Grigas (2002) notes the existence of 'deformed individualism'. Todeva (1999), who carried out a Hofstede cultural survey among Polish students, has discovered differences between internalized and perceived norms of behaviour. Because of different research tools, a significant discrepancy can be found between what people perceive and communicate in public as the 'national cultural norm', and what they have internalized as cultural attitudes and norms of behaviour. Whatever the reasons, this split is an important characteristic of the transformation environment that needs to be taken into account by businesses, educators and policy makers.

An emerging value gap between 'traditional' and 'innovative' parts of society

The complex transformation environment cannot simply be evaluated by measuring the 'mean of the temperature in a hospital', so to speak. It is necessary to look into the diversity of its demographic–professional subgroups. Findings show that younger people (especially under the age of twenty-four) and people with higher education and higher positions, tend to be more egalitarian, rely on spontaneous organizational solutions and place higher emphasis on individual freedom and personal economic objectives, as contrasted with the rest of society. We can thus observe the coexistence of at least two cultural preferences. On the one hand, there is a 'traditional' part of society, with its bureaucratic, hierarchy-based preferences, while on the other there is a more dynamic or 'innovative' part emerging, with a spontaneous, entrepreneurial and market-based value system. It is an enduring question as to what should be done for their peaceful and constructive coexistence in a globalized knowledge economy that tends to sharpen existing differences between the potential winners and losers of transformation.

Institutional specifics of the transformation environment

The transformation of the requirements for business in CEECs is associated first and foremost with transformation in the institutional environment, i.e. the more or less gradual replacement of central planning institutions with those fit for the market economy. The success of business organization was no longer determined in the political circles of state institutions, but in the market. Enterprises became independent, privately owned economic units with free market entrance and exit possibilities, relatively flexible labour regulation, and free competition that enabled individual economic achievement and motivation (Lawrence and Edwards 2000).

Although the collapse of the system of central planning in CEECs happened more or less overnight, the actual market economic framework was not so quick to emerge and fill this certain institutional vacuum (Murrel 2003). However, the process of (re-)constructing the institutional framework in Eastern Europe was much quicker than in Western European countries, where the evolution of this framework lasted for decades or even centuries. The transformation of Eastern European economies was guided in accordance with a neoliberal Washington consensus package of reforms as formulated by international financial institutions and reinforced by the EU (in the case of the new EU member states from CEE) (Žėruolis and Jucevičius 2003). The neoliberal reform package is often criticized for unilaterally imposing the principles of privatization, liberalization and macroeconomic stabilization on CEECs, disregarding (or even at the expense of) other basic elements of the economic system such as social, organizational or informational capital supporting the proper functioning of formal institutions (Stiglitz 1999). The market reforms contributed little to trust building among different agents in society (state institutions, enterprises, professional associations, individuals, etc.) and to the process of collective learning (Storper et al. 1998). The American neoclassical theory with its emphasis on the macroeconomic aspects of transition has predominated, while the neo-institutionalist approach, with its emphasis on the role of institutions in economic development, was relatively disregarded (Murrel 2003). However, it is exactly the institutional systems, such as corporate governance, industrial and inter-firm relations or educational and vocational training systems that determine the competitive outcomes of transformation.

Systems of corporate governance and industrial relations

The dramatic change in firms' ownership and control mechanisms affected all stakeholders, both inside and outside. The evolution of corporate governance in CEECs depended largely on the chosen strategy of privatization. However, in most cases it produced wide managerial autonomy, i.e. largely non-existent mechanisms of control over managers. This was at the expense of small stakeholders such as employees or minor stockholders. The ownership of large former state enterprises was concentrated in the hands of insiders who were oriented to short-term profit and to consolidating their market share. The absence or deterioration of trust-based relations impeded the development of tripartite social dialogue institutions (i.e. between government, enterprises and employees). Although established *de jure*, in most cases these institutions remain ineffective, due to the absence of a culture of dialogue and the prevailing economic interests of lobby groups at the policy-making level. Meanwhile, the labour union movement remains too weak and fragmented to provide an effective counterbalance.

Inter-company relations in technology transfer

Inter-company networks are an important precondition for inter-agent learning and innovation activities. However, hierarchical structures both inside and outside companies have done little to promote trust-based horizontal relationships. Cooperation between companies as well as between companies and universities in research and development remains at unacceptably low levels (Jucevičius 2004). Some inter-company cooperation can be noticed at the political level (i.e. representing collective interests in the state institutions) but this type of association does little to promote innovation. The findings of the doctoral research indicate that Lithuanian managers score lower on their orientation to innovation than most of their North and South European counterparts (i.e. in the Scandinavian countries, France and Belgium). The Achilles' heel of all CEECs is that their economic growth remains driven by traditional economic factors, such as cheap labour and capital, while the innovation sectors of the economy remain underdeveloped.

Management education and vocational training (VET)

Vocational education and training (VET) is one of the areas undergoing fundamental post-Soviet restructuring, whereas higher education in business and management is a newly emerged area. Laužackas (1999) notes that the Soviet system was characterized by a bureaucratic system of vocational training with a high degree of centralization at the state level, which had certain traits in common with South European systems of VET. The last decade can be characterized by the subsequent decentralization of the system, with the delegation of these competences to the state-owned professional schools and private colleges. International organizations (OECD 2002) and various experts (De Rooij 2002) acknowledge that Lithuania has created the basic legal and institutional conditions for modern open vocational training in line with the EU Lisbon agenda. However, the situation in terms of actual implementation is less optimistic. Dialogue between companies, educators and policy makers is very fragmented due to the absence of such a tradition. Employers remain reluctant to participate in codrafting and cofinancing training programmes. There is an enduring lack of a culture of innovation among social agents, as well as little sharing of information and knowledge (Laužackas 2002). The quality of vocational training may also be brought into question, especially in light of the competences for the knowledge economy. Managers educated during the Soviet period usually have backgrounds in engineering and little knowledge of general management (Lawrence and Edwards 2000). On the other hand, the younger generation of professional managers (up to 35–40 years) usually possess American-style generalist MBAs (Novikova 2003).

The brief analysis presented above indicates the coexistence of various institutions and forms of governance. Such coexistence is probably the most characteristic trait of the transformation environment. It is possible to conclude that in most institutional aspects we can observe the coexistence of institutions characteristic of hierarchy-based and market-based systems. Both of these systems, however, are based on low levels of inter-agent trust. Jucevičius (2004) claims that one can observe the emergence of elements of horizontal functional networks such as social dialogue structures, as found in, for example, Germany. Their functioning, however, remains limited due to underdeveloped social capital, such as lack of traditions in cooperation and consensus building.

Challenges for higher education in business management in the context of transformation

The cultural and institutional complexities of the transformation process imply a very special role for education. The system of education and vocational training is more than just one important institutional aspect of the transforming capitalist system. Compared with other institutional factors, it has the most direct effect on the cultural values of people who enter the work organization. It may therefore produce a significant spillover effect on other elements of the system – cultural and institutional – especially in the age of the emerging knowledge economy. But what qualities and directions should higher education in business management take to meet contemporary business needs and ensure a successful outcome of continuous transformation?

- Higher education in management should build the competences necessary for successful participation in innovative partnership networks. This means promoting the values of networking and providing students with interdisciplinary competence, which would enable them to work in groups with different kinds of expertise (Engestroem 1995). It also means the promotion of entrepreneurship and innovation at all levels of education.
- Future managers must have well-developed critical thinking skills, which remains a particularly huge challenge for post-Soviet countries. A study by the World Bank (1996) has shown that students from the former Soviet bloc score very highly on awareness of facts, but very low on the use of knowledge in unanticipated circumstances. It means that the education system rooted in the teaching facts paradigm needs to gravitate towards the learning paradigm.
- Higher education in management must equip students with competences for managing the complexities of continuous transformation. The previously discussed cultural diversity inside the country and organizations, if appropriately managed, may be an excellent source of synergy rather than conflict. The values of traditional and innovative parts of society can be constructively accommodated within the organization; it demands, however, not only tolerance, but also self and social astuteness on the part of a manager (Ferris *et al.* 2004). Competences in double- and triple-loop learning, as well as communication skills inside the organization, may emerge as crucial in this respect.
- Higher education and vocational training should consolidate the social partners (companies, professional associations, state/municipal institutions) and build bridges of trust inside the community, aimed at formulating and implementing various joint programmes. Cooperation and trust could spill over into other areas of the system, such as corporate governance or industrial relations. The involvement of businesses in education and training programmes could also contribute to their increased prestige (especially in the case of vocational training).
- Higher education in business management should fully embrace the concept of lifelong learning, to enable individuals to transfer skills, knowledge and understanding from one context to another (Erault 1994). Theoretical knowledge should underpin and complement reflection upon practice.
- Higher education institutions in business management should not only equip their students with competences for learning and networking, but develop into the learning organizations themselves. This means becoming a part of international business school networks and promoting sharing of competence inside and outside the institution.

All of the challenges indicated above are important not only to the post-Soviet states of Central and Eastern Europe, but also to consolidated western systems of higher education. Dismantling Taylorist structures and mentality, building effective partnership networks and modern learning competences remain issues of common concern. Despite cultural and institutional specifics, any open system needs to embrace the competences necessary for managing complexity and change, to ensure continuing processes of collective learning among its members and continuous regeneration of its patterns of innovative activity.

Note

1 Fitoussi (1996) notes that the post-Soviet economic transformation has confirmed many institutional assumptions and recipes formulated by the economic growth theories. Maniokas (2003) analyses the overall impact of Europeanization (i.e. adjustment of the national institutional system to the EU regulatory impact) on the EU member states on the basis of Central and Eastern European countries because in these countries such impact can be more easily 'filtered' and identified.

References

Bučiūnienė, I. (1995) 'Darbo motyvacijos kitimas Lietuvos pramonės įmonėse rinkos santykių formavimosi laikotarpiu', unpublished thesis, Kaunas University of Technology.
Buck, B. (2002) 'Verslumas – naujas iššūkis profesiniam rengimui' ['Entrepreneurship as a new challenge for vocational training'], *Profesinis rengimas: tyrimai ir realijos*, 5.
Cooper, C.L. (1982) 'Review of Geert Hofstede: "Culture's Consequences"', *Journal of Occupational Behaviour*, 3 (2), 123.
De Rooij, P. (2002) 'Profesinis rengimas Europos kontekste' ['Vocational Training in the European Context'], *Profesinis rengimas: tyrimai ir realijos*, 5, 20–6.
Downes, R. (1996) 'Economic transformation in Central and Eastern Europe: the role of regional development', *European Planning Studies*, 4 (2), 217–25.
Drucker, P. (1994) *Post-Capitalist Society*, Harper Business.
Engestroem, Y. (1995) *Training for Change*, London: ILO.
Erault, M. (1994) *Developing Professional Knowledge and Competence*, London: Falmer Press.
European Centre for the Development of Vocational Training (CEDEFOP) (2001) 'Training and learning for competence', Second report on vocational training research in Europe.
Ferris, G.R., Anthony, W.P., Kolodinsky, R.W., Gilmore, D.C. and Harvey G.M. (2004) 'Development of political skill', in Ch. Wankel and R. DeFillippi (eds) *Rethinking Management Education*, Greenwich: Information Age Publishing.
Fitoussi, J.-P. (1996) 'After communism, is there a middle way?', in W. Streeck and C. Crouch (eds) *Political Economy of Modern Capitalism: mapping convergence and diversity*, London: Sage.
Grigas, R. (2002) 'Šiuolaikinio lietuvio nacionalinio būdo bruožai: nerimą keliančios trajektorijos (sociosofinė kritinė apžvalga)' ['The features of the national character of contemporary Lithuanians: the worrying trends'], *XXI amžius*, 6 November: 13.
Hall, P.A. and Soskice, D. (eds) (2001) *Varieties of Capitalism: the institutional foundations of comparative advantage*, Oxford: Oxford University Press.

Hampden-Turner, C. and Trompenaars, F. (1997) 'Response to Geert Hofstede', *International Journal of Intercultural Relations*, 21 (1), 149–59.
Hancke, B. (2001) 'Restructuring in French industry', in P. Hall and D. Soskice (eds) *Varieties of Capitalisms*, Oxford: Oxford University Press.
Handy, Ch. (1999) *Understanding Organizations*, 4th edn, London: Penguin Books.
Hofstede, G. (1980) *Culture's Consequences*, London: Sage Publications.
—— (1991) *Cultures and Organizations: Software of the Mind*, London: HarperCollins Publishers.
—— (1996) 'Riding the waves of commerce. A test of Trompenaar's "model" of national culture differences', *International Journal of Intercultural Relations*, 20 (2), 189–98.
—— (2001) *Culture's Consequences: Comparing Values, Behaviors, Institutions and Organizations Across Nations*, 2nd revised edn, London: Sage Publications.
Holden, N. (2002) *Cross-Cultural Management: a Knowledge Management Perspective*, Harlow: Pearson Education Limited.
Jaffee, D. (2001) *Organization Theory: Tension and Change*, Boston: McGraw Hill.
Jucevičius, G. (1995) 'Dvigubo gyvenimo sindromo tyrimas', unpublished manuscript, Kaunas University of Technology.
—— (2004) 'Integrated approach to management models in the context of economic transformation: cultural and institutional perspectives', summary of doctoral thesis, Kaunas University of Technology.
Kolman, L., Noorderhaven, N.G., Hofstede, G. and Dienes, E. (2003) 'Cross-cultural differences in Central Europe', *Journal of Managerial Psychology*, 18 (1–2), 76–88.
Kruzela, P. (1995) 'Some cultural aspects on Czech and Russian management', in B. Machova and S. Kubatova (eds) *Uniqueness in Unity: the Significance of Cultural Identity in European Cooperation*, Munich: SIETAR Europa.
Laurent, A. (1983) 'The cultural diversity of western conceptions of management', *International Studies of Management and Organization*, 13 (1–2), 75–96.
—— (1986) 'The cross-cultural puzzle of international human resource management', *Human Resource Management*, 25 (1), 91–102.
Laužackas, R. (1999) *Sistemo-teorinės profesinio rengimo kaitos dimensijos*, Kaunas: VDU.
—— (2002) 'Profesinio rengimo plėtra žinių visuomenės ir konkurentabilios ekonomikos amžiuje' ['Development of vocational education in the era of knowledge society and competitive economics]', *Profesinis rengimas: tyrimai ir realijos*, 5, 26–40.
Lawrence, P. and Edwards, V. (2000) *Management in Western Europe*, London: Macmillan Business.
McSweeney, B. (2002a) 'Hofstede's model of national cultural differences and their consequences: a triumph of faith – a failure of analysis', *Human Relations*, 55 (11), 89–118.
—— (2002b) 'The essentials of scholarship. A reply to Geert Hofstede', *Human Relations*, 55 (11), 1363–72.
Maniokas, K. (2003) *ES plėtra ir europeizacija: Vidurio ir Rytų Europos valstybių įsijungimas į Europos Sąjungą*, Vilnius: Eugrimas.
Marcinkevičiūtė, L. (2003) 'Lietuvos įmonių darbuotojų motyvavimo modelių ypatumai besikeičiančios rinkos sąlygomis', unpublished thesis, Lithuanian University of Agriculture.
Maurice, M., Sellier, F. and Silvestre, J.-J. (1982) *Politique d'éducation et organization industrielle en France et en Allemagne*, Paris: Presses Universitaires de France; trans.

(1986) *The Social Foundations of Industrial Power: A Comparison of France and Germany*, Massachusetts: MIT Press.

Melnikas, B. (2002). *Transformacijos: visuomenės pokyčiai, naujas tūkstantmetis, valdymas ir savireguliacija, Rytų ir Vidurio Europa*, Vilnius: Vaga, Sapnų sala.

Meyer, K.E. (2000) 'International business research on transition economies', working Paper No. 32, Centre for East European Studies, Copenhagen Business School.

Mockaitis, A.I. (2002) 'The influence of national cultural values on management attitudes: a comparative study across three countries', unpublished thesis, Vilnius University.

Murrel, P. (2003) 'Institutions and firms in transition economies', in C. Menard and M. Shirley (eds) *Handbook of New Institutional Economics*, Kluwer Academic Press.

Nasierowski, W. and Mikula, B. (1998) 'Culture dimensions of Polish managers: Hofstede's indices', *Organization Studies*, 19 (3), 495–509.

Novikova, J. (2003) 'How institutional framework affects the formation of capitalism in countries in transition: following the path or finding new ways?', MA thesis, Lund University.

OECD (2002) *Reviews of National Policies for Education: Lithuania, Education and Skills*.

O'Reilly, J. (1996) 'Theoretical considerations in cross-national employment research', *Sociological Research Online*, 1 (1). Online. Available at: www.socresonline.org.uk/1/1/2.html (accessed 1 November 2003).

Porter, M. (1990) *The Competitive Advantage of Nations*, New York: Free Press.

Ravallion, M. (1994) 'Economic transformation in Eastern Europe and the distribution of income', *Economica*, 2–61 (242), 253–4.

Richardson, Th.J. (1994). 'Making markets: economic transformation in Eastern Europe and the post-Soviet states', *Russian Review*, 53 (3), 473–4.

Stiglitz, J. 'Whither reform? Ten years of the transition', keynote address at the World Bank Annual Conference on Development Economics, Washington, DC, April 1999.

Storper, M., Thomadakis, S.B, and Tsipouri, L.J. (ed.) (1998) *Latecomers in the Global Economy*, London and New York: Routledge.

Todeva, E. (1999) 'Models for comparative analysis of culture: the case of Poland', *International Journal of Human Resource Management*, 10 (4), 606–23.

Trompenaars, F. (1984) 'The organization of meaning and the meaning of organization – a comparative study on the conceptions and organizational structure in different cultures', unpublished thesis, University of Pennsylvania.

—— (1993) *Riding the Waves of Culture: Understanding Cultural Diversity in Business*, London: Economist Books.

Varga, K. (1986) *Az Emberi es Szerveti Eroforras Fejlesztese*, Budapest: Akademiai Kiado iln.

Whitley, R. (1992) *European Business Systems*, London: Sage.

—— (1999) *Divergent Capitalisms*, Oxford: Oxford University Press.

Wilkinson, B. (1996) 'Culture, institutions and business in East Asia', *Organization Studies*, 17 (3), 421–47.

World Bank (1996) *World Development Report 1996: From Plan to Market*, Washington, D.C.: The World Bank.

Žėruolis, D. and Jucevičius, G. (2003) 'Strateginis matmuo Lietuvos ekonominėje politikoje – turinys ir lyginamoji analizė', Lithuanian Military Academy, Centre of Strategic Research.

Chapter 12

Competence development for the knowledge-driven economy

Daiva Lepaitė

Contemporary educational systems face many demands from developments in the knowledge-driven economy (KDE). These demands, constituted in particular by human resource development needs in the changing work environment both globally and locally, call for the development and application of 'competences'. The meaning and value of 'competences' are by no means straightforward. Transferability is a much-discussed feature of a 'competence' but, as will be argued below, 'competences' have other features which are less widely discussed but which are also important educationally. Research and discussions relating to the development of competences are especially focused upon the study programmes which are being designed for different levels and phases of educational systems. It will be argued later that 'competences' and their development should not be seen in a narrow way. One of the consequences of this important point is that the development of competences (properly understood) cannot be separated from the development of an individual's wider knowledge, skills, attitudes, personality characteristics and values.

'Competences' have emerged as a major goal and preoccupation of secondary education[1] in European countries alongside subject/discipline knowledge. The curriculum of vocational training has traditionally stressed training for specific professional fields but now attempts to develop transferable competences oriented to the wider perspective of the career development of individuals across their working lives. The need for transferable competences and for an appropriate form of educational provision for their development has also become a preoccupation and major goal of higher education.

The nature and implications of competence development in the context of higher education requires sustained critical research. The research literature relating to a number of aspects of this question is extensive.[2] An important context in which this discussion is situated is the prominent trend in contemporary higher education towards massification and expansion. This trend is investigated by Teichler (1988) and Scott (1993, 1997), among others.[3] The processes taking place at higher education level affect its intersection with Lithuanian secondary, vocational training. Lithuanian researchers have researched aspects of higher education and vocational training (Jucevičienė 1997, 1999a, 1999b,

Zavadskas 1999, 2000) and attention has been given to such matters as the vocational curriculum, qualifications, standards and programme design, and change processes in relation to vocational training (Šernas 1995, 1998, Laužackas 1997, 1999, 2000). However, research into the development of competences in higher education has been neglected.

In a KDE a person's competence and their potential for transformation and development is central. In exploring the role that higher education might play in the development of these competences, it is important to focus attention in more detail on how the notion of a 'competence' is being understood.

The nature of competence

At first sight, the notion of 'competence' is an inherently specific one: a person possesses a competence to do x or y. The notion of 'competence' is also used in a more general sense, but this needs careful articulation if it is to have meaning. In order to develop a person's competence in a specific activity it is necessary to define not only the structure of the activity with which the competence in question is associated, but also the level of the competence being aimed at. Both the nature of the competence being developed and the level of competence being aimed at should properly inform educational planning. It is important, for example, that the right level of competence being aimed at for particular students is properly judged.

As indicated earlier, it is important to insist that 'competence' should not be understood narrowly,[4] but holistically, to include personal characteristics, values and attitudes, as well as the practical ability to perform tasks. A certain interdisciplinarity or breadth of perspective is therefore inherent in the proper understanding of 'competence' and its development, as seen in relation both to the design of competence development programmes (Barnett 1992, 1993) and human resource development in organizations (Rothwell and Kazanas 1994, Rothwell 1996, Von Krogh and Roos 1996). Further, the concept of 'activity' with which competences are associated should not be understood merely in terms of performance in merely functional or instrumental tasks but as including activities which are autonomously chosen by the individual in pursuit of his or her self-realization and personal satisfaction (White 1997, Dahrendorf 1982).

It is possible to categorize the nature and levels of 'competence' in a number of ways. In relation to the nature of 'competence', 'holistic competence' can be regarded as the skill (or, more accurately, composite of skills) to evaluate a new situation, to choose appropriate actions defined by a perception of their efficiency or aptness in other respects, and to involve and express in the process a range of personal values, attitudes and motives.

In relation to competence levels a number of distinctions can be made relating to levels in the activity to which the competence in question is related. In the case of business studies, for example, it is possible to distinguish the following competence levels. For operational performance in work (the first general level of activity) *behaviourist competence* (the most elementary competence) is necessary, corresponding precisely to specific workplace requirements and consisting of segmented parts. For work improvement (the second general level of activity) *additive competence*, based not only on acquired behaviour but also on broader knowledge and initiative, is needed. *Integrative competence*, involving capacities for various kinds of recognition, thinking and action going in important respects beyond the routine, is necessary for subsequent general levels of activity which involve the initiation of change and development. At the higher levels of activity, *holistic competence* is required.

Competences thus form a hierarchical structure. In addition, competence clusters can be identified, which overlap[5] with each other and which can be described as clusters of instrumental competence, cognitive competence, personal competence and social communication competence respectively. In the cluster of instrumental competence, for example, the skills involved have a clearly operational nature. In the cluster of cognitive competence, overlapping skills call for non-standard activity, but the development of these skills (problem-solving skills, analytical and critical-thinking skills, abstraction and 'learning to learn' skills) are applied in many different contexts of application. The notion of 'a context of application' is very significant for a proper understanding of 'competence'. Without a specific context of application, talk of the kinds of general skills which have been referred to as constituting competence clusters makes little sense. In secondary (vocational) school programmes these skills are usually embedded in clear contexts of application, thereby being given relatively clear meaning. In higher education, however, these contexts are often lacking and therefore talk of these skills is often undefined, incoherent and empty.

Research project

'Competence' has become an especially important phenomenon for the field of business and in relation to organizations in which added value is created by a high level of human competence potential. In these environments, the effective realization of personal potential is one of the indicators of the KDE. Business programmes in higher education are therefore a particular focus for research in relation to competence development.

The present chapter reports a research project which developed a curriculum competence level identification methodology in the case of business programmes. The research methods adopted in the investigation included the following:

1   A research literature analysis relating to the framework of activity levels and corresponding competence levels; to the international classification of programmes; and to the identification of the relationship between activity level, competence level and programme level. This research literature was referred to in order to design a model matrix of competence levels and scopes. In addition, the research literature contributed to the illumination of

the framework of business curriculum design, the scope of competences and the trends of competence development in programmes of upper secondary (vocational) and higher education studies.
2   Document analysis, relating to the standards of programmes and programme regulations which helped to identify the 'overlapping competences',[5] which are developed both in upper secondary (vocational) and higher education programmes, and to specify the criteria of competence levels and scopes in the clusters of overlapping competences.
3   A content analysis of programmes conducted in order to distinguish the competences being developed and to evaluate the scopes and level of development. The specific focus of the research was business programmes and the analysis of the various programmes under review included the content structure of courses, the conceptualization and nature of the competences being developed, the indicators taken as signifying the achievement of the competences and the extent to which competence levels are indicated.

The research sample consisted of the following programmes (n = 22)

1   At secondary level, secondary school programme – modules of economic literacy (n = 10) and entrepreneurship development programme of vocational school (n = 1);
2   At tertiary level, non-university business programme with subject/discipline manual (n = 1), business administration programme of undergraduate level (n = 2) and programme of business administration and management of master's level (n = 8).

At the upper secondary (vocational) education level, the following programmes were analysed:

- *Secondary education programmes* developed for the institutions of secondary education in Lithuania (modules: My Economy, Enterprise, International Market, Computer Modelling, Economy, How to Become a Leader, Way to Success, Bank Competition and Simulation Sales on Stock Exchange, Management and Economic Simulation, Simulative Enterprise). While performing this analysis it became evident that the goals set in the programmes are related to entrepreneurship training and the implementation of economic literacy, irrespective of the learner's future career plans.
- *The Entrepreneurship programme of vocational training* that also corresponds to the purposes of entrepreneurship training in Lithuanian institutions.

At the higher education level, the following programmes were analysed:

- *Non-university study programmes.* These programmes are a new phenomenon of higher education in the new colleges being established.

- *University study programmes* (in Lithuanian and foreign universities) which confer the business administration Bachelors and management and business administration Masters degrees and are selected by geographic clusters: Europe, the USA, Asia and Pacific Rim region (Australia, New Zealand).

The full details of this research project and its methodology are indicated elsewhere (Lepaitė 2003). Here there is space only to indicate a number of the central research findings and to draw out a number of general issues requiring further discussion.

General research findings

1. There is considerable complexity in the kinds of capacities being sought for development under the description 'competences' in the various programmes of study looked at. In higher education programmes, there was a great variety in the kinds of feature accommodated within competence descriptions. Cognitive competences, particularly emphasized in the higher stages of education, include skills such as problem-solving, analysis and learning how to learn, which go far beyond mere operational capacity and are in themselves complex. The cluster of cognitive activity also often involves the skills of global thinking and acting as well as various kinds of reflection upon experience and self-reflection. The structure of the personal competence cluster often includes extended and complex capacities such as effective citizenship, undertaking responsibility, self-understanding, career development and taking risks, which clearly involve wide-ranging forms of understanding, values, attitudes and qualities of character (such as responsibility). The composition of these competence clusters defies attempts to reduce them to matters of operational activity and is clearly related to the notion of 'holistic competence' outlined earlier. In programmes at upper secondary level (vocational) it was similarly apparent that the competences developed in the same competence clusters emphasize different skills. In the cluster of instrumental competence attention is paid to general technical knowledge, quality assurance skills and the stimulation of an appropriate 'commercial attitude'. The expansive skills of reasoning and intellectual flexibility, which enter the cognitive competence cluster, are seen as central to possibilities for work improvement. Personal characteristics are important across all competence levels. The research project explored the complex and interrelated nature of these 'competences' at the level of particular courses with reference to matters of location, overlap and coherence, with respect to 'clusters' using a matrix model to identify relevant considerations (Lepaitė 2003).
2. It is clear that the kinds of competences being aimed at in the programmes studied cannot be seen as separate from each other. In the cluster of personal competence, for example, social interaction and teamwork are some-

times presented as separately developable skills, but this is scarcely coherent. This general point can be illuminated by many examples: communication skills, for example, cannot be separated from broader personal qualities.
3 In relation to a person's ability to act appropriately and effectively in a diverse and constantly changing environment, what is crucial is the possession by the person of relevant competences and not merely formal qualifications. A qualification is a formal recognition (within an examination and certification system) of a certain level of achievement. However, the acquired qualification might not necessarily indicate a person's competence.
4 In the context of modern organizations, the term broader term 'activity' rather than 'work' tends to be used, indicating that human resource development is being construed more richly than in mere functional terms.
5 The notion of 'holistic' competence is of major importance. This overall capacity is expressed, *inter alia*, in the ability to apply knowledge in varied and unpredictable situations and in different contexts and levels of action. 'Holistic' competence clearly consists of a composite range of personal qualities and capacities (see above).
6 The 'choice of appropriate actions' is an important aspect of the exercise of competence. This is part of the exercise of judgement which is central to 'competence' and which involves the integration of motives, personal characteristics and value attitudes.
7 The different kinds of competence level identified earlier tend to be developed in the following characteristic ways:
  - Development of operational behaviourist competence (Level 1) is based on behaviouristic methodology and functional content in mastery learning;
  - Development of additive competence (Level 2) is defined by more behaviouristic than cognitive design principles, and a transaction approach in curriculum implementation;
  - Development of integrative competence (Level 3) is based on more cognitive than behaviouristic design principles, and a transformation approach in curriculum implementation;
  - Development of holistic competence (Level 4) occurs when implementing design principles of cognitive and constructivist methodologies, and a transformation approach in curriculum implementation.
8 A number of general conclusions were reached with respect to the programmes of business studies. In the curriculum of business programmes in upper secondary (vocational) education programmes there is an emphasis upon the achievement of operational activity in specific fields via the development of *behaviourist competence, particularly personal behaviour competence in particular contexts*, although the development of analytical and problem-solving skills is not neglected. These programmes are complemented by programmes of general education which emphasize the develop-

ment of economic literacy and entrepreneurship. In business programmes at Bachelors and Masters level in higher education, the cluster of cognitive competence requires the development of problem-solving and analytical skills. Skills of critical thinking and synthesis are emphasized, which should help students to identify different premises, to evaluate them, to foresee different variables and thereby to achieve competences which extend beyond the routine. However, these skills tended to be rather restricted in their conception and application. There was insufficient attention to the creation of new strategies and methods, in part because programmes (especially in the USA) tended to put too much weight on quantitative forms of analysis, as if quantitative methods alone could adequately conceptualize and solve business problems. Attention is therefore needed to other forms of analysis which would help to develop the kinds of holistic competence described earlier. The research showed that certain elements of Masters degree programmes were conducive to the development of competence conceived in this holistic way. Problem solving, leadership and interpersonal skills, (involving cognitive, social interaction and teamwork competences) are integrated into management competence in these courses. The nature and complexity of organizational, international and problem-solving contexts in any programme, and the extent to which management competence was seen as integrating an appropriately broad range of competences, indicated the differences of developed competence level and scope among the programmes of different levels. In Lithuania non-university programmes tend to neglect the development of holistic competences because competence development is rather fragmented and lacks appropriate forms of integration.

Recommendations and issues for discussion

In the light of the research undertaken, the following recommendations and issues for discussion that are significant for the Lithuanian context have been identified:

1 Learners find it difficult to evaluate competences which they are trying to achieve, because there is an emphasis in the programmes upon the achievement of qualifications. In the Lithuanian context it is therefore recommended that competence levels (behaviourist, additive, integrative and holistic) in different professional fields be identified, articulated and discussed along with the contexts of learning in which these competence levels could form the basis of competence development. It should thereby be made possible for learners themselves to evaluate their competence development.

2 Questions which need to be considered by those who design programmes of competence level development include the following:

A In relation to the definition of competence levels:
  i What behaviour is being sought and how it is learnt? (As in behaviourist competence.)
  ii What variables relating to behaviour are required for given competences? (As in additive levels of competence.)
  iii How does the evaluation of variables influence the perception and implementation of needed behaviour changes? (As in integrative level of competence.)
  iv What is involved in the complex judgements and capacities involved in the highest levels of competence? (As in holistic competence.)
B In relation to the implementation of competence-based programmes, it is important to prepare descriptions of activity variations in the form of cases, in order to help learners to understand the diversity and scope of an activity, to enable them to identify central aspects of variations so that they can be appropriately recognized and responded to in future and to prepare appropriate training materials.
3 As the realization of personal potential is of individual value in competence development and may be treated as human resource development in the regional context, the KDE provides opportunities to employ competence for regional development. Competence transferability remains the main feature relevant to this situation. From the educational point of view, the programmes and curriculum have to be designed to enable the learners to foresee the potential of their competence development.

Notes

1 Report of the Symposium 'Secondary Education in Europe' (Key Competences for Europe 1997) distinguished the following competences: 1. Political and social competence defined by the skill to undertake responsibility; 2. Competences related to the skill of living in a multicultural society; 3. Skills of oral and written language; 4. Information skills; 5. Longlife learning skills for personal, professional and social improvement.
2 For example, contemporary trends in vocational training considered in relation to contemporary changes in global markets and organizations are analysed in terms of modern philosophical conceptions of vocational training by Pring (1995), White (1997), Avis (1996), Gleeson (1996) and Hyland (1997); in terms of vocational training policy by Esland (1996a, 1996b), Gleeson and Hodkinson (1995), Hodkinson (1996) and Pring (1995); in terms of policy implementation by Raffe (1994) and Neber (1994); in terms of trends of the design of programme development which stress competence development by Heidegger (1999) and Laur-Ernst (1999) in Germany, Brown (1998) in England, Ellstrom (1998, 1999) in Sweden, Resnick and Wirt (1996) and Tucker (1996) in the USA, and Nijhof (1999), Nijhof and Streumer (1998) in the Netherlands; and in terms of future directions for research into vocational training by Achtenhagen (1994, 1998).
3 Maassen (1997) analyses the quality of European higher education in relation to contemporary trends and historical perspectives. The basic principles relating to educational innovations in higher vocational education are highlighted by Van Meel and

De Wolf (1994). The development of colleges as postsecondary education institutions in America is analysed by Boyer (1987).

4 On the relationship between qualifications and competence see, for example, Otter (1992), Spencer and Spencer (1993), Sandberg (1994), Velde and Svenson (1996) and Achtenhagen (1994). For Lithuanian discussions see Jovaiša (1993), Laužackas (1997, 1999), Bitinas (2000), Jucevičienė and Lepaitė (2000).

5 The author, while developing the research design, suggested 'overlapping competences' as a working definition.

References

Achtenhagen, F. (1994) 'How should research on vocational and professional education react to new challenges in life and in the workplace?', in W.J. Nijhof and J.N. Streumer (eds) *Flexibility in Training and Vocational Education*, Utrecht: Uitgeverij Lemma.

—— (1998) 'General versus vocational education – demarcation and integration', in W.J. Nijhof and J.N. Streumer (eds) *Key Qualifications in Work and Education*, Dordrecht: Kluwer Academic Publishers.

Avis, J. (1996) 'The myth of the post-fordist society', in W. Hutton (ed.) *Knowledge and Nationalhood: education, politics and work*, London: Cassell.

Barnett, R. (1992) *Improving Higher Education: Total Quality Care*, London: SRHE & Open University Press.

—— (1993) *The Limits of Competence*, London: SRHE & Open University Press.

Bitinas, B. (2000) *Ugdymo filosofija*, Vilnius: Enciklopedija.

Boyer, L.E. (1987) *College: the Undergraduate Experience in America*, New York: Harper & Row, Publishers.

Brown, A. (1998) 'Designing effective learning programs for the developments of a broad occupational competence', in W.J. Nijhof and J.N. Streumer (eds) *Key Qualifications in Work and Education*, Dordrecht: Kluwer Academic Publishers.

Dahrendorf, R. (1982) *On Britain*, London: British Broadcasting Corporation.

Ellstrom, P. (1998) 'The meaning of occupational competence and qualification', in W.J. Nijhof and J.N. Streumer (eds) *Key Qualifications in Work and Education*, Dordrecht: Kluwer Academic Publishers.

—— (1999) 'The role of labour market programmes in skill formation: the case of Sweden', in W.J. Nijhof and J. Brandsma (eds) *Bridging the Skills Gap Between Work and Education*, Dordrecht: Kluwer Academic Publishers.

Esland, G. (1996a) 'Knowledge and nationhood: the new right, education and the global market', in W. Hutton (ed.) *Knowledge and Nationalhood: Education, Politics and Work*, London: Cassell.

—— (1996b) 'Education, training and nation-state capitalism: Britain's failing strategy', in W. Hutton (ed.) *Knowledge and Nationalhood: Education, Politics and Work*, London: Cassell.

Gleeson, D. (1996) 'Post-compulsory education in a post-industrial and post-modern age', in W. Hutton (ed.) *Knowledge and Nationalhood: Education, Politics and Work*, London: Cassell.

Gleeson, D. and Hodkinson, P. (1995) 'Ideology and curriculum policy: GNVQ and mass post-compulsory education in England and Wales', *British Journal of Education and Work*, 8, 5–19.

Heidegger, G. (1999) 'Scenarios of work, technology and education for the post-2000 period', in W.J. Nijhof and J. Brandsma (eds) *Bridging the Skills Gap Between Work and Education*, Dordrecht: Kluwer Academic Publishers.

Hodkinson, P. (1996) 'Careership: the individual, choices and markets in the transition into work', in W. Hutton (ed.) *Knowledge and Nationalhood: Education, Politics and Work*, London: Cassell.

Hyland, T. (1997) 'Silk purses and sows' ears: NVQs, GNVQs and experiential learning', *Cambridge Journal of Education*, 24, 233–43.

Jovaiša, L. (1993) *Pedagogikos terminai*, Kaunas: Šviesa.

Jucevičienė, P. (1997) 'New approaches to the development of Lithuanian higher education in the context of system developments in the Western World', in C. Wulf (ed.) *European Studies in Education: Education for the 21st Century*, vol. 7, New York: WAXMANN.

—— (1999a) 'Lietuvos aukštojo mokslo reformos galimas posūkis: edukologinis vertinimas' ['A possible turn of the Lithuanian higher education reform: the educational perspective'], *Proceedings of the Conference 'Lithuanian Science and Industry: Facing Technologies of 21st Century'*, Kaunas: Technologija.

—— (1999b) 'Universitetinės studijos profesinio rengimo koncepcijos kontekste' ['University studies in the context of the concept of vocational training'], *Proceedings of the Conference 'Higher Education Systems and Didactics'*, Kaunas: Technologija.

Jucevičienė, P. and Lepaitė, D. (2000) 'Kompetencijos sampratos erdvė' ['The scope of the concept of *competence*'], *Socialiniai mokslai*, 2, 44–50.

Key competencies for Europe (1997), Report of the symposium 'A Secondary Education for Europe', Strasbourg: Council for Cultural Cooperation.

Laur-Ernst, U. (1999) 'Integrated learning of complex qualifications', in W.J. Nijhof and J. Brandsma (eds) *Bridging the Skills Gap Between Work and Education*, Dordrecht: Kluwer Academic Publishers.

Laužackas, R. (1997) *Profesinio ugdymo turinio reforma: didaktiniai bruožai*, Kaunas: Leidybos centras.

—— (1999) *Sistemo-teorinės profesinio rengimo kaitos dimensijos*, Kaunas: Vytauto Didžiojo universiteto leidykla.

—— (2000) *Mokymo turinio projektavimas: standartai ir programos profesiniame rengime*, Kaunas: Vytauto Didžiojo universiteto leidykla.

Lepaitė, D. (2003) *Kompetencijų plėtojančių studijų programų lygio nustatymo metodologija*, Kaunas: Technologija.

Maassen, P. (1997) 'Quality in European higher education: recent trends and their historical roots', *European Journal of Education*, 32 (2), 111–27.

Neber, H. (1994) 'Knowledge utilization: promotion through training in situated access', in W.J. Nijhof and J.N. Streumer (eds) *Flexibility in Training and Vocational Education*, Utrecht: Uitgeverij Lemma.

Nijhof, W.J. (1999) 'Inserting transferable skills into the vocational curriculum', in W.J. Nijhof and J. Brandsma (eds) *Bridging the Skills Gap Between Work and Education*, Dordrecht: Kluwer Academic Publishers.

Nijhof, W.J. and Streumer, J.N. (eds) (1998) *Key Qualifications in Work and Education*, Dordrecht: Kluwer Academic Publishers.

Otter, S. (1992) *Competence or Competencies? Holism or vocationalism in higher education?*, vol. 1.3, The New Academic.

Pring, R.A. (1995) *Closing the Gap: Liberal Education and Vocational Preparation*, London: Hodder & Stoughton.

Raffe, D. (1994) 'The new flexibility in vocational education', in W.J. Nijhof and J.N. Streumer (eds) *Flexibility in Training and Vocational Education*, Utrecht: Uitgeverij Lemma.
Resnick, L. and Wirt, G. (eds) (1996) *Linking School and Work: Roles for Standards and Assessment*, San Francisco: Jossey-Bass Publishers.
Rothwell, W.J. (1996) *ASTD Models for Human Performance Improvement: Roles, Competencies, and Outputs*, American Society for Training and Development Publishers.
Rothwell, W.J. and Kazanas, H.C. (1994) *Human Resource Development: a Strategic Approach*, Massachusetts: HRD Press Inc.
Sandberg, J. (1994) *Human Competence at Work – an Interpretative Approach*, Gotenberg: Bass.
Scott, P. (1993) *The Meanings of Mass Higher Education*, London: SRHE & Open University Press.
—— (1997) 'The crisis of knowledge and the massification of higher education', in R. Barnett and A. Griffin (eds) *The End of Knowledge in Higher Education*, London: Cassell.
Šernas, V. (1995) *Profesinė pedagogika*, Vilnius: Leidybos centras.
—— (1998) *Profesinės veiklos didaktika*, Vilnius: Presvika.
Spencer, L.M. and Spencer, S.M. (1993) *Competence at Work*, New York: John Wiley & Sons, Inc.
Teichler, U. (1988) *Changing Patterns of the Higher Education: the Experience of Three Decades*, Jessica Kingsley Publishers.
Tucker, M.S. (1996) 'Skills, standards, qualifications system, and the American workforce', in L. Resnick and G. Wirt (eds) *Linking School and Work: Roles for Standards and Assessment*, San Francisco: Jossey-Bass Publishers.
Van Meel, R. and de Wolf, H. (1994) 'Major issues for educational innovation in higher vocational education in the Netherlands', *European Journal of Education*, 29 (2), 135–45.
Velde, C. and Svensson, L. 'The conception of competence in relation to learning processes and change at work', paper presented at the 4th Conference on Learning and Research in Working Life, Steyr, Austria, 1996.
Von Krogh, G. and Roos, J. (1996) 'Arguments on knowledge and competence', in G. von Krogh and J. Roos (eds) *Managing Knowledge: Perspectives on Cooperation and Competition*, New York: SAGE Publications.
White, J. (1997) *Education and the End of Work: a New Philosophy for Work and Learning*, London: Cassell.
Zavadskas, E.K. (1999) *Išmintis neateina savaime*, Vilnius: Technika.
—— (2000) *Pasirinkome teisingą kelią*, Vilnius: Technika.

Chapter 13

Concepts of a service university

Arild Tjeldvoll and Auksė Blažėnaitė

The object of our investigation in this chapter, the concept of the service university, has been the subject of considerable international discussion (see, for example, Cummings 1995, 1998, Tudiver 1999, Tjeldvoll 2000). While the service university is not a new phenomenon (Roszak was already attacking the idea in his 1968 essay on 'The delinquent academy'), it has received fresh attention in the context of the expansion of higher education across the world, the demand for universities to generate funding from sources other than government grant, and policies aimed at extracting economic benefit from the research, teaching and 'intellectual property' locked in higher education institutions. Under new liberal economic policies, higher education institutions have been placed under market requirements in which their 'offer' to society is expected to be demand- rather than supply-driven and their relationship to their 'customers' (formerly known as students) based on a service culture.

'Societies in transition' are in transition towards, among other things, exactly this sort of liberal economy, and hence their universities are being pushed in the direction of this same service culture. The present chapter expands on the factors which have been recently influencing the development of higher education institutions towards the service model and then distinguishes some different versions of this model in the form of: the Enterprise University, the Corporate University and the Entrepreneurial University. Finally, it considers which of these models might most suitably be developed in the context of 'societies in transition'.

Challenges for university development

For hundreds of years, the university has served as a custodian and conveyor of knowledge, wisdom and values. Following the tradition of Alexander von Humboldt, the university has been regarded as a space for uncompromising freedom of opinion and expression, and as a site which nurtures critical discourse. With their universal outlook in probing and searching, universities are supposed to maintain an atmosphere and level of intellectual ferment and questioning hardly seen in other institutions (Mauch 2000: 25–44). Recently, a major dilemma for the university has emerged: it must be both sufficiently stable to sustain the ideals of academic freedom and institutional autonomy, and sufficiently responsive to remain relevant to the society which supports it, particularly in relation to societal needs which require illumination by the creation and supply of knowledge. Responsiveness to society requires on the part of the university the development of a dynamic environment which is capable of responding to market demands. However, in spite of the fact that the conventional notions of university service derive from the well-established American land-grant experience, universities still tend not to be the most entrepreneurial institutions.

In the developed countries as well as in 'societies in transition', a number of global factors have emerged which pose a significant question mark against the ability of universities to respond coherently in terms of their existing processes, norms and traditions to the demands which have been described (Davies 2001: 27). These demands are related to factors such as the salience of market forces, industrial and technological development, new modes of creating scientific knowledge, the impact of lifelong learning, and the need for new role models for students and academics. The market has been 'colonizing' societies, especially those in transition, as well as institutions. Liberal market ideology has been having quite drastic effects on the university throughout the world. The State in many contexts has reduced its financial support to universities, and universities therefore turn to the market to find new ways of strengthening their budgets and feel pressured into accepting external assignments that bring in extra funds. An increasing number of researchers (Tudiver 1999, Slaughter and Leslie 1997, Currie and Newson 1998, Barnett 1994, Etzkowitz and Leydersdorff 1997, Ruch 2001, Bok 2003) agree that the service-oriented university tends to embody a business model. Having introduced elements of market competition with the objective of increasing institutional efficiency, the traditional research university is becoming more and more commercialized and entrepreneurial. The entrepreneurially minded university, trying to survive in the competitive market, struggles for students, for faculty members, for revenues and for academic prestige. In this context, learning and research come 'to be valued in terms of their ability to be translated into cash or merchandise' (Shumar 1997: 5), and society's need for studies with a distinct practical dimension leads to a priority being given to 'professional studies'. However, when the market-oriented university finds its niche in the system, it is natural to fear that the intensifying market forces with their calls for enhanced productivity, as part of an emerging knowledge-driven economy, are about to sweep aside fundamental academic values and traditions and replace them with the demands of the marketplace.

The worlds of global economic, political and technological interdependence, innovation and competitiveness, newly experienced by 'countries in transition', have become fundamental realities impinging upon the vitality of the contemporary university. Since the industrial development of society has been increasingly dependent upon knowledge, and education has become one of the major economic resources, contemporary universities have been asked to direct their efforts towards programmes and initiatives that may gain some technological advantage for society. Moreover, continuing pressure on market-minded universities from governments and the industrial sector to develop applied research and make available education in forms of delivery congenial to companies and public sector organizations (Gibbons 1998) has become commonplace. It is very likely, however, that these processes and forces are in tension with the traditional essence of the university, the academic ethos of free discussion and exchange of ideas and experimental results (Soares and Amaral 1999: 12).

The perception of the kinds of knowledge with which a university is properly concerned has been changing (Cowen 1996). As other contributors to this volume have emphasized, a new form of knowledge production – Mode 2 – has emerged (Kvil 1998). The demands of Mode 2 knowledge production place considerable demands on the university, especially the service university. A number of considerations have led to the emergence of the service university, in addition to those mentioned above, including an increasing emphasis upon lifelong learning and mass higher education.

The presence of more mature and more diversified clientele, with experience and attitudes very different from those of standard higher education students, have brought about major changes in teacher–student relationships, in the 'content' proposed for study, in teaching methodologies, and in the organization of disciplines and of the institutions themselves (Price 1989: 61). Service-oriented universities have been faced with the question of the relevance of their study programmes to their students. Such universities have begun to respond to the new demands with the introduction of in-service courses and new part-time taught Masters courses, many of which are vocational in their nature (Jarvis 2000: 53).

Students are no longer simply 'consumers' of knowledge as in the past. As a result of mass higher education, the socio-cultural background and motivation of the students has changed dramatically. Some students have only an instrumental attitude to study and do not have much ability to learn independently. For these and other reasons the academic standards of universities are under threat. Professors constitute another important segment undergoing critical change at the service university. On the one hand, the shift in their relationship to people and institutions inside and outside the university has become a most dramatic source of discontent, since, under pressure from the state and the market to become more managerial and more entrepreneurial, universities are looking for management tools which may seem to supplant academia. Within the institution, where strong academic staff used to have the main power in decision making, a new group is about to take over. The administration expands at the expense of the professors. It increases dramatically both in size and amount of resources, and it starts operating the university mainly from an administrative point of view, which seriously undermines the value of the academic experience and scientific competence that holds higher education together. On the other hand, in the light of towering entrepreneurism, the faculty is becoming largely contracted 'knowledge workers', or producers of 'useful knowledge'. Research at UK universities (Hay *et al.* 2002) suggests that academics today are perhaps more entrepreneurial than might be first expected: they are creative, favour achievement and require autonomy. Research confirms that institutions of higher education in 'countries in transition', such as Lithuania, have been successfully developing significant capabilities in fields of activity rather different from conventional or traditional mainstream academic research and education (American Institute 2004).

The service university: conceptual foundations

How can the university, an institution accustomed to slow decision making and a long maturation process resulting from lengthy discussions and the formation of consensus amongst peers and their units – faculties, departments, or even disciplines (Soares 1999: 13), operate effectively, when it encounters the entrepreneurially oriented milieu?

Against the background of the established trend towards entrepreneurialism in contemporary higher education, it is useful to review several existing service oriented university concepts and to suggest a particular model of the service university – which we shall call the Critical Service University – as the most appropriate and defensible model, drawing its major characteristics from other related conceptions of the university such as the seminal Service University model, the Enterprise University, the Corporate University and the Entrepreneurial University.

The seminal Service University

More than a decade ago, research was carried out to identify and describe the newly emerging notion of the service university (Cummings 1995, Tjeldvoll 2000). However, the 'seminal' Service University appears too narrow and tenuous from a contemporary perspective (Cummings 1995). This concept is designed to be competitive with other higher education institutions in meeting the needs expressed by private business and public bureaucrats, and is characterized by professional schools, client-tailored training programmes, professionally oriented short-term courses demanded by business clients and professional studies required by the state, and applied research which is responsive to the information needs of the public and private market. However, it is characteristic of the 'seminal' model of the Service University that its work is carried out without an appropriately critical dimension. For example, it tends not to make use of the critical perspectives supplied by philosophers, sociologists or critical political scientists and economists, and many of its staff are temporary employees with no tenured positions. The control and management of the academic labour force, and central planning for contracting of service, is inattentive to central values of the university (Cummings 1995). The Service University on this model resembles a higher education 'supermarket'.

The Enterprise University

Findings of research carried out at Australian universities suggest the emergence of another new institutional type, the Enterprise University (Marginson and Considine 2000). The 'enterprise' model captures both economic and academic dimensions; nevertheless, for many in higher education the concept of 'Enterprise' provokes 'an image of shady villainy, a fifth column gnawing away at the basic values that define a university, a wolf masquerading as a milk-cow' (McNay 2002: 20).

The Enterprise University dwells between the public academic institutions and the private companies (Marginson and Considine 2000). Its purpose is defined by forms of strong executive control, and the university mission takes a distinctly corporate character, and the strengthening of the university's steering core takes place at the expense of the dynamism of academic cultures.

In its pure form the goal of the Enterprise University is not the fulfilment of a range of social, economic and cultural purposes, but serving its own corporate self as an end in itself (Marginson and Considine 2000: 243).

The university welcomes outside funding; under-funding drives a 'pseudo-market' in fee incomes, soft budget allocations for special purposes and contested earnings for new enrolments and research grants.

In respect of academic work, departments and disciplines contest with institutes, research centres and other entities. The academic core of the university is often side-stepped (Marginson and Considine 2000), and academic disciplines are often seen as an obstacle. In general, research (mostly applied and commercial) and scholarship survive, but are now subjected to the systems of competition and demonstrable performance. Definitions of quality and lines of accountability are drawn less from traditional public-sector and political cultures, and more from the private sector and the culture of economic consumption, whether expressed through university–student relations, university–industry relations, or university–government relations.

Thus, the Enterprise University joins a mixed public–private economy to a quasi-business culture and to academic traditions. However, the institution often works around or against academic cultures rather than through them. Moreover, a preoccupation with external relations basically ruins its internal community and eventually drives the university towards losing its identity.

The Corporate University

The Corporate University is a model successfully operating in the higher education market. According to OECD, there are over 1,600 such institutions functioning in the world (Salmi 2001), most of them competing with traditional universities, especially in the area of continuing education, and serving both smaller companies and corporate giants. At the classroom level, the Corporate University looks and behaves like a traditional university, but as one looks further up the organizational hierarchy, it appears to be more like a business and less like an academic institution.

Different from the Enterprise University, the Corporate University works under one of any combination of the following three modalities: with its own network of physical campuses, as a virtual university, or through an alliance with existing higher education institutions.

Among characteristics of such universities are the blending of business management with academic pursuits, the shift in the balance of power toward students and away from faculty, and the absence of tenure. Research and scholarly productivity are excluded or at least significantly downplayed at the Enterprise University. Basic research and scholarship is excluded (Ruch 2001).

A successful Corporate University operates with a yearly budget of hundreds of millions of dollars, manages numerous learning and training sites all over the world, and employs thousands of professionals, who are now able to consider a new set of career options (Ruch 2001).

Only some Corporate Universities have been officially accredited and can grant formal degrees in programmes at the associate, baccalaureate, Masters and doctoral level. At the Corporate University, more than at any other kind of market-oriented university, the teaching of critical thinking and free inquiry is neglected.

It is evident that the voices of academics are muted in relation to the voices of executives and business people in such universities. Therefore, it should be seriously doubted not only whether the Corporate University is able to contribute to the advancement of knowledge, but also whether it even attempts to achieve this and to instil academic values and grant academic freedom.

The Entrepreneurial University

In order to illuminate the features of the critical Service University, the model of the service university which we favour, it is appropriate to look at the concept of the Entrepreneurial University (Clark 1998), which is the most widely developed conception of a market-oriented institution of higher education. The experiences of European universities have revealed that, in crisis, the university is able to change its organization and its relations to its surroundings in a successful way; it can safeguard its economy and, at the same time, show excellence as a research institution. The necessary measures or 'pathways' to be taken by an entrepreneurially minded university when the state as patron becomes less prominent, basically constitutes the backbone for this new mode of the university.

A strengthened steering core and the quality and capacity of the central leadership, form the background for the Entrepreneurial University that wishes to survive in the new national and international context. It is important that the top leadership have high academic standing, preferably acknowledged internationally. The academic quality is crucial in order both to understand the mission and idea of a university, and to create authority and legitimacy amongst colleagues in knowledge production. Equally important is the executive or management competence and capacity of the university.

The second characteristic of a successful university according to this model is the establishment of units for external activities at the local level. These are professionalized outreach offices working on knowledge transfer, industrial contact, intellectual property development, continuing education, fundraising, or even alumni affairs (Clark 1998). The units are closely attached to academic departments. The purpose of these units is to engage in applied and commissioned research and provide other services required by external users in the local, regional, national or international surroundings.

A discretionary funding base is a major requirement for the Entrepreneurial University. Taking a more direct responsibility for its budget and competing for new projects and funding, the university acquires flexibility in economic terms, constructing a widening and deepening portfolio of income from research councils as well as campus services, student fees and alumni fundraising. Having investment money ready may be decisive for competitive success. Even though state funding is decreasing, this source is still important, not least for those activities at the university that do not have a particular market value. Thus, the university ought to become more effective in negotiating with the state, as well as achieving 'competition competence' in relation to funds from public and private programmes for research, nationally and internationally.

On this model, traditional academic values firmly rooted in academic departments (an 'academic heartland') is seen as critical. For a university to really become entrepreneurial, it is nevertheless crucial to motivate professors to be innovative and supportive of the entrepreneurial idea without sacrificing their academic integrity. They must be involved in revenue-generating external activities, seeing them as positive for their academic work as well as an opportunity to improve their salaries.

The further feature of an entrepreneurial university is the challenge to establish a new 'entrepreneurial culture' whilst preserving traditional values. This should take the form of a 'trademark' which will create feelings of belonging among all members of the institution, and create an identity among both students and staff.

Which of the modes of the market-orientated university is likely to dominate higher education in the 'countries in transition'? What dangers should be acknowledged in such societies in relation to the service-oriented university? Since market forces are likely to claim sovereignty over higher education (Aronowitz 2000: 194), preserving institutional autonomy, safeguarding academic prestige, academic intelligence, and upholding university values as well as academic freedom might have crucial implications for the future of a 'country in transition'.

The seminal Service University, the Enterprise and the Corporate universities might serve as effective agents in the competitive market, where educators have to respond quickly to changing knowledge, to the introduction of new technologies, and to training for new jobs. But even a flexible entrepreneurially oriented university – with a strengthened steering core, able to think strategically and to put into effect the necessary changes, possessing the expanded developmental periphery and a diversified funding base – might be inferior to the existing modern research university if it is devoid of a sufficiently robust academic heartland and academic research.

The critical Service University

How important for the university is retaining its academic heartland? Can academic freedom survive in an institution of higher education which is predominantly financed by producing services to meet economic criteria? What kind of an entrepreneurial higher education institution would be able to preserve fundamental university values and characteristics such as intellectual integrity, critical inquiry, and commitment to learning and understanding appropriately conceived? What should be the balance between the drive for profits and academic prestige?

Research suggests that successful market-oriented and entrepreneurially minded universities are those which join three elements together:

- an entrepreneurial capacity to create and exploit income-earning opportunities;
- organizational coherence, bringing with it a capacity to focus performance;
- strong academic cultures (Marginson and Considine 2000).

Then, as Clark (1996: 52–61) pointed out, a university that pursues innovation has to possess the following: an ambitious idea, a change-oriented and integrated administrative core, a funding base which enables new orientations and programmes, a developmental periphery, a developing entrepreneurial culture and appropriate forms of autonomy (Clark 2001: 20). A critical Service University is the model which best encapsulates these features.

In an ideal scenario, the critical Service University has acknowledged the new ideological and financial realities which have been outlined, particularly the fact that the state is no longer able to provide as much financial support as it has in the past. The university has therefore succeeded in finding other funding sources and has been able to maintain the best possible relations with the state as an ongoing important client. It has also successfully competed for the research programmes offered by foundations and has been able to identify niches in the market for its research and education products. By its own initiatives, the university has achieved financial independence. The university is able to produce competitive revenue-generating services for public and private clients, resulting in a budget that makes it possible to sustain independent research and educational policies and programmes. Above all, however, the critical Service University uses its budget to keep up with international academic standards. Teaching programmes in the arts and sciences are maintained, and its researchers are free to carry out critical research on the state bureaucracy and corporate life. Professors' salaries are decent and competitive, signalling a continued high social status for research and higher education. The critical Service University has been able to strike a balance between individual academic freedom, institutional autonomy and accountability toward taxpayers and business. At the same time as it is serving these clients, it is creating the financial independence which enables it to carry out its traditional critical function in a democratic society.

The Service University in 'countries in transition'?

Researchers point out major hazards confronting 'societies in transition'. There is a danger that such societies may build a model of the Service University of an impoverished kind, and end up with all their higher education being driven merely by business values. Could we envisage the scenario of a critical Service University for a country creating an innovative university and trying to extract greater economic benefit from the activities generated by higher education institutions, whilst at the same time preserving the traditional aims and values of the university?

Even this optimistic model should be carefully scrutinized and a number of questions clarified. Given the need for institutions to be flexible, is there a danger that a concern for client priorities is likely to result in an orientation towards short-term market needs, instead of dealing with the issues which relate more directly to academic study in its various aspects? It is also vital to inquire if, having adopted a new model, the university is still able to perform its classical mission, of developing theoretical knowledge, carrying out fundamental research, and pursuing its critical function in a democratic society. As Duke (1992: 64) inquires, how much diversity of values, purposes and activities can the university tolerate? Could it be suggested instead that only dedication to the fundamental traditional understanding of the university mission might prevent it from becoming merely a profit-making centre which sells auxiliary activities and commodities in the market? With the development of the entrepreneurial culture at the university, what happens to core academic values? These are the questions to be answered by young democratic societies. Clearly, the role of higher education in social and economic development, and the specific role of the Service University in this development stands in need of further critical evaluation. The critical service university model, as we have characterized it, is a promising candidate for negotiating the tensions we have identified, but that promise needs to be tested by detailed investigation and research.

References

American Institute (2004) 'University to business: serving the market', project report, Kaunas: The American Institute.

Aronowitz, S. (2000) *The Knowledge Factory: Dismantling the Corporate University and Creating True Higher Learning*, Boston: Beacon Press.

Barnett, R. (1994) *The Idea of Higher Education*, Buckingham: The Society for Research into Higher Education and Open University Press.

Bok, D. (2003) *Universities in the Marketplace: the Commercialization of Higher Education*, Princeton and Oxford: Princeton University Press.

Clark, B.R. (1996) 'Case studies of innovative universities: a progress report', *Tertiary Education and Management*, 2 (1), 52–61.

—— (1998) *Creating Entrepreneurial Universities: Organizational Pathways of Transformation*, Oxford: Pergamon Press.

—— (2001) 'The Entrepreneurial University: new foundations for collegiality, autonomy, and achievement', in M. Shattock (ed.) *Higher Education Management. Education and Skills*, 13 (2), 9–24.

Cowen, R. (1996) 'Last past the post: comparative education, modernity and perhaps post-modernity', *Comparative Education*, 32, 151–70.

Cummings, W.K. 'The Service University', paper presented at the Annual Conference of Comparative and International Education Society (CIES), Boston, March 1995.

—— (1998) 'The Service University in comparative perspective', special issue of *Higher Education*, Amsterdam: Kluwer Academic Publishers.

Currie, J. and Newson, J. (1998) *Universities and Globalization: Critical Perspectives*, Thousand Oaks, London, New Delhi: SAGE Publications.

Davies, J.L. (2001). 'The emergence of entrepreneurial cultures in European universities', *Higher Education Management*, 13 (2), 25–43.

Duke, C. (1992) *The Learning University: Towards a New Paradigm?*, Buckingham: Open University Press.

Etzkowitz, H. and Leydersdorff, L. (eds) (1997) *Universities and the Global Knowledge Economy: a Triple Helix of University–Industry–Government Relations*, London and Washington: Pinter.

Gibbons, M. (1998) *Higher Education Relevance in the 21st Century*, Washington: World Bank.

Hay, D.B., Butt, F. and Kirby, D.A. (2002) 'Academics as entrepreneurs in a UK university', in G. Williams (ed.) *The Enterprising University: Reform, Excellence and Equity*, Buckingham: The Society for Research into Higher Education and Open University Press.

Jarvis, P. (2000) 'The changing university: meeting a need and needing to change', *Higher Education Quarterly*, 54 (1), 43–67.

Kvil, T. 'Governance in higher education. Some aspects of the systems in Norway and France', paper presented at the Annual Oslo Seminar of The Nordic Network of International and Comparative Education (NICE) Conference, Oslo, November 1998.

McNay, I. (2002) 'The e-factors and organization cultures in British universities', in G. Williams (ed.) *The Enterprising University: Reform, Excellence and Equity*, Buckingham: The Society for Research into Higher Education and Open University Press.

Marginson, S. and Considine, M. (2000) *The Enterprise University: power, governance, and reinvention in Australia*, Cambridge: Cambridge University Press.

Mauch, J.E. (2000) 'The impact of higher education on emerging markets', in M. McMullen, J.E. Mauch and B. Donnorummo (eds) *The Emerging Markets and Higher Education*, New York and London: RoutledgeFalmer.

Price, C. (1989) 'Academics and society: freedom's seamless robe', in C. Ball and H. Eggins (eds) *Higher Education into the 1990's: New Dimensions*, Milton Keynes: Open University Press.

Ruch, R.S. (2001) *Higher Ed, Inc.: the Rise of the For-profit University*, Baltimore and London: The Johns Hopkins University Press.

Salmi, J. (2001) 'Tertiary education in the 21st century: challenges and opportunities', in M. Shattock (ed.) *Higher Education Management. Education and Skills*, 13 (2), 108–28.

Shumar, W. (1997) *College for Sale: a Critique of the Commodification of Higher Education (Knowledge, Identity and School Life, volume 3)*, New York and London: RoutledgeFalmer.

Slaughter, S. and Leslie, L.L. (1997) *Academic Capitalism: Politics, Policies, and the Entrepreneurial University*, Baltimore and London: The Johns Hopkins University Press.

Soares, V.A.M. and Amaral, A.M.C. (1999) 'The Entrepreneurial University: a fine answer to a difficult problem?', *Higher Education in Europe*, 24 (1), 11–21.

Tjeldvoll, A. (2000) 'Preparing Service University research', *Studies in Comparative and International Education*, 5, 7–89.

Tudiver, N. (1999) *Universities for Sale: Resisting Corporate Control over Canadian Higher Education*, Toronto: James Lorimer and Company Ltd., Publishers.

Part V

Universities and social, civic and ethical demands

Chapter 14

Higher education as an agent of social innovation

Brigita Janiūnaitė and Dalija Gudaitytė

Lithuania, along with many societies throughout the world, has been experiencing the phenomenon of social transformation. Social transformations involve complex interrelated political, economic, technological and cultural developments which have a profound impact on the social domain itself and on the lives of people (Melnikas *et al.* 2000). The process of social transformation involves innovations of many different kinds which embody in varying ways and to various extents a vision of the goals implicit in the improvements aimed at. Social innovations relate to many aspects of the ways in which people lead their lives in society and to the norms and values which underpin these lives. Social innovations, which have an impact on the structure of society as well as on the lives of individuals, are a necessary complement to changes in the economic and technological spheres (Melnikas *et al.* 2000), not least because they can empower individuals for adaptation in the context of perpetual change. (On the significance of social and cultural factors in the 'transformation environment' see the chapter by G. Jucevičius in this volume and for a related discussion on community development see the chapter by Leliūgienė and Baršauskienė.)

According to Doppler and Lautenburg (1994), the success of innovation implementation is to a large extent influenced by the following psychological and cultural factors at the level of individuals: a general readiness for change, a sense of embraced personal responsibility and participation in a prevailing culture of confidence. Such 'soft' factors of innovation often have a determining influence upon final results. These preconditions at the individual level for successful innovation have a particular significance in the so-called 'countries in transition'. This is because these countries have experienced a double pressure: on the one hand, they have undergone the radical changes related to the transition from a totalitarian to a democratic society, and on the other hand, they have been subject to equally powerful changes arising from general forces such as the proliferation of information and communication technologies and the phenomenon of globalization. However, social innovations are not only necessary if economic and technological innovations are to be 'successful'. These social innovations are also necessary if the norms and values implicit in the goals of economic and technological innovations are to be properly evaluated: the criteria for a 'successful' innovation should not be simply taken for granted.

Attention is needed to the preconditions of appropriate and successful innovation relating to the various agents through which innovation is realized (individuals, institutions, systems, etc.). This chapter focuses on higher education and explores the role which it can and should play in relation to social innovations and the extent to which it can itself function as an agent of innovation (Scott 1998, Gibbons 1998).

Higher education is an appropriate focus for attention in relation to this matter because the role of higher education as an agent of innovation features as an ingredient in the prominent contemporary debate about the changing mission of higher education at the turn of the present century. In this debate, a central theme is the appropriate balance to be struck between, on the one hand, the traditional orientation of higher education towards liberal education and the academic (with its implications for conceptions of 'quality' and for criteria for student admission) and, on the other hand, the orientation of higher education towards the wider needs of society (with its implications for a broader view of what higher education should be seeking to achieve and for promoting access to it as part of the development of 'mass higher education'). The Communication from the European Commission 'The Role of the Universities in the Europe of Knowledge' (2003) points out that the knowledge society depends for its growth on the production of new knowledge, its transmission through education and training, its dissemination through information and communication technologies, and on its use through new industrial processes or services. Universities are unique in that they take part in all these processes and can in various ways make a significant contribution to these goals. The Communication raises a number of key questions about how universities can better make a contribution of this kind.

However, it is important not to take an uncritical approach to the claim that universities do indeed have a contribution to make to these developments or that this contribution is an obvious one. More specifically, it is important to ask critical questions about whether universities should act as agents of social innovation, and, if so, in what way? This chapter addresses these questions, with particular reference to 'countries in transition' in general and to Lithuania in particular.

The chapter has four sections, relating to the context of societal transformation in the Baltic region, the role of agents in social innovation, conceptions of higher education and the role of higher education as an agent of innovation respectively.

Context of societal transformation in the Baltic countries

All conceptions of education, including higher education, are related to, and need to be understood in the light of, particular cultural, social and other conditions which require analysis, not least in historical perspective (Bowsma 1990). The ideal of higher education is, at least to a significant extent, mutable and context specific. Therefore, a discussion on higher education as an agent of social innovation in 'countries in transition' such as those in the Baltic region requires some consideration of the transformation processes which these counties have experienced. Lithuania, in common with other 'societies in transition', was forced to live in a rather closed way during the Soviet era, isolated from the centre of European culture and its evolution. Today these societies have entered the free and democratic world, and have to adjust to the expectations and requirements of that world in their various aspects. A number of important questions arise concerning the nature of the changes which these societies confront, the contradictions which the changes embody and the extent to which the changes are global or local in character. In addressing these questions we shall be referring in particular to Lithuania. The social changes happening in Lithuania in the post-Soviet era involve two stages: revolutionary and evolutionary. Both of these stages have been influenced by processes which originated and took shape outside the geographical and socio-cultural boundaries of the country.

The distinguishing feature of the first, revolutionary, stage (roughly from 1988 to 1992) is the articulation of new political, economic, cultural and social attitudes, the emergence of new contexts of public discussion and the conferring of legitimacy on new ways of thinking and acting. At this stage political, cultural and legitimacy structures (the background of the civic and political community and the framework of the state institutions) were changing more rapidly than economic and social ones.

The distinguishing feature of the second, evolutionary, stage (roughly since 1992) is an institutionalization of the various articulations of the revolutionary stage and their practical realization in part through their transformation into the norms of social life. At this stage economic and social structures have been changing rapidly and new interacting strata in society have become apparent. The norms, forms and institutions of public, political and economic life have become strong.

Both stages of development reflect developments in the West: the development of the service sector and the decline of industry, an increase in bureaucratization, the extension and omnipresence of information and communication technologies, increasing cultural variety and tolerance towards different values, and many other economic, cultural, political and social developments including the emergence of social differentiation and specialization.

Continuing changes result in specific consequences. The societal processes of the recent decade have been more rapid than the changes in values, attitudes and 'life skills'. People have been slow in changing their lifestyles in reaction to new political, cultural, economic and social conditions. This phenomenon results in certain manifestations of psychological instability, social disintegration and disrespect for the civic and legal domains in contemporary Lithuania. An individual encounters unfamiliar problems and is not able or simply does not want to address them. Eventually, a solution is sought by delegating personal responsibility to the authorities. On the one hand, a society which becomes more democratic expects people to assume responsibility for solving their own problems, whilst on the other hand the state has an obligation to help people to implement their choices and guarantee for them the legitimate principles of major human rights and opportunities. However, in a context of transformation this latter task becomes more difficult: social conflict and social exclusion are two major obstacles preventing rights and opportunities from being realized.

The concept of social exclusion is a complex one. Social exclusion can be defined as an involuntary isolation from the main opportunities for an individual's social development, and is often characterized by poor choice options, and poor social relations with family members, friends and other members of society. In Lithuania, a demand that individuals assume personal responsibility for their own welfare coincided with weak social security provision and the emergence of a number of new social risks (for example, unemployment and homelessness). Social exclusion is objectionable because it is unjust, but it can be objected to on other grounds. According to Lundvall and Johnson (1994), one of the most important reasons for trying to bring about social inclusion is that modern societies cannot be innovative and strive for economic and social goals without involving every citizen in the creation and use of knowledge. In particular, it is important for citizens to develop the practical knowledge which will enable the society to innovate, reconstruct and confront economic, technological and social challenges, including those relating to technological innovations, which have a particular significance for individuals. The main role of education in this context is to facilitate the process of adaptation so that technologies can be used effectively in striving for economic and social goals. (For more detail on cultural features relating to contemporary Lithuania see the chapter by G. Jucevičius in this volume.) It is the process of 'social innovation' which opens the way for the innovations of other kinds to appear. How should agents of innovation act in order to stimulate appropriate activities of social innovation?

The role of agents of social innovation

In analysing the notion of an agent of innovation it is necessary at the outset to define the concept of social innovation. It is important to recognize that whilst the term 'innovation' often carries with it an implication that the innovation in question is good, social innovations per se, in common with other innovations, are not necessarily valuable. The educational implications of this important point will be addressed in due course. According to Prigogine (1997), *social innovations* involve changes of various kinds: economic (e.g. new material stimuli, schemes of labour pay), organizational–managerial (e.g. new organizational structures, new forms of labour organization, decision making, decision control, etc.); social–managerial (e.g. internal changes in organizational relations, self-governance, new bodies of governance); legal and educational (e.g. teaching/learning methods and strategies). It is useful to define the concept of the innovation agent and the various functions of agency in very general terms. The present discussion draws on the activity model of the innovation agent provided by Havelock (1973). The agent of innovation is regarded as any person or organization who facilitates a planned change or valued new development. The various identifiable functions of an agent of innovation include: *solution giver*, *process helper*, *resource linker* and *catalyst*. Each of these functions will be discussed briefly in turn. The implicit context of the discussion is a social organization such as a business, although we believe that the functions apply more widely to social innovations of other kinds.

Solution giver To be an effective solution giver, the agent of innovation not only has to have definite ideas about what the change should be. The agent also has to know when and how to offer these ideas, and how to help them to be adopted.

Process helper Process helpers can assist in the recognition and definition of the need for change, in the diagnosis of problems, in the setting of objectives relating to the acquisition of relevant resources, and in the identification of options for decision.

Resource linker Effective problem solving requires bringing together needs and resources, which may be of many kinds, including resources of human time, energy and motivation. A resource linker brings people together and helps in the finding and most effective use of resources.

We think that the main function of the agent of innovation, in some sense encompassing all of the above, is that of *catalyst*. What is characteristic of the change agent as a catalyst? According to Havelock (1973), most people do not want any change: they want to keep things the way they are. Therefore, change agents are needed to overcome inertia and to pressure the system to start working on its problems. Agents of innovation show discontent with the status quo and activate the process of problem solving.

How do people become effective catalysts? The hardest task for a catalyst is to perceive specific situations from the point of view of the leadership of the existing system and thereby to understand when and how a particular situation can be influenced. The catalyst has to realize that sooner or later he or she will have to confront unjustifiably resistant leadership and to either overcome its resistance or win its support. Another special skill a catalyst must cultivate is developing indigenous leadership for change among people it serves. Disadvantaged minorities are disadvantaged partly because they are disorganized, isolated and powerless. Therefore, the change agent as a catalyst needs to be an organizer and promoter of togetherness, and one who can inspire a feeling of common identity and purpose. A catalyst must also possess qualities of humility, timing, patience as well as the ability to collaborate. A number of contrasts and relationships between social innovations and material–technical innovations can be discerned. Social innovations are more difficult to measure in terms of their effectiveness (economic and otherwise), and what constitutes 'effectiveness' here comes up for scrutiny insistently. Social innovations cannot be introduced in a merely technical way. Social innovations are important preconditions and correlates of material–technical innovations. New attitudes, relations and behaviour are often required by material–technical innovation and have an impact on the extent to which the innovation is adopted. For example, efficiency of production may increase not only because of new equipment, but also because of new methods and stimuli in organizing the social aspects of the process of production. Pure technical and economic innovations do not therefore exist; all of them involve some social aspects and consequences. These important and neglected aspects of technical innovations should be considered when the innovations are planned (Prigogine 1997).

Can higher education fulfil the various functions of the catalyst of social innovation, and in what way? Our view is that higher education should descend from the ivory tower to play a role of this kind, although certain dangers need to be recognized and avoided.

Conceptions of higher education

The last century was *inter alia* an era of dynamic technologies, in which individuals became both the subjects and the objects of technologies. Given that technological innovations as well as social innovations are value-laden, technological innovators must be humanists in the sense that they are sensitive to the genuine needs of human development. Technological innovators must be able to think systemically, to be versatile, and to have a strong background not only in the technological domain but also in the social sciences and the humanities, all of which should bear fruit in the particular kinds of judgement which technological innovators should exercise.

A long-term tradition of classical universities was to orient their research and studies towards the fundamental objective of primarily non-instrumental liberal education aimed de facto at the elite of society, whereas now the application of wider forms of knowledge (including the practical and the instrumental) to a much broader range of members of society and to the entire social environment (via activities such as applied research and consultancy) has become an equally important objective. Higher education today, therefore, exhibits not only structural but also functional variety.

We consider that the range of different functions of contemporary higher education should be held together and that no one function should predominate over the others (Fullan 1998). Intellectual emancipation (now extended beyond an elite) is an important aim in mass higher education and in the achievement of greater social equality. However, the notion of the service university and of continuing education are also important and should be integrated with the more traditional conception of the university (Gudaitytė and Jucevičienė 2000).

The concept of liberal higher education assigns higher education a specific role in society: to emancipate individuals and society via engagement with intellectual culture (Barnett 1990, Wyatt 1990). The concept of democratic higher education involves the extension of liberal higher education and its emancipatory ambitions to a greater proportion of members of society. It shares with liberal higher education a commitment to academic autonomy and freedom and the importance of academic culture and its related standards. Democratic higher education aspires to become a form of 'mass' higher education, but without sacrifice of the focus and academic standards inherent in the task of emancipation. The concept of the service university has as its centre the aim of giving service of different kinds to society and includes the need to be entrepreneurial (Clark 1998). In the service model of higher education those to whom services are rendered are seen as 'users' and 'clients', and the forces of competition and the market economy may intrude on transactions. The concept of continuing education reflects a demand for flexible learning opportunities throughout life. Associated with this idea is the phenomenon of a learning culture in society in general, and in organizations in particular.

Our view is that all these different forms of higher education have their merits and their place and should not be seen as in opposition to each other.

Any modernization of higher education into a defensible mass system therefore involves a preservation of the older ideals and features of university education reflected in the liberal and democratic models. These ideals and features include the search for truth and objective knowledge, the development of knowledge by sustained research in the various domains of enquiry, the cultivation of rationality and related forms of disposition and character in students, the fostering and protection of impartial and open forums for discussion and debate, and an insistence upon institutional autonomy and academic freedom. These ideals and features of higher education are necessary if universities are to form the intellectual culture of society and individuals and to play its emancipatory role. They are also needed if universities are to play their role as critics of society. Society expects higher education to exhibit these ideals and features and it is right to do so.

In principle, the integration of the different concepts of higher education should result in the empowerment of wider strata of society via high-quality higher education and a greater enrichment of society by the application of the resources of the university in a wider range of ways. For example, narrow specialists in particular professional fields in society can be replaced by specialists who are formed in the light of broad applied knowledge. Individuals will not only have the opportunity to be provided with the general intellectual tools of emancipation but will also have the opportunity to deploy skills and other capacities useful in employment, in this way overcoming social exclusion and contributing in a positive way in the workplace and to society in general (Ahlberg 1999). The continuing presence of liberal and democratic impulses in universities will ensure both that the self-realization of the individual in its broadest sense will not be compromised and that individuals will have the opportunity to acquire the kind of formation which will lead to the development of the forms of human sensibility and wisdom which are necessary if appropriate judgements about matters of value relating to innovations are to be made. The presence of a service dimension to the university alongside its liberal and democratic dimensions will enable the services provided to be governed by moral criteria and associated forms of responsibility. Further, the dimension of continuing education in universities will enable individuals to continue the reflective development of their capacities throughout their lives. Taken together, a contemporary conception of the university which integrates the various ingredients which have been identified specifies a rich vision of a mass form of higher education which situates new imperatives for openness on the part of the university to society and its contemporary needs with a continuing emphasis upon the traditionally central role of the university: the achievement of intellectual and personal emancipation.

The retention of the liberal and democratic ideals and features of higher education, while extending them to embrace the conceptions of the service university and of continuing education, is fraught with complexity and the possibility of conflict (including epistemological and sociological conflict among other kinds). A fuller discussion is needed about the practical ways in which the integration we have called for can be achieved. At present, however, we confine our discussion to matters of general principle.

Given this general conceptualization of the university, how can its role as an agent of social innovation be best viewed?

The role of higher education as agent of social innovation

As mentioned above, the contemporary development of higher education has opened up the possibility that higher education may play a role as an agent of social innovation. Our earlier discussion of agents of social innovation was couched in terms of individual agency. It is nevertheless true that many of the identified aspects of agency can be fulfilled by an institution such as a university. Our discussion of the role of the university as an agent of social innovation will first consider some general aspects of this role and will then turn to more specific aspects.

In general, much of the work of the university will contribute to social innovation, some of it indirectly. A university education will unleash the talents lying within members of society, many of which will find application in social innovations. A vital general contribution of universities to social innovation is the emancipation of the individual and society which has been referred to as particularly characteristic of liberal and democratic conceptions of higher education. The humanities lie at the heart of liberal and democratic higher education and have an important contribution to make, not only to the development of individuals but also to the development of society through, *inter alia*, social innovations. Higher education has an important role in engaging students in reflexive consideration of matters such as the significance and meaning of human existence, and the kind of philosophy of life which is appropriate for a changing world, as part of the formation of persons of integrity who enjoy balance and autonomy. Such matters are particularly apt for consideration in 'countries in transition'. The social sciences deepen knowledge about social processes and changes. The background for any effective social policy is the understanding of the nature and development of social changes and application of the knowledge acquired in practical decision making. Critical sociological analyses of the strengths and weaknesses of social and political organizations and policies is vital in bringing about appropriate social understanding and a culture of reflective thinking in society. Liberal and democratic higher education has the unique role of acting as an independent critical force in society and this role is related to the university's commitment to values related to knowledge, enquiry and the search for truth (dialogue, open-mindedness and constructive critique are among prominent examples of such values). Nothing important to the freedom of society is alien to the university (Barnett 1990, Wyatt 1990). An intellectually emancipated individual will not merely adapt to society but attempt to change it in positive ways, which is particularly important in 'societies in transition'. Thus a greater number of educated people will increase the number of people who can resist becoming victims of corrupt politicians and who will better understand the integrity of social diversity and are able to express appropriate forms of solidarity. This helps society to become civic and to diminish the prevalence of evils such as social exclusion.

It is vital for the health of a democratic society that higher education plays this critical role. According to Carter (quoted in Samalavičius 2003), a university is considered not only 'the most important social institution which preserves the intellectual heritage, but also the most important critic of that society and its ideology'. The university should respect the values intrinsic to its own fundamental mission and be concerned with safeguarding its autonomy against state and private structures of power. In 'countries in transition' this task requires care, as the structures of political and economic power have a number of mechanisms to make the academic community a passive and easily controllable body, reluctant to engage in critical debate because of a fear of losing its modest privileges. This is not, however, to suggest that the university, in its efforts to develop an appropriate critical discourse, should be closed to criticism from society about its style and habits of thinking and activity.

The general contribution which universities can make to social innovation is vulnerable to various attacks, which have been made on liberal and democratic higher education in Lithuania as elsewhere. For example, according to

Samalavičius (2003), for several years Lithuanian educational policy makers have campaigned against the humanities. The humanities have been treated as a suspicious field of 'cultural activity', which do not meet the requirements of contemporary research. This standpoint has become an indirect stimulus for the universities to marginalize the humanities and to reduce the number of disciplines in the study programmes. This kind of policy implies an attempt to restore the positivist mentality, which is inconsistent with the increasing attention to the role of humanities in the universities of the West. A technocratic academic mentality still prevails in Lithuania. Another problem is that in a consumerist society, which is rapidly developing in Lithuania, the demand for knowledge is one of the main criteria for measuring the value of higher education. In the contemporary industry of knowledge the symbolic capital of the humanities is not very big; the humanities face difficulties in functioning in the academic market and competing with the 'currency' of specialized vocational programmes and the programmes of the natural sciences. Contemporary voices claim that the humanities and social sciences are only adjuncts to the fundamental sciences. The humanities are still part of the study programmes of higher education because the policy makers of higher education are tolerant, and society is too indecisive. However, undue specialization in study without a broad background (including a background of study in the humanities) has major drawbacks. It narrows down thought and diminishes understanding. As indicated earlier, specialists in technological areas have to be capable of broad critical and creative thought informed by appropriate human values and sensibility which enables technical problems to be situated within a clear and wise perception of common human and social problems, needs and goals. (For an emphasis on the role of the university in shaping the broad sensibility of students see the chapter by Alexander in this volume.)

The role of higher education as an agent of social innovation is not, however, confined to its general role, important as this may be. Universities can play a more specific role by engaging in a closer way with society and its needs via certain forms of professional training (involving the development of special competences), partnership, consultancy (involving the application of practical knowledge) and research (relating to the accumulation and dissemination of socially significant fundamental and applied knowledge). In these ways higher education can act as a change agent or catalyst in society by playing an active, direct and constructive role in the identification and resolution of society's practical problems. Lithuanian sociologists (such as Grigas 2001, Mitrikas 1996 and others) pay attention to the fact that in 'countries in transition' there is a tension between a strong need for innovation and a tendency to conservatism in action. In order to avoid the tension, it is necessary not only to expand the knowledge of social processes and their changes, thereby remedying decisions based on insufficient and shallow knowledge of social reality, but also to apply a stimulus to the system, which universities are well placed to do. It should be remembered that the first universities were communities of scholars with a rebellious spirit.

Higher education should be able to inspire its students with the same spirit, but specifically in relation to the needs of social innovation, properly understood. The agent of innovation as catalyst, it will be recalled, has to overcome inertia, to 'pressurize' the system to make it start functioning in order to move beyond an unsatisfactory status quo and to enable problems to be solved. Higher education should be able to stimulate a dynamic approach to societal innovations, presenting them as opportunities and not as threats.

The more specific role of the university as an agent of social change and as a catalyst may require study methods and other forms of educational provision which are different from the traditional ones, such as interactive and problem-based methods and other methods of active learning. In this context the importance of traditional disciplines of study is now in question (Barnett 1990).

It will, of course, be vital for universities in their specific contribution to social innovation to ensure that technological innovations are properly related to proper economic, social and personal needs and goals. The intimate relationship between technological and social innovations needs also to be borne carefully in mind. Major technologies relating to many significant social and economic changes (e.g. new ways of production, new products and new forms of organization) are often associated with the phenomenon of 'technological push'. This phenomenon is, however, based on the dubious assumption that technological products determine the social consequences of their use. An alternative approach insists that technological development is determined by social, ecological and political factors. Wyatt (1990) points out that technologies are social constructs and a result of negotiation among social groups, and depend for their implementation upon social factors. This leads to the thought that social innovations need to be considered prior to the consideration of technological innovations. This is but one example of the insights relating to social innovation which the university can help to convey as part of its role as a catalytic agent of innovation.

One clear implication of our discussion in this chapter is that the future of higher education in Lithuania, as elsewhere, requires collaborative discussion and decision making if the potential of higher education as an agent of social innovation is to be fully realized and the dangers and shortcomings of this kind of role on the part of the university are to be identified and avoided.

References

Ahlberg, M. (1999) *A Theory of High Quality Learning and Two Quality Tools Constructively to Evaluate and Promote it*, Helsinki: University of Helsinki.

Barnett, R. (1990) *The Idea of Higher Education*, Buckingham: SHRE/Open University Press.

Bowsma, W.J. (1990) *A Usable Past: Essays in European Cultural History*, Los Angeles: University of California Press.

Clark, B.R. (1998) *Creating Entrepreneurial Universities*, Oxford: Pergamon.

Commission of the European Communities (2003) 'The Role of the Universities in the Europe of Knowledge', Communication from the Commission, Brussels.

Doppler, K. and Lautenburg, C. (1994) *Change Management*, Frankfurt/New York: Campus Verlag.
Fullan, M. (1998) *Pokyčių jėgos*, Vilnius: Tyto Alba.
Gibbons, M.A. (1998) 'A Commonwealth perspective on globalization of higher education', in P. Scott (ed.) *The Globalization of Higher Education*, London: SRHE and Open University Press.
Grigas, R. (2001) *Tautinė savivoka*, Vilnius: Rosma.
Gudaitytė, D. and Jucevičienė, P. (2000) 'Elitinio aukštojo mokslo tapimo masiniu proceso esmė: paradigma ir charakteristikos' ['The process of massification of the elite higher education: paradigm and characteristics'], *Socialiniai mokslai*, 3 (24), 112–22.
Havelock, R.G. (1973) *The Change Agent's Guide to Innovation in Education*, Englewood Cliffs, NJ: Educational Technology Publications.
Lundvall, B.A. and Johnson, B. (1994) 'The learning economy', *Journal of Industry Studies*, 1 (2), 23–42.
Melnikas, B., Jakubavičius, A. and Strazdas, R. (2000) *Inovacijų vadyba*, Vilnius: Technika.
Mitrikas, A.A. (1996) *Socialiniai pokyčiai ir socialinė politika: Lietuva socialinių pokyčių erdvėje*, Vilnius: LFSI.
Prigogine, I. (1997) *The End of Certainty: Time, Chaos and New Laws of Nature*, Oxford: The Free Press.
Samalavičius, A. (2003) *Universiteto idėja ir akademinė industrija*, Vilnius: Kultūros barai.
Scott, P. (1998) *The Globalization of Higher Education*, London: SRHE.
Wyatt, I. (1990) *Commitment to Higher Education*, London: SRHE.

Chapter 15

The role of the university in community development
Responding to the challenges of globalization

Irena Leliūgienė and Viktorija Baršauskienė

In the global world, in the context of the familiar processes of globalization, information and knowledge have become very important in securing the social well-being of nations. Information and knowledge have also become very important in securing the social empowerment and self-realization of individuals. For both societies and individuals, knowledge is a key element in the achievement of important societal and individual goods. Learning has also become an important element in the achievement of these goods. The paradigm of the new economy encompasses not only a learning individual, but also a learning community and a learning society (including institutions and companies). Bauman (2002) argues that the learning process is more important than what is learned. The global economy has replaced the Soviet era slogan 'Learn, learn, learn' with a new one 'Learn to learn', which is seen as a requirement set by the demands of the information society.

Globalization is characterized not only by globally oriented production, information and activity, but also by the globalization of human resources. Investment in human resource development has significantly increased. The development of human resources implies the development of an individual's innate and acquired personal qualities, the enhancement of systemic knowledge possessed by individuals and the exploitation of human capabilities.

Social and political change in Europe, including increasing labour mobility, the development of the new European social policy and the increasingly global nature of social problems has had a profound effect on the aims and character of socio-cultural and socio-educational work conducted in relation to community development. New trends in social development call for dealing in creative and effective ways with such social phenomena as poverty, social exclusion, discrimination, racism, the destruction of traditional social models and the erosion of specific cultural and ethnic traditions.

In recent years, significant research has been devoted to community development. Themes which have attracted the particular attention of researchers include the impact of future technologies on social empowerment in the modern community, the influence of globalization on community development, the nature of community work in the twenty-first century, and the methods and principles of community development (Halal 1998, Passig 1998, Zissen 1998, Smith and Babcock 1998, Babacan and Gopalkrishnan 2001, Appadurai 1990, Brecher and Costello 1994, Craig 1998, Habermas 1987, Kenny 1994). This research effort has also involved a number of Lithuanian researchers (Grigas 2000, Karalius 2000, Nefas 2004, Baršauskienė and Leliūgienė 2001, 2002). Lithuanian researchers Jucevičienė (2002) and Kuzmickaitė (2003), for example, have analysed the role of entrepreneurship in resolving the social problems of community and have advocated the concept of the learning city as an important contributor to community empowerment. (For a related discussion on social innovation see the chapter by Janiūnaitė and Gudaitytė in this volume.)

Although the role of higher education in contributing to community development in its various aspects has been addressed by western scholars Tjeldvoll (1998), Currie and Newson (1998), Cummings (1998) and others, most researchers into community development tend to neglect the role of higher education in this matter. Those researchers who discuss the idea of a service university (Tjeldvoll 1998, Waterhouse 2000) do not tend to deal at length with the broader and more direct ways in which universities might contribute to community development. In the global world, it is difficult to ensure efficient community development (and its corollaries such as social empowerment) without an appropriate exploitation of the intellectual resources possessed by universities as institutions of research and study.

This chapter addresses the general question: What role should be played by a modern university in relation to community development in the context of challenges posed by globalization? In pursuing this question, the chapter has three sections. The first section discusses the notions of community and community development. In the second section, the role of the university in relation to community development is explored, while in the final section some brief examples are offered of the participation of a specific university (Kaunas University of Technology) in community development.

The notions of community and community development

In studies of the notion of 'community' a number of definitions of 'community' can be found. The Lithuanian sociologist Budvytis points out that the American scholar Hillery has found about ninety different definitions. According to Budvytis (1994), researchers do not now attempt to provide a single precise definition of the notion, but illuminate a range of conceptions. At the heart of the notion of 'community' is a certain 'territory' or social space consisting of 'inhabitants' and their interrelationships.

According to Rothman (1979: 24–45), 'community' is a primary form of social organization which emerged on the basis of kinship and is characterized by immediate relations. Wirth (1961: 309–15) defines 'community' as a group of individuals inhabiting a certain territory who are united by common interests, activities and other characteristics. Ife (2001) argues that the concept is used for describing social relations in a group or certain territory (Davis 1977: 1175–80). 'Community' can be seen as the immediate environment of a person which is analysable as a social system (Johnson 1996: 313). Natorp (1921) argues that 'community' is impossible without individuals and that individuals cannot survive without community: in addition, education is impossible without the interaction of these two realities. The task of 'community' is the 'materialization of values', i.e. the formation of individuals by taking them out of chaos, giving them a shape and developing them (Jovaiša 1993: 67).

A 'territorial community' (in the physical and not merely metaphorical sense of 'territory') is a group of people who live in a particular geographical place (nation, city, village, district, etc.). Every territorial community has subgroups and subcultures, as well as activities, institutions and organizations, and is apt for analysis as a particular kind of social environment, with its own characteristic features and problems.

In a survey of communities conducted by Nefas (2004) in Lithuanian municipalities, the question 'What is a community?' produced answers which stressed 'common interests and traditions' as characteristic of groups of people who can be seen as 'communities'.

The notion of community development in the context of globalization

At the end of the last century, a number of scholars from western countries (Della-Pergola 1998, Halal 1998, Passig 1998, Appadurai 1990, Pilgers 1998, Mulgan 1997 and others) attempted to identify the features of community development in the global world

Della-Pergola (1998) argues that ethnic, religious and social diversity, pluralism and multiculturalism have a direct influence on the nature and prospects of community development. International migration also has an impact upon the development of territorial communities. It is developments such as these which underlie the observation of Halal (1998), based on research extending over ten years which is repeated every two years, which indicates that a revolution is taking place which has a profound effect on communities of all kinds. Yet, according to Della-Pergola, an organized community and its institutions continue to play an increasingly important role in today's societies.

Discussing the prospects of the development of social community, Passig (1998) argues that whilst communities, especially local ones, should not be afraid to change, some members of communities are indifferent to change, resistant to change or (especially in the case of older members) frightened of it.

A useful approach to analysing the notions and features of community development is Appadurai's (1990) 'concept of the core' which enables 'drawing a sociological landscape of community development'. The 'concept of the core' encompasses five dimensions: the ethno core, the information and knowledge dissemination core, the technological core, the ideological core and the financial core. A deeper analysis of these dimensions reveals various aspects of the respects in which global considerations have an impact on community development. The global economic crisis, for example, gives rise to very particular demands.

Community development is not, therefore, immune from broader political and ideological pressures. In some quarters there has been an increased emphasis upon community development being seen as a matter of voluntary effort, and here the influence of thinkers such as Etzione (1995) can be seen, with their emphasis on the importance of people assuming responsibility for themselves, their community and their neighbourhood. Such ideas have had an impact on aspects of the policies of governments in western democracies.

Community development (especially in the case of territorial communities) requires competences in the following areas: partnership, organizing, project development and management, entrepreneurship, design and implementation of the educational environment, multiculturalism and social work. All these competences require appropriate relationships between all the agents involved.

The extent to which the acquisition of the competences indicated above can be facilitated by close links with universities will now be addressed.

The role of the university in community development

As indicated earlier, the role which higher education can and should play in developing and empowering communities has been relatively neglected in terms of discussion and research.

Altbach *et al.* (1999) note that universities, which have traditionally educated the elite and served as an institutional basis for teaching and research conceived in primarily academic terms, are increasingly forced to turn outwards to the surrounding world. Already in the 1980s it was noted that the university is increasingly becoming a service provider, in addition to engaging in knowledge creation and dissemination of a kind more traditionally associated with the university (Bowden and Marton 1998). Universities are establishing external units which, by flexibly collaborating with university departments, conduct applied and contractual research (Clark 1995), enabling them to understand more fully, and contribute to, the needs of the environment surrounding the university.

A number of scholars (Tjeldvoll 1998, Clark 1995, Cummings 1998, Marginson and Considine 2000, Waterhouse 2000) focus on the role of universities as service institutions in society and community and the fruits of these discussions can be applied to the role of the university in community development.

At the heart of the notion of the service university is its mediation between researchers and society more generally. In the characterization of the service university terms such as 'enterprise' (applied to academic as well as economic matters), 'academic capitalism', 'entrepreneurial university' and 'corporate university' are prominent. New applications of technology in distance learning are a feature of service universities. Such universities can play an important role in reducing social exclusion in communities. Where service universities are operating effectively, academic communities and local communities have developed and become equal partners, as seen in the creation of partnership networks between universities and communities, the development of joint projects and the like.

Although Bowden and Marton argue that by providing services to the community, serving society and collaborating with it, the university emphasizes learning at the local community level, Markevičienė (2001) notes that while providing services at the local level, higher education institutions at the same time gain opportunities to understand the perceptions of a wider range of participants in the educational process.

In his discussion of the priorities of Oslo University, Tjeldvoll (1998) points to the use of its knowledge for developing society and the community and for maintaining relations with them. Oslo University is meeting government expectations through research related to the life of society and to its needs.

Tjeldvoll claims that universities which seek to adopt a service orientation are facing two key structural requirements: (i) they have to develop the channels of communication with possible stakeholders outside the university; and (ii) the university management has to develop a human resource policy to motivate the best researchers to become involved in service-providing activities.

In the context of community development and empowerment, Waterhouse (2000) gives an interesting example of Derby University, where an organization and infrastructure for meeting long-term community needs has been created. This university is highly sensitive to community expectations, as seen in the organization of various training courses (e.g. in computer literacy) for members of the community. Derby University provides significant intellectual help to community members who are involved in organizing rural tourism and the development of small businesses.

In the view of the authors of this chapter, the contemporary university can and should perform many roles in community development: in the context of the knowledge and information society these roles can be described under the headings of educator, researcher and initiator.

The role of educator is realized by the university through programmes of study devoted, for example, to the formation of social educators in schools and social workers for work in the community more broadly. For example, community socio-educational workers graduating from Lithuanian universities should be able to help in the handling of problems such as lack of initiative, engagement, responsibility and social control among members of the community. An important role is played by continuing education courses, retraining courses and seminars and courses for community workers, where relevant capacities possessed by the university can be deployed to good effect.

Conducting community research is one of the important roles of the university. This kind of research enables the university to diagnose and evaluate matters relating to community development and to offer research-based strategies for further community development.

The university can act as an initiator of new ideas relating to community development in a range of ways.

It can be argued that a university providing the kinds of services to the community which have been described can enable the development of a community into a learning community, where relevant conditions are created for development in the areas of IT, economic, educational, cultural and financial and human resources, among others.

Some examples

To illustrate in practical terms some of the ideas outlined above, we would like to present some brief examples of the role played by Kaunas University of Technology (KTU) in community development. A number of departments of KTU are participating in community development and education. One of the examples of such initiatives is a project 'Kaunas as a Learning City' which is being implemented jointly with Kaunas Municipality.

The project's methodology is based on the view that a learning city creates for its inhabitants, communities and organizations an effective and favourable learning environment and ensures that citizens are constantly learning, acquiring and developing the competences crucial for working and living in today's technology-based world in the global context. This initiative puts into practical effect arguments such as those of Halal (1998) about the impact of information technologies and education on community development and the role of the university in this respect, and ideas such as those of Babacan and Gopalkrishnan (2001) about knowledge and information as the basis of the economic and social development of the community. Relevant to community development and social empowerment and to the role of the university in these processes is Jucevičienė's (1997: 35) definition of social education: 'It is a field of multidisciplinary education science which lays the theoretical foundation for the individual's development (education and self-education) taking into account the social, economic, science and technology-related and especially IT-related changes.'

It can be argued that this project, which has been developed by the KTU Faculty of Social Science Institute of Educational Studies and is being implemented by Kaunas Municipality, by its nature helps KTU to implement the role of service university and community partner, thereby bringing about social empowerment through education.

Another good example of collaboration between KTU and the community is a set of five projects 'Activities in the Field of Community Development' implemented by the KTU Public Policy Research Centre in 2001–03.

The first project 'Community Development in Three Baltic States' was jointly coordinated by KTU and Rutgers University (USA). Within this project, representatives of the local governments, NGOs and universities from three Baltic States went to the USA to familiarize themselves with the best practices in community development. The second project 'The Role of the University in Fostering Local Community' was jointly implemented by Kaunas NGOs, KTU Distance Education Centre, Vytautas Magnus University (Kaunas) and KTU Municipality Training Centre. The remaining three projects are entitled 'Enhancing NGO Capacities: From Learning to Doing', 'Improvement of Teaching in Public Administration' and 'Development of Civil Society Through University Initiatives'.

All these projects, aimed at community development and social empowerment, are implemented by collaborating with other Lithuanian universities, US universities and international foundations.

An important role in implementing the idea of the service university in the interests of community development and social empowerment is played by the Centre of Educational Competence (CEC) at the Institute of Educational Studies of Kaunas University of Technology. The Centre regularly offers various seminars and courses to rural communities, schools and local public servants, disseminating the newest knowledge and innovations. In the context of community development and empowerment, it is also worth mentioning the project 'Training in Community Health' funded by PHARE, the project 'Training of Community Workers' initiated by the Lithuanian Ministry of Social Security and Labour and the EU SAPARD project 'Ecology of Rural Family'. Within these projects, lecturers of the CEC delivered seminars to the community workers of various Lithuanian regions on social work, social policy, communication psychology and action research, in this way realizing the role of the university as community educator.

Realizing the role of the university as community researcher, KTU scholars are investigating the enabling conditions for establishing community centres in towns and villages, the possibilities of team work in the community in promotion of healthy life styles, the integration of senior citizens into community life, and the social–educational functions of the community centres working with children.

Research evidence indicates community needs in Lithuania which universities are well placed to meet. Penčylienė (2002), in her research 'A study of possibilities of mobilizing the local community for team work', interviewed the leaders of several institutions in a particular community (church, community centre, secondary school, kindergarten, building company, community shelter, police office and health care centre). The interview data indicated a willingness on the part of most of the leaders to become more involved in community activities, but a strong perception on their part that it was necessary for an outside institution to take the initiative in stimulating and supporting appropriate forms of activity. The university has a clear opportunity in these situations to take such initiatives and enable local communities to take responsibility for their own development. As global experience confirms, an important resource requiring mobilization in community development, and in the support of socio-educational workers, is voluntary effort. In Lithuania volunteering as a phenomenon emerged only after the country regained independence, and is only in the early stages of development compared to western countries. Lithuanian universities have a major role to play in the training and support of volunteers.

The study completed by Kvietkauskaitė (2004), 'Opportunities for building a sense of community among neighbourhood inhabitants', involved a survey of adult residents and gymnasium pupils in one of the neighbourhoods of Kaunas city. Its results showed that only 5.4 per cent of community members are involved in volunteering-based activities or NGOs. Only 14.4 per cent of pupils in gymnasiums are engaged in school community activities; only 10.9 per cent of neighbourhood residents take part in meetings which discuss ways of improving community activities. However, the same respondents pointed out that there is too much crime in the neighbourhood (65 per cent of the respondents), too little support given for the disabled (49.5 per cent), a lack of places where people can spend their free time (48.5 per cent), and a messy and noisy environment (45.5 per cent). This implies that at least some members of neighbourhoods and communities in Lithuania are aware of community needs to be met but not sufficiently aware of the importance of their own initiative and capacity in meeting these needs. Universities have a role to play in empowering members of neighbourhoods and communities to address the needs of these neighbourhoods and communities in an effective way. Whilst, as Della-Pergola (1998) points out, an organized community and its institutions are increasingly important in the global world and diverse contemporary society, the significance of initiative at the neighbourhood and community level should not be underestimated, and the university has a central role to play in stimulation and support of this initiative.

The KTU experience in performing educational, research and initiator roles in community development has inspired us to undertake a deeper analysis of these roles and the potential of the university to make yet further contributions to them. As a result, we intend to conduct more in-depth studies of other Lithuanian and western universities in community development.

Globalization poses particular problems for community development in Lithuania, including the encouragement of civic initiative, social engagement and the responsibility of community members in solving increasingly complex socio-educational problems. We have sought to indicate not only that Lithuanian universities have opportunities for making a real contribution to problems of these kinds, but also that universities in all contexts have similar kinds of opportunity which should be grasped in an appropriate way.

References

Altbach, P.G., Berdahl, R.O. and Gumport, P.J. (eds) (1999) *American Higher Education in the Twenty-First Century: Social, Political and Economic Challenges*, Baltimore and London: The Johns Hopkins University Press.

Appadurai, A. (1990) 'Disjuncture and difference in the global cultural economy', in M. Featherstone (ed.) *Global Culture: Nationalism, Globalization and Modernity*, London: Sage Publications.
Babacan, H. and Gopalkrishnan, N. (2001) 'Community work partnership in a global context', *Community Development Journal*, 36 (1), 3–17.
Baršauskienė, V. and Leliūgienė, I. (2001) *Sociokultūrinis darbas bendruomenėje. Užsienio šalių patirtis*, Kaunas: Technologija.
Bauman, Z. (2002) *Globalizacija: pasekmės žmogui*, Vilnius: Strofa.
Bowden, J. and Marton, F. (1998). *The University of Learning*, London: Kogan Page.
Brecher, J. and Costello, T. (1994) *Global Village of Global Pillage: Economic Reconstruction from the Bottom Up*, Boston: South End Press.
Budvytis, S. (1994) 'Bendrios kaip sociologinis objektas' ['Communities as a sociological object'], *Filosofija. Sociologija*, 1, 24–34.
Clark, R.B. (1995) *Places of Inquiry: Research and Advanced Education in Modern Universities*, Los Angeles: University of California Press.
Craig, G. (1998) 'Community development in a global context', *Community Development Journal*, 33 (1), 2–17.
Cummings, W.K. (1998) 'The service university in comparative perspective', *Higher Education*, 35 (1), 12–17.
Currie, J. and Newson, J. (1998) *Universities and Globalization: Critical Perspective*, London, New Delhi: SAGE Publications.
Davis, A.F. (1977) 'Settlements: history', in *Encyclopedia of Social Work*, 17th edn, vol. 2, New York: National Association of Social Workers.
Della-Pergola, S. 'The role of community in socio-demographic trends', paper presented at the conference 'The Role of the Community Center in an Era of Uncertainty and Rapid Change', Jerusalem, December 1998.
Etzione, G. (1995) *Rights and the Common Good: the Communitarian Perspective*, New York: St Martins Press.
Grigas, R. (2000) 'Nūdienos pasaulio kultūros ir lietuvių bendruomeniškumo problema' ['Culture and communitarianism of Lithuanians in today's world'], in R. Grigas (ed.) *Bendruomeniškumas ir savivalda*, Vilnius: VŠĮ 'Savivaldybių žinios'.
Habermas, J. (1987) *Theorie de l'agir communicationnel*, Paris: Fayard.
Halal, W. 'Future technologies and their impact on communal life', paper presented at the conference 'The Role of the Community Center in an Era of Uncertainty and Rapid Change', Jerusalem, December 1998.
Ife, J. (2001) 'Local and global practice: relocating social work as a human rights profession in the new global order', *European Journal of Social Work*, 4, 5–16.
Jovaiša, L. (1993) *Edukologijos įvadas*, Kaunas: Technologija.
Jucevičienė, P. (1997) *Ugdymo mokslo raida: nuo pedagogikos iki šiuolaikinės edukologijos* ['Development of the education science: from pedagogy to contemporary education studies'], Kaunas: Technologija.
—— 'The Development of Education Science and the Forty Years of Educational Research at Kaunas University of Technology', paper presented at the conference 'Higher Education for Knowledge Society', Kaunas, September 2002.
Karalius, A. (2000) 'Bendruomeniškumo formos ir jų pamatai' ['Forms and foundations of the communitarianism'], in R. Grigas (ed.) *Bendruomeniškumas ir savivalda*, Vilnius: VŠĮ 'Savivaldybių žinios'.

Kenny, S. (1994) *Developing Communities for the Future: Community Development in Australia*, South Melbourne: Thomas Nelson Australia.

Kuzmickaitė, D. (2003) 'Bendruomenės tyrimo metodologijos ypatumai' ['Methodology for community research'], Seminar 'Social Economy in Lithuania: Community Research'. Online. Available at: www.vdu.lt/seki/ (accessed 11 November 2004).

Kvietkauskaitė, J. (2004) 'Opportunities for building a sense of community among the inhabitants of the neighborhood', unpublished thesis, Kaunas University of Technology.

Leliūgienė, I. and Baršauskienė, V. (2002). 'Bendruomeninio ugdymo metodai ir principai: Užsienio šalių mokslininkų požiūris ['Methods and principles of the community education: perspectives of overseas scholars'], *Specialusis ugdymas*, 2 (7), 67–74.

Marginson, S. and Considine, M. (2000) *The Enterprise University: Power, Governance, and Reinvention in Australia*, Cambridge University Press.

Markevičienė, A. 'Paslaugų universiteto veiklos ypatumai mokymosi paradigmos kontekste' ['The features of the service university in the context of the paradigm of learning'], paper presented at the conference 'Aukštojo mokslo sistemos ir didaktika', Kaunas, April 2001.

Mulgan, G. (1997) *Life After Politics: New Thinking for the Twenty-First Century*, London: Fontana Press.

Natorp, P. (1921) *Sozialpädagogik. Theorie der Willenserziehung auf der Grundlage der Gemeinschaft*, Stuttgerd: Frommann.

Nefas, S. (2004) 'Vietos savivaldos rinkimų įtaka demokratijai' ['The influence of local government elections on democracy'], in *Vietos demokratija: bendruomenės dalyvavimas sprendimų priėmimo procese Suomijoje ir Lietuvoje*, Vilnius: M. Rudaičio personalinė įmonė 'Sirta'.

Passig, D. 'The future community', paper presented at the conference 'The Role of the Community Center in an Era of Uncertainty and Rapid Change', Jerusalem, December 1998.

Penčylienė, A. (2002) 'A study of possibilities to mobilize local community for teamwork', unpublished thesis, Kaunas University of Technology.

Pilger, J. (1998) *Hidden Agendas*, London: Vintage.

Rothman, J. (1979) 'Three models of community organization', in F. Cox, J. Erich, J. Rothman and J. Trampman (eds) *Strategies of Community Organization*, Itasca: F.E. Peacock Publishers.

Smith, B. and Babcock, A. 'Virtual association', paper presented at the conference 'The Role of the Community Center in an Era of Uncertainty and Rapid Change', Jerusalem, December 1998.

Tjeldvoll, A. (1998) *A Service University in Scandinavia?*, Oslo: University of Oslo.

Waterhouse, R. (2000) 'The distributed university: higher education reformed', in P. Scott (ed.) *Higher Education Re-formed*, London: Falmer Press.

Wirth, L. (1961) 'The problem of minority groups', in T. Parsons, E. Shils, K. Naegele and J. Pitts (eds) *Theories of Society: Foundations of Modern Sociological Theory*, vol. 1, New York: Free Press of Glencoe.

Zissen, M. 'Settlements in the schools: an emerging paradigm', paper presented at the conference 'The Role of the Community Center in an Era of Uncertainty and Rapid Change', Jerusalem, December 1998.

Chapter 16

Higher education and its contribution to public health

Tackling health inequalities through health policy development in Lithuania

Vilius Grabauskas

Introduction

Equity in health, and solidarity in action through participation and accountability for continued health development, are fundamental values on which the 'health for all' strategy in contemporary Europe is based (WHO Regional Office for Europe 1999). A large body of research carried out over the last two decades throughout the world has clearly indicated that socio-economic inequalities are responsible for large inequalities in health among different populations and various population groups (Fox 1989, Dahlgren and Whitehead 1992, Drever and Whitehead 1997, Kunst and Makenbach 1993, Davey Smith, Blane and Bartley 1994, Padaiga, Grabauskas and Gaižauskienė 1998). It is well documented that among socio-economic variables education is the major contributor to existing inequalities in health – the correlation between lower educational level and low health status is clearly measured by various indicators (Pincus and Callahan 1994, Kalėdienė and Petrauskienė 2000, Grabauskas and Kalėdienė 2002). Educational attainment is a composite socio-economic variable, reflecting various influences on health status and mortality. It is closely associated with occupation, income and many other characteristics related to social support systems. Educational attainment affects access to various resources, health services included, which consequently influences health and longevity (Elo and Preston 1976).

The purpose of this chapter is to illustrate the importance of education and some other related variables for population health, based on research data obtained to date in Lithuania, and thereby to demonstrate Lithuania's efforts to address equality in health issues in developing its national health policy.

Research in health inequalities

Already, prior to the 1990s, national researchers had demonstrated socio-economic inequalities in health in Lithuania, which is a rather homogeneous country. The World Health Organization (WHO) coordinated *Kaunas–Rotterdam Intervention Study* which was carried out in 1971–74 is a case in point here.

It demonstrated large inequalities in self-reported health by level of education in middle-aged men (Appels *et al.* 1986) and mortality of middle-aged men by educational level of their spouses (Bosma *et al.* 1995). It was only through the stimulating role of WHO that systematic research effort into health inequalities began in 1997. Under the auspices of this collaboration Lithuania joined the Health Inequalities Project (Padaiga, Grabauskas and Gaižauskienė 1998). The data from the National Health Information Centre, the Ministries of Education, Health, Social Welfare and Labour, combined with the datasets from a number of research projects – Countrywide Integrated Non-communicable Disease Intervention Programme (CINDI), Health Behaviour Monitoring in Adult Population (FINBALT HEALTH MONITOR), Health Behaviour Monitoring in Schoolchildren (HBSC), National Household Survey, Newborn Register and Accessibility to Health Care Project – constituted the database for a joint analysis (Grabauskas, Misevičienė and Klumbienė 2001, Grabauskas *et al.* 1996, Curry *et al.* 2000, Dičkutė *et al.* 2002). The results of this analysis showed that education, socio-economic group, family income and place of residence were significant predictors of health inequality. Higher education, higher income and urban residence were strongly positively related with self-reported health status as well as with such health behaviours as a reduction in smoking and alcohol consumption and an improvement in healthy nutrition. Up to 50 per cent of all-cause mortality in Lithuania can be attributed to tobacco and alcohol abuse, with a smaller proportion contributed by traffic accidents. Large inequalities in neonatal health by the educational level and marital status of mothers were discovered, with maternal smoking, alcohol and drug abuse accounting for a large proportion of the observed differences. Finally, socio-economic inequalities were found in accessibility to health care, lower socio-economic status predicting worse access to services (Grabauskas and Padaiga 2002).

Education and risk of ill-health

The extent of socio-economic inequalities in health in Lithuania varies depending on the set of health and socio-economic indicators selected. According to the data from the national mortality register, the Lithuanian population experiences large mortality inequalities by different educational groups. University education seems to be a significant protector against premature mortality from all causes, in both men and women. The largest mortality difference was observed in the youngest groups of the Lithuanian population (Figure 16.1), reaching 8.5 to 12.5 times in the ages of twenty-five and thirty.

Similarly, the differences in life expectancy by educational category at different ages using life-table methodology were computed for Lithuanian males and females. As it can be seen from the data presented in Figure 16.2, the life expectancy of males with university education was significantly longer than the national average for that age in all age groups up to seventy years. Males with only primary education had shorter than the average life expectancy for that age

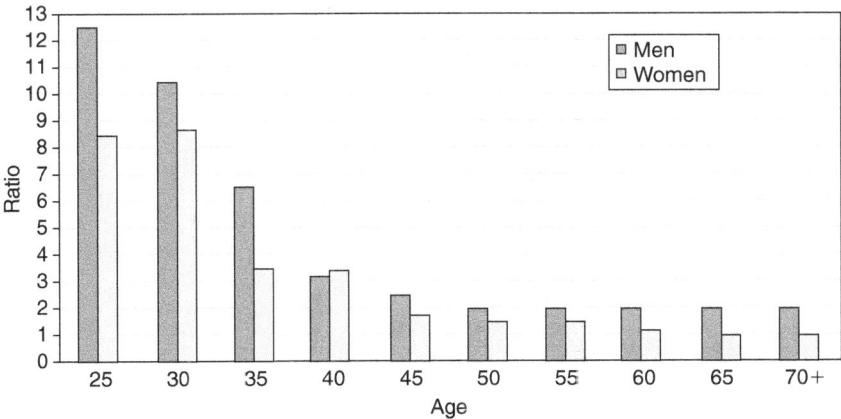

Figure 16.1 Comparison of age-specific mortality between the group with university education and the group with primary education (mortality of the group with university education equals 1).

up to forty-five years of age. It is very impressive that differences in life expectancy are largest in the youngest males, e.g. reaching 11.72 years in the age group of twenty-five. There were no significant differences in life expectancy in males with secondary education.

Although inequalities between national average life expectancy for different age groups and by educational background in Lithuanian females had similar tendencies to those of males, real differences by age were much smaller. As can be seen from Figure 16.2, statistically significant differences in the female group with primary education were observed up to the age of forty-five, while in the group with university education to age of twenty-five only.

It is also important to mention that large gender inequalities by educational category were observed in the Lithuanian population, again, the largest being recorded in the youngest segments of the population. For example, at age twenty-five life expectancy in males with only primary education was 12.12 years shorter than in females of the same age, while in males with university education this difference was 4.71 years only. The observed gender differences in life expectancy gradually decreased with age in all educational categories.

Education as a social phenomenon plays an important role throughout human life. Its impact is significant from birth and even before birth. According to Lithuanian research data (Figure 16.3) the educational level of the mother is a significant contributor to the health of the newborn (Dičkutė *et al.* 2002). Mothers with university education are delivering low birth-weight babies (<2,500 g) substantially less frequently than those in a lower educational category. It is well known that low-birth-weight babies are exposed to all kinds of health risks more frequently than those of normal birth-weight.

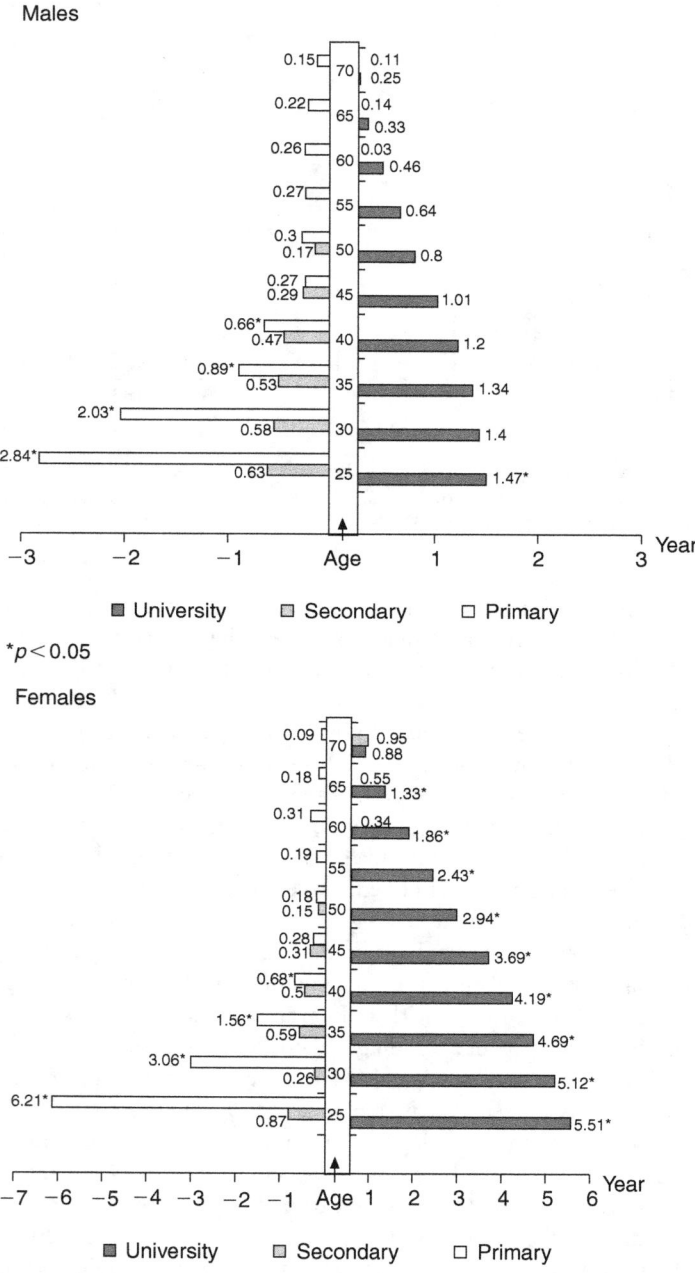

Figure 16.2 Differences in average life expectancy of Lithuanian population by age and educational background.

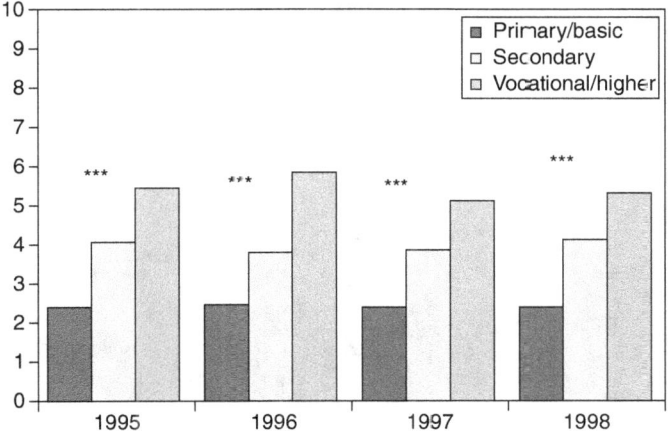

Figure 16.3 Low-birth-weight (<2,500 g) proportions by educational level of mothers.

Note
***p<0.001.

Education and health-conscious behaviour

Numerous research projects prove that alongside socio-economic determinants of ill-health and premature mortality certain life styles play a key role in the development of certain diseases, sometimes called 'diseases of civilization' (World Health Organization 2002). The most important among these 'diseases of civilization' are smoking, diet, alcohol consumption and lack of physical activity. The relationship between some of these diseases and level of education computed from the data of research projects carried out by Kaunas University of Medicine are presented here, again demonstrating significant risk inequalities by educational category.

The smoking habits by educational level in the Lithuanian population are presented in Figure 16.4.

The data presented, first of all, demonstrate that Lithuanian males are more frequent regular smokers than females by each educational category. Second, low educational status is a strong determinant of higher prevalence of smoking habit nationwide: males and females with university education smoke half as much as those with only primary education.

Similarly, as presented in Figure 16.5, Lithuanian males with university education consume significantly less alcohol as compared to those with only primary education. However, the opposite tendencies, although not statistically significant, were observed in the Lithuanian female population.

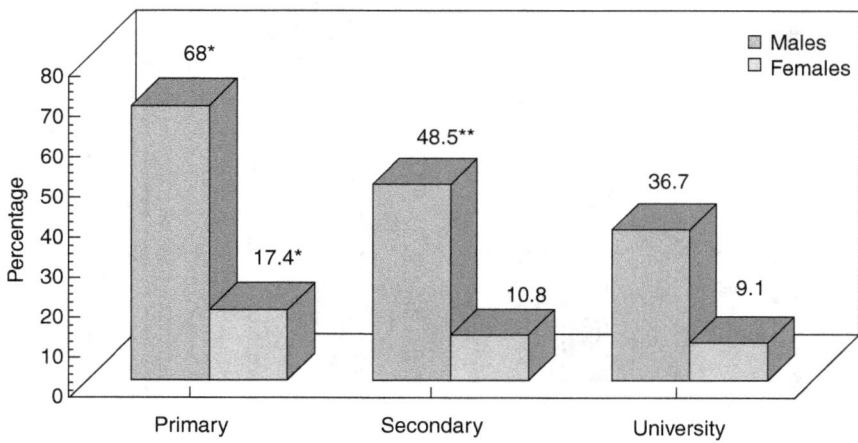

Figure 16.4 Proportion of regular smokers in Lithuanian population by education.

Notes
*p < 0.05 compared with secondary and university education.
**p < 0.05 compared with primary and university education.

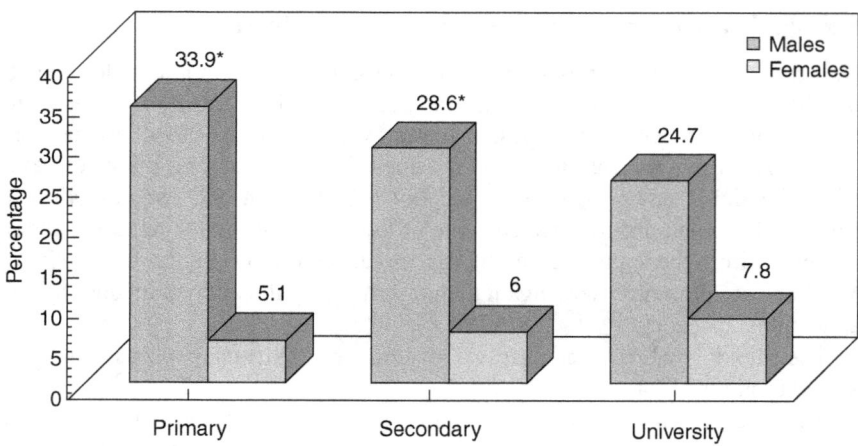

Figure 16.5 Proportion of frequent (weekly) strong alcohol users in Lithuanian population by education.

Note
*p < 0.05.

Changes in health behaviour in relation to educational level

Since 1994 as part of FINBALT HEALTH MONITOR project Kaunas University of Medicine has introduced biennial national monitoring of health behaviours in the adult Lithuanian population (Grabauskas *et al.* 1996, 1998, 2000, 2002). For this purpose, national random samples of 3,000 subjects aged 20–64 are interviewed by mail using a standardized questionnaire. Since the year 2002 this procedure has become an integral part of a larger international effort in health behaviour monitoring and is used for process evaluation purposes of national integrated programmes for the prevention of non-communicable diseases (CINDI HEALTH MONITOR).

Lithuanian health behaviour monitoring data collected since 1994 demonstrate rapid and substantial changes in population behaviours, going in different directions. In this chapter two examples are presented for illustration, one being a success story and another one indicating a certain failure as far as health consequences are concerned.

It is well documented that use of vegetable oils instead of animal fat for cooking is beneficial for health. Strategies to change this habit are of special importance in populations where animal fat is a substantial part of the daily diet. Lithuanian research data have shown that until the 1990s, contrary to an internationally recommended figure of 25 per cent, around 40 per cent of the energy from consumed food was coming from fat, animal fat being the major source (Petkevičienė, Sabaliauskaitė and Žvirėlaitė 1996). Preventive research programmes involving intensive mass media campaigns as well as a considerable increase in variety and choice of food has led to significant changes in nutritional habits. As presented in Figure 16.6, the proportion of persons using mostly vegetable oil for cooking doubled between 1994 and 1998–2000 in both males and females.

Analysing the above changes in relation to the educational level of the Lithuanian population, it is worth emphasizing that these health behaviour changes occur earlier and are more pronounced in males and females with university education (Figure 15.7).

However, some other behaviours, such as smoking habits, did not change in the direction supportive of health. As presented in Figure 16.8, there was a significant increase in the proportion of regular cigarette smokers nationwide, especially in the female population.

One of the possible explanations of these unfavourable trends could be the very aggressive invasion of international tobacco monopolies since the 1990s and deficiencies in national tobacco control legislation or, in many instances, simply failures relating to its implementation. The overall increase in smoking was mainly the result of the increase of this habit in the younger age groups, and in the case of females, even in teenagers. It should be admitted that the data of the last national health behaviour survey show some promising signs. By the

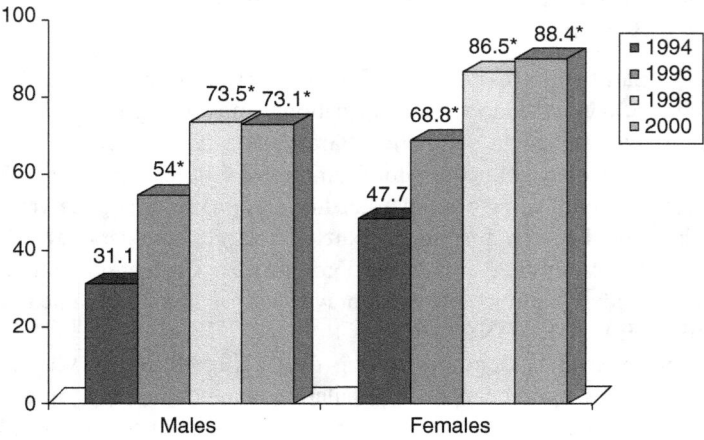

Figure 16.6 Proportion of persons using mostly vegetable oil for cooking in Lithuanian population aged 20–64 between 1994 and 2000.

Note
*p < 0.05 compared with year 1994.

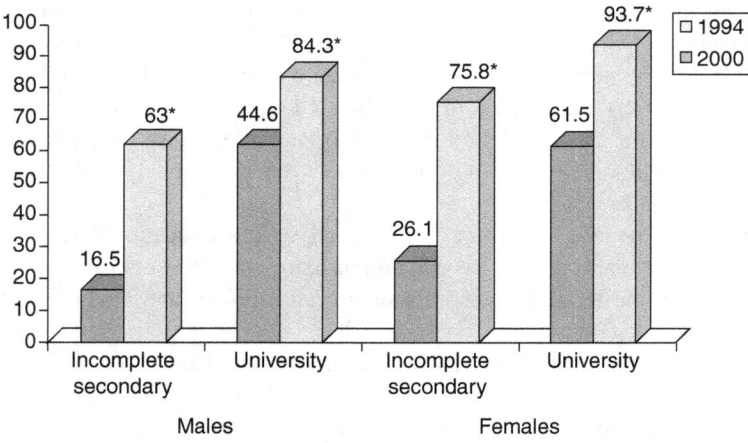

Figure 16.7 Proportion of Lithuanian population aged 20–64 using vegetable oil for cooking, by educational level, 1994 and 2000.

Note
*p < 0.01.

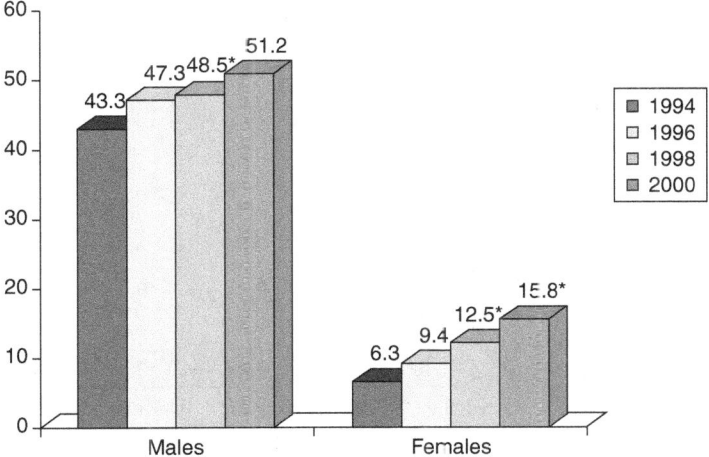

Figure 16.8 Trends in proportion of regular smokers in Lithuanian population aged 20–64 between 1994 and 2000.

Note
*p < 0.05 compared with 1994.

2002 survey, a statistically significant decline in smoking habits was recorded in both genders (unpublished data). This may be a reflection of the introduction of a total ban on tobacco advertising which came into force in May 2000. However, further monitoring of these trends is required.

As can be seen, the above undesirable trends in smoking habits substantially differed when analysed by educational category (Figure 16.9).

The registered trends in smoking habits until 2000 in the male population were mainly determined by an increase in smoking among those with lower education. Among the university degree-holding males there were even some signs of decline. However, that was not so in the case of university degree-holding females, although a difference in overall smoking prevalence compared to females of lower education remained.

Tackling health inequalities through policy development

As a follow-up to earlier and more recent research data, and stimulated by the 'Health for All' (HFA) movement coordinated by WHO, Lithuania initiated its national health policy development even before regaining its independence. Based on the research data available from population-based studies and national statistics, a new national concept of health was developed as a response to the resolution adopted by the re-established Lithuanian Medical Association in

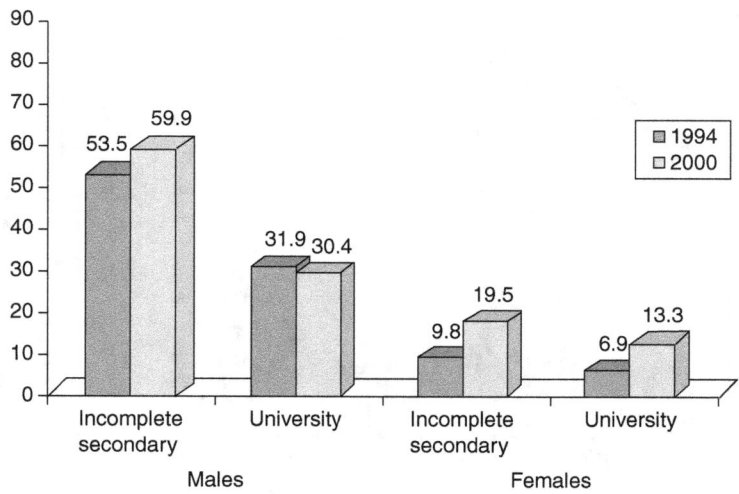

Figure 16.9 Proportion of regular smokers by educational level in Lithuanian population aged 20–64 in 1994 and 2000.

1989. After a nationwide dialogue this concept was approved at the highest political level by a specific parliamentary decision in October 1991, thus becoming a policy document (White Paper) for the reform of the Lithuanian health system. Largely influenced by the long-lasting collaboration with WHO, this concept was based on HFA principles, giving due importance to equality in health, community participation, intersectoriality and balance in health care aspects (Grabauskas *et al.* 1993).

In practical terms it has set the process of health policy implementation based on new health legislation, a participatory process including the health professions, politicians and the public at large, which culminated in bringing all interested parties together at the First National Health Policy Conference with international participation. A first objective health status analysis in postwar Lithuania with trend assessment and international comparison was produced for this conference (ibid.). Further efforts in health policy implementation (Grabauskas 1995a, 1995b, 2000a) led to the development of the Lithuanian Health Programme, adopted by parliament in July 1998 (Grabauskas 1998). Three major objectives aiming to reduce mortality, to increase average life expectancy and to achieve equality in health and health care and in quality of life have been set. The programme contains a separate target on equality which states: 'By the year 2010 differences in health and health care between various socio-economic population groups should be reduced by 25 per cent' (ibid., p. 32). The first step in the strategy to achieve this is defined as follows: 'By the year 2000 inequalities in health and health care between different socio-economic groups should be assessed and indicators for monitoring proposed' (ibid., p. 32). Further on, the problems of health inequalities have to be revised as stated: 'By the year 2005, to supplement health policy by measures aimed at the reduction of inequalities in health and health care' (ibid., p 32). The strategy includes intersectoral collaboration and systematic evaluation of the impact of all legal acts on health inequalities. Also in 1998, the National Board of Health was established by parliament, and is the highest level authority accountable to parliament and responsible for monitoring of health policy implementation. Its first report on national analysis of the health situation focused on social determinants and inequalities in health (Annual Report of the National Board of Health 1998). The report was distributed, presented and discussed on several occasions at international, national, regional and municipal levels. Following the presentation of this report, parliament adopted a resolution requesting that action should focus on ensuring equal rights of access to health for all (by decreasing health differences among the rural and urban population, and populations with different education, income level and age groups) by active cooperation of the state regions, municipalities and non-governmental organizations. All the above means that the problem of inequalities in health is finally on the political agenda and the issue of education is included. Unfortunately, economic constraints, lack of intersectoral cooperation, and frequent changes in government have not allowed more structured development and implementation of strategies aimed at systematically reducing inequalities in health. Nevertheless, the 3rd National Health Policy Conference, held in September 2000, concluded that considerable progress has been made in achieving major objectives and targets, as formulated in the National Health Programme (Grabauskas 2000b, 2000c, 2002).

Conclusions

1 Consistent with data from many other contexts, Lithuanian research data clearly demonstrate that higher education is a significant contributor to the health of a country's population.
2 Low education is one of the composite variables predicting considerably higher mortality in the youngest adult population segments and consequently lowering the economic capacity of the nation due to illness, disability and premature mortality.
3 Higher education is associated with lower prevalence of health behaviour related risk factors for ill-health.
4 Positive changes in health behaviours over time are more pronounced and occur earlier in the population group with university education.
5 Education should be given serious attention and be regarded as a priority in tackling social inequalities, both in developing and implementing national health policy, as well as in public policies at large.

References

Appels, A., Bosma, H., Grabauskas, V., Goštautas, A. and Sturmans, F. (1986) 'Self-related health and mortality in a Lithuanian and a Dutch population', *Social Science and Medicine*, 42 (5), 681–9.

Bosma, M., Appels, A., Sturmans, F., Grabauskas, V. and Goštautas, A. (1995) 'Educational level of spouses and risk of mortality: the WHO Kaunas–Rotterdam Intervention Study (KRIS)', *International Journal of Epidemiology*, 24 (1), 119–26.

Curry, C., Hurrelmann, K., Settertobulte, W. *et al.* (eds) (2000) *Health Behaviour and Health Among Young People*, Copenhagen: WHO/EURO.

Dahlgren, G. and Whitehead, M. (1992) *Policies and Strategies to Promote Equity in Health*, Copenhagen: WHO/EURO.

Davey Smith, G., Blane, D. and Bartley, M. (1994) 'Explanations for socio-economic differentials in mortality evidence from Britain and elsewhere', *European Journal of Public Health*, 4, 131–44.

Dičkutė, J., Padaiga, Ž., Grabauskas, V. *et al.* (2002) 'Ar motinos socialiniai veiksniai, gyvensena ir darbo sąlygos nėštumo laikotarpiu didina naujagimių mažo gimimo svorio riziką Lietuvoje?' ['Do maternal social factors, life style and working environment during pregnancy increase the risk of low birth weight deliveries in Lithuania?'] *Medicina*, 38 (3), 321–32.

Drever, F. and Whitehead, M. (eds) (1997) *Health Inequalities*, London: The Stationery Office.

Elo, I.T. and Preston, G.H. (1976) 'Educational differentials in mortality: United States, 1979–1985', *Social Science and Medicine*, 42, 47–57.

Fox, J. (1989) *Health Inequalities in European Countries*, Aldershot: Gower.

Grabauskas, V. (1995a) 'Health policy development in Lithuania: experience and lessons', in P. Harrington and A. Ritsatakis (eds) *Proceedings of the European Health Policy Conference 'Opportunities for the Future'*, vol. 5, Copenhagen: WHO Regional Office for Europe.

—— (1995b) 'The CINDI Programme in Lithuania – its contribution to national health policy development', in P. Harrington and A. Ritsatakis (eds) *Proceedings of the European Health Policy Conference 'Opportunities for the Future'*, vol. 3, Copenhagen: WHO Regional Office for Europe.

—— (Chair Task Force and ed.) (1998) *Lithuanian Health Programme*, Vilnius: Ministry of Health.

—— (2000a) 'Health policy development in Lithuania', in A. Ritsatakis *et al.* (eds) *Exploring Health Policy Development in Europe*, Copenhagen: European Centre for Health Policy, WHO Regional Office for Europe.

—— (2000b) 'Sveikatos politikos plėtojimas Lietuvoje' ['Development of health policy in Lithuania'], in *Pirmasis reformų dešimtmetis: sveikatos priežiūros sektorius socialinių–ekonominių pokyčių kontekste*, Vilnius.

—— (2000c) 'Sveikatos politikos vystymo procesas Lietuvoje', III nacionalinės sveikatos politikos konferencija 'Lietuvos sveikatos politika XXI amžiuje', Vilnius, 2000 m. rugsėjis ['Process of health policy development in Lithuania', paper presented at the 3rd National Health Policy Conference 'Lithuanian Health Policy in the 21st Century', Vilnius, September 2000], KMU: 5–12.

—— (2002) 'Health targets: the case of Lithuania', in M. Marinker (ed.) *Health Targets in Europe: Policy, Progress and Promises*, BMJ Books.

Grabauskas, V. *et al.* (eds) (1993) 'Lithuanian Health Report – 1990s', a background document for National Conference on Health Policy, Vilnius, 29–30 March 2003, Kaunas: Medical Academy Press.

Grabauskas, V. and Kalėdienė, R. (2002) 'Tackling social inequality through the development of health policy in Lithuania', *Scandinavian Journal of Public Health*, 30, 12–19.

Grabauskas, V., Klumbienė, J., Petkevičienė, J. *et al.* (1996, 1998, 2000, 2002) *Health Behaviour Among Adult Lithuanian Population*, Kaunas Medical Academy, Lithuania and National Public Health Institute, Helsinki, Finland.

Grabauskas, V., Misevičienė, I. and Klumbienė, J. (2001) 'Lėtinių neinfekcinių ligų epidemiologinės situacijos pokyčiai 1987–2000 metais: CINDI programa' ['Changes in epidemiological situation of chronic non-communicable diseases between 1987–2000: the CINDI programme'], *Medicina*, 37 (12), 1511–19.

Grabauskas, V. and Padaiga, Ž. (2002) 'Reducing health inequalities: Lithuania', in J. Mackenbach and M. Bakker (eds) *Reducing Health Inequalities in Health – a European Perspective*, London–New York: Routledge.

Kalėdienė, R. and Petrauskienė, J. (2000) 'Inequalities in life expectancy in Lithuania by level of education', *Scandinavian Journal of Public Health*, 28, 4–9.

Kunst, A.E. and Makenbach, J.P. (1993) *Measuring Socio-Economic Inequalities in Health*, Copenhagen: WHO/EURO.

Nacionalinės Sveikatos Tarybos metinis pranešimas (1998) [*Annual Report of National Board of Health*], Vilnius.

Padaiga, Ž., Grabauskas, V., Gaižauskienė, A. *et al.* (1998) *Equity in Health and Health Care in Lithuania: a Situation Analysis*, Copenhagen: WHO/EURO.

Pincus, T. and Callahan, L.F. (1994) 'Associations of low formal education level and poor health status: behavioral, in addition to demographic and medical, explanations?', *Journal of Clinical Epidemiology*, 47, 355–61.

WHO Regional Office for Europe (1999) *Health 21 – Health for All in the 21st Century*, Copenhagen: WHO/EURO.

World Health Organization (2002) *World Health Report 2002: reducing risks, promoting health*, Geneva.

Chapter 17

Spirituality and citizenship in higher education

Hanan A. Alexander

Over the past quarter century a significant interest has emerged across the western world in the education of spirituality. The growing influence of secularization and democratization has made it possible and necessary at pre-higher education level to educate in one common school system a wide cross-section of people with vastly different visions of what it means to live a good life. In many countries there is a desire for common schools to engage all students in an appropriate study of religious and spiritual matters. This task has required looking for common denominators among non-believers and believers in different faiths (e.g. Jackson 1997, 2004), in the interests of securing appropriate forms of fairness and openness in the educational experience offered. This ambition is in tension with a tendency to approach religious and spiritual matters in common schools via a strategy of 'separation' as in some European countries, including post-Soviet 'countries in transition', whereby religious education in common schools has tended to be conceived in 'confessional' terms and offered as a choice for parents (and in due course for older students) against non-religious courses in 'ethics'. The ambition is also in tension with a strategy of 'exclusion', as in the USA, where the separation of church and state has led to great hesitation in the treatment of spiritual and religious matters in the common school. However, one danger in relation to the ambition of engaging all students in the common school in an appropriate study of religious and spiritual matters is the possibility that the commonalities being appealed to might turn out to be so minimal that youngsters would leave secondary school with little sense of how to relate to these sorts of issues (Noddings 1993, Alexander 2001: 30–6, Dewey 1960). The question to be addressed in this chapter is whether or to what degree this interest in spiritual education, which has to date focused mainly on primary and secondary education, belongs in institutions of higher learning.

To respond to this query requires an exploration first of the purposes of higher education, especially in the 'societies in transition' with which this volume is concerned. I will then consider rival conceptions of democracy and democratic citizenship, in order to explore what it can mean to educate for spirituality in open liberal democratic societies. This will allow me to draw some conclusions concerning the role of spirituality in higher education in democratic 'societies in transition'. It is my thesis that to the extent that higher education should be concerned with the preparation of democratic citizens, and insofar as education in spirituality involves initiation into study of traditions of thought and practice focused on how one should live, then institutions of higher learning should seek to promote the exploration of intelligent spiritual traditions that seek to balance the common or universal with the distinctive or particular. Education in intelligent spirituality, in other words, has a significant role to play in the creation of democratic citizens and so deserves an important place in higher education (Alexander 2001: 198–203, 2004).

Purposes of higher education

Higher education is commonly associated with at least five purposes: (1) to prepare students to understand, conduct or apply research of various kinds, (2) to instruct students in the rational traditions and academic disciplines associated with liberal or advanced learning, (3) to provide vocational training that will enable students to enter the workforce, earn a living, and engage in productive and satisfying labour, (4) to initiate students into the study of substantive visions of the good, and (5) to foster the dispositions and skills required for democratic citizenship (see e.g. Griswold 1962, Rosovsky 1990, Wegner 1978). 'Societies in transition' such as Lithuania and Israel (the former from communism to democracy, the latter from socialism to capitalism) have tended to view the curriculum of higher education at all levels (baccalaureate, masters and doctoral) as a whole serving the first three of these goals. The difference between undergraduate and graduate – pre- and post-baccalaureate – studies, on this view, has to do with level of subject matter expertise aimed at and achieved.

However, the demands of democratization, properly understood, require a reform of the higher education curriculum in 'societies in transition', as elsewhere, so that the fourth and fifth aims are properly addressed also, namely the fostering of the dispositions and skills required for democratic citizenship and (as part of that task) initiation into study of substantive visions of the good. Higher education, in other words, should assume specific responsibility for spiritual, ethical and democratic education.

Specialization in higher education

The rationale for the current specialization-focused orientation to undergraduate education in many European societies is both historical and epistemological. Its roots lay in the emergence of the modern from the medieval university, in which independent, religiously affiliated scholars created communities – colleges – to facilitate their common search for truth. The classical curriculum of late antiquity was well rounded rather than specialized and aimed, at least according to the version advocated by scholars such as Cicero, Quintillian and Boethius, to equip students with the concepts and skills required for republican citizenship. It consisted of the Trivium – grammar, rhetoric and logic – and the Quadrivium – arithmetic (number in itself), geometry (number in space), music (number in time) and astronomy (number in space and time). However, as education came to be conceived in three stages – primary, secondary and tertiary – and as university masters began to specialize in such fields as divinity, law and medicine – and later Greek, Hebrew, Latin, physics, mathematics and metaphysics – the so-called seven liberal arts came increasingly to be seen as the province of secondary studies, leaving higher learning for more focused training (Kimball 1986: 13–42). Yet it is doubtful whether education for civic engagement should end at adolescence and whether the broad education necessary for such engagement can be accomplished properly in the secondary school alone (Alexander 2005a).

This tendency toward specialization at the tertiary level, and away from broad preparation for citizenship, was reinforced by the extraordinary influence during the late medieval period of scholastic philosophy. On the scholastic view there could be no division between the pursuit of truth and learning to live a worthwhile life. This meant that initiation into the rational traditions required engaging a concept of the good, in this case as revealed in scripture. Yet, it also supposed that there is only one way to examine the truth and only one correct way to live (Wolfson 1977).

When the philosophers of the enlightenment began to critique this orientation, they replaced the deductive rationality of Aristotle with the inductive logic of empiricism. The new science that they created was no less absolutist than its scholastic predecessor, only now the absolute truth would be discovered on the basis of human experience within the confines of space and time, rather than in the transcendent realm of Aristotelian spheres or Platonic ideas; and it would be rigorously distinguished from the realm of ethics and values, which would increasingly be seen as the product of unreliable and deeply personal emotions. As the modern European university emerged from its medieval ancestor, its curriculum came to focus on the acquisition of knowledge as defined by the academic disciplines; and as the practical success of the new science was translated into technologies that were connected to the new power elites of industrialization and urbanization, this discipline-based higher education became increasingly identified with instrumental and economic values, with diminishing reference to how one ought to live (Rothblatt 1976, Rothblatt and Wittrock 1993).

Democracy and citizenship in higher education

However, this disconnection between the modern European university and the needs of formation for citizenship in a democratic society is highly problematic. The tendency of the empiricists to believe that the new science would verify objective truth has too often been exploited by political ideologies such as communism, socialism, fascism and colonialism to justify their own agendas, thus maintaining the link between knowledge and power (Apple 1995, Popkewitz 1999). Although the empirical nature of modern science lends itself in principle to public criticism based on tests against experience, post-positivist and postmodern critiques of empiricism and positivism (the intellectual heir of empiricism) have shown at the very least that theoretical expectation often influences how scientific data is interpreted in such a way as to mitigate the impact of such supposedly public and objective criticism (Burbules and Phillips 2000). The overly specialized and narrow curriculum of much European higher education over a good deal of the nineteenth and twentieth centuries, whatever its contribution to the advancement of knowledge and despite the fact that the progenitors of liberal democratic theory were among its scholars, was too often used to prepare the elites of closed societies (Popper 1963) to legitimate objectionable positive conceptions of freedom (Berlin 1958). Rather than promoting political orientations that allow people with competing conceptions of the good to live together in common civil societies, and preparing students to make the substantive choices which citizenship in such societies demands, this education tended to promote a single-minded positivism and belief in a 'one best system' (Tyack 1974).

Whatever the limitations of post-positivist and postmodern critiques of empiricism and positivism, including, for example, Thomas Kuhn's (1996) claim that rival theoretical paradigms are incommensurable or that the meaning of concepts from one research programme cannot be fully understood in another, in their wake we have come to view conceptions of the truth, as well as of the good, as plural, at least in Popper's sense that, even if there is an absolute truth, no one has it in his or her pocket (see Siegel 1987, 1988 and Scheffler 1982). In the absence of definitive and unproblematic criteria to distinguish truth from falsehood, if higher learning is to instruct students in any sort of knowledge at all it will need to prepare them to evaluate ideals and standards of assessment which, if pursued far enough, transcend the confines of space and time; ideals and standards of assessment embedded in conceptions not only of how the world is, but also of how it ought to be (Kant 1997, Hegel 1953). Sovereignty, to use Iris Murdoch's (1970) well-known phrase, belongs to the good. This capacity for strong evaluation (a notion which I will illuminate in more detail later) is, I contend, a basic requirement of democratic citizenship, at least according to one influential way of conceiving democracy. But, what sort of democracy is this, and if rival empirical and ethical theories are incommensurable because data are significantly influenced by expectations, and concepts are only fully comprehensible from within a tradition of thought or practice, how is it possible to prepare students to conduct this sort of assessment in other than arbitrary ways? I will address these questions in the next section by examining a number of leading philosophical theories of democratic citizenship.

Conceptions of democratic citizenship

There is a tension in democratic thought between individual rights on the one hand and the common good on the other. This is connected to related tensions between universalism and particularism, moral minimalism and maximalism, and 'thick' and 'thin' conceptions of democratic citizenship.

Political and comprehensive liberalism

Liberal democratic theory tends to focus on the rights of the individual citizen, expressed, at least according to Rawls' (1971) formulation, in terms of the principles of procedural and distributive justice. The first principle requires that in a just society laws, rules and procedures be applied fairly – equally to all citizens in similar circumstances regardless of irrelevant considerations such as race, religion, gender and ethic origin. This guarantees the right of citizens to choose or not to choose a vision of the good as they see fit. The second principle holds that in a just society resources ought to be distributed equitably so that all citizens, again regardless of irrelevant affiliations, designations or associations, receive a fair share of what the state allocates directly or makes available indirectly by creating stable conditions for commerce and the like. Since the rights guaranteed by these principles are due to all citizens, liberalism is strongly associated with the universalistic impulse in democratic thought.

Michael Walzer (1994) associates this universalistic impulse with what he calls moral minimalism. We can distinguish, writes Walzer, between two different albeit interrelated kinds of moral argument: 'a way of talking among ourselves, here at home, about the thickness of our own history and culture ... and a way of talking to people abroad, across different cultures, about a thinner life we have in common.... There are the makings of a thin and universalistic morality inside every thick and particular morality' (p. xi). Moral terms, Walzer continues (pp. 2–3), 'have minimal and maximal meanings; we can standardly give thin and thick accounts of them ... Procedural justice constitutes liberalism's most minimal, and thus most universal, principle – it requires only a limited degree of substantive moral commitment that is shared across a wide variety of moral traditions'. Rawls (1993) dubbed the political orientation that centres heavily on such procedures 'political liberalism'. Political orientations that embrace various more specific accounts of distributive justice tend to require more substantive, and hence more particularistic, moral commitments; they are in this respect thicker or more maximalist. Callan (1997) and others have referred to this orientation as 'comprehensive liberalism'. Political liberalism requires fewer substantive moral commitments for public purposes than comprehensive liberalism.

Terence McLaughlin (1996a) suggests that conceptions of citizenship can be seen as located on a continuum from 'minimal' to 'maximal'. The more minimal an account of citizenship the less it requires in the way of educational preparation. One main point of Rawlsian 'political liberalism' is to protect the right of citizens to make their own substantive moral choices for their lives as a whole, with only minimum intervention on the part of the state – presumably only to protect the right of all to make their own choices in these matters freely and without interference. In this view, education – at least that supported by the state – should play a very limited role in influencing the substantive moral choices of students about their lives as a whole. As we move from political to comprehensive liberalism, however, the state will be required to shape citizens as liberals in areas which extend beyond the political. Both 'political' and 'comprehensive' liberalism can be seen as requiring, in different ways, forms of education for citizenship whereby students are prepared to achieve various forms and understanding and commitment relating to matters of public policy.

Affiliated liberalism and communitarianism

But this is not the whole story. Those concerned with the rights and roles of communities in democratic societies have raised hard questions about the liberal perspective. These objections divide roughly into two groups: (1) those concerned with the rights of particular ethnic, cultural and religious groups to sustain themselves across the generations in liberal societies and (2) those who challenge the very viability of any account of liberalism or just society without a concomitant substantive conception of political community.

Walter Feinberg's account of 'affiliated liberalism' is one response to the first objection (Feinberg 1998, McDonough and Feinberg 2003). On this view, political liberalism guarantees the right of citizens to affiliate with religious, cultural or other groups as they choose, and thus to inculcate in their children a desire to maintain such affiliations, so that the values maintained by those groups can be sustained across the generations. To deny a group the right of survival is tantamount to denying citizens the opportunity to choose that particular affiliation in the future; and inculcating a preference for affiliation among the children of current members is the most likely mechanism, save perhaps proselytization, of ensuring collective survival.

The second objection relates to the perception that the notion of rational choice presupposed to liberalism requires a broader ethical framework – or deeper philosophical principles – of some kind, which cannot be satisfactorily provided by affiliated liberalism. Communitarian philosophers such as Michael Sandel (1982, 1984), who draw inspiration from the civic republicanism of Aristotle and Cicero, note that Rawls' theory of justice accepts a move made by earlier liberal theorists, especially Immanuel Kant, of prioritizing individual rights over a conception of the common good. Sandel (1984: 1) challenges claims about the priority of the right over the good and the vision of the freely choosing individual which it embodies. Following Aristotle, he argues that 'we cannot justify political arrangements without reference to common purposes and ends, and that we cannot conceive our personhood without reference to our role as citizens, and as participants in a common life' (ibid., p. 5).

On the communitarian view, then, moral minimalism – those universal principles such as procedural justice that diverse ethical traditions have in common – is possible only by virtue of its embeddedness in thicker moral traditions, and thin conceptions of citizenship education require connection to more maximalist visions of the role that citizens ought to play in democratic life. In order to prioritize individual rights, such as that of rational choice, we must first embrace a conception of the common good which recognizes the value of personal autonomy.

Yet this response carries its own set of difficulties. Feminist philosophers such as Nel Noddings (2002), and radical theorists such as Peter McLaren (1989) and Ilan Gur-Zeev (2003), complain that the communitarian preference of the good over the right only compounds the difficulties with moral minimalism mentioned above. How, they ask, does the imposition of a moral tradition thicker than political liberalism resolve the difficulty that even thin conceptions of citizenship inculcate values in children that violate their fundamental right to choice? If the conception of citizenship inherent in political liberalism is too thin to sustain democratic life, the communitarian alternative may be too thick.

Liberal communitarianism

Charles Taylor's discussion of human agency – defined in terms of self-determination, self-expression and strong evaluation – can help to address these sorts of perplexities by delineating a middle-ground between liberal and communitarian democratic theories, along the lines of Tamir's (1993) notion of liberal nationalism, that clarifies how thin a conception of citizenship can be to sustain a viable account of democracy, as well as when it becomes so thick that individualism is stifled. I have called this view liberal communitarianism (Alexander 2004).

Taylor follows Kant in believing that autonomy or self-determination is a 'transcendental condition' of ethics – an assumption we must make for any conception of normative discourse to make sense altogether. Rational choice is not a value to be justified within a particular moral tradition; it is a condition that makes the very discussion of moral alternatives possible (Smith 2002: 65–6).

However, Taylor also follows Hegel in recognizing that for persons to exercise autonomy they must be capable of grounding their choices in some sort of reasoning or understanding; otherwise these choices would not actually be theirs, but a product of caprice. This requires that their choices express ideals or desires they have come to embrace and upon which they can base their decision. To avoid the quagmires of strong subjectivism and radical relativism, this sort of self-expression must entail more than an expression of arbitrary taste, personal whim, or momentary feeling. It requires an appeal to 'horizons of significance' or 'transcendental ideals' embedded in moral traditions sufficiently 'thick' to sustain meaningful moral choices to which competing conceptions of the good give expression, even if we cannot agree on their content (Taylor 1989, 1991).

For self-expression to be meaningful, in other words, we must suppose that people have the capacity to engage in a particular kind of evaluation which involves not merely first order (or 'weak') evaluation – involving first order desires relating to such matters as food, procreation and survival, where the criterion for evaluation is simple preference – but also second order evaluation relating to second order desires – desires about desires – where the criterion for evaluation relates to the worth or value of the desire in a deeper and self-defining sense (Frankfurt 1971).

Strong evaluation of this kind is an essential ingredient of democratic citizenship, grounded in moral traditions sufficiently thick to enable self expression, but not so thick as to squelch self-determination. This view is communitarian in that it assumes that concepts of the common good lie at the heart of any democratic society. But it is also liberal in that it does not suppose that anyone has the single correct conception of the good in his or her pocket, so that people will need to choose in an appropriate way among competing alternatives or, when unable to choose between equally compelling accounts, embrace several that are in tension with one another. Liberal communitarianism, like affiliated liberalism, appreciates the contribution to liberal democracy of a diversity of traditions, but is less tolerant of putative ethical orientations that fail to recognize the degree to which the very possibility of democratic society and ethical discourse are conditional upon the cultivation of human agency.

Democracies need citizens who have the capacity to deliberate and assess the key policy issues that face the societies in which they live, and the evaluative tools for engaging critically with these issues are to be found within particular moral traditions. This requires a robust association with particular orientations, along with a profound commitment to political liberalism; and the preparation of such citizens is a primary task of education in what I call intelligent spirituality – one that balances moral maximalism with moral minimalism in an appropriate way.

Spirituality and the democratic citizenship

It may well be the very thinness of political liberalism, and the moral minimalism of many of the educational, religious and cultural institutions that it spawned, that has sent people on what many call a spiritual quest for answers to how one should live (Alexander 2001: 12–24). But this interest in spirituality is notoriously hard to define, in part because people answer Socrates' question about how one should live in vastly different ways. Consequently, educators at all levels of schooling promote surprisingly different, even contradictory, agendas under the banner of spiritual education.

Dimensions of spiritual education

To clarify this discussion, David Carr and I have recently arranged some of the most significant issues with which spiritual education might be concerned along six dimensions or distinct but interrelated continua (Alexander and Carr 2005).

An approach to spiritual education is confessional or non-confessional to the degree that it aims to teach, convince or inspire youngsters to embrace a particular religious, ethical or cultural point of view. The so-called phenomenological approach to religious education, for example, aims to offer students a sympathetic but non-confessional depiction of a variety of faiths and traditions (Lovat 1991). A conception of spiritual education can be said to be religiously tethered or untethered to the extent that it is tied to a particular historical faith or organized religion (Alexander and McLaughlin 2002).

Other respects in which conceptions of spiritual education differ relate to forms of objectivity and moral authority claimed, the role of personal feelings or experiences invoked, the extent to which a particular view of life is involved, the universality or otherwise of their scope and the role given to the communication of various forms of knowledge and the cultivation of particular sentiments or experiences, such as those of awe and wonder (Alexander 2001: 55–8, Cajete 1994, Carr 1996, Erricker 2004, Gearon 2001, Heubner 1999, McLaughlin 1996b, Ofsted 1994, Walzer 1994).

Extreme and intelligent spiritual instruction

Each of these dimensions can be pursued in an extreme or in a balanced manner. Spiritual instruction can be conducted in a way that is totally confessional, as if no other faith or ethical traditions are worthy of consideration; it can teach about spirituality as a phenomenon alone, without ever asking students to consider embracing any faith or ethical commitment whatsoever; or it can try to foster a particular orientation while concomitantly examining alternatives. Instruction in spirituality might similarly be so totally tethered to a particular religious faith that it ignores all others or, conversely, be totally disconnected from organized religion altogether. Alternatively, it can embrace a particular religion while learning from untethered spiritualities, or promote non-religious forms of spirituality while learning from distinct religious traditions. By the same token, spiritual instruction can focus totally on personal feelings, group solidarity or transcendent reality; or it can look for ways to integrate these sources of spiritual value. It can be so thick that it smothers individuality, so thin that it offers little wisdom concerning how to live, or somewhere in between; and it can focus entirely on knowledge, wholly on affect, or on both.

When practised in an extreme manner, however, instruction in spirituality tends to limit awareness of and capacity for self-determination and self-expression, either because a tradition becomes so all-encompassing that the possibility for a sense of individuality is severely diminished, or because its content becomes so vacuous that there is little of value for the individual to express. Under these circumstances, the possibility for strong evaluation is seriously jeopardized. People will either lack the awareness that they can in fact influence the course of their lives by making choices based on strong values, or they will lack commitment to values on which to base their assessment. Indoctrinatory forms of spiritual education deny essential ingredients of both democratic and ethical discourse relating to the demands of personal self-determination. Extreme spiritual instruction leads toward totalistic, amoral or unethical ideologies – with diminished sense of agency – characteristic of Popper's closed society and Berlin's positive concept of liberty (Alexander 2005b).

Societies seeking to foster democratic values and institutions, and to cultivate citizens capable of taking responsibility for them, require balanced, not extreme, spiritual instruction, which might be justifiably called education in intelligent spirituality (Alexander 2001: 171–213, 2005b). Such an education seeks to empower individuals to make intelligent choices grounded in traditions of ethical thought and practice that express what individuals judge to be most worthwhile. Education in this sort of intelligent spirituality can be conceived in terms of the cultivation of human agency – self-determination, self-expression and string evaluation – through a balanced engagement with spiritual traditions that vary in the extent to which they embody the dimensions indicated earlier.

Spirituality in higher education

Spiritual engagement of this sort ought to be a lifelong pursuit that requires the kind of mature and serious study which only higher learning can provide. It should not be relegated to the education of children and adolescents alone, but should find a significant place in the institutions and curriculum of higher education as well.

Spiritual linkages in institutions of higher learning

We can distinguish between institutions of higher learning on the basis of the extent to which they are linked to a particular spiritual tradition or community. An institution can be said to be highly linked if it has strong ties to a particular faith or culture that is expressed in its history, governance, faculty, student body or curriculum, and less linked if it has few ties of this kind. Many historic European colleges and universities, for example, were founded long ago by religious denominations and maintain varying degrees of linkage to their historic roots, from the positioning of a chapel at the centre of the campus, to the sponsorship of denominational divinity faculties, to religious requirements for particular corporate officers such as deans or faculty members, to the arrangement of academic calendars, to explicit and implicit expectations placed upon students.

In the United States, universities founded by Catholic religious orders – such as the Jesuits – have tended to maintain strong religious linkages. Often, key members of the governing board, the president and faculty members in sensitive theological disciplines are required to have affiliation or sympathy with the faith commitments of these orders. Institutions founded by Protestant churches, on the other hand, have tended to diminish their denominational ties, maintaining no more than an historic chapel or denominational theology school. These linkages are tethered, to greater or lesser degrees, to particular religious traditions. I want to make three points relating to institutional linkages. First, given the significance of moral maximalism to democratic society, highly linked institutions have a particularly important role to play in the education of democratic citizens. It is perhaps here that students are most likely to be initiated into thick spiritual traditions and to acquire the sorts of robust ethical identities democratic citizenship demands. Yet, these institutions may be easily tempted to devote significant energies and resources to promoting their particularist agenda, without paying sufficient attention to the concerns of the wider democratic society of which they are a part. This could prove to be highly problematic for the institutions' faculty and students, who might be drawn to one or another of the spiritual extremes against which I cautioned above. It would also be a great loss to democratic society as a whole, which depends upon input from a diversity of thick ethical traditions in order maintain its liberal procedures and institutions.

Second, it is equally important that institutions with fewer linkages to distinct spiritual traditions actively create opportunities for students to engage in the exploration of the variety of dimensions of spiritual education mentioned above. In addition to curricular obligations, about which I will have more to say below, these institutions need to provide a wide array of religious, political, cultural and intellectual co-curricular activities that will inspire students to explore a variety of spiritual traditions and encourage them to make one or more of them their ethical home. If students have brought such a tradition with them from their family or earlier education, the university should challenge them to re-evaluate their previous commitments, either to reaffirm them or reject them for new ones. And if students have not come with such spiritual backgrounds, it is the university's obligation to provide opportunities to discover or create them. That an institution professes no tie to a particular spiritual tradition does not relieve it of the obligation to assist students in exploring and eventually making in an appropriate way spiritual and moral commitments.

Third, regardless of the degree to which an institution is linked to particular spiritual traditions, it is likely to employ faculty and staff and to admit students who are not committed to those traditions. The argument for balanced or intelligent spirituality articulated above would require that institutions of all degrees of linkage be open in appropriate ways to those who are different from the institutional norm in one way or another.

Spirituality in the curriculum of higher education

The analysis offered here suggests a fundamental shift in current thinking in Israel and Europe about the content of higher education, away from the empirical influence that has dominated the university curriculum for most of modernity, and back to an earlier ethical attitude associated with the seven liberal arts required of republican citizens. At the forefront of this shift is the recognition that the pursuit of truth is first a moral activity grounded in such virtues as honesty, integrity, humility and literacy, not an instrumental activity associated with moving up the social, corporate or academic hierarchies. Truth can only be pursued once we have a sense of the knowledge most worth advancing and are imbued with the values – Israel Scheffler called them the 'cognitive emotions' – that will enable us to advance it (Scheffler 1991).

On the undergraduate level, this means that the exploration of alternative moral and spiritual traditions needs to become much more central than has been the case to date. Students need to examine competing accounts of the cultural, historical, religious and philosophical underpinnings of the democratic forms of life in which they are being educated to engage, so that they will become competent to raise questions and make judgements about the knowledge worth advancing and the life worth living. Following Richard Peters (1965), such exposure is required in some degree of both depth and breadth; students should understand their own commitments in some depth and be able to relate them to a variety of alternatives (see Phenix 1964). The distribution I have in mind, however, would be based more on competing moral and spiritual traditions than on the rational disciplines or forms of knowledge emphasized by Peters (also Hirst 1974, Hirst and Peters 1970, Schwab 1982).[1] Indeed, the sort of examination needed to foster the robust ethical affiliations required of democratic citizens would need to be multi-disciplinary, allowing students not only to examine a variety of traditions but also to do so from a host of different methodological points of view. This certainly does not preclude the other sort of discipline- or vocation-orientated studies for which higher education is well known. But it does imply that students will be better prepared to make choices about specialized studies once they have acquired some of the tools of strong evaluation that can be learned from the sort of moral and spiritual engagement I am proposing.

When it comes to graduate studies, this analysis suggests that the masters and doctoral degrees be imbued with broad moral, as well as specialized, professional or epistemological significance. To become an expert in a particular field of inquiry or practice entails not only that one learn research methods and advanced knowledge, but also that one critically engage with the purposes and meanings of that field for wider society, including its ethical dilemmas and moral perplexities. One should understand why the field is worthy of time, attention and resources, and be willing to accept an obligation to become a steward of the discipline, transmitting and transforming it across the generations.[2]

Education in intelligent spirituality should play a prominent role, therefore, in how we conceive both the institutions and the content of higher learning in transitional societies, as elsewhere. When a proper balance is achieved between moral maximalism and moral minimalism, this approach lies at the heart of the robust ethical identities democratic citizenship requires, and provides the ethical context in which it is possible for citizens to realize their potential for human agency by exercising self-determination, self-expression and strong evaluation.

Notes

1 It is well known that Hirst repudiated this view later in his career.
2 The term 'steward of the discipline' comes from the Carnegie Initiative on the Doctorate, of the Carnegie Foundation for the Advancement of Teaching. See Sullivan 2004, and www.carnegiefoundation.org/CID.

References

Alexander, H.A. (2001) *Reclaiming Goodness: Education and the Spiritual Quest*, Notre Dame: University of Notre Dame Press.
—— (2004) 'Moral education and liberal democracy: spirituality, community, and character in open society', *Educational Theory*, 53 (4), 367–87.
—— (2005a) *Democracy, Knowledge Growth, and the Education of Citizens: Emerging Trends in Israeli Higher Education*, Iyunin Behinukh.
—— (2005b) 'Education in ideology', *The Journal of Moral Education*, 34, 1.
Alexander, H.A. and Carr, D. (2005) 'Philosophical issues in spiritual education and development', in G. Roehlkpart *et al.* (eds) *Handbook of Spiritual Development and Adolescence*, Thousand Oaks, CA: Sage.
Alexander, H.A. and McLaughlin, T.H. (2002) 'Education in religion and spirituality', in N. Blake *et al.* (eds) *The Blackwell Guide to the Philosophy of Education*, Oxford: Blackwell.
Apple, M.W. (1995) *Knowledge and Power*, 2nd edn, New York: Routledge.
Berlin, I. (1998) 'Two concepts of liberty', in H. Hardy and R. Hausheer (eds) *The Proper Study of Mankind: an Anthology of Essays*, London: Pimlico.
Burbules, N. and Phillips, D.C. (2000) *Postpositivism and Educational Research*, Lanham, MA: Rowman and Littlefield.
Cajete, G. (1994) *Look to the Mountain: an Ecology of Indigenous Education*, Ashville, NC: Kivaki Press.
Callan, E. (1997) *Creating Citizens: Political Education and Liberal Democracy*, Oxford: Clarendon Press.
Carr, D. (1996) 'Rival conceptions of spiritual education', *Journal of Philosophy of Education*, 30, 159–78.
Dewey, J. (1960) *A Common Faith*, New Haven: Yale University Press.
Erricker, C. (2004) 'A manifesto for spiritual activism: time to subvert the branding of education', in H.A. Alexander (ed.) *Spirituality and Ethics in Education: Philosophical, Theological, and Radical Perspectives*, Brighton: Sussex Academic Press.
Feinberg, W. (1998) *Common Schools and Uncommon Identities: National Unity and Cultural Difference*, New Haven: Yale University Press.
Frankfurt, H. (1971) 'Freedom of will and the concept of a person', *Journal of Philosophy* 67 (1), 5–20.
Gearon, L. (2001) 'The corruption of innocence and the spirituality of dissent: postcolonial perspectives on spirituality in a world of violence', in J. Erricker, C. Ota and C. Erricker (eds) *Spiritual Education: Cultural, Religious, and Social Difference – New Perspectives for the 21st Century*, Brighton: Sussex Academic Press.
Griswold, A.W. (1962) *Liberal Education and the Democratic Ideal*, New Haven: Yale University Press.
Gur-Zeev, I. (2003) *Destroying the Other's Collective Memory*, New York: Peter Lang.

Hegel, H.W.F. (1953) *Reason in History*, Indianapolis: Bobbs-Merrill.
Heubner, D. (1999) *The Lure of the Transcendent*, Mahwan, NJ: Lawrence Erlbaum.
Hirst, P.H. (1974) *Knowledge and the Curriculum*, London: Routledge & Kegan Paul.
Hirst, P.H. and Peters, R.S. (1970) *The Logic of Education*, London: Routledge & Kegan Paul.
Jackson, R. (1997) *Religious Education: an Interpretive Approach*, London: Hodder & Stoughton.
—— (2004) *Rethinking Religious Education and Plurality*, London: RoutledgeFalmer.
Kant, I. (1997) *Prolegomena to Any Future Metaphysics*, Cambridge: Cambridge University Press.
Kimball, B.A. (1986) *Orators and Philosophers: a History of the Idea of Liberal Education*, New York: Teachers College Press.
Kuhn, T.S. (1996) *The Structure of Scientific Revolutions*, Chicago: University of Chicago Press.
Lovat, T. (1991) *What is this Thing Called Religious Education?*, Wentworth Falls: Social Science Press.
McDonough, K. and Feinberg, W. (2003) 'Liberalism and the dilemma of public education in multicultural societies', in K. McDonough and W. Feinberg (eds) *Citizenship Education in Liberal Democratic Societies: Teaching for Cosmopolitan Values and Collective Identities*, Oxford Oxford University Press.
McLaren, P. (1989) *Life in Schools*, New York: Longman.
McLaughlin, T.H. (1996a) 'Educating responsible citizens', in H. Tam (ed.) *Punishment, Excuses, and Moral Development*, Aldershot: Avebury.
—— (1996b) 'Education of the whole child?', in R. Best (ed.) *Education, Spirituality, and the Whole Child*, London: Cassell.
Murdoch, I. (1970) *The Sovereignty of Good*, London: Routledge & Kegan Paul.
Noddings, N. (1993) *Educating for Religious Belief and Unbelief*, New York: Teachers College Press.
—— (2002) *Educating Moral People: an Alternative to Character Education*, New York: Teachers College Press.
Ofsted (1994) 'Spiritual, moral, social and cultural development', an Ofsted Discussion Paper, Office for Standards in Education, UK.
Peters, R.S. (1965) *Education as Initiation*, London: Evans.
Phenix, P.H. (1964) *Realms of Meaning: a Philosophy of Curriculum for General Education*, New York: McGraw-Hill.
Popkewitz, T.S. (1999) 'A social epistemology of educational research', in T.S. Popkewitz and L. Fendler (eds) *Critical Theories in Education: Changing Terrains of Knowledge and Politics*, New York: Routledge.
Popper, K.R. (1963) *The Open Society and Its Enemies*, London: Routledge.
Rawls, J. (1993) *Political Liberalism*, New York: Columbia University Press.
—— (1971) *A Theory of Justice*, Cambridge: Harvard University Press.
Rosovsky, H. (1990) *The University: an Owners Manual*, New York: Norton.
Rothblatt, S. (1976) *Tradition and Change in English Liberal Education*, London: Faber & Faber.
Rothblatt, S. and Wittrock, B. (eds) (1993) *The European and American University Since 1800*, Cambridge: Cambridge University Press.
Sandel, M. (1982) *Liberalism and the Limits of Justice*, Cambridge: Cambridge University Press.

—— (1984) *Introduction. Liberalism and Its Critics*, Oxford: Basil Blackwell.
Scheffler, I. (1982) *Science and Subjectivity*, Indianapolis: Hackett.
—— (1991) *In Praise of the Cognitive Emotions*, New York: Routledge.
Schwab, J. (1982) *Science, Curriculum, and Liberal Education*, Chicago: University of Chicago Press.
Siegel, H. (1988) *Educating Reason: Rationality, Critical Thinking, and Education*, New York: Routledge.
—— (1987) *Relativism Refuted: a Critique of Epistemological Relativism*, Dordrecht: Reidel.
Smith, N. (2002) *Charles Taylor: Meaning, Morals, and Modernity*, Cambridge: Polity.
Sullivan, W. (2004) *Work and Integrity: the Crisis and Promise of Work in America*, San Francisco: Jossey-Bass.
Tamir, Y. (1993) *Liberal Nationalism*, Princeton: Princeton University Press.
Taylor, C. (1989) *Sources of the Self*, Cambridge: Harvard University Press.
—— (1991) *The Ethics of Authenticity*, Cambridge: Harvard University Press.
Tyack, D.B. (1974) *The One Best System: a History of American Urban Education*, Cambridge: Harvard University Press.
Walzer, M. (1994) *Thick and Thin: Moral Argument at Home and Abroad*, Notre Dame: University of Notre Dame Press.
Wegner, C. (1978) *Liberal Education and the Modern University*, Chicago: University of Chicago Press.
Wolfson, H.A. (1977) *From Philo to Spinoza: Two Studies in Religious Philosophy*, New York: Behrman House.

Chapter 18

Higher education, scientific research and social change

Sir Brian Heap

Ontogenesis of science in higher education

One of the major contributions which higher education makes to a community is its scientific research, teaching and development. There is increasing recognition by government and by the business community that this scientific resource is critical to business innovation and competitiveness. In the UK there have been a large number of government-led initiatives – for example, through the *Lambert Review of Business–University Collaboration* (Lambert 2003), the establishment of regional Science and Industry Councils and the development of 'third stream' funding for higher education (to sit alongside funding for teaching and for research) – focused on knowledge transfer. Other chapters in this volume explore the dynamics of this relationship more fully (see especially those by Radošević and Kriaučioniené on innovation systems and Lukoševičius on knowledge transfer). The importance of the scientific resource of higher education extends much wider than this, however, for science, engineering and technology (SET) are applied to all spheres of human life; they underpin developments in what we eat and drink, in how long and how well we live, in our physical and mental security, in our housing and transport, in our interconnectedness, in the richness of the lives we enjoy and in our capacity to improve or destroy our fragile planetary environment. Science informs all these spheres of life and provides the basis for policy which addresses them. It is especially important therefore to have in our universities people who can both contribute to such policy formation and provide independent critical scrutiny of such policies. These are some of the functions of science and higher education which I shall explore in this chapter.

Advances in science, engineering and technology have become major drivers of economic development in industrialized countries and have attracted the attention of those that are in transition. These advances have also become the focus of general attention because the creation of new knowledge has promoted debates about ethical content and acceptability. This was not always the case as is clear in the book of Boden *et al.* (2004), which will now be summarised.

Historically, four phases can be identified in the story of science: 'pre-science',

'science for gentlemen', 'professional science' (Boden *et al.* 2004: 15) and 'industrialized science'. 'Pre-science' describes the time when people knew by observation that certain things happened but they could not explain them, as in the eclipse of the sun or the periodic flooding of the Nile. Academies existed at this time but only in the form found in Ancient Greece, where the name was used to describe groups of people rather than institutions. 'Science for gentlemen' was the period from about the fifteenth to the nineteenth centuries when scientific theories were developed around which much modern science still revolves. Natural philosophers sought to explain the world through understanding God's will and his creativity. This was the time of Newton, Leibnitz and Boyle, and institutions emerged such as the *Accademia Nazionale dei Lincei* in Rome, the Royal Society in London, and the *Académie des Sciences* in Paris. Towards the end of this period the needs of industry for research and trained personnel became prominent and the civic university came into evidence with the formation of the Victoria University of Manchester and the *Kaiser Wilhelm Gesellschaft* in Germany. The motivation in the UK was the need to address the perception that British industry was losing its competitiveness. The third era, 'professional science', portrays a later level of sophistication in terms of both intellectual coherence and codification. Greater emphasis was placed on knowledge production, extensive and prolonged education, career structures, and research networks facilitated by the growth in communication systems. The fourth era, 'industrialized science', describes the present, postmodern apparatus whereby capitalization for major scientific research projects depends on public–private partnerships; imperatives to calculate the real economic costs of research are pre-eminent; 'outsourcing' of more routine testing and research to the places where it can be done most cheaply, and the 'quality assurance' and 'kitemarking' of research and the establishments where it is done.

Boden *et al.* (2004: 15) distinguish between the organic change that followed each of these historical developments, and intentional change that is driven by policies initiated because they are perceived to achieve a certain goal within the industrial, social or military ambit. These policies are based on evidence that investment in science leads to economic advantage. In the mid-1990s an econometric study of the relationship between publicly funded basic research and economic performance indicated that the rate of return was 28 per cent. However, numerous assumptions were made, including the important limitation that such studies measure average rather than marginal rates of return and that they vary greatly across fields and sectors (Martin *et al.* 1996: Table 1). In the late 1990s, the Committee for Economic Development in the USA calculated similar returns on R&D investments, at that time roughly double the average historical return to stock market investments (Popper 1995: 1). With such evidence it is unsurprising that science, engineering and technology (SET) have undergone a remarkable expansion in more developed economies. In fact, 90 per cent of all the scientists born in the human race are alive today. As governments accept the relevance of SET to wealth creation, quality of life and, latterly, security, there is little wonder that investments are substantial, organizational structures ever more complex, and the chorus of demand for accountability and transparency increasingly strident.

Universities are major, though not exclusive, producers of new knowledge. In some instances state or private research organizations with minimal or no teaching function receive a greater significance. Profound changes have taken place in recent decades in respect of institutional cohesion, employment structures, resources and their management, research priorities and their evaluation, and the evolution of global networks (Gibbons *et al.* 1994: 145; European Commission 2001: 1). Tenure has virtually disappeared, career paths and career choices have diversified, while small research groups have learned to flourish through networking. Activities have shifted towards research projects so that many research workers can boast a portfolio of short-term projects that provide a mix of basic science funded by research councils, and others that are funded directly by users and stakeholders who demand quick returns to specific questions of an applied nature (Boden *et al.* 2004: 136).

One consequence of this diversity is that the historical vision that portrays science as autonomous, apolitical and ethically neutral has changed. No longer is the vision concerned solely with the pursuit of truth (Ravetz 1973: 1, Wolpert 1993: 25). Instead, the boundaries have become increasingly blurred, partly through the mechanisms of funding and the demands of the funding bodies, and partly because the timescale from discovery to application may be greatly foreshortened. In biotechnology, for instance, industry-sponsored basic research into gene regulation can result in the incorporation of genetic engineering into medicine and agriculture within a single decade rather than three.

In the UK, government strategies and policies have had a far-reaching effect on research within higher education (Chancellor of the Duchy of Lancaster, 1993: 1). 'Curiosity-driven' (academic) science that exists as a discrete and independent activity which should not be interfered with by management and funding controls is rigorously defended. Ideally, it should be funded by public monies or by private foundations or organizations dedicated to the production of knowledge for its own sake and for the public good. It is the seedbed of new ideas and breakthroughs. Belatedly, the European Union has been persuaded of its significance, and lobbying to have large sums dedicated to basic science and young scientists in Framework Programme 7 has been intense! The idea of launching a European Research Centre to organize the distribution of EU funding of fundamental research has gained momentum with the strong intention to increase the quality and visibility of European research globally. 'Useful science', as it is now known, is that which contributes to wealth creation and quality of life, supported by public and private funds competitively acquired, with outputs that are transferred to users. This model implies linearity, which is both misleading and an oversimplification; an interactive model more accurately describes what happens in reality between scientists, industry and end-users. 'Commodified science' funded by governments or by private organizations goes further because it refers to scientific knowledge produced in the context of its application rather than with the potential for transfer to end-users (Boden *et al.* 2004: 27). Hence, in today's increasingly technologically-driven world, the trend in SET research has accelerated in favour of work that will lead to increased competitiveness with a focus on what you do best, or at least better than your neighbours or distant countries – fitted kitchens in Germany, financial services in London and Manhattan, automobiles in Japan, knitwear producers and shoemakers of Italy. The UK's list of science and technology includes pharmaceuticals, chemicals, telecommunications, hydrocarbons, biotechnology, agriculture, electrical engineering and computer software.

Inevitably, the management and organization of research within centres of higher education and research organizations have been exposed to a radical overhaul through the application of market-based solutions based on accountability and accounting practices. As we have already noted, this process is not unprecedented, because during the mid-nineteenth century it was perceived that British industrial competitiveness also lagged behind other countries and this led to the emergence of a new structure for higher education, namely, the civic university. However, rather than considering the new forms of higher education or governance of research that have emerged, the latter dealt with expertly elsewhere (Boden *et al.* 2004), we now examine the origins of new knowledge and how far policies that aim to promote SET in society should be at the centre of government.

Excellence as a benchmark

The remarkable benefits of the modern era have come from scientific research and the talents and dedication of some of the very best minds and research teams in the world. Yet, science is difficult and costly to do well. The word 'excellence' is frequently used to describe basic science that is, by nature, a long-term pursuit and usually associated with a unique array of non-commercial, non-market institutions and organizations that govern the exploration of new areas. The Royal Society, the UK's Academy of Science, has always been linked with such research endeavour. Three years after its foundation it set out its motto *Nullius in verba* – a determination to withstand dogma and to verify all statements by an appeal to facts (Second Charter 1663). This was in keeping with the still remaining Renaissance academies in Europe – the *Académie des Sciences* in France and the *Accademia dei Lincei* in Italy. This central tenet continues to underpin all of modern science: respect for, and scrupulous attention to empirical evidence, which embodies the idea that good science can be identified and is worth more than bad science.

A.E. Housman once began a book review, 'there is much in this book that is true and much that is new. But that which is true is not new and that which is new is not true.' Is there anything new or true to say about excellence? At least we should be reminded that one of the qualities of excellence is that it is not always predictable. Sir Hermann Bondi, former Chairman of the UK's Natural Environment Research Council, quoting Lord Leverhulme, used to say that half the money spent by his Council was wasted, but he did not know in advance which half. A former Director General of the UK Research Councils once asked his Chief Executives to invest only in those projects that would be successful, but rapidly withdrew his remark when asked if he only invested in shares that increased in value!

The concept of excellence is not only about surpassing others in terms of originality and creativity, it is fundamental to the type of innovation that translates discovery and invention into application. Pavitt (2000: 1) has argued that high-quality academic papers arising from publicly funded work in prestigious universities and institutions have been the major source of USA patents in recent years. Businesses gave greatest attention not to immediately useful knowledge but to the benefits of trained researchers familiar with the latest research techniques and results, background expertise and membership of leading-edge international networks. For these and many other reasons he also argued that there were strong reasons for supporting policies in Europe that ensure high-quality academic research that is mainly publicly funded and frequently interdisciplinary.

The challenge for Europe's citizens is to grasp a corporate vision for an adventure in the pursuit of knowledge that they have displayed at other times of their history. It is essential to create a climate of well-justified confidence in scientific and technological progress, restore self-assurance in the processes of accountability and equity, and enhance the opportunities that exist for rewarding collaboration that can promote synergy and economies of scale if managed positively. To promote excellence at all levels has to be the priority of any administration, but it requires great skill and sensitivity in its nurture and application if it is to inform policy. The cautionary words of Oliver Goldsmith should be recalled – 'we must touch weakness with a delicate hand. There are some faults so nearly allied to excellence, that we can scarce weed out the fault without eradicating the virtue.'

Policies informed by science

People engaged in higher education, academies and learned societies of all types seem to share the ambition of advising their administrations. Yet the relationship is a complex one. Science itself is not democratic – scientific truth is addressed by experiment and observation, not by counting votes and heads. Science needs openness, and the story of Lysenkoism in the former Soviet Union, or of global warming as viewed by a sceptical administration, shows what can happen to science in a society where political orthodoxy determines what is acceptable and what is not, or where political/industrial imperatives are more highly valued than the best international evidence available, which may point to a different solution. The free exchange of ideas on which science depends can be threatened by political correctness, and the scientific community needs to be alert to this.

The world is now a complicated place. It always has been, but the pressures now are greater than ever: bigger population, tougher international competition, and rapid consequences of taking the wrong decisions. Decision makers (not only in government) can now make gross mistakes which are bigger than ever, and the technology of instant communication means that they are immediately exposed to universal critique.

Science that forms the basis of advice is a public good and has real value in its own right. It needs to flourish despite the pressures of market forces, it needs to be accountable, and it needs to be listened to if the phrase 'evidence-based policies' is to become redolent of meaning. Managers facing major investment decisions to exploit their research have to rely on expert advisory panels or similar mechanisms to supply the quality assurance function of peer-reviewed journals. Journals publish excellent science that opens up new fields of research and new ways of thinking about particular scientific issues, and good science that is judged sufficiently meritorious and subsequently used by other scientists to inform their own thinking. On the other hand, science carried out for commercial or military purposes may not always be published (or peer-reviewed) in the open literature. (In passing, it is notable that the defence spend in the USA has subsidized an enormous amount of science in universities and other institutions, more than anywhere else.)

Three consequences follow. First, you need good scientists to consult. Second, decision makers must, and increasingly do, recognize when they are dealing with a science-related issue. And third, we all need to distinguish good science from bad science. The decision maker has to understand the options available and the foreseeable consequences of each. Lord May of Oxford, when Chief Scientific Advisor at the Cabinet Office, stressed the need for a transparent and objective system that ensures scientific advice is thoroughly comprehensible and rigorously tested. In addition, governments need to be forewarned of potentially controversial issues at an early stage, to ensure that the best scientific advice can be marshalled, that consultations are broadly based involving all interested parties, and that new knowledge is translated into publicly acceptable policies (Office of Science and Technology 2001: 1).

For some issues, scientific analysis is essential to inform policy (e.g. stem cells, population policy, energy options, bovine spongiform encephalopathy (BSE), foot-and-mouth disease, nanotechnology). Other issues arise as a result of scientific advance and therefore need scientific understanding (e.g. cloning, GM crops). Diplomatic science has a place, but when the converse occurs, as in nations that attempt to exclude foreigners from certain laboratories and conferences, it can result in undiplomatic science. Yet, in bringing these values to bear on public life, we must recognize the limits of science and science advice.

Science is fallible because theories change, and knowledge expands and contradicts earlier thinking. Science can also be misconstrued, as in the case of the flawed paper on autism that linked the condition to measles–mumps–rubella (MMR) vaccination. As the UK's Chief Medical Officer, Sir Liam Donaldson, has said 'if the paper had never been published, then we wouldn't have had the controversy, we wouldn't have had the seed of doubt sown in parents' minds which has caused a completely false loss of confidence in a vaccine that has saved millions of children's lives around the world' (Oldstone 2004: 275). The measles virus is remarkably contagious and one in 300,000 cases lead to progressive neurological disorders; routine vaccination has reduced its incidence in the USA alone from four million a year to just forty (ibid.).

Janasoff (1997: 221) believes the UK has relied too much in the past for analysis of complex issues on character and experience, thereby consolidating power in relatively few individuals. The USA has probably erred too far the other way, putting too little faith in people and too much in formal analysis and a simplistic reading of complexity by hearings, congressional oversight and media investigations. In both cases, the dangerous drift away from the world that people experience and inhabit now demands an even greater dialogue between decision makers and critics, so that uncertainties in science and policy are debated openly and honestly. This may take the form of expensive and protracted judicial reviews, such as the Phillips Report on BSE in the UK, which took three years to complete and £30 million to fund (not recommended), or in-depth inquiries performed within the existing academic framework, such as the Royal Society's Report on the foot-and-mouth epidemic that took less than twelve months to complete at a fraction of the cost. The latter has the clear advantage of speed and economy.

Science is not everything. Nobody (sensible) imagines for one moment that you can make and implement policy on the back of scientific advice alone, or that science will give compelling, unambiguous answers to deep social questions. Bad science did not cause the spread of BSE; it was bad agriculture and bad governance. But to pretend that science has nothing to offer would be equally fatuous because scientists themselves are best qualified to judge science. Not only is there a role for academies to recognize and reward talent and to participate in policy making and science advice, but there is a growing demand that they should shore up the science base against anti-science factions which can come in various forms – e.g. certain special-interest groups, scaremongers and Luddites, often of the intellectual or quasi-intellectual type.

There is an interesting codicil. Not only do you need demonstrably good scientists in such instances, you need demonstrably impartial scientists. Historically, these came from academia and independent people, i.e. those with private incomes who owed no allegiance to anyone. Too often, the nearest we have to independent academics are the retired, some of whom are in the House of Lords, now radically restructured. The supply of overtly independent bench scientists is threatened by policies energetically pursued in many countries to drive academia and industry together. This is not a minor matter. Academic biologists and corporate researchers have often become indistinguishable, with special awards being given by governments for collaborations between the two sectors, for behaviour that used to be cited as a conflict of interest. Efforts are now made either to avoid or to document potential conflicts of interest, so that the nature of the advice is transparent and not called into question. The significance of credibility was brought out when 1,100 people in the UK were asked by MORI opinion pollsters – whom do you trust to provide information? Family doctors registered 50 per cent of votes, advisory bodies to government composed of different viewpoints 40 per cent, pharmacists and chemists 20 per cent, environmental groups, nurses, veterinarians and scientists 10 per cent, with negative responses in descending orders of magnitude for government, patients, animal welfare groups, farmers, religious organizations, media, industry and retailers. Clearly, the trusted independent expert is not the answer to everything, but if we let the species become extinct we are in trouble.

Cooperation and social change

The modern trend of fostering business–university collaboration for the purpose of economic benefit can take several forms. 'Technology-push' is seen in communities influenced by the transfer and exploitation of new knowledge from a regional centre of excellence. The Greater Cambridge Technopole is a typical example, strongly influenced by curiosity-driven research in the University of Cambridge, with its 25,000 students, staff and academics and income of about £460 million p.a. The Technopole area is 176,000 hectares around the city, contains 44,000 people, consists of 3,500 high-tech companies, 50,000 employees in multidisciplinary companies, and has a venture capital scene estimated at £1.5 billion. There has been a steady growth in the flow of knowledge into industry, not only locally but also nationally and internationally; some 120 inventions and five spin-off companies are created annually (Cambridge Enterprise, December 2004). Numerous myths have had to be dispelled (though some remain), including the idea that angels in shining clothes are waiting to solve the financial problems of the university in the form of unlimited investment. The emerging mantra is: 'get it right and the inventors, the universities, industry and society can all benefit' (Dr Richard Jennings, personal communication).

The city of Enschede in the region of Twente, Netherlands, with its long-standing history as a major textile centre, provides an example of 'market-pull', following its serious decline in manufacturing during the second half of the last century. A new science-based Technical University was created in 1964 which has grown to about 8,000 students and academics. University starter schemes have encouraged the formation of spin-off companies and since 1985 the success rate, measured as companies that still exist, has been about 70 per cent. The emphasis on a mix of engineering projects that include environmental, chemical and medical engineering has created a new entrepreneurial climate replacing classical academic attitudes, a multidisciplinary economy that has succeeded the former monodisciplinary one, and a significant impact of R&D companies on the local economy, boosted by government incentives for the establishment of start-up companies.

Other examples of the crucial importance of centres of excellence as drivers of social reparation and renewal can be seen in countries in transition. Capacity building in post-apartheid South Africa has invoked linkages with international centres of excellence, as in the initiative of the National Research Foundation of South Africa and the Royal Society. The project formed linkages between scientists in four historically-black universities in South Africa and those in UK laboratories. Similarly, NATO's Science for Peace Programme has created collaborations between scientists in nations of the NATO Alliance and those of the former Soviet Union, the Commonwealth of Independent States (CIS). Research outputs have been harnessed to develop 'spin-off' companies and to provide new knowledge for end-users such as CIS environmental agencies. This latter programme has been a stunning example of turning SET into societal benefit, through industrial initiatives and environmental projects concerned with clean water supplies and pollution. It has created over 2,500 fellowships for CIS scientists working with colleagues in NATO countries and has embodied the sentiments of the distinguished physicist Freeman Dyson: 'the most useful contribution that scientists can make to the abolition of war has nothing to do with technology. The international community of scientists may help to abolish war by setting an example to the world of practical co-operation across barriers of nationality, language and culture' (Gardner 2004).

Such is the importance of cooperation that we may digress briefly to examine components that underlie the growth of networking. Vogel (2004: 1128) has argued that cooperation is one of the main reasons why humans have managed to survive in almost every ecosystem on Earth. She acknowledges that Darwinian evolutionists brought up on the central role of competition have real problems with the origins of cooperation and asks questions about whether cooperative urges are programmed in our genes, are we taught by our culture to play well with others? are we driven by outdated urges that don't make sense today?

Cooperation may be hard wired, which would help to explain why it increases the chances of survival, as proposed in the well-known theory of kin selection, that is, passing on one's genes to the next generations (Hamilton 1964: 1). Cooperation may occur as a result of reciprocal altruism, namely, that by helping unrelated individuals one's fitness is increased, as long as the recipient can be reasonably expected to return the favour (Trivers 1971: 35). Direct reciprocity means that you help somebody who might help you; indirect reciprocity that your cooperation will be returned not by the recipient but by another individual (Nowak *et al.* 2004: 793).

The Royal Society's programme in South Africa enhanced the quality of science in historically black universities by cooperation between UK project leaders and historically disadvantaged black scientists in South Africa. This generous act sponsored by the UK government resulted in scores of graduates reaching higher degree levels where previously there were none. Comments from distinguished UK scientists included the following: 'young scientists from historically black universities have contributed a lot – I'd take more like them any time'; and 'co-operation isn't a one-way street – the biodiversity in South Africa is stunning ... before I joined this programme I hadn't realized how important the country was'. Examples of direct reciprocity at work!

NATO's Science for Peace Programme has provided for the first time Internet technologies and communication networks between partner nations in Caucasian and Central Asian nations, the so-called Virtual Silk Highway. A Turkish–French satellite system interconnects three Caucasian and five Central Asian new independent states (and now Afghanistan) with the World Wide Web. The objective, to link scientists together and to enhance education and training in schools and universities, has been saluted as an outstanding success and has gained a further round of funding. Here, people were willing to help others who won't pay them back, but by doing so they built a reputation for cooperation so that others who observed this behaviour would be more likely to cooperate – indirect reciprocity, or 'doing good and talking about it'!

Humans excel at large-scale collaborations – transportation networks, energy networks, sending robots to Mars, European Framework programmes and the Human Genome Project, to name but a few. Evolutionary biologists believe that such forms of cooperation cannot be explained by indirect reciprocity and that to keep such behaviour on track a series of rewards and punishments are needed (strong reciprocity). Game theory tells us that in laboratory games designed to enable players to earn money and then be given a chance to spend some of their earnings, to reward those who cooperate and to punish those who cheat, an innate sense of 'fairness' emerges that leads people to reward do-gooders and punish cheaters. Such is the nature of large-scale cooperation.

As we have already observed in the ontogenesis of science, networking and the creation of knowledge through large-scale collaborations (Gibbons *et al.* 1994: 34; mode 2) have become prominent in modern scientific research. In Europe, research council funding has had a significant impact internally by stimulating this activity during the last five decades. However, it is only in recent decades that European research councils have ventured into transnational and international cooperation through opening their research programmes to other nations, by capacity building in developing countries (indirect reciprocity), or by investment in large-scale initiatives such as the world-leading centre at CERN Geneva (strong reciprocity). The question is whether a new plane of cooperation could be reached through the establishment of a European Research Council that includes science, arts and humanities, and whether the continuing growth of cooperation with the rapidly emerging Asian bloc could counterbalance the American colossus of science.

Comment

Higher education and scientific research are in the vanguard of change that will affect the future of greater Europe and beyond. The economic case for investment in science and research has been frequently advanced, based on evidence that a strong public science base supports improvements in human welfare. A recent study found that 1 per cent growth in public R&D led to a 0.17 per cent increase in the total factor productivity in the long run, and increased with the share of public science conducted in universities (cited in HM Treasury 2004: 149), though any linear relationship between education and wealth has been disputed by others (Patten 2004). Notwithstanding, the European Council at its Barcelona Summit meeting in 2002 agreed that the overall spending on R&D and innovation should be increased to 3 per cent of GDP by 2010 and that two-thirds of this investment should come from the private sector. The serious challenge that faces the EU is shown by the evidence that only Finland and Sweden have attained the 3 per cent target so far (EASAC 2004) and that while the USA has reached the figure of 2 7 per cent, the gap between the EU and the USA has doubled at constant levels since 1994.

This relationship between higher education, scientific research and social change is an important one, given the considerable sums of public (government) money spent on basic research. The outputs from centres of higher education and the science base are not easily measured, since basic research is a rich source of the skills required to translate new knowledge into practice, it provides an enhanced ability to solve complex technological problems and it is an 'entry ticket' into the world's stock of knowledge, providing the ability to participate effectively in networks and to absorb and exploit the resulting knowledge and skills (Pavitt 1991: 109, Martin *et al.* 1996: 1). It also improves our ability to reach informed decisions and to formulate policies (Chancellor of the Duchy of Lancaster, 1993: 1). Consequently, any initiative to establish a European Research Council should focus on research and scholarship driven by curiosity that looks at the longer term and develops informed and democratic citizens, rather than be narrowly focused on applicability and exploitation potential in the short term. It should operate in a way that endorses the importance of independence, excellence and transparency, and invests in young academics.

Higher education and scientific research are international by nature, and the scale of their activities and aspirations are increasing rather than declining – e.g. human genome, climate change, infectious diseases, particle colliders, large data sets. National networks and facilities have been crucial to this process, and the development into international ones is unprecedented. This trend seems set to continue in relation to things that we value, such as wealth, health, food, environment and security. The greatest challenge, however, is to enquire how far the ancient virtue of wisdom will be pursued, because without it lies opportunism and exploitation of knowledge rather than the discovery of its conceptual utility for the greatest good as distinct from its instrumental use. As Pope John Paul II argued – 'the pre-eminence of the profit motive in conducting scientific research ultimately means that science is deprived of its epistemological character, according to which its primary goal is discovery of the truth. The risk is that when research takes a utilitarian turn, its speculative dimension, which is the inner dynamic of man's intellectual journey, will be diminished or stifled' (quoted in Patten 2004).

Acknowledgements

I am greatly indebted to many colleagues for stimulating discussions and insights, and in particular to Dr Peter Collins and Dr Keith Root at the Royal Society and Dr Richard Jennings of the Research Services Division, University of Cambridge.

References

Boden, R., Cox, D., Nedeva, M. and Barker, K. (2004) *Scrutinising Science: the changing UK government of science*, UK: Palgrave Macmillan.
Cambridge Enterprise (2004) Online. Available at www.enterprise.cam.ac.uk/about/statistics.htm (accessed 14 December 2004).
Chancellor of the Duchy of Lancaster (1993) *Realising our Potential: a Strategy for Science, Engineering and Technology*, London: HMSO.
EASAC (2004) 'Towards 3%: attainment of the Barcelona target', European Academies of Science Committee (EASAC) Policy Report no. 1. Online. Available at: www.easac.org (accessed 18 January 2005).
European Commission (2001) *Internationalization of Research: Institutional Innovation, Culture and Agency in the Framework of Competition and Co-operation* (INNOCULT), Project Final Reports.
Gardner, K. (2004) 'Security through science', presentation for NATO Science Committee, Brussels. Online. Available at: www.nato.int/science (accessed 18 January 2005).
Gibbons, M., Limoges, C., Nowotny, H., Schwartzman, S., Scott, P. and Trow, M. (1994) *The New Production of Knowledge*, London: Sage.
Hamilton, W.D. (1964) 'The genetical evolution of social behaviour', *Journal of Theoretical Biology*, 7 (1–16), 17–52.
HM Treasury, Department of Trade and Industry, and Department for Education and Skills (2004) *Science and Innovation Investment Framework 2004–2014*, London: HMSO.
Janasoff, S. (1997) 'Civilization and madness: the great BSE scare of 1996', *Public Understanding of Science*, 6, 221–32.
Lambert, R. (2003) *Lambert Review of Business–University Collaborations: final report*, Norwich: HMSO.
Martin, B., Salter, A., Hicks, D., Pavitt, K., Sharp, M. and von Tunzelmann, N. (1996) 'The relationship between publicly funded basic research and economic performance', Science Policy Research Unit, University of Sussex, Brighton, UK.
Nowak, M. and Sigmund, K. (2004) 'Evolutionary dynamics of biological games', *Science*, 303, 793–9.
Office of Science and Technology (2001) *Code of Practice for Scientific Advisory Committees*, London: Department of Trade and Industry.
Oldstone, M.B.A. (2004) 'Immune to the facts', *Nature*, 432: 275–6.
Patten, C. Distinguished lecture 'Save British Science', University College London, 18 November 2004.

Pavitt, K. (1991) 'What makes basic research economically useful?', *Research Policy*, 20, 109–19.
—— (2000) 'Why European Union funding of academic research should be increased: a radical proposal', *Science and Public Policy*, 27, 455–60.
Popper, S.W. (1995) 'Measuring the economic and social benefits of fundamental science', Critical Technologies Institute (MR-708.0-ostp), Washington, DC: Rand.
Ravetz, J.R. (1973) 'Tragedy in the history of science', in M. Teich and R. Young (eds) *Changing Perspectives in the History of Science*, London: Heinemann.
Second Charter (1663), in *Year Book of the Royal Society 2005*, London: The Royal Society.
Trivers, R.L. (1971) 'The evolution of reciprocal altruism'. *Quarterly Review of Biology*, 46, 35–57.
Vogel, G. (2004) 'The evolution of the golden rule', *Nature*, 303, 1128–31.
Wolpert, L. (1993) *The Unnatural Nature of Science*, London: Faber and Faber.

Part VI

Universities, societies and transitions in perspective

Chapter 19

The audit and 'embrace' of quality in a higher education system under change

Barbara Zamorski

Introduction

The chapters of this book reflect the wide-ranging expectations which are today laid upon our systems of higher education – and perhaps nowhere more so than in 'countries in transition', which simultaneously face challenges of social, political and economic reconstruction in an increasingly competitive environment. Expanding the scale and role of higher education is, however, of little benefit unless this role is *well* played and unless the quality of work in our higher education institutions and the quality of learning for which they are responsible is *high*. It is this dimension of the *quality* of higher education on which I wish to focus in this chapter.[1]

To begin with, however, it is important to note some of the factors that are challenging the development of the quality of higher education.

Challenges to the maintenance or development of the quality of higher education

First, it is becoming more and more difficult to see the boundaries of the higher education landscape. The harder we look at the landscape – in order to fix the picture, to concentrate the eye, to fully understand what is happening and its consequences and implications – the more the images move. This is because higher education is becoming the all-encompassing solution to all problems. Higher education is required to create, for example, scientific knowledge, economic wealth, a skilled labour force and worthy, informed and active citizens. And we all feel this responsibility and obligation. Each time we teach a class, write a research proposal, share or transfer our intellectual capital, attempt to write articles, books and papers that are economically useful as well as academically sound, we feel not only the privilege of these pursuits but also these multifaceted pressures. And, unfortunately, the pressures may cancel out the privilege. A recent OECD report makes this point well. It begins: 'The University is no longer a quiet place to teach and do scholarly work at a measured pace and contemplate the universe as in centuries past. It is a big, complex, demanding, competitive business requiring large-scale ongoing investment' (OECD 2004: 3). The authors comment:

> The challenge for institutions is to manage a more complex portfolio of aims and funding; to differentiate themselves in an increasingly competitive environment; and to protect and maintain academic quality and their ability to deliver over the long term.
>
> (OECD 2004: 3)

For 'countries in transition', which are relying on their higher education systems to do all that the OECD outlines in this statement and more, in effect, the boundaries of expectation, alarmingly, begin to expand beyond the eye's horizon.

Second, during the last twenty years or so, the massification of higher education has developed rapidly. For example, an article in the *Times Higher Educational Supplement* (THES) reported on an OECD study of global education trends. It states: 'Half the developed world's young adults now complete a higher education course ... An average of 50 per cent of people across thirty countries enter higher education at some stage in their life, and a third gain a degree or a masters qualification.' Some countries have now reached 70 per cent participation and could reach up to 80 per cent soon (THES 2004: 11).

This is obviously not a trend that will diminish. As we are all aware, the OECD, the World Bank and the European Community, among other agencies of analysis, prediction and influence, regularly publish reports that demonstrate how crucial higher education is to our futures. For example, an authoritative European Commission report *Measures to Improve Higher Education/Research Relations in Order to Strengthen the Strategic Basis of the European Research Area* (2003a) suggests that there are two possible future scenarios for the role of higher education and research in Europe. Crudely characterized, in the first scenario, called 'Riding the Wave', the authors write: 'Higher Education and Research will develop in which ever ways market forces take it' (ibid., p. 27). Higher education and research will become little more than a commodity, primarily open to a market of demand, and subject to those people and multinational organizations who can afford it. The second scenario 'A Second Renaissance' is 'essentially a pro-active scenario in which higher education and research systems are asked to play a fundamental structural role in supporting new notions of competitiveness and social cohesion in the face of trends – such as de-industrialization, privatization and short-termism – that can have undesirable effects' (European Commission 2003a: 27). Not surprisingly, the preference is for the second scenario, where we will all be required to become lifelong learners and intellectual workers.

Third, following on from the issue of massification, is the resulting challenge of the diversity of higher education. There is more diversity in student access points, student access pathways, student motivations and expectations and student abilities, than ever previously experienced by universities. Consequently, there is also further diversity in the now wider portfolio of curricula and qualifications that are being offered and accredited in higher education. For example, in the United Kingdom, many universities now offer a taught doctorate, the Doctorate of Education or Ed.D, which only came into being just over a decade ago. The Ed.D is interesting because it is a doctorate utilized to enhance professional and career development rather than disciplinary understanding or advancement. And in 2001, the Foundation Degree was introduced in the United Kingdom. This is a two-year, work-based degree that is concerned with employability and up-skilling the workforce. Foundation Degrees are available in approximately twenty-five different subjects, many of which would have been considered either outside of, or peripheral to, higher education curricula until very recently.

A fourth factor challenging the maintenance or development of the quality of higher education in many parts of the world is the European drive to map and accredit non-formal and informal learning, for non-traditional access to further or higher education. This drive is rapidly gaining force across the whole Europe. EU programmes to develop common European principles of accreditation for non-formal and informal learning are taking place under the now all-enveloping umbrella term of lifelong learning. (See, for example, the European Commission report *Making a European Area of Lifelong Learning a Reality* (2001)). Indeed the notion of lifelong learning itself, as a key agenda item for economic development, may begin to dissolve the reasonably fixed boundaries between higher education and other sectors of education, and gradually reconfigure the status and position of universities in its wider reach.

The scope of the higher education curriculum is therefore being stretched to embrace the training and education of a far wider range of disciplines, professions and vocations than before. As reported to me recently by a senior academic during some research on learning and teaching in different disciplines: 'We don't teach a discipline, we train people for a profession.' One of the implications of this curricular drift is that course design, the delivery and access of a higher education programmes, the teaching and learning methodologies utilized by students and teachers and the accreditation processes – currently in the hands of universities – may increasingly lie in the hands of a number of stakeholders outside of the university. The extent to which the university will remain central to these processes in the future or begin to fall away to the margins remains to be seen.

The final factor I would briefly mention is that higher education now takes place in widely diverse physical locations and virtual spaces. In addition to traditional classes in university buildings, we have the expansion of work-based learning, where much of the learning happens either at the students' workplaces or in their homes. The use of technology and distance learning in virtual spaces creates other new, still to be fully understood and exploited, learning arenas. Pedagogical space now has few boundaries left.

Determining, maintaining and improving quality in this kind of higher education scenario is an extremely complex task. Areas for debate by universities at this point might include, for example, what exactly it is that we are, or that we should be, looking at, and what is it that we wish to improve. A short, non-exhaustive list that instantly comes to mind would consist of service to teaching and learning, to knowledge production and transfer, to the economy, to the community and civil society, and social justice. No doubt we could expand on this list.

So a key question currently exercising the minds (and probably also the hearts) of academics is: What is the universities' future role in the 'embrace' of and 'control' of quality in a variety of virtual, physical and intellectual environments attempting to serve a multiplicity of purposes? In line with this diffusion and fragmentation of higher education, the role of 'audit' is gaining prominence as a way of gathering up and keeping a grip on the loosening threads of quality development; a not unnatural impulse towards seeming cohesion and unity. This is this issue I will now consider.

Quality and audit

Quality appears to have become a 'catch-all' concept for the achievement of competitive edge in higher education, and there is genuine anxiety about leaving the issue of quality merely to the academics (however misplaced that anxiety may be). Unsurprisingly, much time and many resources in higher education are now being spent on defining, maintaining, improving or auditing quality, and much of that by governments and agencies that lie outside of the university itself. The urge to centralize, standardize and minutely track, monitor, measure and record higher education processes may relieve some of the anxieties felt by politicians. But this urge may also have inadvertently trapped us in a suffocating embrace of control and fear that diminishes our motivation and ability to innovate and develop creatively.

In the UK, the quality assurance mechanisms and audit systems are particularly elaborate, and in spite of sympathetic government messages suggesting that such bureaucracy is being reduced, the growth of centralizing agencies continues to proliferate. In higher education, universities and higher education institutions (HEIs) are now subject to a complex multiplicity of quality bodies, templates and guidance. The Higher Education Funding Council for England (HEFCE) and the other UK funding councils offer overall direction of policy for universities, but layers of regulation and requirements from other national bodies generate frustration and confusion rather than support for vision and action. In 1997, the Quality Assurance Agency for Higher Education (QAA) was established to provide an integrated quality assurance service for UK higher education. This is undertaken by QAA providing reference points that define clear and explicit standards of quality and good practice, and reviewing quality through institutional audit and academic review. Highly specified qualification frameworks, subject benchmark statements, institutional programme specifications, student progress files and a Code of Practice are either offered or required in these processes.

A further mechanism of quality measurement in universities is the Research Assessment Exercise (RAE). The RAE is a national exercise which is conducted at approximately five-year intervals in order to assess the quality of UK research in individual universities and disciplines. Submissions are assessed by panels of experts drawn from the academic community and are given grades. Significant funding consequences follow these grading decisions, and, as a result, the RAE is the subject of some controversy. For example, the vice-chancellor of a large university recently wrote a strong critique of the RAE, suggesting that the £20 million that the next exercise will cost to run is a 'wasteful exercise' because we can already predict which fifteen universities will top the poll and capture over 50 per cent of the research funding (Knight 2004).

In 2004, the Committee of University Chairmen's (CUC) guide for governors in HEIs has included, for the first time, a code for governance in order to support higher education in developing high standards. An Office for Fair Access (OFFA) has come into being, in order to regulate fair access to higher education for under-represented groups. And finally, in the interests of accountability and transparency, performance indicators in higher education, providing comparative data on performance of universities and colleges on a range of factors, are published each year, as are league tables of results.

It would be all too easy to continue with this list, which is growing rather than diminishing. UK managers and academics in higher education are struggling hard to work coherently and effectively within this burdensome and high-maintenance network of external imposition and 'support', many suggesting that this network is being created and implemented in an ethos of crisis and, as a result, is producing unintended and counter-productive consequences.

Similar trends can now be discerned at a European level. As noted earlier, the EC is increasingly pro-active in developing a European Research Area (ERA) and education and training systems that work towards future global EU economic and educational supremacy. EC documentation expressing alarm at lack of progress on this trajectory, with subsequent strategies and programmes of remediation, prevail. For example, in an EC interim report *Education and Training 2010* (2003b), the authors write:

> In March 2001, the European Council adopted three strategic goals (and thirteen associated concrete objectives) to be attained by 2010: education and training systems should be organized around quality, access, and openness to the world. A year later, it approved a detailed work programme ('Education & Training 2010') for the attainment of these goals and supported the ambition of the Ministers for Education to make education and training systems in Europe '*a worldwide quality reference by 2010*'.
>
> (European Commission 2003b: 3)

Quality is certainly the primary goal here, as access and openness can only follow if this first goal is achieved. Faced by this 'urgent' challenge, the report then suggests strongly that: 'In particular, the Commission feels that as from 2004 a mechanism should be put in place to monitor progress achieved on the basis of annual reports forwarded to the Commission by the Member States' (European Commission 2003b: 4). So we begin to import yet more layers of audit.

Of course, any rational and sensible person could make what appears to be a good case for quality audits and all their concomitant attendants, and there may well be gains arising from these audits. The bigger question, however, concerns what we may be losing by using such audits. A challenge for 'societies in transition' is to ensure that on our journeys of change we do not lose on our way those aspects of higher education that are of most value. To what extent can homogeneous and standardized criteria and frameworks of quality address diversity, fragmentation and uncertainty in higher education?

It can be argued that those taking on the mantle of higher education governance and management through a 'command and control' structure begin to uncouple higher education endeavour from management. This results in a dislocation between university governance and academic cultures, and is a key factor in the growing fragility of university 'identity' – which, as we have seen, is something already at risk. A major fault line is developing between those who wish to impose such quality frameworks of criteria and those who are subject to them. Hence, the concept of quality is moving from a focus of debate and insight that is intrinsic to the learning process of students and teachers, to a formalized discourse where quality is defined, stabilized, imposed and measured in terms of particular outcomes and products. Some would argue strongly that the concept of quality has narrowed to little more than compliance to standards. (See the discussion of the dominance of discourses of technical rationality by Richard Smith in his contribution to this volume.)

It is not difficult to find informed arguments and critiques that alert us to the long-term dangers that this current form of 'quality' improvement is taking. Two researchers and social commentators can be said to epitomize the wide-ranging criticisms which have emerged.

Frank Furedi, a Professor of Sociology, writes passionately about the unintended and worrying consequences of auditing for quality:

> It's time to speak out against the raw politics and crude economics ruining our universities ... The university has become one of the most audited institutions in society. Every aspect of university life, from teaching to student progression and modes of assessment and research is systematically audited. One of the consequences of this is the erosion of university autonomy. Academics are expected to work according to criteria established by external auditors, civil servants and politicians. Auditing does not merely measure, it alters and ultimately transforms how a university works. Inside every uni-

versity, an ever-expanding [...] of auditing and quality assurance experts help institutionalize the values imposed by the education bureaucracy. This group of auditors plays an important role of weakening the integrity of the intellectual activity pursued ... The auditing ethos forces people to submit to a regime that seeks to quantify and inspect their efforts, promoting bite-sized, standardized efforts that can be easily measured, weighed and served to infantilized customers ... Auditing encourages the adoption of dumbed-down pedagogy and practices. Thus we are no longer interested in what students have learnt, but whether they have achieved a course's 'learning outcomes'.

(Furedi 2004: 22)

Making a slightly different point, but similarly uneasy about unintended consequences, John Elliott, a Professor of Education, writes: 'What is going on is the concealment of one kind of reality about human activities in order to construct another kind of reality about them, one which renders them amenable to social/economic control in the name of quality assurance.' Considering audit of quality in higher education specifically, he quotes from Strathern (2000):

For Strathern it is these 'invisible to audit' processes that are critical for the production of research quality, and these are essentially marked by relationships of trust within the organization ... Performative cultures ... imply a low level of trust in the 'professionalism' of their employees. The more persuasive the gaze of audit the less the trust invested in the moral competence of its members to respond to the needs of the people they serve.

(Elliott 2001: 197)

Thus our notions of 'quality' and 'standards' become confused or conflated through the device of 'audit'. We lose the added value of intrinsic academic motivation that a low-trust culture persistently diminishes and we begin to concentrate our energies and resources on creating a simulacrum of quality. This simulacrum involves the creation of an unreal representation that not only diverts our attention and resources from genuine reality, but also refocuses our decision making and resource distribution for quality improvement on misleading information and analysis.

Michael Power, now a professor in the London School of Economics, but an auditor in his former professional life, critically outlines the rise of quality audit and accountability in public life. In his book, *The Audit Society: rituals of verification* (1999), he argues that the 'huge and unavoidable social experiment' of audit that we appear to be trapped in is perverse in its effects. He writes that:

Pressures exist for audit and inspection systems to produce comfort and reassurance, rather than critique. If this argument is true and auditing systems are primarily about reaffirming order, then it will be interesting to see how auditable outcome-based performance measurement progresses in the face of system decay, especially given political rhetoric of zero tolerance for poor performance.

(Power 1999: xvii)

I would suggest that although universities may not be in decay, they may be a little lost, and thus vulnerable to this 'perverse' pressure.

As I indicated earlier, there is no lack of powerful critique of what is becoming the dominant form of quality maintenance. We have to advance our thinking and consider alternatives. I would now like to briefly note how those at the heart of academic life might conceptualize quality differently in universities. There are obviously many ways of doing this, but for the purposes of this chapter I will suggest only four. I offer them as indicators for exploration at this point, rather than as fully expanded ideas.

Alternative indicators of quality

Quality as pluralism

Faced by changing relationships between universities and students, where students begin to conceive of themselves as customers or clients, it seems only natural that national agencies and individual universities are beginning to attend to the quality of teaching and learning more closely. To this end, formulaic frameworks and centrally produced teaching guides are being put in place. Some academics find this a worrying trend, as it appears to diminish the crucial importance of 'pluralism' in intellectual endeavour and debate. I quote a typical response from Tim Birkhead, a Professor of Behavioural Ecology. He argues that lecturers should 'discover the joys of eccentricity and leave uniformity to the clones'. He is worried about the 'obsession of uniformity' suggesting that:

> Many academics feel that the powers that be would prefer all academics to be clones, giving uniform lectures in a uniform style, with a uniform structure to feed the uniform notebooks of uniform undergraduates to justify their uniformly good marks. The recent idea that undergraduate lectures should follow a more uniform format is a retrograde step.

Using ecological analogies, he writes:

> Animals that reproduce asexually are a bit dull and are most likely to become extinct because they lack the genetic variation that might allow them to cope with a changing environment. Since variety is the spice of life, it is bizarre that some of those who work in higher education should be hell bent on eliminating it.

(Birkhead 2004: 23)

I have found it interesting that in my own research on differences in teaching and learning in the different disciplines, there are indications (small yet) of convergence of discourse, pedagogy and even curriculum (Zamorski 2004).

Quality as passion

Quality, I have been told many times, also resides in the passions, obsessions and determination of individuals. Academics pursue diligently their search for knowledge, delight in the beauty and elegance of mathematics, strive to understand and pass onto their students the humanity in history, and obsessively and perhaps even ruthlessly investigate, create and invent new knowledge, ideas and products in science. And it is their values and moral imperatives that drive them to look for and educate students who are cognitively active and intellectually adventurous. Such quality indicators are not so easy to define, articulate or measure. Our questions here are: Can we impose or force quality of this kind? How can we create or maintain the environments and conditions in which this kind of intrinsic motivation can flourish? For instance, in my own research in higher education, I have been interviewing deans of schools and faculties in different disciplines. There was much that was different, but there were two commonalities (Zamorski 2004). One was their passion for their subjects and disciplines. I was swept away by their enthusiasm; I wanted to join every school/subject or discipline by the end of each interview that I conducted. The second commonality was their negativity towards the imposition, the language and bureaucracy of quality criteria and audit, which they saw as the main inhibition of the intellectual environments that they were striving to enhance. They assumed that their interest in research – knowledge creation or discovery – and their urge to work at the highest intellectual level with their students would and should be self-evident. Why create an artificial layer of 'quality' that rarely touches or meets, let alone overlaps, with the reality?

Quality as responsibility

The research I am engaged in also indicates that academics make a strong connection between 'quality' and 'responsibility'. As part of their personal values and academic identities, academics report that 'quality' in higher education is manifested and practised (or achieved) through fulfilling their responsibilities. And their responsibilities are twin – towards their disciplines and towards their students. Senior academics made it clear in interviews that they had limited loyalty to their universities, little to governmental agencies, but much to their discipline and to their students.

Quality as equality and inclusion

Of course 'equality' and 'inclusion' are not the same issues, but they stem from a similar concern; that of social justice and civil society – a fourth indicator of quality in higher education. Academics report that universities should not only have a role in helping to develop these aspirations, but that they should also locate equality and inclusion at the heart of their practice, so that they are central to the lived experience of all in university cultures and environments.

But this is not always the case. Paradoxically, it seems that the more recent impositions for developing quality are the ones that interfere most with what they hope to achieve on these issues. For example, in the UK, Deem, Tlili and Morley (2004) have been investigating staff experiences on equality in higher education across a number of universities. As part of this research, they are examining the relationship between equality and quality for all university staff. So far, they suggest that in spite of EU legislation poor equity continues in higher education in the UK. They argue that in fact the equality agenda and the quality culture are in tension. A primary reason for this is that 'audit is so dominant' in the quality culture and discourse. They suggest that quality (audit) has little to do with equality and equity, as it is mainly associated with the new 'managerial project', which is often concerned with 'impression management'. That is, 'quality' is for 'consumers' rather than staff (Deem, Tlili and Morley 2004).

In another example from my own research, a senior academic reported to me despairingly that: 'Nothing will get past the government unless it has the word "standards" in it.' He wondered: 'How do we create that feeling of well-being, which is essential, not peripheral, to being a human being? That is about inclusion. Inclusion is a matter of "quality" in education.' He argued that we now live in a negative culture, based on the premise of deficit models of citizenship and humanity that standards and audit attempt to remedy, maintaining that 'We can never achieve inclusion and equality in this kind of culture.'

Conclusion

'Quality' in higher education discourse should be a good and positive word. But now the use of the word is sliding to negative meaning, often provoking reactions of cynicism and even hostility. Extrinsic imposition of quality maintenance – narrowed, centralized and standardized in conception – has to some extent displaced the energies, motivation and focus of the academic away from quality development which grows out of personal and professional responsibilities and the excitement and determination to pursue and create knowledge. Instead it has moved to grudging and game-playing compliance.

So we are left, a little stranded perhaps, with a situation that is unsatisfactory, and with questions still requiring serious deliberation. For example: Where do we find quality? What do we look for? Is it in targets, procedures, infrastructures, planning documents and benchmarks, or is it primarily located in people's intentions, attitudes, behaviour, values, and in a sense of personal or professional excitement or obligation? Certainly policies, procedures and resources can help make manifest the human intentions that underpin and motivate us. But is it in our heads and hearts that quality actually begins? The intrinsic desire to improve quality resides in most of us. However, new contexts, environments, cultures, rules and procedures can inhibit these natural desires. Has genuine quality thus been reduced to a 'polite' and compliant attendance to the policies and the procedures that impose and audit standards and improvement of quality? Are we losing the 'added value' of authentic care for and in higher education?

For 'societies in transition', which are looking to their higher education systems to successfully propel them into a twenty-first century by addressing the needs of both economic prosperity and a fulfilled and informed citizenry, determining the interrelationship of the what, why and how questions of quality is crucial. As the authors of the OECD report on 'Securing a Sustainable Future for Higher Education' (OECD 2004) note in their final paragraph:

> The challenges for governors and managers of higher education institutions are therefore related to how best they can introduce appropriate management techniques and incentives into their institutions in a way which will respond to these pressures, but without undermining the fundamental mission of the institutions. This is one of the greatest challenges in public service today.
>
> (OECD 2004: 66)

Note

1 This chapter is based on a keynote address to the UNIQUAL conference on Quality in Higher Education held in Vilnius, 7 October 2004.

References

Birkhead, T. (2004) 'Why the best academics are just like sperm', *Times Higher Educational Supplement*, 3 September: 23.

Deem, R., Tlili, A. and Morley, L. (2004) 'The equity in European higher education debate in the twenty-first century: preliminary findings from an investigation of staff experiences of current equality policies in UK higher education institutions', PowerPoint presentation at the European Conference on Educational Research (ECER), University of Crete, September 2004.

European Commission (2001) *Making a European Area of Lifelong Learning a Reality*, Brussels: European Commission. Online. Available at: europa.eu.int (accessed 2 September 2004).

—— (2003a) *Measures to improve Higher Education/Research Relations in Order to Strengthen the Strategic Basis of the ERA*, Luxembourg: Office for Official Publications of the European Communities. Online. Available at: europa.eu.int (accessed 5 August 2004).

—— (2003b) *Education and Training 2010: the Success of the Lisbon Strategy Hinges on Urgent Reforms*, Brussels: Commission of the European Communities.

Elliott, J. (2001) 'Characteristics of performative cultures: their central paradoxes and limitations as resources for educational reform', in C. Husbands (ed.) *The Performing School*, London: Routledge.

Furedi, F. (2004) 'Clipboard versus the mortarboard', *Times Higher Educational Supplement*, 17 September: 22.
Knight, P. (2004) 'Opinion', *Education Guardian*, 12 October: 5.
OECD (2004) *On the Edge: Securing a Sustainable Future for Higher Education*, France: OECD Publications. Online. Available at: europa.eu.int (accessed 1 September 2004).
Power, M. (1999) *The Audit Society: Rituals of Verification*, Oxford: Oxford University Press.
Times Higher Education Supplement (*THES*) (2004) 'Graduates reap high returns on degree', 17 September: 11.
Zamorski, B. 'Beginning to explore the research/teaching nexus in higher education through different disciplines . . . and being led off on a tangent', paper presented at the European Conference on Educational Research (ECER), University of Crete, September 2004.

Chapter 20

Universities and societies
Traditions, transitions and tensions

Terence McLaughlin

The aim of this chapter is to draw together some central elements in the wide-ranging discussions in this volume of questions relating to universities and societies in transition and to situate these central elements in a broader critical perspective. Given the detailed and complex nature of many of the contributions, the focus of this chapter is necessarily selective in its attention to central elements in the discussions. Many detailed matters of great interest and importance are not addressed here. For the purposes of this chapter, it is helpful to locate matters roughly under three general categories: transitions, traditions and tensions.

Transitions

The claim that various kinds of *transition* are taking place in societies, in the world as a whole and in higher education has been a recurring and dominant theme in the volume. In our introduction, David Bridges and I identified three contexts of transition central to the concerns of the collection: (1) political, cultural and economic transitions relating to societies in Central and Eastern Europe which were part of the former Soviet Union such as Lithuania: 'countries in transition' in a very specific sense; (2) transitions involving societies throughout the world relating to the phenomena of globalization and the knowledge economy, and relatedly (3) transitions involving institutions of higher education involving such matters as the application of market principles, a demand for wider participation, an expansion in kinds of learning and teaching, and a 'deconstruction' of some of the defining features of the university (identity of place, time, scholarly community, student community and academic discipline or subject).

The general notion of *transition* indicates that certain changes are taking place which are moving something from one state or condition to another. An obvious general question which arises in relation to the notion of a 'transition' is a factual one: are the alleged changes actually taking place? The discussion in the volume tends not to be preoccupied by factual questions about the transitions under consideration, but focuses on questions relating to the *meaning* and *significance* of the transitions and to their *value*. Transitions per se are, after all, neither necessarily transparent nor valuable. For example, Cowen (Chapter 1 in this volume) urges us to be aware that notions such as 'social progress' (implicit in 'stages of development') require interpretive and normative attention.

Transitions in countries in transition

The contributors in the volume tend to accept that most of the transitions described in relation to 'countries in transition' are in fact taking place (implying that at least some of them are inevitable) and that other transitions may need to be secured in the face of obstacles (thereby implying that they are valuable). It would be wrong, however, to see the dominant concerns of the contributors as focused solely upon how the 'countries in transition' can succeed in 'catching up' with their western neighbours who have enjoyed a 'head start' in achieving the transitions. Many contributors raise critical questions about the meaning, significance and value of the transitions themselves.

On the meaning and significance of the transitions, several contributors stress the importance of avoiding an overly simple view of aspects of 'transition' as straightforwardly interpretable and transferable from western contexts to 'countries in transition'. Giedrius Jucevičius' account (Chapter 11 in this volume) of the specific cultural and other features of the Lithuanian context relevant to proposed 'transformations' is instructive in this regard (see also the discussion by Musiał – Chapter 8 in the volume – of contextual features of the Baltic Sea region in general). Janiūnaitė and Gudaitytė (Chapter 14 in the volume) emphasize the need for 'countries in transition' to take account of the human and social prerequisites, preconditions and implications of proposed transformations. A recurring theme in these and other contributions is the need to take account of the persisting residue of Soviet thinking prevalent in such countries, with its implications for sensibility, attitude, confidence and motivation in relation to the economic, civic and political demands of liberal democratic societies. Many contributors are in principle receptive, therefore, to Robert Cowen's warning of the need to attend to the normative, institutional and environmental specificities of particular societies in the face of a temptation to see the processes involved in the 'transfer' of concepts, values and policies from one societal context to another in terms of the application of technical solutions to a contextual and abstract problem.

The discussion in the volume extends beyond the meaning and significance of the transitions to their value. There is a general realization that the transitions are not cost free for 'societies in transition', and pose, as Jucevičienė and Vaitkus point out (Chapter 3 in this volume), not only opportunities but also 'multiple challenges'. Janiūnaitė and Gudaitytė draw attention to certain manifestations in contemporary Lithuania of psychological instability, social disintegration, disrespect for civic and legal domains, social conflict and social exclusion arising from the transitions. As Anthony Giddens (2002: 46–8) has pointed out in his discussion of globalization, more autonomy for individuals is not necessarily a good thing: choice, for example, when subverted by anxiety, can bring about forms of addiction and the need for self-identity to be created and recreated in various ways. Giddens identifies as one of the consequences of globalization 'the end of tradition' understood not as its disappearance but the decline of 'tradition lived in the traditional way', namely in the light of its internal claims to truth (ibid., p. 43 cf Chapter 3. On the wide-ranging changes which Giddens argues that globalization is bringing about in relation to sexuality, relationships, marriage and the family see Chapter 4). One of the major challenges which preoccupy Jucevičienė and Vaitkus arises from the fact that, despite a successful recent track record of transition (including one of the world's fastest growing economies and a steadily rising proportion of the young population in higher education), the national identity and resources of Lithuania are seriously challenged by the phenomenon of 'brain drain'. At the time of writing, for example, it is estimated by some sources that between 200,000 and 250,000 Lithuanians emigrated from the country after its accession to the European Union on 1 May 2004 and that a total of between 284,000 and 314,000 Lithuanians will be working outside the country in 2006 (Jesuits Province in Lithuania and Latvia, January 2006).

The transitions also pose threats to the national identity of 'countries in transition' in other ways. Giddens points out that the influence of globalization is not only to 'pull away' power from local or national contexts but also to 'push downwards', creating new pressures upon local autonomy and cultural identity and also to 'squeeze sidewards', creating new zones of an economic and cultural kind within and across nations (op. cit., p. 13). Richard Smith (Chapter 2 in this volume), following Readings (1996), points out that the economic and other pressures of globalization have led to the increasing internationalization of culture. 'National culture' and the nation-state (both now weakened in different ways) are no longer the main focus of the university in the way suggested, from the nineteenth century onwards, in the thinking of German scholars such as Humboldt. According to Readings, the university no longer has a 'national cultural mission' and 'is no longer linked to the destiny of the nation-state by virtue of its role as producer, protector, and inculcator of an idea of national culture' (Readings 1996: 3): instead, 'excellence' in the modern university becomes defined in contextual, technicist and competitive terms. Given the Soviet dominance for much of the last century of 'countries in transition', the role of higher education in relation to national culture has taken a rather different form in these contexts from that indicated by Readings. However, Lithuania, in common with other 'countries in transition', defended its valued national culture and identity for many years under Soviet occupation. It is ironic that, having successfully defended its national culture and identity under Soviet influences, Lithuania and the other countries in transition should now face erosion of their culture and identity by global forces (on these matters see, for example, McLaughlin and Jucevičienė 1997).

A realization of the costs to 'societies in transition' of some of the transitions in which they are involved should lead naturally to a deeper questioning of the value of the transitions themselves. Many of the contributors to the volume are alert to Cowen's warning to the 'countries in transition' not to exchange an educational system based on a Soviet form of 'deductive rationality' (where a broad social vision is translated directly into forms of educational provision) for an educational system based on a new kind of 'deductive rationality' involving an uncritically accepted discourse of international economic Darwinism.

However, it is appropriate for 'societies in transition' to draw more upon critical appraisals of phenomena such as 'the learning society' from western sources, some of which will be indicated shortly. Such resources should enable an enrichment of the kinds of broader judgement implicit in the wide-ranging forms of 'intelligence', extending well beyond those required for the mere 'implementation' of transitions, invoked by Robertas Jucevičius in his discussion of 'the intelligent country' (Chapter 5 in this volume). Part of the 'intelligence' characteristic of an 'intelligent country' should consist in a full consideration of the sorts of questions about the meaning, significance and value of the transitions which have been pointed to.

Transitions throughout the world

One of the most prominent transitions throughout the world discussed by contributors to the volume is that of globalization, which, according to Anthony Giddens, is a term which 'has come from nowhere to be almost everywhere' (2002: 7). The need for globalization to be properly understood and evaluated in the full range of its processes and implications (economic, political, technological and cultural) scarcely requires emphasis (on these matters see, for example, Giddens 2002 esp. Chapter 1, Held *et al.* 1999, Singer 2002). Given the complexity of globalization, however, the evaluative task here is by no means straightforward (see, for example, Giddens 2002: 17).

One of the most troubling features of globalization is summed up by Friedman's remark, quoted by Peter Singer, that the most basic truth about globalization is that 'no one is in charge' (Singer 2002: 11). Giddens observes that, at least at present, globalization is not 'a global order driven by collective human will. Instead, it is emerging in an anarchic, haphazard fashion, carried along by a mixture of influences' (op. cit., p. 19). Questions of control as well as evaluation loom large in relation to globalization.

The contributors to the volume do not assume that globalization is a straightforward good. Janiūnaitė and Gudaitytė, for example, draw attention to the human and social preconditions and correlates of material–technical innovations, to the need for the genuine needs of human development to be kept in clear focus and to the need to form citizens so that they are able to make judgements about the value of proposed innovations. Some ethical critiques of globalization are wide ranging. Giddens, for example, argues that globalization presents us with a vision not only of a 'global village' but of 'global pillage' (Giddens 2002: 16). Singer draws radical implications from his insistence that the question of how we should live together in 'one world' has an inescapably ethical dimension (2002: 13). For Singer, there is no moral justification for our 'circle of concern' for the well-being of others to be limited at the boundaries of a nation (or, one might add, an entity such as the enlarged European Community) (Singer 2002, Chapter 5). Singer has recently restated his well-known argument to the effect that our obligation to help a stranger in need in another (and perhaps very distant) country is as great as the obligation to help our neighbours or compatriots. He argues that someone who sees a child in danger of drowning in a shallow pool and who fails to offer assistance when they are in a position to do so with minimal inconvenience is doing something seriously wrong. Similarly, Singer argues, the vast majority of people in the developed nations of the world fail to offer assistance to distant sufferers when they are able to do so by using their disposable income on other than 'frivolities and luxuries, things of no more importance to us than avoiding getting our shoes and trousers muddy' (op. cit., p. 157). Therefore, argues Singer, such people are no better morally than the person who passes by a child in danger of drowning in a pool (see op. cit., Chapter 5). Whatever the merits of this particular argument, it is clear that globalization invites extensive ethical assessment. Singer discusses four major challenges, of an ethical kind, to the role of the World Trade Organisation in relation to the development of globalization: that it places economic considerations ahead of concerns for the environment, animal welfare and human rights, that it erodes national sovereignty, that it is undemocratic and that it increases inequality and leaves the world's poorest people worse off than they would otherwise have been (op. cit., p. 55. See also Chapter 3).

Two contributions to this collection in particular offer resources for the kinds of ethical assessment that are needed in response to ethical challenges of these, and other, kinds. At the most general level, Hanan Alexander (Chapter 17 in this volume) insists that citizenship, properly conceived, requires citizens to be equipped to engage in 'strong evaluation', including evaluation of conceptions of the good and their ethical implications in a way which can be interpreted as including consideration of 'the meaning of life' (for recent philosophical discussion of the notion of 'the meaning of life' see Cottingham 2003). At the more specific level, Flavio Comim (Chapter 6 in the volume) offers a perspective on development which provides criteria for the kind of broad ethical evaluation which is required. Comim points out the inadequacy of conceiving development merely in terms of increasing economic growth and insists that human well-being more generally conceived (including aspects of well-being which are irreducible to the economic) need to be brought into the picture. For Comim, following Amartya Sen's 'capability' approach to human development, what is crucial is the enlargement of choices of people as 'ends in themselves' to achieve a range of goods (including quality of life and well-being) in which a form of autonomous freedom is prominent. What is at stake is not merely the provision of resources but of the ability of persons to convert resources into valued functionings and capabilities. This approach gives concrete guidance in the evaluation of phenomena such as globalization.

Another prominent transition discussed by contributors to the volume relates to the emergence of 'the learning society' (and related notions such as 'the knowledge economy' and 'lifelong learning'). Palmira Jucevičienė (Chapter 4 in this volume) indicates how the notion of 'the learning society' is contested and variably interpreted (as in the quoted cultural, technological and democratic conceptions outlined by Jarvis). The contributors in the volume, however, tend not to engage sufficiently with fundamental critiques of the concept of the 'learning society' which are prominent in western discussions.

For example, Frank Coffield (2000a), as a result of the ESRC research programme into 'The Learning Society: knowledge and skills for employment' (see Coffield 2000b), observes that in the UK there is 'widespread and deep-seated disagreement about the characteristics of such a society' (Coffield 2000a: 3) and claims that research into the use of the term has shown that 'political and educational discourse surrounding a learning society was shot through ... by extreme conceptual vagueness' (op. cit., p. 3). Coffield identifies ten (non-exhaustive) models of the 'learning society' (op. cit., pp. 7–27) and argues that the lack of agreement on any one model means that we have to abandon talk of *the* learning society (op. cit., p. 28). For Coffield, a lack 'of consensus on definitions, aims and basic values' (op. cit., p. 28) will, *inter alia*, hamper the implementation of new approaches to lifelong learning, a notion which he sees as having become almost indistinguishable from that of the learning society (op. cit., pp. 5–6). In addition to lack of clarity about the meaning of the notion of a 'learning society', Coffield also claims that much of the discourse relating to the notion in the UK contains ' "factual" assumptions and assertions ... unsupported by any hard evidence or which have since been seriously questioned' (op. cit., pp. 3–4). For Coffield, 'lifelong learning' 'has remained an evidence-free zone, under-researched, under-theorized, unencumbered by doubt and unmoved by criticism' (op. cit., p. 4): it is, claims Coffield, 'an area which is awash with unsubstantiated generalities, armchair musings and banalities without bite' (op. cit., p. 7).

Coffield raises critical questions in relation to each of the ten models of the learning society which are identified (op. cit., pp. 7–27). In relation to *skills growth*, for example, Coffield argues that 'the alleged link between investment in education and economic performance is a *belief* rather than an established research finding' (op. cit., p. 8). In relation to *a learning market*, disadvantages and adverse effects need to be carefully considered (op. cit., pp. 12–14). In relation to *the centrality of learning* model, there is critical inattention to the notion of *learning* itself and to the meaning and justification of favoured forms of learning such as 'key skills' (op. cit., pp. 19–23). A general point made by Coffield is that the discourse of the 'learning society' and 'lifelong learning' often embodies a view of learners 'in an overly simplistic manner as individual, rational and calculating human capitalists' (Coffield, op. cit., p. 29). Attention is needed, for example, to the uneven distribution of relevant social, economic, cultural and human capital among individuals and to wider questions of politics, power and inequality.

It is clear, therefore, that the notion of a 'learning society' (and the related notion of 'lifelong learning') does not specify an unambiguous set of generally agreed goals which can be aimed at. Whilst this is recognized by a number of contributors to the volume, fuller critical assessment of notions such as the 'learning society' is needed in the 'countries in transition', as elsewhere.

Transitions in higher education

Transitions in higher education have been a major focus of discussion in the collection as a whole. Much discussion of the contemporary university is concerned with a range of developments which invite us to extend our conception of its aims, values and purposes. The variety of expectations now made of contemporary universities is apparent in Richard Smith's five 'dimensions of responsiveness' now demanded of them: to their national and cultural setting; to the demands of the national and local economy; to international and global concerns; to international 'league tables' of performance in research and other terms; and to ideals of education such as the emancipation of the human spirit and the broadening of the horizons of the individual. The resultant policy pressures bearing upon universities are discussed and criticized by a number of contributors, including Barbara Zamorski (Chapter 19 in this volume). At the level of strategies for teaching, learning and assessment, familiar advocated policies relate to such matters as 'active' learning, flexible modularity, credit transfer, the accreditation of non-formal and informal learning, non-traditional access routes, 'service learning' and the development of a variety of physical locations and virtual spaces in which the activities of higher education take place.

This section will focus on a number of general transitions affecting universities relating to focuses of teaching, learning and research. Broader questions about the aims, values and purposes of universities, which relate to the 'traditions' of universities, will be considered in the next section.

Many of the transitions relating to university teaching, learning and research are highly controversial. For example, in relation to the alleged importance of the role of higher education in developing the skills base necessary for future economic development, Dunne *et al.* argue, on the basis of an empirical study of skill development in higher education in the UK, that little thought has been given to central theoretical and empirical matters, including those relating to implicit assumptions about skill transfer (Dunne *et al.* 2000: 106). In relation to matters of conceptualization, Dunne *et al.* found that the range of labels employed to identify the kinds of specific valued achievements being sought via higher education in the area of skills were various in their description of the category of the achievement (skills, competences, attributes) and in their descriptions of other features of the achievement ('transferable', 'personal', 'common', 'key', 'core', 'generic', etc.) (Dunne *et al.* 2000: 108). These labels, often used to identify sets or lists of valued skills, were seen as subject to rapid and unpredictable change and as 'theoretically and empirically threadbare' (ibid.) not least because they have usually been formulated without the involvement of those involved in developing the skills in the context of higher education. The notion of 'key skills' was discovered to be ambiguous as between skills which are seen as central to a particular discipline and those which are seen as more generic in that they support study in any discipline (ibid.). The research casts doubt on any assumption that 'generic' skills transfer from one context to another in a straightforward way (op. cit., pp. 108–9). Rather, Dunne *et al.* argue, 'The discourse on generic skills, and all its variants, is confused, confusing and underconceptualized. Employers and policy makers alike have been seduced by the slogans, with scant consideration of their definition, characteristics, transferability or utility' (op. cit., p. 131). Dunne *et al.* point out that although employers used a common vocabulary with respect to skills, this concealed a great variety of specific kinds of context-related capacity: an example in this respect is the wide range of activities covered by the term 'communication skills' (op. cit., p. 121). This tendency to employ what Ronald Barnett refers to as a uni-dimensional label to a multi-dimensional skill (quoted in op. cit., p. 127) has great implications for the possibility and even coherence of the notion of 'transferable skills' (ibid.). For Dunne *et al.* it is important to acknowledge the implications of their finding that 'global generic descriptors hide enormous variation in actual skill use' (op. cit., p. 127).

This point is recognized by a number of contributors to the volume. Daiva Lepaitė (Chapter 12 in the volume) is alert to the need to avoid unduly narrow conceptualizations of the notion of 'competence'. Lepaitė notes that the term 'competence' covers a range of levels and kinds of capacity which need to be carefully identified, not least in relation to training programmes. She is cautious about the coherence and possibility of general competences and insists that competences (properly understood) should not be seen as separable from each other or from the development of an individual's wider knowledge, skills, attitudes, personality characteristics and values. Lepaitė's conception of 'holistic competence' (akin to Robertas Jucevičius' notion of 'intelligence' in its emphasis on the ability to apply knowledge in varied and unpredictable situations and in different contexts and levels of action) raises the question of whether the richness of the qualities and capacities involved can be properly captured in the notion of a 'competence' (on the notion of competences see, for example, Barnett 1994).

A further transition relating to teaching, learning and assessment in universities is a transition from 'Mode 1' to 'Mode 2' knowledge in the terms conceptualized by Michael Gibbons and discussed, among others, by Jucevičienė and Vaitkus in this volume. According to Gibbons, Mode 2 knowledge, in contrast to its Mode 1 counterpart, is produced in the context of application under the aspect of 'usefulness', collaboratively determined by a range of 'actors', transdisciplinary, dynamic ('problem solving capacity on the move'), varied in the skills used in problem solving, heterogeneous, flexible in its organizational structures (temporary teams and networks), varied in its sites of knowledge creation (multi-national firms, small hi-tech companies, government institutions, national and international research programmes, etc.), socially accountable, and quality controlled according to wide criteria (Gibbons 2000). Interestingly, Gibbons insists that the nature of Mode 2 knowledge production invites evaluation from perspectives other than the merely scientific and technological, since the problems addressed often involve the values and preferences of different individuals and groups: the humanities therefore have a role to play in the reflexivity involved in Mode 2 knowledge production, as do various forums for the expression of public concern, including public controversy (ibid.). Gibbons holds that the emergence of Mode 2 knowledge production challenges universities traditionally engaged in Mode 1 knowledge production in various ways: to share their resources with, and seek collaboration with, other knowledge-producing institutions, to change the work environments of academics, to change the system of rewards and career paths for the Mode 1 academic (to give proper weight to the demands of transdisciplinarity and application) and to revise the undergraduate curriculum to emphasize skills application in real world contexts (Jansen 2000).

Mode 2 knowledge production escapes serious critical analysis by the contributors to the volume. An evaluation of the implementation of Mode 2 forms of knowledge production in South Africa may have some lessons for implementation of the notion in 'countries in transition'. The findings of a recent study concluded that Gibbons' claim about the inevitability of transition to Mode 2 knowledge needs to be modified in the light of the complexities of organizational and cultural aspects of university life, resistance to the replacement of Mode 1 orientations by professors, the lack of willingness and readiness of the partners to engage in new forms of knowledge production and the dominance of organizational rather than epistemological considerations in partnerships forged (Jansen 2000). There are hints in some of the contributions to the volume that similar difficulties arise in Lithuania. Further work has called into question deeper aspects of the theory itself, including the nature and coherence of the distinction between the modes, the over-dichotomization of the distinction, Gibbons' position on whether Mode 2 knowledge production is seen as supplanting Mode 1 or coexisting with it, the respects in which Mode 2 depends on Mode 1, the importance of continuing Mode 1-based undergraduate courses and the general need to secure Mode 1 knowledge production in any university committed to adequate research and teaching (on these matters see, for example, Muller 2000).

The discussion in this section of two prominent 'transitions' in higher education, the emphasis on skills development and on the emergence of Mode 2 knowledge production, is intended to exemplify the general point that many of the proposed transitions are problematic conceptually and empirically. It is therefore highly appropriate that 'countries in transition' are not merely embracing the transitions but contributing to appropriate criticism of them.

Traditions

Questions relating to tradition surface in a number of ways in the collection: reference has already been made to 'the end of tradition' as an alleged consequence of globalization and its influence upon 'countries in transition'. In this section, however, attention will be focused on tradition in relation to universities. Many of the discussions in the volume imply that, despite the force of the various transitions relating to universities which have been noted, something of the 'traditional' role of the university (most notably its role in relation to the promotion of independent critical thinking, emancipation and the broadening of horizons) should be preserved.

It is important to note at the outset that the notion of *tradition* with respect to universities is not unproblematic. Gordon Graham (2000) cautions that a 'purism' about the aims, values and purposes of universities is not only out of place, but has in fact never been in place. The 'traditions' of universities have always been plural. Graham argues, for example, that a concern with knowledge and the pursuit of learning for their own sake rather than for some external practical end has always coexisted in universities, including ancient universities, with a concern to provide forms of practical training (ibid., pp. 19–21. See also Chapter 1). Richard Smith reminds us that the universities of Europe originated as professional training grounds for doctors, lawyers and priests, and Hanan Alexander brings into focus the range of purposes which universities have traditionally served. It is instructive to note, as Megone (2005: 117) has pointed out, that the term 'the virtual university' was first coined by Cardinal Newman in *The Idea of a University* in the nineteenth century and applied to the University of London because of the spatially dispersed nature of its constituent colleges.

Notwithstanding these points, it is widely felt that a fundamental role of the university requiring preservation and protection relates to its role in relation to criticism and to human development and emancipation. In relation to criticism, Ronald Barnett observes that the critical role of the university requires that it must maintain 'vigorously and vigilantly a discourse of critique, of commentary and of fearless evaluation' (Barnett 1997: 36. See also Chapter 3). Barnett argues that higher education should not confine itself to a narrow account of 'critical thinking', but rather be concerned with a widely conceived form of 'criticality' of increasing expansiveness in relation both to *level* (ranging from 'skills' of critical thinking to unrestricted 'critique') and to *domain* (extending beyond disciplines of knowledge to the self and the world) (op. cit., pp. 7–8). For Barnett, the full emancipatory potential of 'criticality' can only be realized when it is seen as embodied in qualities of persons – 'critical being' – in the various domains and when the level of 'criticality' achieved in each domain extends far beyond the level of 'skills' of critical thinking and of instrumentality (ibid.). The 'traditional' concern of the university with human development and emancipation is reflected in Allan Bloom's observation that the question of the nature of the human being is at the heart of a liberal education (1987: 21).

These aspects of the 'traditional' role of the university cannot, it is argued, be reduced to, or governed solely by, economic considerations and instrumentalities, and should be preserved and protected as an important aspect of the aims, values, teaching and research of universities. This conclusion finds support among contributors to the book for at least two broad reasons.

First, several contributors argue that economic considerations, seemingly paradoxically, are not only harmonious with a 'traditional' dimension to the university but actually require it. A number of the contributors point to the need in economic and business contexts for higher-level generic, analytic and synthesizing skills (together with their related sensitivities), which cannot be developed merely through training in narrowly defined vocational skills. Significant here are Robertas Jucevičius' notion of 'intelligence', Daiva Lepaitė's notion of 'holistic competence' and Giedrius Jucevičius' report that research by the World Bank has shown that students from the former Soviet Bloc score very highly on tests for factual knowledge, but poorly on the use of knowledge in unanticipated circumstances. Radošević and Kriaučionienė (Chapter 9 in the volume) argue that the most important contribution of universities to national innovation systems is in the development of high-level problem-solving skills. Many contributors agree with David Bridges (Chapter 7 in the volume) that the kinds of higher-level skills and sensitivities at stake can often be developed, and perhaps developed better, through the study of traditional academic university subjects such as Greek philosophy

The second reason relates to the range of issues raised in the volume which invite the critical and humanizing attention of the university. As was clear from the discussion in the last section, the range of transitions currently in play (such as globalization, the learning society, the promotion of skill development and the emergence of Mode 2 knowledge production) are ripe for critical exploration with respect to their meaning, significance and value. (On the importance of wide-ranging kinds of criticism in the context of the learning society see, for example, Barnett 1997, Chapter 12). Arūnas Lukoševičius (Chapter 10 in the volume) echoes the concerns of a number of contributors in his insistence that the university has a role in defining the social and human needs of a country and in balancing them against the potentially 'wild' and 'uncontrolled' development of technologies. Arild Tjeldvoll and Auksė Blaženaitė (Chapter 13 in the volume), in their articulation and defence of the 'critical service university', argue that such institutions should retain contact with their 'robust academic heartlands' in order to perform their traditional critical function in a liberal democratic society. The notion of 'supercomplexity' discussed by Jucevičienė and Vaitkus has important human and evaluative dimensions, as do various aspects of Mode 2 knowledge production. Janiūnaitė and Gudaitytė insist that extension of liberal higher education and its emancipatory ambitions to a greater proportion of members of society is an important 'social innovation' which needs to be secured, and they provide a robust defence of the place of the humanities as part of this education. In their discussion of the role of the university in community development Irene Leliūgienė and Viktorija Baršauskienė (Chapter 15 in the volume) include its role as 'educator' in relation to social educators in school and to social and community workers. Brian Heap (Chapter 18 in the volume) argues that scientific research and scholarship should not be driven solely by short-term concerns with applicability and exploitation, but by curiosity and long-term considerations relating, *inter alia*, to the development of informed democratic citizens. Following Pope John Paul II, Heap argues that the development of a form of wisdom is required in relation to scientific development and its role in society. The benefits for health associated with higher education, which Vilius Grabauskas outlines (Chapter 16 in the volume), cannot be seen as relating solely to the provision of information. Comim brings out how the role of education in relation to human development, properly conceived, can no longer be seen as merely instrumental (as in the creation of 'human capital' for the promotion of growth and development conceived economically), but as also having a constitutive role in the achievement by persons not only of functionings but of capacities to choose and discriminate between possible livings as part of a form of autonomous agency.

The role of higher education in the development of citizenship is a context in which the importance of some of the 'traditional' roles of the university are emphasized. Alexander sees the ability to engage in 'strong evaluation' of world views (and their related ethical and other implications) as an important part of citizenship and argues that this capacity involves the development of a form of 'intelligent spirituality'. The invocation of 'spirituality' is open to question here, at least in a non-religious university, because the category of the 'spiritual' is one which itself might be expected to be problematized as part of 'strong evaluation': another consequence of globalization (on the role of higher education in education for citizenship see, for example, Arthur and Bohlin 2005, Annette and McLaughlin 2005. On the educative tasks which arise for democracy in the context of globalization see Giddens 2002, Chapter 5).

The two broad kinds of reason outlined above point towards a widely felt need among the contributors to preserve central aspects of the 'traditional' role of the university, even if not in a fully articulated 'tradition'. The critical and humanizing roles of the university are not, however, straightforward and require careful restatement, not least in the light of intellectual developments and 'transitions' which are not unrelated to developments such as globalization. (On the wide range of complex matters arising here see, for example, Barnett 1990, 1994, 1997, Barnett and Standish 2003, Blake, Smith and Standish 1998, Bloom 1987, Bok 2003, Delanty 2001, Fuller 1989, Graham 2002, Maskell and Robinson 2002, Readings 1996, Robinson and Katulushi 2005.)

The contributors to the volume have little to say about how, in detailed terms, the 'traditional' critical and humanizing role of the university can be protected and preserved in the contemporary climate. A recent proposal for reform of university undergraduate education, by Martha Nussbaum (1997), which unites the critical and humanizing roles of the university in an interesting way, is worthy of consideration by 'countries in transition'. Nussbaum uses the term 'liberal education' to refer to 'a higher education that is a cultivation of the whole human being for the functions of citizenship and of life generally' (ibid., p. 9). The 'liberal' in this conception refers, in Nussbaum's view, to a 'liberation' of the mind 'from the bondage of habit and custom, producing people who can function with sensitivity and alertness as citizens of the whole world' (ibid., p. 8). According to Nussbaum, central to higher education, properly conceived, is 'the cultivation of humanity' at the heart of which is the development of three capacities. First, the capacity for critical examination of oneself and one's traditions – for living 'the examined life' (ibid., p. 9), which involves the development of appropriate forms of critical questioning and attitude and their related requirements of reasoning, skill and judgement (cf ibid., Chapter 1). Second, the capacity for people to 'see themselves not simply as citizens of some local region or group but also, and above all, as human beings bound to all other human beings by ties of recognition and concern' (ibid., p. 10), in this way coming to realize possibilities of communication and fellowship with, and responsibility for, other people throughout the world and achieving an understanding of how 'common needs and aims are differently realized in different circumstances' (ibid., p. 10; cf ibid., Chapter 2). The third capacity is development of a critical 'narrative imagination': 'the ability to think what it might be like to be in the shoes of a person different from oneself, to be an intelligent reader of that person's story, and to understand the emotions and wishes and desires that someone so placed might have' (ibid., pp. 10–11; cf ibid., Chapter 3). Nussbaum sees these three capacities as necessary but not sufficient for the development of intelligent citizenship: scientific and economic understanding, among others, are very important. However, Nussbaum self-consciously restricts her account to the humanities and the social sciences, and to selected, particularly controversial, elements in these domains.

Nussbaum herself draws attention to one implication of this conception, which is not a feature of European Higher Education: the idea of 'a core of common studies that is essential to the good life for each and every person' (Nussbaum 1997: 31). For Nussbaum this should include a compulsory requirement to study philosophy and the humanities (particularly the arts), with appropriate attention to multicultural considerations (properly conceived). The precise nature of this curriculum is, of course, difficult to specify. As Nussbaum herself notes, 'It is relatively easy to construct a gentleman's education for a homogeneous elite. It is far more difficult to prepare people of highly diverse backgrounds for complex world citizenship' (Nussbaum 1997: 295).

Although Nussbaum's proposal is developed in the context of the United States, and is therefore subject to the important points made earlier about the dangers of conceiving 'transfer' in a contextual and abstract way, the general contours of the proposal may be worth considering by 'countries in transition'. The respects in which the proposal needs adaptation to local contexts (through, for example, greater attention to local culture and identity) require detailed attention and consideration. It may be that an appropriately modified proposal of this kind may help, in part, to provide and secure the 'traditional' critical and humanizing elements of the university about which the contributors are concerned. After all, striking innovations in relation to the various 'transitions' which have been discussed may require parallel innovations in relation to other aspects of the life and work of the university seen as important.

Tensions

A characteristic feature of the discussion throughout the volume has been its attempt to acknowledge, conceptualize and judge a complex series of tensions of different kinds both at the theoretical and the practical levels.

A number of such general tensions can be pointed to here. First, a range of tensions arise for 'countries in transition' in judging the respects in which they should, on the one hand, welcome the 'transitions' which are having an impact on them (such as 'globalization' and its related concepts and processes) and, on the other hand, temper or resist the impact of these 'transitions' in the interests of protection against the potential and actual harms indicated earlier. Second, a range of tensions arise at the general level in judging the relative merits and demerits of 'transitions' such as globalization, the 'learning society' and its related notions. Third, a range of tensions arise in relation to the various aims, purposes and priorities of the contemporary university. As Bridges argues, on the one hand it is a reasonable aspiration both that a community which contributes public funding to higher education should expect that the system should bring an economic return and that the application of knowledge available in universities to business should be facilitated. However, on the other hand Bridges also cautions that the university should maintain vigilance in guarding its own central commitments (to systematic and sustained learning and enquiry, to academic discipline in scholarship and research and to academic virtue in its various aspects). Many would echo Janiūnaitė and Gudaitytė's claim that the various functions of higher education should be pursued together, and Smith's claim that its various aims and purposes need to be kept constantly in equilibrium and responded to in a contextually sensitive way. However, the reality of incompatibilities, conflicts and hard decisions looms large. Tensions in relation to the aims, purposes and priorities of the contemporary university also surface in tensions in relation to the relative merits and demerits of particular notions relating to teaching and research such as 'skills', 'Modes 1 and 2 knowledge production' and the precise ways in which the 'traditional' critical and humanizing functions of the university can be preserved and defended in the contemporary context.

General tensions of these kinds are mirrored by more detailed tensions of one kind and another relating to particular matters of policy and strategy. It will be recalled that all these tensions are felt not merely at the theoretical but also at the practical level, where they surface in particular institutions, enterprises and contexts.

The tensions arise in part from the complexity of the conceptualizations and judgements involved in the matters at stake and the force of the considerations in play on either side of the tensions in question. In this situation, it is hard to specify a range of criteria for the making of adequate judgements. In the context of judgements about the aims, purposes and priorities of contemporary universities, Richard Smith cautions that any attempt to formulate and articulate these in an explicit way runs the risk of being captured by illicitly dominant and pervasive instrumental or technical reason ('the default language of our time'), where the specification of means to the achievement of preordained ends is central and where aims and purposes stated at a high level have a tendency to be transmuted into an instrumental form behind superficially reassuring rhetoric. Smith argues that while instrumental reason has its indisputable place and value, it is limited in its capacity to illuminate fundamental questions of human value, including educational value. Smith urges us to proceed in a pragmatic way in relation to the differing demands that contemporary societies place upon their systems of higher education, whilst keeping in view our 'best understanding' of what a university is for and nurturing the five forms of responsiveness which he specifies. In effect, Smith is recommending here a form of 'practical judgement' or 'practical wisdom' in relation to the matters at stake.

A form of 'practical judgement' or 'practical wisdom' seems appropriate also in judging the other tensions arising in relation to the discussions in this volume. How these qualities of judgement and wisdom should be characterized and developed invites extended consideration. At least one ingredient in this process is informed and detailed communication and discussion. The involvement of 'countries in transition' in the ongoing international debate about the matters at stake which this volume has sought to bring about augurs well for the development of these capacities, both in the 'countries in transition' themselves and beyond.

References

Annette, J. and McLaughlin, T. (2005) 'Citizenship and higher education in the UK', in J. Arthur and K.E. Bohlin (eds) *Citizenship and Higher Education: the Role of Universities in Communities and Society*, London: RoutledgeFalmer.

Arthur, J. and Bohlin, K.E. (eds) (2005) *Citizenship and Higher Education: the Role of Universities in Communities and Society*, London: RoutledgeFalmer.

Barnett, R. (1990) *The Idea of Higher Education*, Buckingham: The Society for Research into Higher Education and Open University Press.

—— (1994) *The Limits of Competence: Knowledge, Higher Education and Society*, Buckingham: The Society for Research into Higher Education and Open University Press.

—— (1997) *Higher Education: a Critical Business*, Buckingham: The Society for Research into Higher Education and Open University Press.

Barnett, R. and Standish, P. (2003) 'Higher education and the university', in N. Blake, P. Smeyers, R. Smith and P. Standish (eds) *The Blackwell Guide to the Philosophy of Education*, Oxford: Blackwell Publishing.

Blake, N., Smith, R. and Standish, P. (1998) *The Universities We Need: Higher Education after Dearing*, London: Kogan Page.

Bloom, A. (1987) *The Closing of the American Mind: How Higher Education has Failed Democracy and Impoverished the Souls of Today's Students*, New York: Simon and Schuster.

Bok, D. (2003) *Universities in the Market Place: the Commercialization of Higher Education*, Princeton University Press.

Coffield, F. (2000a) 'Introduction: a critical analysis of the concept of a learning society', in F. Coffield (ed.) (2000b) *Differing Visions of a Learning Society: Research Findings*, vol. 1, Bristol: The Policy Press.

—— (ed.) (2000b) *Differing Visions of a Learning Society: Research Findings*, vol. 1, Bristol: The Policy Press.

Cottingham, J. (2003) *On the Meaning of Life*, London: Routledge.

Delanty, G. (2001) *Challenging Knowledge: the University in the Knowledge Society*, Buckingham: The Society for Research into Higher Education and Open University Press.

Dunne, E., Bennett, N. and Carre, C. (2000) 'Skill development in higher education and employment', in F. Coffield (ed.) *Differing Visions of a Learning Society: Research Findings*, vol. 1, Bristol: The Policy Press.

Fuller, T. (ed.) (1989) *The Voice of Liberal Learning: Michael Oakeshott on Education*, New Haven and London: Yale University Press.

Gibbons, M. (2000) 'Appendix: some attributes of knowledge production in Mode 2', in A. Kraak (ed.) *Changing Modes: New Knowledge Production and its Implications for Higher Education in South Africa*, South Africa: HSRC Press. Online. Available at: www.hsrcpress.ac.za (accessed 9 January 2005).

Giddens, A. (2002) *Runaway World: How Globalisation is Reshaping Our Lives*, 2nd edn, London: Profile Books.

Graham, G. (2002) *Universities: the Recovery of an Idea*, Thorverton: Imprint Academic.

Held, D., McGrew, A., Goldblatt, D. and Perraton, J. (1999) *Global Transformations: Politics, Economics and Culture*, Cambridge: Polity Press.

Jansen, J.D. (2000) 'Mode 2 Knowledge and institutional life: taking Gibbons on a walk through a South African University', in A. Kraak (ed.) *Changing Modes. New Knowledge Production and its Implications for Higher Education in South Africa*, South Africa: HSRC Press. Online. Available at: www.hsrcpress.ac.za (accessed 9 January 2005).

Jesuits Province in Lithuania and Latvia. Online. Available at: www.skrynia.lt (accessed 20 January 2006).

McLaughlin, T. and Jucevičienė, P. (1997) 'Education, democracy and the formation of national identity', in D. Bridges (ed.) *Education, Autonomy and Democratic Citizenship: Philosophy in a Changing World*, London: Routledge.

Maskell, D. and Robinson, I. (2002) *The New Idea of a University*, Thorverton: Imprint Academic.

Megone, C. (2005) 'Virtue and the virtual university', in S. Robinson and C. Katulushi (eds) *Values in Higher Education*, St Bride's Major, Vale of Glamorgan, Aureus Publishing on behalf of the University of Leeds.

Muller, J. (2000) 'What knowledge is of most worth for the Millennial citizen?', A. Kraak (ed.) *Changing Modes: New Knowledge Production and its Implications for Higher Education in South Africa*, South Africa: HSRC Press. Online. Available at: www.hsrcpress.ac.za (accessed 9 January 2005).

Nussbaum, M.C. (1997) *Cultivating Humanity: a Classical Defence of Reform in Liberal Education*, Cambridge, MA: Harvard University Press.
Readings, B. (1996) *The University in Ruins*, Cambridge, MA: Harvard University Press.
Robinson, S. and Katulushi, C. (eds) (2005) *Values in Higher Education*, St Bride's Major, Vale of Glamorgan, Aureus Publishing on behalf of the University of Leeds.
Singer, P. (2002) *One World: the Ethics of Globalization*, New Haven and London: Yale University Press.

Index

Aaltonen, M. 126
Aarhus University 129–30
About Södertörns högskola 128
Abramson, H.N. 162
access 114
Adorno. T. 33
Afele, J.S.C. 76
Ahlberg, M. 222
Alcamo, J. 100
alcohol consumption 238, 241, **242**
Alexander, H.A. 8, 10, 224, 250, 251, 252, 256, 257, 258, 259, 297, 302; and Carr 257; and McLaughlin 258
Altbach, P.G. 21, 230
Amaral, A. 24, 203
American Institute 204
Annette, J. 304
Annual Report of the National Board of Health 247
Appadurai, A. 228, 229
Appels, A. 238
Apple, M.W. 253
Arbonies, A.L. 74
Archibugi, D. 165
Argyris, Ch. 46, 58
Aristotle 252, 255
Aronowitz, S. 207
Arthur, J. 304
Ashby, E. 21
audit, quality and 284–8
Auriol, L. 138, 143
Australia: educational reforms 14, 24; Enterprise University 205; higher education and regional development 120
Austria, relationship between employment and share of population with third level education **142–3**

Babacan, H. 228, 232

Babcock, A. 228
babies, low-birth-weight 239, **241**
Bainbridge, W.S. 164
Balaz, V. 139
Baltic region: context of societal transformation 216–18; regional context 121–3; regional universities 7, 120–1; supranational region as an action space for the university 127
Barnett, R.: 22, 33–4, 44, 45, 47, 55, 62, 63, 191, 202, 221, 223, 225, 300, 302, 303, 304; and Standish 304
Barrow, C.W. 24
Baršauskienė, V. 8, 215, 228, 304
Bartley, M. 237
Basic Needs approach 93–4, 95
Bastid, M. 19, 21
Bauman, Z. 61, 227
Bayh-Dole Act, US 137, 149, 161
Beal, R.M. 76
Beck, U. 64
Becker, G. 90
Becker, R.F.J. 21
Beech, J. 24, 25
Belgium: relationship between employment and share of population with third level education **142–3**; universities 14
Bereday, G.Z.F. 17
Berg, A. 138
Berlin, I. 253, 259
Bernhardt, D.C. 76
Birkhead, T. 288
Bjønåvold, J. 60
Blaas, W. 165
Blake, N. 31, 304
Blane, D. 237
Blaženaitė, A. 8, 120, 303
Bleiklie, I. 22

Bloom, A. 302, 304
Blumenthal, D. 136
Bobe, M. 120
Boden, R. 266, 267, 268
Bohlin, K.E. 304
Bok, D. 202, 304
Bondi, Sir H. 269
Boshier, R. 57, 58
Bosma, M. 238
Bowden, J. 62, 63, 64, 230, 231
Bowden, R. 23
Bowsma, W.J. 217
Bozeman, B. 163, 166, 167, 169
brain drain 7, 43, 44, 51–3, 152, 172
Brazil 14, 26
Brecher, J. 228
Bridges, D. 4, 7, 9, 44, 65, 66, 126, 137, 155, 161, 293, 303, 306
brokerage 115
Buchbinder, H. 166, 168
Bučiūnienė, I. 181
Buck, B. 178
Budvytis, S. 228
Bulgaria: graduates in science and technology *151*; high-tech and medium-high-tech manufacturing and knowledge-intensive services *140–1*; lifelong learning *153*; public expenditure on tertiary level education *152*; R&D expenditure *146*; R&D personnel *144–5*; relationship between employment and share of population with third level education **142–3**; relative number of graduates and annual changes *147*; unemployment rates 146
Bullock, M. 111
Burbules, N.C. 4, 253
business management, transformation and 179–80

Cajete, G. 258
California, University of 120
Callahan, L.F. 237
Callan, E. 254
Callister, T.A. 4
Caloghirou, Y. 162, 166
Cambridge, University of: apex university 21; Estates Department 105; i10 project 108, 109; learning community 4; origins of this publication 9; research 272; role in learning region 65; Technopole area 272
Cambridge Enterprise 272
Capability Approach (CA) 94–8

Caracostas, P. 162, 165
Carayannis, E.G. 165, 166
Carnoy, M. 3
Carr, D. 257, 258
Castells, M. 72, 127
Castro, C.M. 21
catalyst, function of 219–20
Central and Eastern European countries (CEECs): functional transformation of universities 143–51; higher education as a building block of national innovation systems 138–43; role of higher education in national innovation systems 135–8, 157–8; transformation 178–9; transformation of requirements for business 183–4
Chancellor of the Duchy of Lancaster 267, 275
Charles, D.R. 107, 123
Chatterton, P. 107, 120
Cheng, Y.Ch. 53
Child, J. 58
China: educational principles 6; education system before 1949 20; osmotic translations 18–19; Soviet influence 14, 19
Choo, C.W. 74, 76, 79
Cicero 251, 255
Cimdiņš, P. 61
citizenship: conceptions of democratic 254–7; in higher education 8, 250–1, 252–3, 304; requirements 297; spirituality and democratic 257–9
Clark, B.R.: 21, 44, 206, 207, 208, 221, 230
Coffield, F. 56–7, 60, 298
Comim, F. 7, 43, 297
communitarianism: affiliated liberalism and 255–6; liberal 256–7
communities of practice 58, 62
community, concept of 228–9
community development: in the context of globalization 229–30; role of the university 8, 227–8
competence: additive 192, 195; behaviourist 192, 195; development for the knowledge-driven economy 190–1; holistic 191, 192, 194, 195, 300, 303; integrative 192, 195; nature of 8, 191–2; recommendations and issues for discussion 196–7; research findings 194–6; research project 192–4
complexity 47
Considine, M. 205, 208, 230

Conway, C. 166, 169
Cooke, P. 125
Cooper, C.L. 180
cooperation and social change 272–4
Coppola, B.P. 172
corporate governance 184
Corporate University 201, 205–6, 207
Costello, T. 228
Cottingham, J. 297
countries in transition: challenges for university development 202; focus 1; knowledge economy 7, 43–4; learning society 7, 62; the path of post-Soviet 61–2; service university in 209; technology transfer 8, 162–3, 169–70, 172–3; transitions in 294–6
Coupe, T. 161, 168
Cowen, R. 6, 13, 19, 23, 25, 26, 203, 294, 296; and Jones 19
Cowey, M. 72
Craig, G. 228
critical society 59
Croatia, innovation expenditures in manufacturing, by economic activity **139**
Cronin, B. 80
Crossan, M. 58, 63
Cubillo, J. 81
Cummings, W.K. 201, 204, 228, 230
Currie, J. 202, 228
Curry, C. 238
Cyprus, graduates in science and technology *151*
Czech Republic: graduates in science and technology *151*; high-tech and medium-high-tech manufacturing and knowledge-intensive services *140–1*; innovation expenditures in manufacturing, by economic activity **139**; knowledge-intensive businesses 139; lifelong learning *153* ; public expenditure on tertiary level education *152*; R&D expenditure *146*; R&D personnel *144–5*; ranking of sources of information by importance for enterprises *150*; relationship between employment and share of population with third level education **142–3** ; relative number of graduates and annual changes *147*; unemployment rates 146

Dahlgren, G. 237
Dahrendorf, R. 191
Daines, G.P. 166, 168
Damijan, P.J. 138, 139

Davenport, T.H. 74
Davey Smith, G. 237
Davies, J.L. 202
Davies, L. 66
Davies, W.K. 62
Davis, A.F. 229
De Luca, J.V. 76
De Rooij, P. 185
Dearing Report 35
Dedijer, S. 76
deductive rationalities 6, 19; and transitologies 23–5
Deem, R. 22, 290
Delanty, G. 44–5, 47, 62, 64, 65, 121, 304
Della-Pergola, S. 229, 234
Delors, J. 59
demand 114–15
democracy and citizenship in higher education 252–3; conceptions of democratic citizenship 254–7; spirituality and democratic citizenship 257–9
democratic society 58
Denmark, relationship between employment and share of population with third level education **142–3**
Department for Education and Employment (DfEE) 60, 104, 120
Department for Education and Science 104
Department for Trade and Industry, HM Treasury and Department for Education and Skills 104
Derby University 231
development: concepts of 7, 87–8, 297; human 92–8
Dewey, J. 13–14, 34, 250
Dičkutė, J. 238, 239
diet 241, 243, **244**
Domar, E. 89
Donaldson, Sir L. 270–1
Downes, R. 177
Drever, F. 237
Drucker, P. 165, 177
Duke, Ch. 62, 65, 66, 120, 209
Duncan, R. 58
Dunne, E. 59–60, 299–300
Durvy, J.N. 169
Dyker, D.A. 166
Dyson, F. 273

EASAC 275
East Anglia, University of 105
East of England Development Agency 108
Easterly, W. 135

Eckstein, M. 17
Economic and Social Research Council (ESRC) 56, 57, 60
education: constitutive value of 92–8; exploring the full potential 98–100; instrumental value of 88–92; role in development 87–8
Edwards, V. 179, 181, 183, 185
Egorov, I. 165, 166
Elkjaer, B. 58
Elliott, J. 287
Elo, I.T. 237
Elsner, D. 61
Enders, J. 24, 124
Engestroem, Y. 186
Enroled Senate Bill 102 162
Enschede, Technical University 272
Enterprise University 201, 205, 207
Entrepreneurial University, 201, 206–8
Erault, M. 186
Erricker, C. 258
Estonia: graduates in science and technology *151*; higher education and regional development 120; high-tech and medium-high-tech manufacturing and knowledge-intensive services *140–1*; learning society 61; lifelong learning *153*; public expenditure on tertiary level education *152*; R&D expenditure *146*; R&D personnel *144–5*; relationship between employment and share of population with third level education **142–3**; relative number of graduates and annual changes *147*
Ettore, B. 76
Etzione, G. 230
Etzkowitz, H. 165, 166, 202
European Centre for the Development of Vocational Training 178
European Commission: *Education and Training 2010* 103, 112, 113, 285–6; *Entrepreneurship in Europe* 166, 169; Green Paper on innovation 162, 165; *Innovation Policy* 165; *Internationalization of Research* 267; *Making a European Area of Lifelong Learning a Reality* 283; *Measures to Improve Higher Education/Research Relations* 282; 'National actions to implement lifelong learning in Europe' 60, 165; 'The role of the Universities in the Europe of Knowledge' 216; White Paper on education and training 59, 169
European Council 103

European Union (EU): communication services 139; graduates in science and technology *151*; high-tech and medium-high-tech manufacturing and knowledge-intensive services *140–1*; innovation expenditures in manufacturing, by economic activity **139**; lifelong learning *153*; new member states 176–7, 183; public expenditure on tertiary level education *152*; R&D expenditure *146*, 275; R&D personnel *144–5*; ranking of sources of information by importance for enterprises *150*; relative number of graduates and annual changes *147*; scientific research 267; technology transfer 162–3, 165; vocational training 178
European White Paper 32, 33
Eurostat 146
excellence 36–7; as a benchmark 268–9

Feinberg, W. 255
Ferris, G.R. 186
Figueiredo, M. 21
Finland: higher education and regional development 120, 124, 125, 126; R&D expenditure 275; relationship between employment and share of population with third level education **142–3**; technology policy 165–6
Fischer, S. 138
Fitzpatrick, S. 19
Florida, M. 107
formal rules and structures 181
Foss, N.J. 55
Fox, J. 237
France: education system 178; relationship between employment and share of population with third level education **142–3**; unemployment rates 146
Frankfurt, H. 257
Fraser, S.E. 15
Freeman, C. 135, 136
Freire, P. 14, 99
Friedman, G. 76
Fukuda-Parr, S. 93
Fuld, L.M. 76
Fullan, M. 220
Fuller, T. 304
Fulton, O. 24
Furedi, F. 285–7

Gaižauskiene, A. 237, 238

Gardner, K. 273
Gazeta Wyborcza 122
Gearon, L. 258
Genscher, H.D. 121
Germany: coordinated capitalist system 177; management education 178; Nazi era 6, 18–19; relationship between employment and share of population with third level education **142–3**; university model 20; vocational-technical education system 13
Geroski, P.A. 169
Geuna, A. 151
Gibbons, M.: 45–6, 63–4, 164, 168, 203, 216, 267, 274, 300–1
Giddens, A. 64, 294–5, 296–7, 304
Global University Network for Innovation *see* GUNI
globalization: attitudes to 296–7, 298, 304; challenges of 227–8; community development in the context of 229–30; of culture 6; social innovation 215; university strategies 121
Goddard, J. 107
Goldsmith, O. 269
Gopalkrishnan, N. 228, 232
Gopinathan, S. 24
Gorman, M.E. 168
government, role of 164, 169–70
Grabauskas, V.: 8, 238, 243, 246, 247, 304; and Kalėdienė 237; and Misevičienė and Klumbienė 238; and Padaiga 238; and Šveikauskas 44; Padaiga, Grabauskas and Gaižauskienė 237
graduates, relative number and annual changes *147*
Graham, G. 302, 304
Grant, N. 19
Greece: economic status 176; relationship between employment and share of population with third level education **142–3**
Green, A. 60
Griffin, A. 5
Grigas, R. 182, 224, 228
Grippenberg, P. 74
Griswold, A.W. 251
growth, theories of 88–92
Gudaitytė, D.: and Jucevičienė 49, 221; Janiūnaitė and 8, 66, 228, 294, 296, 303, 306
GUNI (Global University Network for Innovation) 120

Gur-Zeev, I. 256

Habermas, J. 228
Halal, W. 228, 229, 232
Hall, P.A. 177, 178, 180
Halliday, F. 124–5
Hamilton, W.D. 273
Hampden-Turner, C. 180
Hancke, B. 179
Handy, Ch. 179
Hans, N. 16
Harrod, R. 89
Havelock, R.G. 219
Havrylyshyn, O. 138
Hay, D.B. 204
Hayhoe, R. 19, 20, 21
health: changes in health behaviour in relation to educational level 243–5; education and health-conscious behaviour 241–2; education and risk of ill-health **238–41**; policy development 8, 237; research in health inequalities 237–8; tackling health inequalities through policy development 245–7
Health Inequalities Project 238
Heap, B. 8, 304
HEFCE 23, 65, 66, 108, 116, 284
Hegel, G.W.F. 263, 256
Heidegger, M. 34, 35
Held, D. 296
Henningsen, B. 121, 128
Herring, J.P. 77
Heubner, D. 258
hierarchy, approach to 181
Higginson, J.H. 14
higher education: as an agent of social innovation 8, 135–6, 215–16; bridging role in technology transfer 164–5, 170–3; challenges for higher education in business management 185–7; changing relations with the state 47–8; conceptions of 220–2; democracy and citizenship in 252–3; development for knowledge society 43–4; features relevant to the development of the knowledge economy 44–8; learning for intelligent organizations 80–1; links with society 48–9; links with state 50; Lithuanian 48–51; new links with disciplines 47; new links with society 45–6; public expenditure on *152*; purposes of 251–3; qualities as a facilitator of knowledge economy 50–1; role as agent of social innovation 222–5;

specialization in 251–2; spirituality in 259–61; spirituality and citizenship in 250–1; transitions in 299–301
Hirst, P.H. 261
HM Treasury 275
Hobrough, J. 165
Hofstede, G. 179, 180, 181, 182
Holden, N. 180
Holmes, B. 17–18
Horkheimer, M. 33
Housman, A.E. 268
Human Development Report 89
Humboldt, A. von 201
Humboldt, W. von 20, 35–6, 295
Hungary: graduates in science and technology *151*; high-tech and medium-high-tech manufacturing and knowledge-intensive services *140–1*; knowledge-intensive businesses 139; lifelong learning *153*; public expenditure on tertiary level education *152*; R&D expenditure *146*, R&D personnel *144–5*; relationship between employment and share of population with third level education **142–3**; relative number of graduates and annual changes *147*; unemployment rates 146
Husén, T. 57, 58
Hutchins, R.M. 57

Iceland, graduates in science and technology *151*
ICT: integration into business and social processes 136; revolution 2
identity: of the discipline or subject 5; of place 4; of the scholarly community 4–5; social 58; of the student community 5; of time 4; university 286
Ife, J. 229
industrial relations 184
information society 74
informational economy 72
innovation: expenditures in manufacturing by economic activity **139**; higher education system as a building block of national innovation systems 138–43; national systems 8, 135–8, 157–8; role of higher education in national innovation systems 135–8, 151–7; social *see* social innovation; systems perspective 136; value 73–4; virtual space for 79; ways of developing technological innovations in 1999 *170*

instrumental reason (technical reason) 32–4
intellectual property 112–13
intelligence: concept 7, 75–6, 300, 303; economic 77; educational 77; and the intelligent country 74–6; as interpreted information 76–7; legal 77; market or business 77; political 77; scientific and technological 77
intelligent country 78–80; concept 7, 72; core components 79; intelligence and 74–6; transitions 296
intelligent organizations 80–1
inter-company relations in technology transfer 184
international educational transfer, 'double problem' of 13–16, 25–6; classic approaches 16–18; deductive rationalities and transitologies 23–5; osmotic problem 18–20; transfer problem 20–3
interpretation 75
Iran, religious principles 19
Ireland: economic status 176; relationship between employment and share of population with third level education **142–3**
Israel: curriculum of higher education 260; society in transition 251
Italy, relationship between employment and share of population with third level education **142–3**

Jackson, R. 250
Jaffee, D. 179
Jasanoff, S. 271
Janiūnaitė, B. and Gudaitytė 8, 66, 228, 294, 296, 303, 306
Jansen, J.D. 301
Japan: education system 178; German influence 20, 26; learning society 60; Meiji era 19–20, 26; university reform 13–14
Jarvis, P. 57, 61, 62, 65, 203, 298
Jelenc, Z. 60, 61–2
Jennings, R. 272
Jequeir, N. 76
Jesuits Province in Lithuania and Latvia 295
Jõgi, L. 61
John Paul II, Pope 275, 304
Johnes, G. 90
Johnson 229
Johnson, B. 218

Jones, C. 19
Jones-Evans, D. 164, 165
Jovaiša, L. 229
Jucevičienė, P. 7, 9, 44, 47, 51, 62, 190, 228, 298; 'Development of the education science . . .' 232; Gudaitytė and 49, 221; McLaughlin and 295; 'New approaches to the development . . .' 190; and Tautkevičienė 64; 'The concept of *intelligence* . . .' 81; 'Universities on the way..'; and Vaitkus 7, 172, 294–5, 300, 303
Jucevičius, G. 1, 8, 179, 182, 184, 185, 215, 218, 294, 303; Žėruolis and 179, 183
Jucevičius, R. 7, 9, 74, 296, 303
Jullien, M.-A. 15

Kaldor, N. 89–90
Kalėdienė, R. 237
Kant, I. 253, 255, 256
Karalius, A. 228
Karczewski, W.A. 122
Katulushi, C. 304
Kaukonen, E. 166
Kaunas University: of Medicine 241, 242; of Technology (KTU) 8, 9, 49, 66–7, 126, 156, 168, 232–4
Kazanas, H.C. 191
Keep, E. 60
Kenny, S. 228
Kettunen, J. 126
Kim, T. 21, 24
Kim, W.C. 73
Kimball, B.A. 252
Kitagawa, F. 103
Klauss, R. 168
Kliebard, H. 34
Klimašauskienė, R. 46
Kloftsen, M. 164
Klumbienė, J. 238
Knight, P. 285
knowing organization 74
knowledge: economy 7, 43, 44–8, 72–4; generation and transfer 163–4; internationalization 47; management 74; organization 58, 63–4; production 300–1; society 7, 45; workers 46, 47
knowledge-driven economy (KDE) 190–1
knowledge-intensive services (KIS) *139–41*
Koivunen, S.
Kolman, L. 181

Komninos, N. 73, 79
Koschatzky, K. 169
Kraujutaitytė, L. 44
Kriaučionenė, M.: 136; Radošević and 161, 171, 172, 265, 303
Kruzela, P. 181
Kuhn, T. 253
Kunst, A.E. 237
Kuzmickaitė, D. 228
Kvietkauskaitė, J. 234
Kvil, T. 203
Kwiek, M. 3, 122

Lado, A.A. 166
Lajunen, L.H.J. 126
Lambert R. 113, 114–16, 265
languages 31
Latvia: graduates in science and technology *151*; higher education and regional development 120; high-tech and medium-high-tech manufacturing and knowledge-intensive services *140–1*; innovation expenditures in manufacturing, by economic activity **139**; lifelong learning *153* public expenditure on tertiary level education *152*; R&D expenditure *146*; R&D personnel *144–5*; ranking of sources of information by importance for enterprises *150*; relationship between employment and share of population with third level education **142**; relative number of graduates and annual changes *147*
Laurent, A. 180
Lauwerys, J.A. 17
Laužackas, R. 184, 185, 191
Law, W. 19
Lawrence, P. 179, 181, 183, 185
learning organization 74
learning regions 7, 65–7, 74
learning society 55–6; cultural model 57; democratic model 58; educational perspectives 56–8; managerial perspectives 58–9; nature and significance of 56–9; the notion of the 59, 298–9; potential of universities in the development of 62–5; review of policies and practices of the development of learning societies 59–62; sociological perspectives 59; technological model 57–8; transitions 298
Lee, M. 24

Leliūgienė, I. 8, 215, 228, 304
Leney, T. 60
Lepaitė, D. 8, 46, 77, 194, 300, 303
Leslie, L.L. 202
Leverhulme, Lord 269
Leydesdorff, L. 165, 166, 202
liberalism: affiliated and communitarianism 255–6; political and comprehensive 254–5
lifelong learning 24–5, 56, 59, *151–3*, 299
Lithuania: brain drain 7, 44, 51–3, 172; changes in health behaviour in relation to educational level 243–5; changing functions of universities and their role in a national innovation system 151–7; competence research project 192–7; cultural background 180–3; education and health-conscious behaviour 241–2; education and risk of ill-health 238–41; features of higher education as a knowledge economy development facilitator 7, 44, 48–51; graduates in science and technology *151*; health inequalities 237–8; health policy development 8, 237; higher education 44; higher education and regional development 120; high-tech and medium-high-tech manufacturing and knowledge-intensive services *140–1*; learning society 61; life expectancy **240**; lifelong learning *153*; oil refinery industry 78–9; partners of innovation activities **156**; public expenditure on tertiary level education *152*; R&D expenditure *146*, 171; R&D funding *155*; R&D personnel *144–5*, 153, 171; ranking of sources of information by importance for enterprises *150* ; relationship between employment and share of population with third level education **142–3**; relative number of graduates and annual changes *147*; role of higher education as part of national innovation system *153–4*; social transformation 215, 217–18; tackling health inequalities through policy development 245–7; technology transfer 166; university employment 105
Lithuanian Science and Technology White Paper 171
Longworth, N. 56, 59, 60, 62
Lönnberg, H. 126
Loogma, K. 61
Lovat, T. 258

Lucas, R. 90
Lukoševičius, A. 5, 8, 172, 265, 303
Lundvall, B.A. 165, 218
Luton, University of 106
Luxembourg, unemployment rates 146
Lyotard, J.-F. 33, 37

Mahnke, V. 55
Majcen, B. 138, 141
Makenbach, J.P. 237
Mallinson, V. 16
management education 184–5
managerial perspectives on the learning society 58–9
manufacturing: high-tech and medium-high-tech and knowledge-intensive services *140*
Mao Zedong 6, 19, 20
Marchese, T. 4
Marcinkevičiūtė, L. 181
Marginson, S. 205, 208, 230
Markevičienė, A. 231
Martin, B. 266, 275
Marton, F. 62, 63, 64, 230, 231
Maskell, D. 304
Massachusetts Institute of Technology 161
Mauborgne, R. 73
Mauch, J.E. 201
Maurice, M. 130
May, Lord 270
Mayer, S. 165
Mayhew, K. 60
Mazzarol, T. 106
Mbeki, T. 31
McBrierty, V. 169
McDonough, K. 255
McGivney, V. 60
McLaren, P. 256
McLaughlin, T. 9, 254, 258, 295, 304
McLean, M. 17
McNay, I. 205
McSweeney, B. 180
Megone, C. 302
Melnikas, B. 177, 215
Merricks, L. 56
Merton, R.K. 167
Meyer, K.E. 176
Middlehurst, R. 95
Mikula, B. 181
Mill, J.S. 58
Millennium Development Goals (MDGs) 99
Miller, D. 58
Misevičienė, I. 238
Mitrikas, A.A. 224

Mockaitis, A.I. 181
Morley, L. 290
Moso, M. 74
Mowery, D.C. 137, 148, 149
Muldur, U. 162, 165
Mulgan, G. 229
multiversity 47, 63
Murdoch, I. 253
Murrel, P. 176, 183
Musiał, K. 7, 10, 66, 294

Nasierowski, W. 181
National Committee of Enquiry into Higher Education 60
National Research Council and Russian Academy of Sciences 165
National Research Foundation of South Africa 273
national systems of innovation 8, 151–7
NATO 273, 274
Natorp, P. 229
Nefas, S. 228, 229
Nelson, R.R. 136, 143, 156–7
Netherlands: educational reforms 24; relationship between employment and share of population with third level education **142–3**; unemployment rates 146; vocational training 178
Newman, J.H. 302
Newson, J. 202, 228
New Zealand, educational reforms 14, 24
Nieminen, M. 166
Noah, H. 17
Noddings, N. 250, 256
Nonaka, I. 58
Nordmann, A. 164
Novikova, J. 185
Nowak, M. 273
Nussbaum, M. 32–3, 95, 97, 304–5

Ochs, K. 24, 26
OECD 128, 135, 165, 185, 281–2, 291
OECD/IMHE 103
Office for Fair Access (OFFA) 285
Office of Science and Technology 270
Ofsted 258
Okamoto, K. 60
Oldstone, M.B.A. 271
O'Reilly, J. 179
Øresund University 127, 128–9
Oslo University 231
osmotic problem 15, 16–18
osmotic translations 18–19
Otto, H.U. 19

Oulu, University of 126, 129

Padaiga, Ž. 237, 238
Pandya, D. 165
Participatory approach 93–4, 95
Passig, D. 228, 229
Passin, H. 20
patents, 168
Patten, C. 275, 276
Pavitt, K. 148, 150, 269, 275
Pedler, M. 58
Penčylenė, A. 233
Peters, R.S. 261
Petkevičienė, J. 243
Petrauskienė, J. 237
Phenix, P.H. 261
Phillips, D. 24, 26, 253
Phillips Report on BSE 271
Pilger, J. 229
Pincus, T. 237
Plato 252
Poland: graduates in science and technology *151*; higher education 122–3; higher education and regional development 120; innovation expenditures in manufacturing, by economic activity **139**; learning society 61; lifelong learning *153*; private sector provision 3, 122; public expenditure on tertiary level education *152*; R&D expenditure *146*; R&D personnel *144–5*; relative number of graduates and annual changes *147*; Soviet model of education 14; student cultural survey 182; unemployment rates 146
policies informed by science 269–72
Popkewitz, T.S. 253
Popper, K.R. 253, 259
Popper, S.W. 266
Porter, M.E. 23, 177
Portugal: graduates in science and technology *151*; relationship between employment and share of population with third level education **142–3**
Poškienė, A. 44
Power, M. 287–8
Preston, G.H. 237
Price, C. 203
Price, R.F. 19
Prigogine, I. 218, 220
process support 115–16
Puukka, J. 126

quality: alternative indicators of 9, 288–90;

assurance 24, 284; and audit 9, 284–8; challenges to the maintenance or development of 281–4; as equality and inclusion 289–90; of higher education 281, 290–1; as passion 289; as pluralism 288–9; as responsibility 289
Quality Assurance Agency for Higher Education (QAA) 284

R&D: consultancy and R&D contracting mode 149, 150; contract 137; demand for 141, 148, 152; expenditure *144–6, 155*, 157, 275; implosion of 143; institutes 122, 153; personnel *144–5,* 153; public 275; theories 90–1
Radoševič, S. 136, 139, 141; and Auriol 138, 143; Dyker and 166; and Kriaučionenė 8, 161, 171, 172, 265, 303
Radovan, M. 74
Rainbird, H. 60
Ranson, S. 62
Ravallion, M. 177
Ravetz, J.R. 267
Rawls, J. 94, 96, 254
Ray, D. 91
Raymond, L. 76
Readings, B. 36, 295, 304
Regional Development Agency 112
regional universities: as identified with subunits of the nation 125–7; multiple identification patterns 129–30; role 65
regional university: as a concept 123–4; models of 127–9
regionalism, nationalism and internationalism 124–5
Reich, R. 23
research, scientific 265–8
Research Assessment Exercise (RAE) 285
research capacity and business development 110–12
researchers 64–5
Rhoten, D. 3
Richardson, Th.J. 177
Ringer, F.K. 19
Rip, A. 169
Robb, C. 93
Robertson, D. 43, 62, 66
Robinson, I. 304
Robinson, J. 89–90
Robinson, S. 304
Robson, B. 120
Roco, M.C. 164
Rodrigues, S. 58
Rohrs, R. 20

Rojec, M. 138, 139
Romania: graduates in science and technology *151*; high-tech and medium-high-tech manufacturing and knowledge-intensive services *140–1*; innovation expenditures in manufacturing, by economic activity **139**; lifelong learning *153*; public expenditure on tertiary level education *152*; R&D expenditure *146*; R&D personnel *144–5*; relationship between employment and share of population with third level education **142–3**; relative number of graduates and annual changes *147*
Romer, P. 90
Rocs, J. 191
Rosovsky, H. 251
Rostow, W. 88
Roszak, T. 201
Rothblatt, S. 21, 44, 62, 63, 252
Rothman, J. 228
Rothwell, W.J. 191
Rowley, J. 74
Royal Society 266, 268, 271, 273–4
Ruch, R.S. 202, 206
Russia, innovation expenditures in manufacturing, by economic activity **139**
Rutgers University 232

Sabaliauskaitė 243
Sadler, Sir M. 14, 16
Sahay, R. 138
Sala-i-Martin, J. 91
Salmi, J. 205
Samalavičius, A. 223, 224
Sandel, M. 255
Sandström, U. 127
Sayetat, F. 169
Scheffler, I. 253, 261
Schiller, F. 35
Schmiemann, M. 169
Schön, D. 56, 58
Schreiwer, J. 24, 26
Schuller, T. 49
Schultz, T. 90
Schwab, J. 261
Schwartzman, S. 21
science in higher education 265–8, 274–6; cooperation and social change 272–4; excellence as a benchmark 268–9; policies informed by science 269–72
Scott, P. 44, 62, 65, 190, 216

self-directed learner 58
Sellier, F. 180
Sellin, B. 60
Selvarantnam, V. 21
Sen, A. 87, 88, 94, 96–7, 297
Senge, P. 58, 74
Šernas, V. 191
service university 8, 201; challenges for university development 201–4; conceptual foundations 204–8; in countries in transition 209; critical 8, 208–9, 303; seminal model 204
Shumar, W. 202
Siegel, H. 253
Silvestre, J.-J. 180
Simpson, R. 20
Singer, P. 296, 297
skills: development and transfer 299–300, 301; growth 298; higher-level 106–7, 303; intelligence and 7; key 300; knowledge and 24; problem-solving 303
Slaughter, S. 202
Slovakia: graduates in science and technology *151* high-tech and medium-high-tech manufacturing and knowledge-intensive services *140–1*; innovation expenditures in manufacturing, by economic activity **139**; knowledge-intensive businesses 139; lifelong learning *153*; public expenditure on tertiary level education *152*; R&D expenditure *146*; R&D personnel *144–5*; ranking of sources of information by importance for enterprises *150*; relationship between employment and share of population with third level education **142–3**; relative number of graduates and annual changes *147*
Slovenia: graduates in science and technology *151*; high-tech and medium-high-tech manufacturing and knowledge-intensive services *140–1*; innovation expenditures in manufacturing, by economic activity **139**; learning society 61–2; lifelong learning *153*; R&D expenditure *146*; R&D personnel *144–5*; ranking of sources of information by importance for enterprises *150*; relationship between employment and share of population with third level education **142–3**; relative number of graduates and annual changes *147*
smart communities 79

Smarzynska-Javorcki, B. 138
Smith, A. 5
Smith, B. 228
Smith, N. 256
Smith, R.: 6, 59 295, 299, 302, 306–7; Blake, Smith and Standish 304
smoking 238, 241, *242*, 243, **245**, **246**
Soares, V.A.M. 203, 204
social change, cooperation and 272–4
social identity 58
social innovation: higher education as an agent of 8, 215–16, 222–5; the role of agents of 218–20
societies in transition 202, 250–1
society, traditional and innovative parts of 182–3
Socrates 257
Södertörn University College 127, 128
Soete, L. 44
Solow, R. 88, 89
Sörlin, S. 125–6, 127
Soskice, D. 177, 178, 180
Soutar, G.N. 106
Soviet Union *see* USSR
Spain, relationship between employment and share of population with third level education **142–3**
specialization in higher education 251–2
spirituality and citizenship in higher education 250–1, 304
Stacey, R.D. 73, 79
Standish, P. 304
Stankevičiūtė, J. 9, 74
Stankewicz, R. 137, 149
Stationery Office 60
Steiner-Khamsi, G. 24, 26
Stephan, P.E. 166, 169
Stiglitz, J. 183
Storper, M. 176, 177, 183
Sunker, H. 19
supercomplexity 7, 47, 63, 303
Sutton, H. 76
Šveikauskas, V. 44
Švietimo aprūpinimo centras 61
Švietimo kaitos fondas 61
Swan, T. 89
Sweden: higher education and regional development 120, 124, 125, 127; R&D expenditure 275; relationship between employment and share of population with third level education **142–3**
symbolic analysts 46

Takeuchi, H. 58

Talvi, M. 61
Tamir, Y. 256
Tanaka, M. 20, 21
Tautkevičienė, G. 64
Taylor, C. 256
Taylorist structures 178, 179, 181, 186–7
teachers 14, 64
teaching capacity and business development 109–10
technical reason *see* instrumental reason
technology transfer 8, 161–5; the bridging role of higher education 164–5, 170–3; the generation of knowledge for the purposes of 168–9; inter-company relations 184; policies and the role of government 164, 169–70; positive and controversial sides of 163, 165–7; ways of developing technological innovations in 1999 *170*
Teichler, U. 123, 190
Teixeira, P. 92
tensions 306–7
Thomas, D. 95
Times Higher Education Supplement 37, 282
Tjeldvoll, A. 10, 201, 204, 228, 231; and Blaženaitė 8, 120, 303
Tlili, A. 290
Todeva, E. 182
Toffler, A. 76
Tokyo, University of 20, 21
Tomiak, J.J. 19
Tornatzky, L.G. 166
Törnqvist, G. 127
traditions 302–6
transfer problem 15, 20–3
transformation: challenges for higher education in business management in the context of 185–7; concept 177; cultural and institutional context 179–80; cultural specifics of the transformation environment 180–3; implications for business management 179–80; institutional specifics of the transformation environment 183–5
transition(s) 293–301; concept 176–7; in countries in transition 294–6; in higher education 299–301; in societies 1–3; throughout the world 296–9; in universities 3–6; *see also* countries in transition; societies in transition
Trivellato, P. 60
Trivers, R.L. 273
Trompenaars, F. 180

Tudiver, N. 201, 202
Turkey: innovation expenditures in manufacturing, by economic activity **139**; public expenditure on tertiary level education *152*; ranking of sources of information by importance for enterprises *150*
Tyack, D.B. 253

Umeå, University of 126
unemployment rates 146
Underwood, J.D. 73, 76
United Kingdom (UK): curricula and qualifications 283; developing a regional collaborative infrastructure 107–8; East of England 106–7; educational reforms 14, 23–4; government strategies 265, 267; higher education and regional development 120; learning regions 65, 66; learning society 60–1; managed university 22–3; quality assurance 284; relationship between employment and share of population with third level education **142–3**; science 265; university investment 103–4; university reform 13; vocational training 178
United Nations Development Programme (UNDP) 94
United States of America (US): educational initiatives 59; German influence 20; higher education and regional development 120; higher education model 3, 21; liberal market economy 177; management education 178; R&D expenditure 171, 275; religion and universities 259; research universities 21; technology transfer 161–2; university reform 13, 24
universities: aims and purposes 6 30–8; changing functions in Lithuania and role in national innovation system 151–7; functional transformation in CEE 143–51; as hubs of economic activity 104–7; knowledge-diffusion function of CEE universities 146–8; knowledge-generation function of CEE universities 143–6; knowledge utilization function of CEE universities 148–51; potential in the development of the learning society 62–5; regional 65; religious ties 259–60; role in community development 8, 230–2; role in regional development 7, 65–7, 103–4; role in relation to 'quality' 9; role in social innovation 8; role in

universities *continued*
   technology transfer 8; traditions, transitions and tensions 9, 293; transitions in 3–6, 299–301
university: apex 21; citational 21–2; conceptions of the 30–8; identity 286; as an institution of learning 64–5; as a knowledge organization 63–4; 'managed' 22–3; regional 123–4; responsiveness of the 30–1; role in community development 8, 227–8, 230–2; role as educator 231, 304; role in regional economic development 103–4, 113–17; service *see* service university; traditional role 302–6; world models 21–3
University of Cambridge 105
Unterhalter, E. 96
Uphoff, N. 100
USSR: educational principles 6; educational reform 13–14; imposition of educational ideas 26; model of education 14; osmotic translations 18–19

Vaitkus, R. 172, 294–5, 300, 303
value innovation 73–4
Van der Wende, M. 46
Varga, K. 181
Vartiainen, P. 126
Vegh, C. 138
Vera, D. 58, 63
Vidzeme University College 123
Viiri, A. 126
virtual innovation system 79
vocational training 178, 184–5
Vogel, G. 273
Von Krogh, G. 191
Vozikis, G.S. 166

Walters, G. 20

Walzer, M. 254, 258
Wan, H. 88
Ward, D. 120
Waterhouse, R. 62, 228, 230, 231
Webster, A. 148
Webster, F. 5
Wegner, C. 251
Weiss, A. 58
Wenger, E. 58
Westlund, H. 124, 127
White, J. 191
Whitehead, M. 237
Whitley, R. 177, 180
Wijk, R.V. 58
Wilkinson, B. 179
Williams International 78–9
Wirth, L. 228
Wisker, G. 96
Wittrock, B. 252
Wolfson, H.A. 252
Wolpert, L. 267
work goals, approach to 182
World Bank 186, 303
World Development Report 91, 98
World Health Organization (WHO) 237–8, 241; Regional Office for Europe 237
World Trade Organization 297
Wyatt, I. 221, 223, 225

Yonezawa, A. 24
Young, M.F.D. 57
Yukos 79

Zamorski, B. 9, 10, 110, 289, 299
Zavadskas, E.K. 191
Žėruolis, D. 179, 183
Ziedonis, A.A. 137, 149
Zissen, M. 228
Žvirėlaitė 243

For Product Safety Concerns and Information please contact our EU
representative GPSR@taylorandfrancis.com
Taylor & Francis Verlag GmbH, Kaufingerstraße 24, 80331 München, Germany

www.ingramcontent.com/pod-product-compliance
Lightning Source LLC
Chambersburg PA
CBHW060552230426
43670CB00011B/1793